Beck, Charlotte H.,
1937-

The fugitive legacy.

$49.95

Southern Literary Studies
Fred Hobson, Editor

The Fugitive Legacy

The Fugitive Legacy

A Critical History

CHARLOTTE H. BECK

 LOUISIANA STATE UNIVERSITY PRESS

Baton Rouge

Copyright © 2001 by Louisiana State University Press
All rights reserved
Manufactured in the United States of America
First printing
09 08 07 06 05 04 03 02 01 00
5 4 3 2 1

Designer: Amanda McDonald Scallan
Typeface: Janson Text
Typesetter: Coghill Composition Co., Inc.
Printer and binder: Thomson-Shore, Inc.

Library of Congress Cataloging-in-Publication Data

Beck, Charlotte H., 1937–
    The fugitive legacy : a critical history / Charlotte H. Beck.
        p.   cm. — (Southern literary studies)
    Includes bibliographical references (p.) and index.
    ISBN 0-8071-2590-3 (alk. paper)
    1. Fugitives (Group)   2. American literature—Southern States—History and criticism.   3.
American fiction—Southern States—History and criticism.   4. American literature—20th
century—History and criticism.   5. American fiction—20th century—History and criticism.
    6. Southern States—Intellectual life—1865–   7. Influence (Literary, artistic, etc.)   8.
Southern States—In literature.   I. Title.   II. Series

    PS261.B44   2000
    810.9′975—dc21   00-044389

Excerpts from "Place and Time: The Southern Writer's Inheritance," by Eudora Welty, are reprinted by
permission of Russell & Volkening, Inc., as agents for the author. Copyright © 1954 by Eudora Welty,
renewed in 1982 by Eudora Welty.

The paper in this book meets the guidelines for permanence and durability of the Committee on Production
Guidelines for Book Longevity of the Council on Library Resources. ♾

In memory of Cleanth Brooks

Contents

Acknowledgments

Tracing the Fugitive legacy has proved to be a long and wide-ranging quest that could neither have been conceived of nor carried out without the assistance and encouragement of a host of individuals. I wish to acknowledge first the senior scholars, themselves Fugitive legatees to one extent or another, who inspired and encouraged me in the initial stages of this project: Joseph A. Bryant, Jr., Thomas Daniel Young, Lewis P. Simpson, R. W. B. Lewis, and, especially, the late Cleanth Brooks, to whom this volume is dedicated. Interviews and informal communications with these and others who have firsthand knowledge of the persons, places, and events that figured in this literary saga—such as Peter Taylor, David Madden, and Mr. Brooks—have added a vibrancy to an already fascinating story.

For giving me access to and permission to employ essential primary materials, I express my gratitude to the following literary executors and surviving relatives: John Burt, the Robert Penn Warren Papers; John Michael Walsh, the Cleanth Brooks Papers; Barbara Thompson Davis, the Katherine Anne Porter Papers; Robert Giroux, the Flannery O'Connor Papers; Mary Jarrell, Randall Jarrell's letters; Frank Bidert, the Robert Lowell Papers; Kathleen Donohue Berryman, John Berryman's letters; Helen Ransom Foreman, John Crowe Ransom's letters; Nancy Tate Wood, Caroline Gordon's letters; Helen Tate, the Allen Tate Papers; and the permissions departments of Farrar, Straus & Giroux, Inc., of Russell and Volkening, and of the *Kenyon Review*.

For granting me access to, and assistance with the documentation of, archival materials, I especially thank, along with their assistants, Patricia C. Willis, curator of American literature at Yale's Beinecke Rare Book and Manuscript library; Marice Wolfe, curator of special collections, Vanderbilt University; Margaret Sherry, curator of special collections, Firestone Library, Princeton University; Beth Alvarez, curator of special collections, MeKeldin Library, University of Maryland, College Park; H. T. Holmes and Forrest W. Galey, Archives and Library Division, Mississippi Department of Archives and History, Jackson, Mississippi; Leslie A. Morris, curator of manuscripts, Houghton Library, Harvard University; Nancy Bray, curator of the Flannery O'Connor Collection, Ina Dillard Russell Library, Georgia College, Milledgeville, Georgia; and Jami Peelle, special collections librarian, Kenyon College, Gambier, Ohio.

For permission to quote my own previously published essays, I thank the following editors and publishers: Mark Royden Winchell, editor of *The Vanderbilt Tradition: Essays in Honor of Thomas Daniel Young* (Louisiana State University Press, 1991); Richard J. Kelly and Alan K. Lathrop, editors of *Recovering Berryman: Essays on a Poet* (University of Michigan Press, 1993); William J. Spurlin and Michael Fischer, editors of *The New Criticism and Contemporary Literary Theory, Connections and Continuities* (Garland Press, 1992); and the editors of the *Southern Literary Journal* and the *Flannery O'Connor Bulletin*.

Part of the research for this project was facilitated by funds and released time granted by the Russell D. Parker Faculty Development Fund at Maryville College, Maryville, Tennessee; by two James Still Summer Fellowships at the University of Kentucky in Lexington, in 1986 and 1992; and by a National Institute for the Humanities Summer Seminar stipend (Yale, 1989) and a Travel-to-Collections grant (Harvard, 1991).

I also thank my patient and encouraging friends from the Robert Penn Warren Circle, especially James A. Perkins, Lucy Ferriss, John Burt, James Grimshaw, Robert Koppelman, William Bedford Clark, Mary Louise Weaks, and James Justus, as well as others who have been most generous in their interest, assistance, and support, notably Alice Brown, director of the Appalachian College Association; Mark Royden Winchell, Clemson University, who read and commented on the manuscript; and Fred Hobson, senior adviser to LSU Press, who read the manuscript several times and provided helpful suggestions for revision.

Even with the help of those mentioned above, this manuscript would never have become a book without the active assistance of two indispensable persons: John Easterly, my patient and thorough editor at LSU Press, and Raymond W. Beck, my husband, who has devoted untold hours to assisting me with the editing, revising, and preparing of this manuscript for publication. The support of these two faithful and true believers can neither be overestimated nor sufficiently appreciated.

PART I

The Critical Legacy

1 / A Tale of Three Cities

I n 1922, when the *Fugitive*, a magazine of verse, first appeared in Nashville, its editors could scarcely have realized to what extent they were participating in the birth of modernism in American letters. During the first three decades of the twentieth century, the atmosphere in Nashville was not entirely conducive to high culture. As Louis D. Rubin, Jr., put it, "Although the people of Nashville . . . like to refer to their city as 'the Athens of the South,' . . . the capital city of Tennessee did not in the early 1920's possess much in the way of literary tradition."[1] It was, in fact, this lack of cultural stimulation that brought together a group of Nashvillians later known as the Fugitives. At that relatively peaceful moment between the world wars, the threatened triumph of industrialism had not yet transformed Fugitives into Agrarians, nor had the Scopes trial lent credence to H. L. Mencken's opinion, as set forth in his 1920 essay, that Tennessee deserved to be called "the Sahara of the Bozart." There was time for such esoteric pursuits as the writing and criticism of poetry.

And yet, by 1937, all but one of the four major Fugitives had fled—only to

1. Louis D. Rubin, Jr., *The Wary Fugitives: Four Poets and the South* (Baton Rouge: Louisiana State University Press, 1978), 1.

take up similar tasks elsewhere and, in so doing, transform themselves from a regional into a national force in cultural history by helping to develop an entire generation of outstanding literary men and women. Not only did the former Fugitives attract to their new campus homes the most promising young would-be writers and establish new literary journals in which their pupils and protégés could begin publishing, but they and their heirs were also important forces in revolutionizing college curricula and methods and making creative writing and literary criticism legitimate activities in English departments across the nation. For the Fugitives themselves, the roles of mentor and sponsor were natural and positive outgrowths of their professional lives as teachers and editors. For their heirs, membership in the post-Fugitive circle was an aspect of personal and professional maturation that proved to be invaluable in the beginnings of their careers but gradually weakened as they took their places in the literary community.

From its beginning, the Fugitive legacy has been subject to what Harold Bloom has called "the anxiety of influence," whereby "one poet [also read "critic" and "fictionist"] helps to form another" and "strong poets . . . wrestle with their strong precursors, even to the death," while "weaker talents idealize," and "figures of capable imagination appropriate for themselves."[2] For some of the Fugitives' heirs, allegiance to their mentors was almost absolute for the greater parts of their careers; for others the Fugitive connection was only one of many factors that would account for their rise in the literary world. All, however, whether they would admit it or not, benefited in the beginning of their writing careers from relationships, of varying strengths, with one or more members of the Nashville group.

From a gathering of Nashvillians in search of "cultural entertainment," the original Fugitive group ultimately evolved into a workshop in the writing of poetry led by John Crowe Ransom. During its most active period, between 1921 and 1925, the group not only included Ransom, Donald Davidson, Allen Tate, and Robert Penn Warren, destined to become famous men of letters, but also Merrill Moore, Jesse and Ridley Wills, Sidney Hirsch, William Yandell Elliott, Alec Stevenson, and Stanley Johnson, the *other* Fugitives. Members would bring their newly composed poems to the meetings and submit them to their peers for constructive criticism. By 1922, the group made the publication of the *Fugitive* the focus of their activity, thereby extending their influence beyond Nashville for the first time. The journal provided a

2. Harold Bloom, *The Anxiety of Influence: A Theory of Poetry* (New York: Oxford University Press, 1973), 5.

handy outlet not only for the members' creative efforts but also for codifying their aesthetic theories. John Crowe Ransom's best poems—"Philomela," "Judith of Bethulia," "Bells for John Whiteside's Daughter," "Captain Carpenter," and others—were first published in the *Fugitive*. Davidson and Tate also published their poems, and the work of Robert Penn Warren and Laura Riding was introduced. During its three years of publication, the *Fugitive* also attracted submissions from such well-known poets as Robert Graves, Hart Crane, William Alexander Percy, Louis Untermeyer, and John Gould Fletcher—along with poets who were never to achieve recognition outside its pages. This mixture of unknown, outside, and in-house acceptances became the pattern for the journals its members later established or edited. Also a part of the pattern was the holding of a poetry contest, after the example of the *Dial*, the *Lyric*, and *American Poetry*, and the inclusion of critical essays and reviews, mostly Ransom's, which further proliferated his critical theories. The *Fugitive* published quarterly until 1925, when the rigors of putting out a magazine proved too onerous to sustain. By 1929, with the development of the Agrarian movement, the agendas of the editors began to change from literary to sociopolitical concerns.

Although the Fugitive group included Vanderbilt professors and students, it was never officially connected with or even encouraged by the university. As George Core has stated, Edwin Mims, head of the English Department, became notorious for his treatment of the Fugitives: "More than for anything else that he did, including his published work, Mims will be remembered as the man who scuttled a graduate fellowship for Allen Tate in classics; who did not retain Robert Penn Warren after his three years of teaching at Vanderbilt in the early thirties; and who above all allowed Ransom, indeed almost encouraged him, to leave Vanderbilt for Kenyon College in 1937." Walter Clyde Curry, Mims's successor and a member of the Fugitive group, became anathema to the former Fugitives by "more nearly following than departing from Mims's arbitrary and highhanded example."[3] By making no effort to keep Warren, Tate, or Ransom, Vanderbilt University inadvertently was responsible for the expansion of the Fugitive legacy to other campuses and urban centers in a geographical area no longer southern and regional.

Many members of the Fugitive movement eventually taught courses in literature and in writing, both creative and expository. For some, like Tate,

3. George Core, "Vanderbilt English and the Rise of the New Criticism," in *The Vanderbilt Tradition: Essays in Honor of Thomas Daniel Young*, ed. Mark Royden Winchell (Baton Rouge: Louisiana State University Press, 1991), 20, 21.

teaching was a last resort when writing would not pay the bills or put food on the table. For Davidson, Warren, and Ransom, the college classroom became an opportunity to propagate their artistic theories and develop a coterie of young disciples.

John Crowe Ransom was the first influential teacher among the Fugitives. Beginning with Davidson and Tate and continuing with Cleanth Brooks and Andrew Lytle, Ransom taught his students a mode of thought, characterized by wit and irony, that Louise Cowan has called "the key to the attitude behind the whole Southern approach to writing." Moreover, not just potential writers but all of Ransom's students were for a time exposed to what would soon be called the New Criticism. According to Thomas Daniel Young, "when Ransom first taught the freshman required course in literature at Vanderbilt, there were six Shakespearean plays. When he had taught that course for six or eight years, he had those plays down to one act of one play [*Hamlet*]. What he was interested in was not those people[s'] getting a knowledge of Shakespeare but their learning to read poetry."[4] Ransom's unorthodox, neo-Socratic method led some students to conclude that he habitually came to class unprepared; but the best minds grasped what he was driving at, and his reputation as a teacher steadily grew. The last Vanderbilt class to come under his tutelage included such lifetime friends and colleagues as Peter Taylor and Randall Jarrell.

Donald Davidson's long teaching career earned him much admiration from Vanderbilt students over several decades. The first to attain literary stature was Jesse Stuart, who, in Davidson's words, "came to Vanderbilt in 1932 because he had heard about the Fugitive poets and wanted to study with them. . . . He did not complete his M.A. program at this time, mainly because his nearly completed M.A. thesis was destroyed in a fire that destroyed his dormitory, Wesley Hall. Donald Davidson lost a large portion of his and his family's possessions in the same fire. But almost immediately after his year at Vanderbilt, he began to write and publish his poetry and fiction." Davidson frequently championed the cause of writers such as Stuart and Mildred Haun against the objections of his Fugitive colleagues, who summarily rejected all so-called regional writings submitted to the journals they edited. Despite his political and aesthetic conservatism, Davidson also consistently defended literary criticism and creative writing as proper activities for the college class-

---

4. Louise Cowan, *The Fugitive Group: A Literary History* (Baton Rouge: Louisiana State University Press, 1959), 201; Thomas Daniel Young, interview by author, Atlanta, Ga., October 30, 1985.

room. Many of his protégés, both at Vanderbilt and at the Bread Loaf School, where he spent his summers, would attain literary reputations. But most would have agreed with the fiction writer Robert Drake that "at every one of Davidson's classes my soul might be required of me."[5]

Because Allen Tate realized early that he did not want to be a university professor, he became the most itinerant Fugitive of them all. By mail and through personal association, Tate kept up lively discussions with young literary acquaintances as well as with his Fugitive-Agrarian cohort. Certainly the early careers of almost every participant in the Fugitive legacy would have been quite different without Tate's patronage. Not only did he invite them to his homes in New York, Clarksville, Monteagle, and Princeton, but he was instrumental in locating teaching jobs and, more important, publishers for their first books. Ever a believer in tradition, Tate was later to wonder, in his memorial essay "Young Randall," why none in Jarrell's cohort of young writers chose to form a "post-Fugitive group."[6] Some, like Peter Taylor, were only too glad to retain those associations, but others, like Randall Jarrell, would eventually loosen the ties that bound them to their former patron and mentor.

Robert Penn Warren was a natural teacher whose associations with his more talented students often extended beyond the classroom at Vanderbilt, Southwestern (now Rhodes College), and Louisiana State University. Disarmingly humble about his classroom teaching, Warren functioned best in one-to-one relationships with such writers as Jesse Stuart, Randall Jarrell, Robert Lowell, and Peter Taylor. As an editor of the *Southern Review*, Warren helped to introduce Taylor and Eudora Welty to the literary world. Warren seldom wrote blurbs or reviews of his protégés' work, but he could be counted on to include them in the many anthologies he would edit. Warren wrote incisive introductions to the collected stories of such young fiction writers as Jesse Stuart, Caroline Gordon, Katherine Anne Porter, Eudora Welty, and Peter Taylor that would influence all future evaluations of their work.

After the Fugitives' activities ceased, several members of the group, including Ransom, Davidson, and Tate, became Agrarians and turned their attentions from poetry to political and economic theory. In their 1930 mani-

5. Donald Davidson, "The Southern Writer and the Modern University," in *Southern Writers in the Modern World* (Athens: University of Georgia Press, 1958), 66; Robert Y. Drake, "Donald Davidson and the Ancient Mariner," *Vanderbilt Alumnus* 49 (1964): 18–22.

6. Allen Tate, "Young Randall," in *Randall Jarrell, 1914–1965*, ed. Robert Lowell, Peter Taylor, and Robert Penn Warren (New York: Farrar, Straus & Giroux, 1967), 232.

festo *I'll Take My Stand*, Robert Penn Warren also published an essay, "The Briar Patch"; but in a 1984 communication, he asked to be called "a contributor to *I'll Take My Stand*"—not "an agrarian." Mark Royden Winchell has stated correctly that "the major Fugitive-Agrarians always saw themselves as writers more than polemicists, and it is by their literary productivity and legacy that they must be judged." While Agrarianism distracted the former Fugitives from the writing of poetry and criticism, it added to their circle Andrew Lytle and Cleanth Brooks and made an art form, as Martha Cook has demonstrated, of the Agrarian essay.[7]

In 1935, this tale of three cities shifted from Nashville to Baton Rouge, where Governor Huey Long was attempting to transform LSU into a major university, in Thomas Cutrer's words, by acquiring a "faculty, football team, and live tigers."[8] The implementation of Long's plan made possible the hiring of Robert Penn Warren and Cleanth Brooks and led to the establishment of the *Southern Review*. Before the "Brooksandwarren" era, as Robert Lowell called it, had ended in 1942, the Fugitive legacy would include not only Lowell but Peter Taylor, Albert Erskine, Leonard Unger, George Marion O'Donnell, and David MacDowell—all Vanderbilt alumni who came to LSU for graduate study under former Fugitive-Agrarians.

The idea of publishing the *Southern Review* actually came, in 1935, from LSU president James Monroe Smith. The *Review*'s editors—Robert Penn Warren, Cleanth Brooks, and Charles Pipkin—subsequently sent out a form letter to such well-known writers as Sherwood Anderson, E. E. Cummings, T. S. Eliot, and F. Scott Fitzgerald asking them to contribute to a review that would not, despite its title, "aim at a sectional program, nor . . . have an academic bias."[9]

Because of Pipkin's influence and the other editors' Agrarian backgrounds, the *Review* did include essays on historical, political, and economic topics. While many of these articles were written by former Agrarians such as Davidson, Lytle, and Herbert Agar, essays by Kenneth Burke, Sidney Hook, and other non-Agrarians attest to the cosmopolitan outlook of the

7. Robert Penn Warren, annotations to author's manuscript, 1986; Mark Royden Winchell, introduction to *Vanderbilt Tradition*, 7; Martha E. Cook, "The Artistry of I'll Take My Stand," *Mississippi Quarterly* 33 (1980): 425–32.

8. Thomas W. Cutrer, *Parnassus on the Mississippi: "The Southern Review" and the Baton Rouge Literary Community, 1935–1942* (Baton Rouge: Louisiana University Press, 1984), 36.

9. Form letter from Robert Penn Warren, Cleanth Brooks, and Charles Pipkin to Sherwood Anderson and others, March 23, 1935, *The Southern Review* Papers, Beinecke Rare Book and Manuscript Library, Yale University, New Haven, Conn.

journal. The early issues contained such memorable articles as Brooks's analysis of *The Waste Land* and Ransom's controversial "Shakespeare at Sonnets," as well as such well-known stories as Andrew Lytle's "Jericho, Jericho, Jericho," Katherine Anne Porter's "Old Mortality," and Eudora Welty's "Petrified Man." The *Review*'s policy of printing "a long group of poems by a single author so that the reader may be able to get a real sample of the poet's work" was generally applauded by its contributors, except when the poet was unable to provide as many acceptable poems as the editors required.[10] John Berryman and Randall Jarrell were among the young poets whose careers profited from the opportunity to publish extensively in the *Southern Review* under the editorship of Brooks and Warren.

Lively interactions between LSU and Kenyon College characterized the years 1937–42, when Gambier, Ohio, along with Nashville and Baton Rouge, formed the post-Fugitive triangle. John Crowe Ransom moved to Kenyon in 1937 after he had been the focus of bitter controversy with Vanderbilt's administration over status and compensation and despite letters of dire warning from such partisans as Allen Tate and a keep-Ransom campaign led by Vanderbilt students Randall Jarrell and Peter Taylor. Jarrell followed Ransom to Kenyon as English instructor and tennis coach, as did Peter Taylor and Robert Lowell, who would earn their baccalaureate degrees there. During Ransom's long teaching career at Kenyon, his students included poets Anthony Hecht and James Wright, members of a group of World War II veterans who used their GI benefits at Kenyon. Robie Macauley put it best when he said, "Like my friends Robert Lowell, Randall Jarrell, and Peter Taylor, I had been drawn there because I heard that Ransom was a great teacher."[11]

The *Kenyon Review* began at the request of Kenyon president Gordon Keith Chalmers, whose wife, the poet Roberta Teale Swartz Chalmers, believed that Kenyon College was a likely home for an important journal. When he hired Ransom, President Chalmers, at Robert Frost's suggestion, had already determined that Ransom would edit the review. Unlike the *Southern*, the *Kenyon Review* had no sociopolitical program but was rather to be devoted to "the discussion of values in literature" and to the "presentation of the best imaginative writing."[12] Like the *Southern Review*, its early issues contained essays that have attained autonomous status, such as Philip Rahv's

10. Robert Penn Warren to James Agee, March 3, 1936, ibid.

11. Robie Macauley, *"The Kenyon Review, 1939–1970," Tri-Quarterly* 43 (1978): 72.

12. Marian Janssen, *"The Kenyon Review," 1939–1970: A Critical History* (Baton Rouge: Louisiana State University Press, 1990), 11; Macauley, *"Kenyon Review,"* 73.

"Pale Face and Red Skin" and George Marion O'Donnell's "Faulkner's Mythology." In addition to the writing of former students Lowell, Jarrell, and
Taylor and such established writers as Dylan Thomas, Wallace Stevens,
W. H. Auden, and Boris Pasternak, the *Kenyon Review* helped to develop new-
comers such as Flannery O'Conner, John Ciardi, Reed Whittemore, Howard
Nemerov, and Mona Van Duyn. Ransom's editorial style was no less magisterial than Warren's at LSU. His typical phrase, "We don't quite like it
enough," accompanied rejected manuscripts to writers now both famous and
forgotten.

The Fugitive legacy was also extended through the schools of criticism
which Ransom conducted at Kenyon in 1948, 1949, and 1950. Believing that
"the next great strategic move of English studies" would be "toward the critical side," Ransom advertised that his summer sessions would develop teachers of English who could "form literary judgments."[13] Lecturers included
such imposing members of the literary establishment as Kenneth Burke, William Empson, L. C. Knights, Eric Bentley, Philip Rahv, F. O. Matthiessen,
and Austin Warren, as well as Ransom, Tate, and Brooks. After three successful summer sessions, Ransom arranged with Indiana University at Bloomington to continue the schools under the same structure and leadership until
1972. At Indiana, the schools of criticism carried on the Fugitive legacy's pattern of northern dispersal. Ransom and the *Review* were to remain at Kenyon,
and Gambier would be Ransom's home until his death.

Other journals edited by the Fugitives' friends and heirs were also vital to
the careers of the former Fugitives and their mentees. After the *Southern Review* suspended publication in 1942, the *Sewanee Review*, edited at various
times by Allen Tate and Andrew Lytle, essentially took over its function in
promoting younger members of the post-Fugitive circle, including Peter
Taylor and Flannery O'Connor. Other journals with ties of varying strength
to the former Fugitives were the *American Review*, the *Virginia Quarterly Review*, the *Partisan Review*, and *New Directions*. For members of the circle wanting to publish in these magazines, the influence of former Fugitives would
differ according to who edited the particular journal at the time. Although
these reviews paid their contributors modest amounts for their writing—Tate
consistently refused to become involved with any publishing operation that
did *not* pay its contributors—a writer could certainly not depend on them for
a significant portion of his or her livelihood. Consequently, the best of them

13. Thomas Daniel Young, *Gentleman in a Dustcoat: A Biography of John Crowe Ransom*
(Baton Rouge: Louisiana State University Press, 1976), 341.

also sought to publish in such popular magazines as the *New Yorker*, the *Atlantic Monthly*, and the *Nation* and in women's magazines such as *Harper's Bazaar* and *Mademoiselle*.

The Fugitive Legacy: A Critical History explores the impact, crucial though often unacknowledged, of the Nashville Fugitives as teachers, editors, and mentors. Their protégés have received considerable scholarly attention only as individuals or in relation to small groups of closely related writers within single literary genres. The many-faceted career of Robert Penn Warren has provoked much interest, but no one has sufficiently noted the number of young writers whose successful careers he helped to develop. The critical revolution brought about by Cleanth Brooks and the New Criticism, an obvious outgrowth of the Fugitive movement, has been treated, and *mis*-treated, mainly as an independent phenomenon. Studies of Randall Jarrell, Robert Lowell, and John Berryman have provided insight into their individual careers and into how they, like their mentors, functioned in small circles. Similarly, a plethora of able critics and scholars have explored in considerable depth the careers and relationships of Andrew Lytle, Katherine Anne Porter, Caroline Gordon, Eudora Welty, Peter Taylor, and Flannery O'Connor, while others, notably feminists, have demonstrated how the women in the group interacted with and sustained one another. No one has described how these writers became part of a larger phenomenon, the Fugitive legacy, whose influence extended far beyond the parameters of southern literature.

The cultural importance of the Fugitives has too often been confused with the narrow politics of Agrarianism and relegated to a reactionary piety for regionalism and dead tradition. *The Fugitive Legacy: A Critical History* focuses instead on the Fugitives' most vital contribution: their sponsorship of those writers who, in their own ways, have continued what began in Nashville, Tennessee, in the 1920s. In his postscript to *Writers of the Modern South*, Louis D. Rubin, Jr., asked, "Who would think to link the work of Randall Jarrell and James Dickey with that of John Crowe Ransom and Allen Tate?"[14] Within the still-widening circle of the Fugitive legacy, such disparate talents and personalities did indeed become a force to be reckoned with in American letters.

14. Louis D. Rubin, Jr., *Writers of the Modern South* (Seattle: University of Washington Press, 1963), 237.

2 / The Editorial Legacy

When the Fugitives decided to cease publishing their poetry magazine, it seems unlikely that any of them knew that their editorial days were only beginning. The bonds that connected the former Fugitives and their protégés had solidified long before, one by one, they left Nashville for New York, California, Oxford University, Baton Rouge, and Gambier, Ohio. How long those connections would remain close and whether the Fugitive legacy would spread to succeeding generations of poets, critics, and fiction writers was to a great extent dependent on how often, and under what conditions, their work would appear in print. Rather than depending on a few literary magazines and reviews, not all of them friendly, former Fugitives Allen Tate, Robert Penn Warren, and John Crowe Ransom would find themselves, sometime within the next fifteen years, serving as literary editors once again.

Those who have written on the history of the literary journals differentiate sharply between the so-called little magazines, like the *Fugitive*, and the quarterlies, such as the *Southern*, *Kenyon*, and *Sewanee*. The little magazines were, as Monroe Spears put it, both "experimental" and "ephemeral," largely products of the "exciting, rebellious, and unpredictable" 1920s and bearing such racy titles as *Broom*, *Blast*, and *Transition*. They were mostly published abroad, at low cost, and were "carefree about deadlines and business matters, living very much for the moment." Their mission was to publish new, avant-garde poetry and fiction; but they had little or no interest in criticism. A literary review, or quarterly, is, in contrast, a "noncommercial magazine, uncompromisingly highbrow in character, which publishes criticism of literature and to some extent of the other arts in the form of essays, book reviews, and chronicles, together with fiction and poetry selected according to the kind of high standards defined and employed in the criticism." To an extent, also, the two types of publications that involved the former Fugitives had different antecedents and lines of development. The *Fugitive*, for example, resembled the New Orleans *Double Dealer, Dial, Little Review*, and *Poetry*, while the three southern quarterlies, according to G. A. M. Janssens, had the following "genealogy": the *Dial* led to the *Hound and Horn*, in turn to the *Symposium* and the *Southern Review*, which then spawned the *Kenyon Review*, the (new) *Sewanee Review*, and finally the *Partisan Review*.[1]

In their own individual evolutions, however, the *Southern, Kenyon*, and *Sewanee Reviews* must also claim the *Fugitive*, a typical "little" magazine, as their common progenitor. Although the *Fugitive* was like others of its genre—devoted to the publication of poetry, published on a shoestring, and destined to live a mere four years—it lacked the Bohemian panache and the unconventionality of the typical twenties rag. From the beginning, as its advertisement proclaimed, the *Fugitive* was a middle-of-the-road publication, presenting new poets but also seeking contributions from "the best modern poets," mostly, but not necessarily, from the South.[2] And although publishing poetry remained its major concern, the *Fugitive*, almost from the beginning, began to slip in some editorials that engaged in critical controversy. As a result, working on the *Fugitive* allowed its editors—Ransom, Tate, and Warren—to develop the practical experience and critical judgment that paved the way for their much larger successes as editors of the quarterlies. Though Donald Davidson's contributions to the editing and management of the *Fugitive* were as important as Tate's, Ransom's, and Warren's, his decision to remain at Vanderbilt University effectively foreclosed any opportunity he might have had

1. Monroe Spears, "The Function of Literary Quarterlies," in *American Ambitions: Selected Essays on Literary and Cultural Themes* (Baltimore: Johns Hopkins University Press, 1987), 111, 110; G. A. M. Janssens, *The American Literary Review: A Critical History, 1920–1950* (The Hague: Mouton, 1968), 29–30.

2. *Fugitive* 1 (April–December 1922), advertisement page, *The Fugitive* Collection, Donald Davidson Papers, Jean and Alexander Heard Library, Vanderbilt University, Nashville, Tenn.

to edit a literary magazine after the *Fugitive* because that university had no interest in putting out the Fugitives' sort of journal.

At first, the *Fugitive* was an unlikely vehicle for training editors destined for individual distinction. It began as a group project in which all members were "editors in the matter of choice of contents of the journal and of decisions on policy." An editor was designated for each month to work with a committee of two more Fugitives on the upcoming issue of the magazine. Such a plan predictably led to frustrations so that as early as 1923, some in the group wanted to designate a single editor. Ransom remained "dead against" the plan because, as Louise Cowan surmises, he "opposed having his name appear in a subordinate position." In summer 1923, however, Allen Tate and Stanley Johnson "took matters into their own hands by drawing up a plan for a yearly organization of the magazine." Tate and Johnson wanted to make Donald Davidson editor, with Tate as his assistant. Although Tate was the youngest in the group, most of the members agreed, since, as Jesse Wills wrote to Davidson, "You and Allen are the logical candidates for the positions named therein. Without honor or title you have done most of the work up to now. With or without, you will probably continue to do most of it."[3] In the summer of 1923, Tate took over as managing editor, and Davidson, after much hesitation, finally accepted the position of editor in chief.

From the beginning, however, Ransom was commonly considered the editor of the *Fugitive* because he wrote most of the editorials while others, Davidson and Tate in particular, performed the managerial duties. Ransom's editorials in the *Fugitive* were among his first pieces of published criticism and germane not only to subsequent criticism but also to his future editorship of the *Kenyon Review*. His review of *On English Poetry* by the internationally known British poet Robert Graves was Ransom's first attack on free verse and his opening salvo against modernist poetics. Ironically, the Graves review also opened a debate between Ransom and Tate, an outspoken defender of modernism despite his own use of traditional poetic forms.

Any account of the Fugitives' editorial legacy must emphasize the importance, often from behind the scenes, of Allen Tate. Although he would actually serve as editor in chief of only one review, the *Sewanee*, and for only two years, Tate was a major player in all four publications. His work on the *Fugitive* prepared Tate for his own future involvement with the southern critical quarterlies.

Tate was not content for long merely to answer mail and be one of many

3. Cowan, *Fugitive Group*, 74, 122, 120, 121.

poets publishing in the *Fugitive*. In the fourth issue, that of December 1922, he published an editorial essay entitled "Whose Ox?," concerning "the relation of traditional form to modern poetry." "Whose Ox?" was not only Tate's answer to Ransom's remarks on poetic form in the Graves review but also his first published defense of modernist poetics in the manner of his idol T. S. Eliot, who, Tate believed, had "demonstrated the necessity, in some cases, for an aberrant versification." Far from defending the spate of "mediocre" free verse then being written, Tate attributed opposition to the new poetics to personal taste and allegiances among poets. It was a question, therefore, of "Whose Ox?" (is being gored). Apparently taking the editorial as an attack on their traditional poetics, both Davidson and Ransom called for emendations but finally published Tate's essay. Davidson would later call it "a brilliant piece of work," adding that "none of us, except John could write such an editorial." Ransom remained firmly on the side of traditional prosody, demonstrating as much in "The Future of Poetry," in the February 1924 issue, to which Tate would reply in "One Escape from the Dilemma" in the April 1924 issue.[4]

This exchange on the cutting-edge topic of free versus metric verse not only contains the genesis of both Ransom's and Tate's consistent positions on poetic form, but it also foreshadows the way the *Southern* and *Kenyon* reviews would enliven the dialogue about poetry by becoming the arena of polite but pointed critical controversy, frequently involving one or more persons from the post-Fugitive circle.

Robert Penn Warren first became involved in the *Fugitive* when his poem "Crusade" was nominated for the Nashville prize in the *Fugitive*'s first poetry contest. For the August–September 1923 issue, Tate, Warren's former roommate, accepted "After Teacups," a poem owing much to Eliot's "The Love Song of J. Alfred Prufrock." Thereafter, Warren consistently published his poems in the *Fugitive*, among them "A Face in the Crowd," the poem that closes each collection of his poetry. As early as 1923, Tate had written to editor Davidson that "that boy is a wonder, or I'm much mistaken, and deserves election to the Board." Warren was invited to replace Tate as assistant editor in 1924 but refused, thinking that it would be "a thankless bit of drudgery of no particular significance." In the last year of the magazine's publication, however, Warren became its coeditor, along with Tate, responsible for soliciting contributions and selecting the poems for each 1925 issue. Although Warren wrote no editorials for the *Fugitive*, his contribution to the manage-

4. Ibid., 84.

ment of the magazine was significant enough that his departure from Vanderbilt to begin graduate work at the University of California was a factor in the
Fugitive's demise.[5] Like Ransom and Tate, Warren had, through his involvement with the *Fugitive*, gained experience in the evaluation of poetry and in
the management of a journal that would serve him well when he became one
of the editors of the *Southern Review*.

Warren's future coeditor, Cleanth Brooks, first became involved with aca-
demic writing at Vanderbilt in 1928 with a student publication called *Facets:
An Anthology of Verse*. Though *Facets*, in Mark Winchell's opinion, made no
impression on the literary scene, it did publish a few good writers, such as
Henry Blue Kline, who contributed to *I'll Take My Stand*, and Richmond
Croom Beatty, who later became a distinguished professor of English at Vanderbilt. The magazine was entirely the work of Vanderbilt students, including
Brooks, who took part in its publishing and distribution. On one occasion, he
even drove over to Sewanee to ask advice of W. S. Knickerbocker, then editor
of the *Sewanee Review*, unaware that Knickerbocker was neither an effective
editor nor a friend of the Vanderbilt group.[6]

Soon after their involvement with the *Fugitive* came the turbulent days in
which the energies of Ransom, Tate, Davidson, and other former Fugitives
were directed toward the publication of their Agrarian symposium *I'll Take
My Stand* in 1930. Although none of the twelve southerners who contributed
essays to the symposium claimed the position of editor, the organizational
and editorial tasks involved afforded Tate, primarily, and Ransom further
useful experience and widened their network of literary and philosophical allies—as well as enemies. With the historian and journalist Herbert Agar,
Allen Tate edited a sequel, *Who Owns America* (1936), in which Cleanth
Brooks and eight of the twelve contributors to *I'll Take My Stand* published
essays. Cutrer calls it a "loosely knit symposium" that was "a disappointment
to its editors."[7] Brooks's and Warren's interest in the Agrarian cause had
passed its climax, for they were deeply involved by then in the *Southern Review*; and Tate had gone on to other projects.

Tate first rose to editorial prominence as regional editor of the *Hound and
Horn*, formerly an undergraduate magazine at Harvard University. Lincoln
Kirstein and Varian Fry, who began as undergraduate editors, would continue

---

5. Ibid., 261, 182, 125; Joseph Blotner, *Robert Penn Warren: A Biography* (New York: Random House, 1997), 41, 45.
6. Mark Royden Winchell, *Cleanth Brooks and the Rise of Modern Criticism* (Charlottesville:
University Press of Virginia, 1996), 26, 36.
7. Cutrer, *Parnassus on the Mississippi*, 126.

with the journal throughout its life, to be joined in 1932 by regional editors Allen Tate, Yvor Winters, Ezra Pound, and R. P. Blackmur as the magazine became national in scope. Tate had contributed to the magazine several years before 1929, when Blackmur asked him to "write reviews for us more or less regularly—poetry and criticism." Three months later, Tate was asked to submit "any essays on hand or that you are planning to write"; and two years after that Tate became regional editor for the South to the delight of editors Bernard Bandler and Blackmur. (Yvor Winters would edit for the Pacific states.) Kirstein and Bandler hoped that the regional editors would procure for the review manuscripts "we would not otherwise know about and [about] which you would probably be in a position to instruct us."[8] Tate's Fugitive-Agrarian associations indeed gave him immediate access to such "manuscripts."

The *Hound and Horn*'s last two years (1932–34) were its best, in Lincoln Kirstein's opinion, because Tate and Winters were regional editors. Although Tate is said to have "sponsored the Southern agrarians, mainly his friends from the days of the *Fugitive* . . . and some new recruits to that group," Tate's ability to get his friends' work published seems to have been limited. Earlier, under Kirsten's editorship, the magazine accepted Katherine Anne Porter's first mature story, "Flowering Judas," in 1929, and published Caroline Gordon's "The Ice House" in 1931, before Tate became regional editor. The only piece of fiction Tate seems to have obtained for the journal during his editorship was his own first short story, "The Immortal Woman"; and when Tate obtained critical essays from his post-Fugitive brethren, he sometimes encountered stiff opposition from his coeditor Yvor Winters. Tate tried unsuccessfully to promote John Crowe Ransom's famous essay "Poetry: A Note in Ontology," later published in the *Kenyon Review*; an article on Ransom by Robert Penn Warren caused dispute among the editors and was never published in *Hound and Horn*; and a Ransom essay on Henry James was canceled. When considering articles on Agrarianism, Tate sometimes voted against his fellow Fugitives. Davidson's "Sectionalism in the United States," for example, was published in volume 6, number 4 (Summer 1933) over Tate's objections (Tate disagreed with Davidson that a "provincial society" was necessary for literature). The only other Agrarian contributions during Tate's editorship were reviews by Andrew Lytle and Frank Owsley.[9]

After the demise of the *Hound and Horn*, the *Southern Review* was the Fugi-

8. Janssens, *American Literary Review*, 127–28.
9. Ibid., 128, 130–31, 132, 134–35.

tive legacy's next editorial accomplishment. Janssens calls it the "closer heir," rather than the *Symposium* and *Partisan Review*, to the tradition of the literary review as established by the *Dial* and *Hound and Horn*: "Although it was edited in the South it appealed to a national audience. Its temper was conservative but its pages were open to dissenting views if they were intelligently and persuasively expressed. The strength of the *Southern Review* lay in its consolidated body of contributors and in its unobtrusive but intelligent editorship."[10] Because Cleanth Brooks and Robert Penn Warren were its editors, it became a means to express the former Fugitives' aesthetic standards, directly in critical essays and indirectly through the fiction and poetry they chose for its pages.

After their involvement with the *Southwest Review* at Louisiana State University, it would have been remarkable had Brooks and Warren *not* published a journal there. Warren liked to tell how, one Sunday afternoon in 1935, LSU president James Monroe Smith took him and Albert Erskine for a ride in his black Cadillac and asked whether a superior review could be established at LSU. Warren replied that it could be done if contributors were paid fairly, if writers were given " 'decent company between the covers,' " if "editorial authority were sufficiently concentrated to allow the magazine its own distinctive character and quality," and if the publication could be free from interference from university committees. Smith accepted Warren's conditions and the *Southern Review* was born. Warren later recalled that in the beginning, Albert Erskine was "as much an editor as he and Brooks" and that the crowded editorial rooms in the agriculture building—no apparent connection with the *Review*'s reputation as an "Agrarian rag"—were the scene of many "arguments, the banging together of opinions and temperaments" that would subsequently end "with an agreement."[11]

According to the *Reveille*, LSU's student newspaper, the *Review* set out to present "essays on social, economic, political, and literary topics; fiction; poetry; and reviews of current books." Charles Pipkin, the other editor, was a more vigorous supporter of the nonliterary component than were the former members of the Agrarian group. Pipkin's bust stands without inscription in the present offices of the *Review*, anonymous to staff and visitor alike, mutely signifying his virtual absence from most annals of the *Review*'s early days. Mark Winchell in fact calls Pipkin "the odd man out" even when he "was

10. Ibid., 29.
11. Robert Penn Warren, "Then and Now . . . A Review in Review," *LSU Outlook*, January 1981, n.p.

the magazine's ostensible editor," partly because of his demanding position as graduate dean but mainly because he wanted more social science emphasis in the magazine. In his amusing December 1, 1937, letter to Allen Tate, Cleanth Brooks let his Fugitive mentor in on a project targeted at Pipkin: "Tinkum and Albert and I have been working up a parody of 'The Waste Land' for extremely private circulation. Our *Waste Land* is the Southern Review office, and the dead which have been buried is an MS on social science which we hope will remain interred in the filing cabinet. At present we have only a few scattered fragments, but you can see the relevance of the following: 'O keep the Pip far hence that's friend to men / Or with his nails he'll dig it up again.' "[12] Although under Pipkin's influence, the quarterly would devote considerable space to political and sociological essays, the pendulum was destined to swing toward literature. The *Southern Review* therefore proved to be one of the last expressions of the Agrarian movement and the first of the influential southern literary quarterlies.

Because Robert Penn Warren and Cleanth Brooks were well-known for having published essays in *I'll Take My Stand* and *Who Owns America*, respectively, the new journal was automatically tarred with the Agrarian brush. The suspicions of the Southern Methodist wing of the *Southwest Review* to that effect were largely responsible for the schism between the Dallas and Baton Rouge editors and the subsequent founding of the *Southern Review*. And in fact, only two of the twelve contributors to *I'll Take My Stand*, Stark Young and Henry Blue Kline, failed to publish in the *Southern Review*. The literary world was to be surprised, however, when the journal became better known for literary criticism, poetry, and fiction than for its generous airing of political and economic treatises. As Janssens points out, however, the *Review* not only weighed in consistently against scientific positivism, but it also included essays that joined its literary and nonliterary emphases. Cleanth Brooks's "The Vision of W. B. Yeats," for example, asserts an absolute separation between poetry and science.[13]

Although Brooks and Warren were indisputably the driving forces behind the *Southern Review*, the other Fugitives also played important roles. Janssens calls Tate "the most important adviser of the *Southern Review*." Not only was he the first outside the Baton Rouge circle to be informed about the possibil-

---

12. Rhonda Cabot Tinterelli, *"The Southern Review, 1935–1942: The Intellectual History of a Cultural Quarterly"* (Ph.D. dissertation, Louisiana State University, 1980), 40; Winchell, *Cleanth Brooks and the Rise of Modern Criticism*, 96.

13. Janssens, *American Literary Review*, 214–15; Cleanth Brooks, "The Vision of W. B. Yeats," *Southern Review* 4 (Summer 1938): 116–42.

ity of creating the *Review* and regularly called on for advice about contributors to cultivate and special projects to undertake, but Tate was also expected to contribute his own writing regularly. His essay "The Function of the Critical Quarterly" (volume 1, number 3, 1935) was his first and most important contribution.

In this influential essay, as George Core has written, Allen Tate drew "a blueprint," not just for the *Southern Review* but for all three of the southern literary quarterlies with which he would be involved.[14] Tate laid out his own notions of how a quarterly should be run and made very plain that the strength and durability of such a publication would require high editorial standards and a united front, consisting not only of the quarterly's editors but also of their circle of allies. Writing not long after the demise of the *Hound and Horn* and the *Symposium*, Tate could cite only T. S. Eliot's *Criterion*, which would be around for three more years, as an example for the editors to follow.

After wryly remarking that literary reviews existed mainly "for acquainting unpopular writers with one another's writings," Tate proceeded to set forth some principles he thought essential. Such a publication must be subsidized and must attach as much importance to "creative" work as to critical essays. Moreover, the review must bear a weighty responsibility to its clientele: "to supply its readers with coherent standards of taste and examples of taste in operation; not mere statements about taste." The journal should, moreover, pay all contributors but be loyal to the regular ones, accepting most of their work and paying them more than "for the casual manuscript, however good, that [the editor] found on his desk this morning."[15] Tate thus recognized that a successful review required not only a stable source of revenue but also an editor who had contacts in the literary world. With university funding behind it and the Fugitive network surrounding it, the *Southern Review*, Tate implied, had every opportunity to succeed.

The crucial role which the *Review* played in the careers of such Fugitive heirs as critics Cleanth Brooks and Robert Penn Warren, poets Randall Jarrell and John Berryman, and fiction writers Andrew Lytle, Katherine Anne Porter, Caroline Gordon, Eudora Welty, and Peter Taylor is chronicled in

14. George Core, "The Literary Quarterly in the South," in *"The Southern Review" and Modern Literature, 1935–1985*, ed. Lewis P. Simpson, James Olney, and Jo Gulledge (Baton Rouge: Louisiana State University Press, 1988), 187.

15. Spears, "Function of Literary Quarterlies," 45, 47, 52.

subsequent chapters in this book. For young writers like John Berryman, the *Southern Review* filled what they perceived as a near vacuum. In *Love and Fame*, Berryman's autobiographical account of his own beginnings, he re-called that for poets trying to publish in the late 1930s, it was "Solely the *Southern Review/* Not *Partisan* yet." Through the force of its editorial empha-ses, the *Southern Review* was also responsible for the spread of the New Criti-cism (see Chapter 3), not only through essays and reviews written by former Fugitives and their circle, Cleanth Brooks especially, but also through the poetry, fiction, and criticism it published and the established writers those choices emphasized. The *Review* promoted modernist poets, particularly Eliot and W. B. Yeats, and tended to reject poetry with philosophical or other didactic agendas. In general, it favored formal prosody over free verse. In fic-tion, the editors, according to Janssens, "admired complex novels with com-plex characters and psychological situations, and with a fine moral discrimi-nation matched by a corresponding complexity and appropriateness of style."[16] In covering foreign fiction, the editors of the *Southern Review* were "haphazard" but somewhat more international in their interests than the *Hound and Horn* and less than the *Dial*.

When the *Southern Review* ceased publication in 1942, its physical remains would have literally been reduced to ashes except for the heroic efforts of Cleanth Brooks. After LSU had officially cut off support for the journal in March 1942 and a final issue was published, the *Southern Review*'s staff was unceremoniously ousted from their offices. Maintenance crews began imme-diately to renovate the area for future occupants and tossed the *Southern Re-view*'s valuable papers in the trash. According to Winchell, Brooks, "dis-covering where the files were dumped . . . grabbed a flashlight one sweltering summer night, crawled up into the attic of Allen Hall, and salvaged for pos-terity what was left of the *Southern Review*." Although both Brooks and War-ren would serve on editorial boards of and contribute to the *Sewanee* and *Ken-yon* reviews, and Brooks would be offered the editorship of the *Sewanee*, neither would ever manage another literary magazine. The review they founded and fought to sustain for seven productive years had taken time and energy which they now preferred to devote to their own writing. The *Re-view*'s demise nonetheless left the entire post-Fugitive group in a state of shock. Allen Tate even advised Lytle, on January 26, 1942, to join the armed services because "there will be nothing for writers elsewhere in the next few years, perhaps longer."[17]

Twenty-three years later, the new *Southern Review*, a somewhat bedraggled Phoenix, rose from the ashes of the first. Lewis P. Simpson, who co-edited the new series with Donald Stanford, wrote in 1985 of a "certain continuity" between the old and new reviews. When the editors naturally turned to Brooks and Warren for advice on what tack the resurrected journal should take, Brooks replied that "it should be a direction as different from that of the earlier publication as the literary situation demanded," which would probably mean "a quite divergent road." In fact, in Simpson's opinion, that path would turn out to be "only a relatively different one." Because the editors had been students during the so-called Southern Renaissance, they still idealized that bygone era and desired, if possible, to recreate it. Unlike the former *Southern Review*, however, which was created to air discussions of political, economic, and social issues, the second was to be almost exclusively devoted to literature.

The new series of the *Southern Review* would continue to be indebted to the Fugitive legacy. The first issue presented an essay on Ransom and one on the Agrarians, and a special issue was later devoted to Caroline Gordon. After 1965, the *Review* once again presented essays by such former post–Fugitive-Agrarians as John Crowe Ransom, Donald Davidson, Allen Tate, and Andrew Lytle; essays and poems by Robert Penn Warren and Randall Jarrell; and fiction by Eudora Welty, Katherine Anne Porter, and Caroline Gordon. In general, Simpson states, "Ten numbers given over to the subject of writing in the South have tended to look backward" even though the editors' aim, as stated in an advertising brochure printed in its fourth year, was to show that "contemporary literature matters because it is the consciousness of our own age."[18]

The void left by the passing of the Brooks and Warren *Southern Review* was immediately filled by its sister journal the *Kenyon*, which had begun publishing three years earlier, in 1939. After a brief but serious effort to continue the *Southern* through merger with the *Kenyon Review*, the *Kenyon* became the "legitimate successor," in Janssens's words, "because of personal friendship between Brooks, Warren, and Ransom."[19]

17. Winchell, *Cleanth Brooks and the Rise of Modern Criticism*, 194; Thomas Daniel Young and Elizabeth Sarcone, eds., *The Tate-Lytle Letters: The Correspondence of Andrew Lytle and Allen Tate* (Jackson: University Press of Mississippi, 1987), 178.

18. Lewis P. Simpson, "Introduction: A Certain Continuity," in *"The Southern Review" and Modern Literature*, ed. Simpson, Olney, and Gulledge, 11.

19. Janssens, *American Literary Review*, 29.

The *Kenyon* differed from the *Southern* because it had no "political or re-gional discussion" and because Ransom was so large a presence. In *The Ken-yon Review, 1939–1970*, Marion Janssen offers two answers as to why Kenyon College president Gordon Keith Chalmers recruited Ransom to create the review. His name was suggested by Robert Frost, either out of admiration or because he did not consider Ransom a serious competitor. It is more likely, however, that because Chalmers's wife, the poet Roberta Teale Swartz, had won second place in the *Fugitive*'s 1923 poetry contest, she and her husband harbored warm feelings toward Ransom and the other Fugitives. Janssen also suggests, however, that the fact that Ransom had "helped to edit" the *Fugi-tive* might have been seen as a disadvantage by the professors and administra-tion of this midwestern college, who may have felt that Ransom's Fugitive-Agrarian reputation meant that he was "out of touch, reactionary, and . . . [possibly] racist" and that his group method of running the *Fugitive* was "old-fashioned . . . [and] roundabout." Ransom himself was not without under-standable trepidation when, concerned over lack of institutional support and funding, he wrote to Merrill Moore, "I don't want to edit another Fugitive, or little magazine, which would be wondering if each issue might be the last."[20]

Ransom had not, however, ceased to believe in a group approach to the job of publishing a journal—as long as that group could be filled with his post-Fugitive cronies. In a December 24, 1937, letter to Allen Tate, Ransom described the situation he had been offered:

> [Gordon Keith Chalmers] thinks of its editing as a full-time one-man job, aside from secretarial and business help. Doesn't want to withdraw me from all teaching, and proposed to go out and get another man to be a co-editor with me, both of us to teach half-time. . . . Wants to consider long and hard with me the choice of the man. Names a name or two I don't know and therefore suspect, is more impressed with the idea of [Mark] Van Doren. I held my peace but instantly occupied my mind with the idea of: *Tate*. After Tate, Warren, of course.

Ransom continued for some time to press Chalmers to hire Tate, but the ad-ministration of Kenyon would not agree to give him a salary as high as Ran-som's (higher than anyone else in the Kenyon English Department). Tate went instead to the Women's College of North Carolina, and Warren seems not to have received serious consideration. Philip Blair Rice was hired to

20. Janssen, *"Kenyon Review,"* 11–13; Janssens, *American Literary Review*, 261.

serve as managing editor and teach philosophy, while Norman Johnson, a Harvard graduate, would be secretary and teach a section of English. Steadfastly refusing to accept advisory editors from the Kenyon English Department, Ransom demanded that the board be staffed by people with good reputations in the literary world. In the end, however, he was forced to accept an eclectic group of advisers, including such noted literary persons as Tate, R. P. Blackmur, and Mark Van Doren, joined by Philip Timberlake of the English Department; Paul Rosenfeld, an expert on music; Roberta Teale Swartz, and Eliseo Vivas, a philosopher. Writing to Tate in the fall of 1938, Ransom described Van Doren as "a universal favor[rite] at Kenyon," Swartz as "a thoroughly good though not a high-powered literary person" but "not a meddler," Timberlake as "our local faculty man . . . good though unambitious," and Vivas as "a philosopher . . . an excellent man, friend of Rice's."[21]

The writers who appeared in Ransom's first issue were so familiar that Janssens was prompted to remark that "almost all its contributions could have been taken straight from the *Southern Review.*" Ransom asked Tate to help him find other worthy contributors, and between the two of them, they wrote to Ezra Pound, Ford Madox Ford, Dylan Thomas, and T. S. Eliot, as well as to Tate, Warren, and Blackmur. Although none of these established writers were able to comply, the young men who had followed Ransom from Vanderbilt to Kenyon—George Marion O'Donnell, Robert Lowell, and Randall Jarrell—were only too happy to have their work considered. Jarrell and Lowell were the poets whose work appeared in the first issue. Although O'Donnell submitted poems and volunteered his services as a reviewer, neither met Ransom's ambitious criteria. Ransom wrote to O'Donnell on February 17, 1938, "We don't like them [the poems] quite well enough."[22] O'Donnell's influential article "Faulkner's Mythology" did, however, appear in the third issue.

From the beginning, the *Kenyon Review* became known as the major proliferator of the New Criticism. Among the essays that helped make the New Criticism popular in universities were Robert Penn Warren's "The Love and the Separateness in Miss Welty" (6:246–59), "Melville the Poet" (7:208–23), "Hemingway" (9:1–28), and his most influential theoretical essay, "Pure and Impure Poetry" (5:228–54). Randall Jarrell published his important review of

21. Janssen, *"Kenyon Review,"* 17; Young, *Gentleman in a Dustcoat,* 299–302, 496.

22. Janssens, *American Literary Review,* 266; Janssen, *"Kenyon Review,"* 30–31; Ransom to George Marion O'Donnell, February 17, 1938, *Kenyon Review* Papers, Kenyon College Special Collections in the Olin Library, Kenyon College, Gambier, Ohio.

Marianne Moore's *What Are the Years* in "The Humble Animal" (4:408–10), and Cleanth Brooks, in "Cantankerous and Other Critics" (6:283–88), reviewed *The Anatomy of Nonsense* by Yvor Winters.[23]

Janssen points out that the *Kenyon Review* also published many essays by critics of other opinions. Some were so-called New York intellectuals such as Delmore Schwartz, Lionel and Diana Trilling, Philip Rahv, William Phillips, Dwight Macdonald, Elizabeth Hardwick, Mary McCarthy, Alfred Kazin, and Irving Howe. In his book *A Margin of Hope*, Howe even included Randall Jarrell and John Berryman. Most of these writers were New Yorkers, Jewish, publishing in *Partisan Review*, and interested in leftist politics. These "culture critics," as Ransom called them, joined the New Critics in their "concern for literature as literature and a belief in the value and necessity of literary criticism." Ransom's success as editor resulted in part from his ability to see the worth of such writers whose philosophies differed sharply from his, but it was actually Rice who solicited their contributions.[24] A cursory investigation of the careers of these so-called New York critics reveals, however, that most, if not all, had some connection with the Fugitive network, several having published in the *Southern Review*.

By devoting so much more space to critical essays and reviews than to poetry and fiction, the *Kenyon Review*, like the *Southern Review* before it, displeased those who saw the quarterlies primarily as a place to promote creative writing. In his influential essay "The Age of Criticism," Randall Jarrell (never averse to biting the hand that fed him) complained that the quarterlies "print far too much criticism, and far too much of the criticism that they print is of a kind that is more attractive to critics and to lovers of criticism than it is to poets and fiction-writers and to lovers of poetry and fiction." Jarrell actually wrote the essay for the *Kenyon Review*, but in a letter to his future wife, Mary Von Schrader, he predicted, correctly, that the editors would "think it an unkind tactless piece more or less directed at them, among others—as it is."[25] The *Kenyon* did not publish the essay, although its editorial policies bore out Jarrell's thesis that, largely through the rise of critical quarterlies, his would be an age more noted for criticism than for creative writing. More than ever, poets and fiction writers were forced to expend time and effort on the writing of essays and reviews that might have been devoted to their creative art.

23. Janssen, *"Kenyon Review,"* 113–14, 116.
24. Ibid., 38–40.
25. Randall Jarrell, "The Age of Criticism," in *Poetry and the Age* (New York: Random House, 1953), 65; Mary Jarrell, ed., *Randall Jarrell's Letters: An Autobiographical and Literary Selection* (Boston: Houghton Mifflin, 1985), 270.

Although by the 1950s, the *Kenyon Review* helped to give the New Criticism what Janssen calls a "monopoly position" in American universities, Ransom had become somewhat disenchanted with academic New Critical writing. He therefore saw to it that the *Kenyon Review* published literary analysis from outsiders such as Leslie Fiedler, Richard Ellmann, and Richard Chase. Demonstrating its critical eclecticism, the autumn issue of volume 12 opened a symposium on the critic's profession entitled "My Credo," with essays by Fiedler, Herbert Read, Richard Chase, and William Empson. The following issue (volume 13, number 1) continued the discussion with articles by Cleanth Brooks, Douglas Bush, and Northrop Frye; and the spring (volume 13, number 2) issue concluded with Stephen Spender, Arthur Mizener, and Austin Warren. While Brooks's "The Formalist Critic" was a spirited defense of the New Criticism, the symposium provided a useful presentation of "almost the entire gamut of contemporary critical approaches."[26] It is likely that Ransom not only wanted to place his review on the cutting edge of the critical debate but that he also desired to put some distance between his editorial persona and that of his (friendly) rival Cleanth Brooks.

Despite Ransom's avowed ignorance about fiction, he was determined to make the *Kenyon Review* a journal of considerable importance to talented fiction writers. He therefore requested additional funds in 1940 to enlarge each issue from 128 to 144 pages so that the review might print "some piece of fiction having both technical and imaginative distinction." Ransom was, however, suspicious of the latest fiction. As he wrote to George Marion O'Donnell, "I have the idea that there is nothing to modern fiction but its [predominantly Marxist] ideology." Ransom therefore began by relying on what he called "stories of our sort," that is, by trusted friends such as Caroline Gordon, Katherine Anne Porter, and Andrew Lytle.[27] For the same reason, Ransom was also not averse to printing stories by members of his circle who were not primarily known for their fiction. John Berryman published two stories, "The Lovers" (volume 7, number 1) and "The Imaginary Jew" (volume 7, number 4); Randall Jarrell published two chapters from his novel *Pictures from an Institution* in volumes 15 and 16; and Robert Penn Warren published a portion of *World Enough and Time*, "Portrait of La Grand' Bosse," in volume 12, number 1.

The *Kenyon Review*'s most important contribution to the development of good writing in all fields, but especially fiction, was the establishment of the

26. Janssen, *"Kenyon Review,"* 174–75, 177–78.
27. Ibid., 79, 32.

Kenyon Review Fellowships. In the 1950s, the Rockefeller Foundation, which had refused to subsidize further the publication of the *Kenyon Review*, did fund a request for a program to assist writers whom the *Review* had published and who showed particular promise. A three-year grant of $41,000, beginning in 1952, was renewed in 1956 at $52,000 to underwrite three awards—for poetry, criticism, and fiction—and to provide some funds for administering the grant. The Fellows did not apply directly but were nominated by advisory editors and "literary friends." Noted recipients with post-Fugitive connections included Flannery O'Connor (the only Fellow to be renewed) in 1953 and Andrew Lytle in 1956, as well as Elizabeth Spencer, James Wright, and Robie Macauley. Other Kenyon Fellows were Leslie Fiedler and R. W. B. Lewis, who was awarded a fellowship in criticism for 1954 (almost twenty years before he became Brooks and Warren's collaborator in *American Literature, the Makers and the Making*).[28]

After their receipt of Kenyon Review Fellowships, all eighteen writers, as Janssen puts it, "belonged to Ransom's elect," benefiting from the money and prestige of the awards but most of all from the validation they implied. Although the selection process seems to have been acceptable to those who applied, it obviously did no harm to have been a part of that "elect" through prior association. Defending his selection of Lytle to John Marshall, Ransom wrote: "Lytle has already done three novels, of which at least two are absolutely first-rate, and at his best he has enormous style. I have known him since my Fugitive and Agrarian days at Vanderbilt, and I have the greatest faith in his vitality and potential." Lytle wrote part of *The Velvet Horn* for his fellowship (see Chapter 9), and the *Kenyon Review*'s future editor Robie Macauley reviewed it in the autumn 1957 issue. Having been a student of Andrew Lytle's at Iowa, Flannery O'Connor had a better than average chance at the award, which allowed her to continue writing short stories, when normally only novels could be considered a reliable source of income.[29] Four of O'Connor's most famous stories—"The Life You Save May Be Your Own," "A Circle in the Fire," "The Artificial Nigger," and "Greenleaf"—appeared in the *Review*. The *Review* would probably have published more, except that O'Connor needed the income that her stories could elicit from commercial magazines.

An additional component of the Fugitives' editorial legacy was Ransom's creation of the Kenyon Schools of English. Operating during the summers

28. Ibid., 172–73, 240.
29. Ibid., 174, 307.

of 1948 through 1950, this program of graduate-level courses in English and American literature advertised itself as an "institute for critics," offering "comparative courses of study" during a six-week period between late June and early August. An article entitled "Experiment at Kenyon," written by David Zesner for the *Dallas Morning News*, described the school's purpose: "to recapture the imperative and exciting activity of literary criticism." About seventy-five students, both male and female, would be chosen primarily from young teachers and graduate students in English. The scholars attended classes in the mornings from Monday through Saturday and devoted the afternoons to library research, essay writing, or scheduled conferences with the professors.[30]

The students who attended must have relished the opportunity to study and interact with an auspicious group of literary giants in such informal and pleasant surroundings—though the hot summer temperatures and difficult travel arrangements caused some inconveniences. Ransom drew his faculty from the highest echelons of practicing critics, many, though not all, being his literary friends, and encompassing a range of critical positions. In its first year, the professors included Eric Bentley, Cleanth Brooks, Richard Chase, F. O. Matthiessen, William Empson, Ransom, Austin Warren, and Allen Tate. T. S. Eliot had been invited and expressed interest but eventually declined the offer. Despite the attempt to avoid being thought of as an indoctrination camp for the New Criticism, there is no doubt that the School of English, later carried on at Indiana University at Bloomington, was an important proliferator of the "method." George Lanning, who attended the school in 1950 (and later edited the *Kenyon Review*), reported that he and his colleagues were very "much New Critical" and saw themselves as "early settlers" in the critical wilderness that had been carved out by the New Critical "pioneers" on the faculty.[31]

By 1956, Ransom was ready to retire as editor of the *Kenyon Review*. Rather than allow the magazine to expire, he offered the editorship to Peter Taylor, a *Kenyon Review* adviser since 1953, who seriously considered it but eventually declined, unwilling to surrender so much time and attention from his writing. Other familiar names suggested by Ransom but ultimately rejected by the Kenyon College administration included Allen Tate, Donald Davidson, and Robert Lowell. Randall Jarrell was offered the editorship in

---

30. David Zesner, "Experiment at Kenyon," *Dallas Morning News*, September 5, 1948, *Kenyon Review* Papers; Young, *Gentleman in a Dustcoat*, 387.

31. Young, *Gentleman in a Dustcoat*, 387, 388.

January 1958 but refused it two weeks later, fearing that the position would "interfere too much with my own writing and general peace of mind."[32]

A former Kenyon student, Robie Macauley, ultimately accepted the editorship of the *Kenyon Review*. Although Ransom considered him only "the best next man," he nonetheless described Macauley, in a February 14, 1958, letter to Edward Lund, as "wise and thorough, thoroughly experienced, an excellent critic . . . ; a pretty good fiction writer who has just begun to get a lot better; and a person universally admired and liked." In *"The Kenyon Review, 1939–1970,"* Macauley wrote that in taking Ransom's place, he "respected criticism and wanted to keep up that *Review* tradition—but with more maverick critics than John Ransom had printed. I also wanted to do well by the poets, though knowing that my editorial insight could never equal his. But chiefly I hoped that the *Review* could display some of the new talents in fiction." He hoped to publish not only southern fiction writers like Flannery O'Connor but also such established outsiders as Saul Bellow, John Cheever, and Ralph Ellison. Among the "new talents" Macauley presented were Joyce Carol Oates, Thomas Pynchon, John Barth, V. S. Naipaul, and Doris Lessing.[33]

Although Macauley's selection as Ransom's successor was positively received by such respected contributors as Philip Rahv, Delmore Schwartz, and Karl Shapiro, his editorial experience was, according to Janssen, "negligible, even compared to Ransom's training as one of the editors of the short-lived *Fugitive*." In Janssen's opinion, Macauley failed to keep the *Kenyon Review* vital "because he made it too much of a miscellany, so that it lost its decisive voice, and because he became its editor at an infelicitous time." Despite his high hopes that the *Kenyon Review* could continue to play an important role in the literary scene, Macauley shared the widespread feeling of the 1960s that "the purely literary review was becoming outmoded . . . like a Conestoga wagon in the day of the automobile."[34]

George Lanning, Macauley's successor in 1962, also failed, in Janssen's opinion, "because he lacked imagination, discernment, daring," "published established names and deferred to middle-of-the-road preferences," and attempted to broaden the *Review*'s readership by appealing to common readers and high school students. Lanning's editorship was criticized severely by members of the post-Fugitive group in response to a form letter from Patrick

32. Janssen, *"Kenyon Review,"* 272–76, 279.
33. Ibid., 280; Macauley, *"Kenyon Review,"* 74.
34. Janssen, *"Kenyon Review,"* 315; Macauley, *"Kenyon Review,"* 76.

Cruttwell, a member of the Kenyon College English Department, who chaired a committee charged with studying the future of the *Review*. Tate responded that it needed a great (new) editor, Warren said that it needed to be more experimental, and Robert Lowell wrote the following stinging critique: "The old Kenyon concentrated on criticism, printed too much as people said, yet set a very high standard, and was surely a much better magazine than the present Kenyon, very weak on criticism and reviews. It is a little difficult to know what the Review now stands for not only in criticism, but in fiction and poetry."[35] The *Kenyon Review*, as Ransom founded it, ended ignominiously when, after the college withdrew support in 1969, other colleges and universities interested in taking it over found it too expensive.

George Core cites the *Kenyon Review* under Macauley and Lanning as "a striking example of how a quarterly can move from being major, as it was run by Ransom, to minor, as it was edited by Robie Macauley and then co-edited by George Lanning and Ellington White, all three of whom cut back drastically on formal criticism and published a considerable amount of fiction and poetry together with the kind of reports and digests of opinion that Tate deplored." Core goes on to characterize the *Kenyon Review*'s new series, begun in 1978 under Frederick Turner and Ronald Sharp, as a "minor quarterly" that limited itself by "encouraging innovation and urging its writers to provide copy on everything from cooking to gerontology." When Core wrote in 1985, the new editors, Galbraith Crump and Philip Church, were attempting to reorganize the *Review* "along the lines laid down by Ransom," hoping thereby to make it a major quarterly once more.[36]

Of the three Fugitive-related southern quarterlies, the *Sewanee Review* has had the longest and most colorful history. The first *Sewanee Review* was founded in 1892 by W. P. Trent, a teacher of English and history, who, according to Monroe Spears, wanted to provide the South with "the kind of intellectual milieu in which criticism and literature could flourish." His successor, George Herbert Clarke, editor from 1920 to 1925, formed an early connection with the Nashville group by publishing poems by John Crowe Ransom, Laura Riding Gottschalk, Robert Penn Warren, and Donald Davidson and essays by Davidson and Ransom.[37]

Between 1926 and 1942, under W. S. Knickerbocker, the *Sewanee Review*

35. Janssen, *"Kenyon Review,"* 342–44.
36. Core, "Literary Quarterly," 188–89.
37. Monroe Spears, "The *Sewanee Review* and the Southern Renascence," *South Carolina Review* 25 (Fall 1992): 7–11.

was, according to Spears, "important to the Nashville group mainly as a goad, gadfly, or thorn in the flesh." During Knickerbocker's editorship, there was "a sharp decline in the poetry: nothing more from the Nashville group, and a great deal by Knickerbocker, his family and his friends." A New South man who opposed the Nashville Agrarians, Knickerbocker had published Tate's essay "Poetry and the Absolute" and Ransom's *I'll Take My Stand* essay in 1928, boasting afterward that "the Agrarian movement was launched in these pages," then printing attacks on the Agrarians in subsequent issues. In a letter to Andrew Lytle, Allen Tate called Knickerbocker's *Sewanee Review* a "graveyard for second-rate professors."[38] By 1942, University of the South vice chancellor Alexander Guerry, convinced that Knickerbocker should be removed and that the *Sewanee Review* should be completely overhauled, looked to his contacts in the post-Fugitive circle.

The third period of the *Sewanee Review*, from 1942 to the present, belongs to the Fugitive legacy. At the suggestion of Andrew Lytle, who was teaching at the Sewanee Military Academy, Guerry offered the editorship to Allen Tate. In a January 30, 1942 letter, Lytle advised Tate to get in touch with Guerry and "tell him that now is the time for the *Sewanee Review* to take the place of the *Southern Review*, and that you might take the Academy job until Knickerbocker's contract expired, when you would be made editor of that and do more or less what you have been doing at Princeton."[39]

For reasons that are unclear, Tate did not become editor of the *Sewanee Review* after Knickerbocker's removal. Janssens believes that Tate was offered the editorship but declined the position to "become Consultant in American Letters at the Library of Congress," whereas, Thomas Daniel Young and Elizabeth Sarcone conjecture that "Tate was passed over as editor when it became clear that he would demand funding." Forced to look elsewhere, but only within the post-Fugitive circle, Guerry wired Cleanth Brooks on July 28, 1942, and offered him the editorship. By that time, connections between the editorships of a number of literary magazines had become so interconnected that Allen Tate advised Cleanth Brooks, should he become editor, "to fire all associate editors" because "most of our crowd have been on most of the magazines for the past ten or fifteen years, virtually taking in one another's washing, and I think it advisable to make our influence more effective by concealing it." Guerry apparently had no such trepidations. After considering the offer carefully, Brooks also declined, and, according to Mark Winchell, a

---

38. Spears, "*Sewanee Review*," 9, 7–8; Young and Sarcone, eds., *Tate-Lytle Letters*, 186.
39. Young and Sarcone, eds., *Tate-Lytle Letters*, 181.

subsequent barrage of letters and telegraphs failed to break down his reluctance. His recent experiences at LSU had been disconcerting, to say the least. Moreover, as Winchell records, Brooks felt relieved to be freed of editorial responsibilities and able to concentrate on his own writing.[40] Guerry was finally compelled to place Sewanee English professor T. S. Long in the role of acting editor, with Lytle reluctantly agreeing to serve as managing editor.

The editorship of the *Sewanee Review* was the beginning of some friction between "brothers" Lytle and Tate. Lytle had, according to Young and Sarcone, been "drafted for the job because as one who was already on the faculty, he could hardly refuse." Sincere in his belief that Tate would be a far better choice than he, Lytle actually edited only until the summer of 1943. He returned to his farm, leaving T. S. Long to handle the magazine, although he did return to edit the winter 1944 issue. From the beginning of his editorship, Lytle received considerable help and advice from Tate, perhaps more than Lytle requested. Sensing a "loss of confidence between us" that "had to be acknowledged," Tate wrote Lytle on January 11, 1943 that he had "been blind, but now my eyes are wide, if reluctantly, open to the fact that I shouldn't have taken it upon myself to help you so extensively in getting your editorship under way." Admitting no such discomfort, Lytle replied, on January 14, "Of course, I wanted you to help on the *Review* or I wouldn't have let you. The only thing that has troubled me is this: your usual generosity and affection for your friends has in this instance led you to do almost everything for the magazine of an institution which has less than a claim on you."[41]

Despite such ambivalent feelings, Andrew Lytle nonetheless presided over important changes at the *Sewanee Review*. His Vanderbilt colleague Richmond Croom Beatty thought Lytle had "transformed the old and once distinguished Sewanee Review from . . . a haphazard receptacle of second-rate academic-literary exercises—into a publication with character and difficult standards of excellence."[42] Relying on his Fugitive-Agrarian connections, Lytle published poetry by George Marion O'Donnell, Randall Jarrell, John Berryman, and Robert Lowell; essays by Cleanth Brooks, Allen Tate, and Donald Davidson; a portion of Robert Penn Warren's novel *At Heaven's Gate*; and reviews by Lytle, Lowell, and Davidson.

40. Janssens, *American Literary Review*, 279, 253; Young and Sarcone, eds., *Tate-Lytle Letters*, 149; Winchell, *Cleanth Brooks and the Rise of Modern Criticism*, 197–98.

41. Young and Sarcone, eds., *Tate-Lytle Letters*, 149, 195–96.

42. Janssens, *American Literary Review*, 278.

Allen Tate continued to function behind the scenes of the *Sewanee Review* while serving his term at the Library of Congress. Tate left the door open by volunteering to "solicit manuscripts" since he was "advantageously located for that sort of thing." On October 13, 1943, with unanimous approval of the review's Board of Directors, Guerry once again offered the position to Tate, who, having secured some sizable donations for the running of the journal, finally accepted.[43]

Beginning with the summer 1944 issue, Tate took over control of the *Sewanee Review*, declaring that under his editorship it would "continue in the South the recent service to letters performed by the *Southern Review* from 1935 to 1942." Tate is credited with almost single-handedly transforming the *Sewanee Review* by "having the format of the magazine completely redesigned, paying contributors, introducing prize competitions, and so quadrupling the circulation." His first issue included contributions by Robert Lowell, Katherine Anne Porter, John Crowe Ransom, and his own important editorial "The State of Letters," which Janssens says "epitomizes not only the point of view of the *Sewanee Review* but also that of its fellow quarterlies." Tate pledged that he would feature writers who had not yet made names for themselves in New York and thereby combat the malaise into which American letters had sunk, in his opinion, since the war began. He pledged, in summary, that "whatever the new literature turns out to be it will be the privilege of the *Sewanee Review* to print its share of it, to comment on it, and to try to understand it."[44]

On October 16, 1944, former editor Lytle wrote a complimentary letter to Tate, calling his first issue "very fine" and "loaded against big and little guns." He praised Tate's "notes at the end" as "just right. With no sociology to mar it," then predicted that the *Review* would "not be embarrassed as was the *Southern* by Pipkin." Stating the obvious, Lytle attributed Tate's value to the *Sewanee Review* to the "fact, at least, that you have the widest literary connection in the country."[45]

Tate drew heavily on his post-Fugitive connection throughout his short tenure as editor. Fugitives and their heirs publishing in the 1945 issues included Donald Davidson, Caroline Gordon, Andrew Lytle, Peter Taylor, Randall Jarrell, and John Berryman, as well as such famous outsiders as Wal-

43. Ibid., 279.
44. Ibid., 279, 282–83.
45. Young and Sarcone, eds., *Tate-Lytle Letters*, 203.

lace Stevens, Dylan Thomas, Harry Levin, and Arthur Mizener. All contributors received token pay of about $2.60 a page, though Tate had wanted to pay
$5.[46]

After exactly two years, 1944–46, Tate left the *Sewanee* under a cloud of
scandals relating to his sexual improprieties. The torch was passed to John
Palmer, an LSU undergraduate and graduate student in the days of the *Southern Review*. During his editorship, in Spears's opinion, Palmer "somewhat increased the Southern emphasis, with stories by Porter, Welty, Warren,
Faulkner, and Flannery O'Connor." Clearly the *Sewanee Review* had become
home to the post-Fugitive circle. Not only did it concentrate first on the publication of criticism, then poetry and fiction, but it was, like the *Southern* and
Kenyon reviews before it, especially receptive to submissions from the
"group" and its protégés. When the *Sewanee* held its first writing competition
in 1945, the winners were Randall Jarrell in poetry and Andrew Lytle in fiction. Nor would the post-Fugitive group lose its preeminent position with
the *Sewanee Review* under later editors. When Monroe Spears became editor
(between 1952 and 1961), he pledged to "preserve the character of the magazine as Tate and Palmer had formed it." Spears accordingly made Tate and
Lytle advisory editors and launched a fellowship program with Rockefeller
funding for such young writers as James Dickey and Madison Jones, both
Vanderbilt alumni. By his own admission, Spears "took special pleasure in
publishing Tate, Warren, Ransom, Walker Percy, Flannery O'Connor, and
other major Southern writers," devoting a 1959 issue to the celebration of
Allen Tate's sixtieth birthday.[47] Spears was succeeded as editor by George
Core, a personal friend of Tate and Lytle, who has held the position since
1973. Of the three journals, the *Sewanee Review* was perhaps the most solidly
dedicated to keeping the Fugitive legacy viable.

The Fugitives' editorial legacy began in Nashville with a magazine run by
a group of poets who had no publishing experience. Lewis Simpson has nonetheless attributed to the *Fugitive* "the reopening of the literary realm in the
South," in that it "not only expanded the realm of literary discourse in the
South but pushed its boundaries outward to embrace the modernist discussion of history and tradition."[48] In this expanded terrain shortly thereafter
would emerge three southern quarterlies, all of which rose to unprecedented
importance under the leadership of the Fugitives and their heirs. Not only

46. Janssens, *American Literary Review*, 283.
47. Spears, *"Sewanee Review"*, 9–10.
48. Simpson, "Introduction," 7.

did these reviews spread the Fugitive legacy's provenance, but they helped to make the South an undeniable locus of power and importance in modern letters.

While the present has frequently been called a disadvantageous time for the literary quarterly, these literary magazines, and others like them, not only represent a proud tradition but continue to serve the academic world by publishing a high standard of poetry, fiction, and criticism. Although they compare unfavorably with their predecessors, the continuing *Sewanee* and the new versions of the *Southern* and *Kenyon* reviews have carried the Fugitives' editorial legacy into the last decade of the twentieth century. Ironically, their ability to dominate in the manner of their predecessors has been reduced by the proliferation of a growing number of university-supported literary publications such as the *Georgia Review* (founded by former Agrarian John Donald Wade), the *South Atlantic Journal*, the *Mississippi Quarterly*, and the *South Atlantic Review*, which have followed in their footsteps. In a sense, all of these southern journals share the Fugitives' editorial legacy.

3 / Cleanth Brooks, the New Criticism, and the New Pedagogy

The analyses are as much of the old poems as of the new poems, and those of the old are as fresh and illuminating as those of the new; or at least nearly. What can this mean, but that criticism as it is now practiced is a new thing?
—John Crowe Ransom
Kenyon Review, 1940

Without doubt the Fugitive legacy had its greatest impact in the beginnings of the New Criticism. Although the term itself was yet to be applied, the technique actually began in the regular sessions of the Fugitive group. In 1941, John Crowe Ransom unwittingly gave this method of reading and interpreting a name by publishing a book entitled *The New Criticism*, including theoretical essays about an assortment of "new critics" and ending with Ransom's own defining treatise, "Wanted: An Ontological Critic." Thereafter, the New Criticism came to be associated with Ransom and began to accumulate so many definitions and connotations, so many accounts of its origin and development, as to attain the status of cultural myth.

The New Criticism might have remained a mere moment in literary history had not Cleanth Brooks and his lifelong friend Robert Penn Warren imported the method from Vanderbilt to Louisiana State University, where they incorporated it into the most influential literary textbooks ever to emerge from actual experience in the university classroom. Thereafter, Cleanth Brooks gradually replaced Ransom as the major theoretician of the New Criticism. Through Brooks and his articulation and praxis of what began in Ransom's leadership of the Fugitive meetings, the story of the Fugitive legacy's contribution to literary criticism and pedagogy became perhaps its most fascinating and important chapter.

Ransom's legacy to Brooks might constitute yet another instance of what Harold Bloom would call the "anxiety of influence," illustrating the two Bloomian modes of *clinamen* and *kenosis*, wherein the younger critic both *misreads* and *breaks away from* his precursor. And although Bloom's terminology refers specifically to poets, he finds it possible, with but a slight adjustment, to make room for critics: "Poets' misinterpretations of poems are more drastic than critics' misinterpretations of criticism, but this is only a difference in degree and not at all in kind. There are no interpretations but only misinterpretations, and so all criticism is prose poetry. . . . For just as a poet must be found by the opening in a precursor poet, so must the critic. The difference is that a critic has more parents . . . poets and critics."[1] Brooks's "parents" later included T. S. Eliot and I. A. Richards, but it was John Crowe Ransom, both as poet and critic, who occupied the central position in Brooks's development.

Among Ransom's students between 1921 and 1927 were Donald Davidson, Allen Tate, and Robert Penn Warren, also fellow Fugitives. These unusually talented students were introduced not only to a new way of approaching literature but also to an aesthetic which Tate described as a concoction of "Kantian aesthetics and a philosophical dualism, tinged with Christian theology, but ultimately derived from the Nicomachian ethics." Both in the Fugitive meetings and in Ransom's classes, literary texts were subjected to a method that came to be known as "close reading," involving, in Thomas Daniel Young's words, "line by line, word by word examination of the poem's [later extended to drama and fiction] *texture*." While such analyses might delve into prosody, they were chiefly concerned with diction. All conceivable connotative, denotative, and tropic significances would be considered singly and in interrelating patterns throughout the text. This painstaking and time-consuming exercise—which demands supportive quotation at every propositional point in the demonstration—naturally led Ransom to favor abbreviated texts such as short lyric poems (like those that were read for "Fugitive" criticism), scenes from image-laden drama (Shakespeare, as in Ransom's teaching of *Hamlet*), and short fiction.[2]

1. Bloom, *Anxiety of Influence*, 14, 94.

2. Allen Tate, "A Southern Mode of the Imagination," in *Essays of Four Decades* (Chicago: Swallow Press, 1968), 579–80; Young, interview. In an interview with the author (New Haven, Conn., August 7, 1991), Brooks commented that while it is especially true that in short poems and stories every word must count, longer texts—novels, plays, epic poems—may also be tested by the measurement of organic unity.

Ransom's many activities during the relatively short period around 1923–25 included his editorship of the *Fugitive: A Magazine of Verse* and the composition of his most important poetry for publication in the *Fugitive*. At the time, however, he apparently was not interested in training a generation of critical-minded literature teachers (as he would later do at Kenyon in the schools of criticism). In fact, when Agrarianism came to dominate the thoughts of the former Fugitives, Ransom's classroom methods seem to have changed accordingly. The Kentucky writer James Still's pleasant memories of Ransom's classes in 1929–30 did *not* include a method of attacking a literary text. Lewis Simpson, one of Ransom's students when he taught a summer course at the University of Texas, remembers his coming into the classroom with book in hand but no notes to spend the entire period reading *Daisy Miller* to a somewhat confused class.[3]

How, then, could Hugh Kenner say with confidence in 1976 that Ransom's classroom method was at that time familiar to just about every college freshman in the United States?[4] Probably because Ransom's students during that crucial 1923–25 phase *did* for a time include Cleanth Brooks, who was destined to reinterpret and propagate the New Criticism.

Cleanth Brooks was born in 1906 in Murray, Kentucky, the son of Cleanth Brooks, Sr., a Methodist minister in western Tennessee, and Bessie Lee Witherspoon Brooks. Brooks obtained his preparatory education at the McTyeire School, where he took courses in Latin, Greek, English, math, and history, but none in science. He believed that this curriculum may have played a role in the development of his critical method since "my prep school discipline in reading Latin and Greek—discussing the meaning of passages and parsing them—had prepared me rather directly for this new discipline of literary exploration."[5]

Despite his excellent preparation, Brooks was somewhat overwhelmed by Vanderbilt. Like others who were fortunate enough to be at that particular place during the twenties, he became aware of the literary activity going on

3. James Still, interview by author, Lexington, Ky., August 16, 1986; Lewis P. Simpson, Panel on the New Criticism at Tennessee Homecoming Celebration, Nashville, Tenn., 1987. Ransom taught at the University of Texas during the summer of 1938. Lewis Simpson received his baccalaureate and master's degrees at the University of Texas in 1938 and 1939, respectively.

4. Hugh Kenner, "The Pedagogue as Critic," in *The New Criticism and After*, ed. Thomas Daniel Young (Charlottesville: University Press of Virginia, 1976), 36.

5. Thomas Daniel Young, "Cleanth Brooks at Vanderbilt," 1, unpublished essay, Cleanth Brooks Papers, Yale Collection of American Literature, Beinecke Rare Book and Manuscript Library, Yale University, New Haven, Conn.

there. Among those who were writing and publishing poetry were Ransom, recently author of a collection of poems entitled *Chills and Fever*, and Davidson, of *The Outland Piper*. Volume 3, number 4, of the *Fugitive* had also just appeared, and although the Fugitives were still meeting, Brooks attended only one of their sessions. He decided to major in English, rather than become "a really shifty halfback," after hearing a graduate teaching assistant read Davidson's essay on a story by Rudyard Kipling. Brooks recalled: "This opened a new world for me. It revealed that you could look inside a story and see how it was put together, and could make sensible observations about it. . . . It showed me that the inner workings of a poem or a story were important."[6]

Brooks's epiphanic moment was to come during his senior year when he picked up a book of Ransom's poetry. Brooks did not recall what poems caught his attention. He remembered only that "the scales dropped from my eyes." Not only was Ransom's poetry unlike any he had previously encountered, but he, Brooks, actually *knew* the poet. Impressed also with the "approach" to literature used by Ransom and Davidson, he seized on the concept that "the sense of technique, the structure of a thing is related to the life of the poem and then the life behind the poem."[7]

After Vanderbilt, Brooks began gradually assimilating his own theoretical position, combining Ransom's method with other elements in his background and education to that point. In "Why Critics Don't Go Mad," Ransom hit upon one important similarity between himself and the man who would become his heir in critical theory: that as sons of Methodist ministers, both he and Brooks heard numerous Sunday sermons "where the preacher unpacked the whole burden of his theology from a single figurative phrase of Scripture taken out of context." Asked if he was aware of ways in which a steady diet of Methodist sermons may have contributed to his critical method, Brooks replied that in pastors' and others' homes, a classical education, always in Latin and sometimes in Greek, would train the educated person to "look[ ] mighty close at that word, how it worked."[8]

The striking resemblance of the "homiletic" method of such sermons to New Critical pedagogy may be observed by examining a typical Methodist sermon that might have been presented to small-town congregations in the

6. Ibid., 1, 2; Winchell, *Cleanth Brooks and the Rise of Modern Criticism*, 38.

7. Cleanth Brooks, interview by author, New Haven, Conn., January 10, 1988; Young, "Cleanth Brooks at Vanderbilt," 1–3.

8. John Crowe Ransom, "Why Critics Don't Go Mad," *Kenyon Review* 14 (1952): 334; Brooks, interview, January 10, 1988.

nineteenth- and early twentieth-century South. *The Methodist Pulpit, South*, an anthology, contains a group of exemplary sermons. All begin with a biblical text as epigraph and proceed to elaborate on that aphoristic phrase in every conceivable direction. One sermon, "Angelic Study" by John W. Hanner of the Tennessee Conference, chooses the phrase "What things the angels desire to look into" from 1 Peter 1, 12, as a theme on which to examine the subjects, motivations, and implications of angelic "research" into human affairs. The body of the sermon is organized in a series of rhetorical questions and answers, all based on the phrase *look into*: "What things form the subjects of angelic study?"; "What is implied in the desire of Angels to look into these things?"; and "The Probable Motives of and Instances of Angelic intervention." (The numbered questions are reminiscent of the interpretive exercises in one of Brooks's textbooks.) The phrase *look into* is considered literally and figuratively as if it were a metaphysical conceit. As he set forth various interpretations of the phrase, the preacher could display his wit and rhetorical skill to considerable advantage.[9]

From the philological orientation and rhetorical training that contributed to the "art" of the Methodist sermon, Ransom and Brooks (and even Robert Penn Warren, who was also Methodist) no doubt found it natural to approach a literary text as a rhetorical act based on semantics. Moreover, the critical texts thus produced became lengthy, often ornately elegant products, not unlike Methodist sermons. In short, in Ransom's and his pupils' hands, the literary essay became a rhetorical performance, designed as much to dazzle and confound as to enlighten and convince, but always an *argument* which the critic, as *rhetor*, dominated.

Brooks connected the oratorical style of the southern pastor to the southern predilection toward rhetoric, rather than dialectic. He cited his longtime friend Marshall McLuhan's belief that a southern bent toward rhetoric had resulted from an emphasis in the southerner's education on "the linguistic and legalistic learning of sixteenth-century humanism" as opposed to the New Englander's grounding in "logic and speculative or systematic theology." Therefore, as Brooks extrapolated, southern rhetoric persisted into the twentieth century "in tatters and rags pretty often in the worst kind of pulpit oratory [and] political oratory." As Allen Tate also remarked in his essay "A Southern Mode of the Imagination," "The traditional Southern mode of discourse presupposes somebody at the other end silently listening; it is the rhe-

9. William T. Smithson, *The Methodist Pulpit, South* (1859), 77–89, Special Collections, Hoskins Library, University of Tennessee, Knoxville.

torical mode. Its historical rival is the dialectical mode, or the give and take between two minds, even if one mind, like the mind of Socrates, prevail at the end."[10] This shared exposure to old-style southern rhetoric may well have served both Ransom and Brooks as an unconscious basis for what would become the classical New Critical essay.

After Vanderbilt, Brooks's career took him to Oxford, where he earned his B.Litt. and renewed his acquaintance with Robert Penn Warren. Much later, Warren remembered that when their "paths crossed at Oxford," Brooks made available to him "the opening world of poetry and poetic criticism and theory" and that their "passion for poetry" gave permanent shape to their friendship. Even then their relationship was complementary, with Brooks's appetite "leading him into a devoted study of criticism and theory," while Warren "was already spending night after night trying to write poems." At Oxford, he could take "his midnight efforts" to Brooks for a first reaction based on his growing expertise on poetic theory. Warren could glean from his peer what he had resisted from his masters: "I had heard a lot of subtle and learned talk from old friends like John Crowe Ransom and Allen Tate among the Fugitives back in Nashville, but then I had been so hot at the immediate task of trying to write poems that I had missed a certain enrichment for that practical task." Warren remembered "with perfect clarity" the day when Brooks "thought he had found the bridge between Eliot and Richards," between "the churchman and the positivist." Brooks had already "logically . . . found his ease in a sort of paradox" wherein Eliot and Richards might "shake hands over the poetic instance." Brooks would set forth what Warren called a "doctrine of 'inclusion,' not 'exclusion' " a decade later in "Metaphysical Poetry and Propaganda Art." This "reconcilement of opposite or discordant qualities" led then to Brooks's critical nexus in irony and paradox.[11]

While at Oxford, Brooks finally got to know Ransom when he visited Warren and other friends. Now junior and senior colleagues rather than pupil and teacher, Brooks and Ransom became lifelong friends. Brooks also formed a friendship with Allen Tate while in Paris. When they met at the

10. Marshall McLuhan, "An Ancient Quarrel in Modern America (Sophists vs. Grammarians)," in *The Interior Landscape: The Literary Criticism of Marshall McLuhan*, ed. Eugene McNamara (New York: McGraw-Hill, 1969), 230; Brooks, interview, January 10, 1988; Tate, "Southern Mode," 583.

11. Robert Penn Warren, "Brooks and Warren," *Humanities* 6 (April 1985): 1, 2; Cleanth Brooks, "Metaphysical Poetry and Propaganda Art," in *Modern Poetry and the Tradition* (Chapel Hill: University of North Carolina Press, 1939), 50.

Café des Deux Magots in 1929, Brooks, in his thick glasses, reminded Tate of Eliot's Donne seeing "the skull beneath the skin."[12] Tate later became a trusted critic of Brooks's work and a valuable contact with the literary establishment.

Fortunately for Brooks, the period between his graduation from Vanderbilt in 1928 and his first real "job" at LSU, beginning in 1932, was a time when various ideas and influences could be considered independently. Because Ransom had initially disagreed with Allen Tate on the merits of Eliot's *Waste Land* and had attacked Richards in *The New Criticism*, Brooks, who became an Eliot proponent, thereby declared his independence from Ransom and formed his own synthesis. Still attending to text, still explicatory in method, Brooks established his most influential version of the New Criticism against Ransom, first by deflecting his anxiety of influence onto more remote precursors and then by adopting the principle of organic unity as the criterion for excellence. Brooks's theories became, in simplest terms, a combination of Ransom's critical method with T. S. Eliot's traditionalism and with carefully chosen aspects of I. A. Richards's practical criticism.[13]

An enabling, energizing stimulus to Brooks's development was, however, provided by a stichomythic tension between himself and Ransom that Robert Penn Warren would later call "bloodletting." When his editorship of the *Southern Review* placed him some distance from Ransom, Brooks was ready for a challenge. The first sally took the form of the *Southern Review* editors' response to Ransom's essay "Shakespeare at Sonnets," in which Ransom declared that Donne was a better sonnet writer than Shakespeare. According to Brooks, there was never a question of not publishing the essay; rather, Brooks feared that Ransom might harm himself by coming out so strongly (in an age of unquestioned Bardolatry) against Shakespeare and in favor of Donne. Although Ransom must have destroyed Brooks's letter, as he did all incoming correspondence, his subsequent letter to Tate not only survived but has been quoted frequently, usually without some of Ransom's more cutting references to Brooks and Warren:

The *Southern Review*, by the way, is slipping unless I am greatly mistaken. They are at their high standard by the pure accident that there

12. Allen Tate, "What I Owe to Cleanth Brooks," in *The Possibilities of Order: Cleanth Brooks and His Work*, ed. Lewis P. Simpson (Baton Rouge: Louisiana State University Press, 1976), 125.

13. Charlotte H. Beck and John P. Rhoades, " 'Stanley Fish Was My Reader': Cleanth Brooks, the New Criticism, and Reader Response Theory," in *The New Criticism and Contemporary Literary Theory: Connections and Continuities*, ed. William J. Spurlin and Michael Fischer (New York: Garland, 1995).

are now a good number of fine critics who have no where to market their wares. Their fiction could be greatly improved, and certainly their poetry; and even their criticism, though you and I have often contributed to that. A Review of half their size, all literary, and all of the highest contemporary excellence, would be a distinguished thing. . . .

To bear on this point I enclose a letter from the two Associate Editors. The boys deal pretty pedantically with my poor paper, you will see; I thought when I read it I must have mistakenly sent it to the *Yale Review* and got back an epistle from Miss Helen Macafee. . . . The thing is, I believe, that Cleanth is showing his limitations as a thinker with one thing on his mind at a time, and he is not providing for Red the suggestions and stimuli that Red requires. *Those boys are stale* (I have said this frankly to them).

Although Ransom must have realized that his response was petty, he did follow some of Brooks's suggestions in his revision of the article. As Mark Winchell has pointed out, Ransom and Brooks differed mainly on the question of whether good poetry must form a "logical unity" rather than a "psychological unity."[14] "Shakespeare at Sonnets" was published in the *Southern Review*'s winter 1938 issue.

For his part, Brooks did not hesitate to send the manuscript of his first book of criticism, *Modern Poetry and the Tradition*, for Ransom's "honest reaction." His initial response was perfunctorily tactful: "Thanks for the book. It's fine though you and I have begun to diverge our positions." But Ransom's more considered evaluation, though friendly as always, again cut deeply: "Your position is argued with patient and persuasive logic & illustration. It's an extreme position, as I think, or held with extreme almost dogmatic tenacity. You never discuss any *limit* to complication, and you tend to think that *any* complication in a modern is logical or functional complication."[15] Brooks evidently did not make substantive changes in response to Ransom's objections.

Far from attacking Ransom directly in this volume, Brooks praises both

14. Warren, "Brooks and Warren," 1; Cleanth Brooks, interview by the author, New Haven, Conn., November 15, 1991; Thomas Daniel Young and George Core, eds., *Selected Letters of John Crowe Ransom* (Baton Rouge: Louisiana State University Press, 1985), 233; Winchell, *Cleanth Brooks and the Rise of Modern Criticism*, 200–201.

15. Thomas Daniel Young, "A Little Divergence: The Critical Theories of John Crowe Ransom and Cleanth Brooks," in *Possibilities of Order*, ed. Simpson, 171; Ransom to Brooks, June 20, [1938], Brooks Papers; Young and Core, eds., *Selected Letters of Ransom*, 247.

his poetry and his criticism. Brooks's task in one of the essays, "Metaphysical Poetry and Propaganda Art," is to set forth the components of his own position in regard to *all* precursors. Ransom's definition of "Platonic poetry" supports Brooks's view of the nature of "truth" in poetry, which must call upon for its expression "another order of description from that in which science indulges."[16] For Brooks in this essay, Eliot, Tate, Ransom, and Richards essentially corroborate one another and together present a revolutionary new doctrine of poetic truth. The "enemy" all agree on is the Marxist critic, who sees poetry as a way of advancing "propaganda."

Ransom delayed reviewing *Modern Poetry and the Tradition* in the *Kenyon Review* because of a lengthy article he had already placed in the next issue but promised, in the following one, to "editorialize and give it the very best send-off, with a haggling reservation or two . . . to make the review decently 'objective.' " Although Ransom's "reservations" do not quite damn by faint praise, they nonetheless undercut any favorable commentary by following it with barely civil blame. After initially describing *Modern Poetry and the Tradition* as "able to the point of brilliancy," Ransom complained that "its dialectic skims rather lightly over some of the deep places." After calling Brooks "very likely, the most expert living 'reader' or interpreter of difficult verse," his "plain exposition of passages" both helpful to readers and "definitive," Ransom warns that the "criticism that accompanies it is, must be, speculative." After somewhat ironically paraphrasing the book's thesis—"The new poetry *which Mr. Brooks admires* is *supposed to* represent a return to the English poetic tradition as it stood in the 17th Century" (emphasis added)—Ransom took exception to it on two grounds: that modern poetry, "with all its 'wit' and its 'richness,' has not had the patience to achieve firm metrical structure, and [that] it is equally lacking in firmness of logical argument." Willing to waive the metrical questions as existing outside Brooks's purview, Ransom believed that "the matter of logic might have engaged [Brooks] a little more deeply." On one hand, the Brooks argument is a "spirited and usually convincing performance"; on the other, it is "arrogantly" undertaken.[17]

If Ransom could agree with Brooks in "Metaphysical Poetry and Propaganda Art," he certainly would have objected, as Young points out, to Brooks's statement in "Symbolist Poetry and the Ivory Tower" that "the only

16. Brooks, "Metaphysical Poetry," 47.

17. Young and Core, eds., *Selected Letters of Ransom*, 172; John Crowe Ransom, "Apologia for Modernism, a Review of *Modern Poetry and the Tradition* by Cleanth Brooks," *Kenyon Review* 2 (1940): 248–49.

unity which matters in poetry is an imaginative unity. Logical unity when it occurs in a poem is valued, not in itself, but only as element which may be brought into the larger imaginative unity."[18] Ransom's definition of poetic "structure" made thematic logic the framework upon which the language of poetry coheres.

The next significant round between Brooks and Ransom occurred in 1947 when Brooks's *The Well Wrought Urn* appeared. Though neither combatant had altered his position appreciably, Brooks did not hesitate, this time, to confront Ransom directly. In "Criticism, History, and Critical Relativism," Brooks provided a reprise of the 1939 confrontation as he compared Ransom's criticism with Yvor Winters's with the following "reservations": "Mr. Ransom, in his essay 'Shakespeare at Sonnets,' finds Donne a better lyric poet than Shakespeare because Donne's images 'work out' and Shakespeare's frequently do not. . . . I am inclined to feel that Ransom demands that all images work out as Donne's more 'logical' images work out; and that, in my opinion, is to elevate one admirable poetic strategy into the whole art." Brooks also, as Young points out, comes out squarely against Ransom's "texture-structure formulation" in "The Heresy of Paraphrase," but without mentioning Ransom by name.[19]

In the summer of 1947, Ransom answered Brooks at length in his *Kenyon Review* article "Poetry: I, The Formal Analysis." *The Well Wrought Urn*, according to Ransom, "exhibits all the ingenuity we should expect of [Brooks]." In the task of "conceiv[ing] that difficult object, the unitary poem," however, Brooks had not succeeded, in Ransom's opinion, in his "new role"—to "reassemble and integrate the meanings when he has made it his first duty to dissipate them."[20] Not surprisingly, Ransom also attacked Brooks's dependence on irony and paradox to effect unity. "Ingenious," as Ransom uses it, is no compliment! Any comments Brooks might have made to either article have not survived.

Brooks maintained that although the critics of his (Fugitive legacy) circle could engage in heated arguments, generally in print, they remained friendly in person. He admitted, however, that Ransom's tone in expressing his opposition to Brooks's ideas was often biting, even sarcastic. It is amazing that

18. Young, "A Little Divergence," 185; Brooks, *Modern Poetry and the Tradition*, 66.

19. Cleanth Brooks, *The Well Wrought Urn: Studies in the Structure of Poetry* (New York: Harcourt Brace Jovanovich, 1947), 243–44; Young, "A Little Divergence," 185.

20. John Crowe Ransom, "Poetry: I, The Formal Analysis," in *Selected Essays of John Crowe Ransom*, ed. Thomas Daniel Young and John Hindle (Baton Rouge: Louisiana State University Press, 1984), 193.

though their theoretical differences were never resolved, Brooks and Ransom's collegial relationship prospered in shared enterprises such as Brooks's participation in the Kenyon Schools of English and in polite letters (like the following from Ransom dated August 1, [1939]): "Am delighted to have your long letter this morning. I'm going to take a little time replying. You put your doctrine down with extreme facility and cogency, and I am not feeling in any sense at pains to find wholes in it—I mean holes, a pun, which Empson would probably comment—but I will be at pains to state as precisely as I can what I take to be our differences. They are not wide ones."[21]

When T. D. Young used Ransom's phrase "a little divergence" to characterize the critical debate between Ransom and Brooks, he realized, no doubt, that the adjective "little" is an example of Ransomian irony. The differences, though not "wide ones," were substantive. To Ransom, Brooks always made too much of irony as a unifying device and favored the metaphysical poets too much; to Brooks, Ransom was always a dualist, too ready to sever content from form. Looking back on their confrontations, it appears that Ransom was more than a little threatened by Brooks's audacity, while Brooks seems, if anything, to have been energized and emboldened.

Brooks's lifelong friendship with Robert Penn Warren was important in that it allowed Brooks to replace Ransom with someone who also understood and subsequently represented the most beneficial aspects of the Fugitive legacy to literary criticism. Brooks called their relationship, which began in their undergraduate days, an "overlapping" affair: "I did have the good luck [while a student at Vanderbilt] to meet Red Warren, however, and one or two other seniors, including Andrew Lytle, and continued to see them later on." And so, said Brooks, "Warren and I overlapped four times: one year at Vanderbilt, one year at Oxford, eight years at LSU, and many years here [at Yale]."[22]

During their third "overlap," at LSU, Brooks and Warren encouraged each other in their separate efforts and became inseparable collaborators. Years of teaching, textbook writing, and editing of the *Southern Review* brought the two together, even as they worked individually on their own writing. Brooks was impressed that Warren was already a successful poet and novelist; to Warren, Brooks had the edge in critical acumen. Each provided the other with invaluable feedback, which was always requested and usually acted upon. In short, Robert Penn Warren and Cleanth Brooks became the Wordsworth and Coleridge of the Fugitive legacy, their relationship a mutual

21. Ransom to Brooks, August 1, [1939], Brooks Papers.
22. Brooks, interview, January 10, 1988.

admiration society combining theory with praxis and criticism with poetry. Neither ability manifested itself to the exclusion of the other but passed back and forth through the vital membrane of mutual regard and shared ideas that connected the two wherever they happened to be.

While Warren was teaching at Vanderbilt during the academic year 1932–33 and Brooks had just begun his teaching and editing career at Louisiana State University, they reestablished their friendship by correspondence. The first letter in this series dates from sometime in the spring of 1933, when Brooks, feeling "quite exiled" at LSU, asked Warren, "What about reviewing some books for us—especially poetry and criticism?" LSU, Brooks explained, had begun sharing editorship of the *Southwest Review* with the "Southern Methodists of Dallas"—"hoping to broaden its scope a little and to improve the quality of the articles. [Charles] Pipkin [he explains is] . . . our generalissimo." Warren prefaced his reply, on July 16, 1933, with "You honor me," followed by mock alarm that Cleanth was "pimping reviews for a magazine, and in the end probably writing most of them yourself."[23]

After considerable negotiation, LSU had agreed to enter into a partnership with Southern Methodist University to prevent the demise of the *Southwest Review*. The protagonists in this drama were Charles Pipkin, dean of the Graduate School at LSU, and J. H. McGinnis of Southern Methodist, a New England liberal and the new editor of the *Southern Review*. The latter was distrustful of LSU's partiality toward southern interests: in Thomas Cutrer's words, "McGinnis especially feared the self-effacing but brilliant young Brooks, who although technically neither a Fugitive nor an Agrarian, was by his association with Donald Davidson and John Crowe Ransom at Vanderbilt branded a neo-confederate conservative."[24] By enlisting Warren in the effort as early as 1933, Brooks not only justified McGinnis's fears that the Vanderbilt group would come to dominate the editorship of the *Southwest Review* but paved the way for future editorial partnership with Warren, Pipkin, and Albert Erskine in the *Southern Review*.

The *Southwest Review* continued in partnership with LSU until 1935, when political differences led to their mutually acceptable separation. The incipient tension between McGinnis, and his even more liberal assistant Henry Nash Smith, and the Agrarian views of Brooks and Warren came to a head over a favorable review of Stark Young's novel *So Red the Rose* (1934). Warren

23. James A. Grimshaw, Jr., ed., *Cleanth Brooks and Robert Penn Warren: A Literary Correspondence* (Columbia: University of Missouri Press, 1998), 15–16.

24. Cutrer, *Parnassus on the Mississippi*, 32–33.

assigned the review to Erskine, who, according to Winchell, "endorsed Young's reactionary social vision and declared the paternalistic slave owners of the Old South morally superior to the capitalist employers of our own time." Although the Dallas editors accepted a revised version of the review for the spring 1935 issue, they were confirmed in their opinion that the Baton Rouge editors were bent on making the journal "an Agrarian sheet." On March 20, 1935, Pipkin wrote a letter to the Southern Methodist editors formally dissolving the partnership.[25]

As a direct result of their teaching at LSU, Brooks and Warren became involved in a far more influential venture: the production of textbooks. Brooks recalled that it began in their dissatisfaction with what was available at the time: "The textbooks which were issued to us to teach these students were next to no help at all, because they were an old fashioned sort of thing, still very much in vogue, in which you gave a brief note on the author—where he was born, his education, the circumstances, marriages, interests—and you told about the date of his death, and you [had] some comment maybe on some of the themes of his poems; but then you didn't tell the student how to read [them] at all."[26]

From his experiences in the Fugitive meetings and in Ransom's classes at Vanderbilt, Warren realized that the study of literature, particularly poetry, should be presented to students as a process wherein certain technical elements must be accounted for as they unite with content. The young professors, therefore, took matters into their own hands. As Brooks described it:

> Warren came in one day with something to show me. He had, largely because there was no metrical help at all to the poetry in the textbook, written out a little scheme showing [the students] different kinds of feet, meters, and so on. I looked it over with him, of course, and made some further comments on it, and particularly wanted to propose fattening up the comments on imagery. It wasn't enough to say that the imagery could be decorative or illustrative or so on. Actually, all the *good* imagery, I think I was saying, was *functional*. It was worked out into a little mimeographed thing.[27]

The "little mimeographed thing" was gathered into a paperbound manual that was the ancestor of most literary anthologies to be devised in the follow-

25. Winchell, *Cleanth Brooks and the Rise of Modern Criticism*, 91; Cutrer, *Parnassus on the Mississippi*, 81, 49.
26. Brooks, interview, January 10, 1988.
27. Ibid.

ing half-century. An examination of one of those two extant copies suggests that there are more similarities than differences between that "handout" and the immensely successful and influential textbooks which Brooks and Warren were soon to produce: *An Approach to Literature* (also edited by John T. Purser), *Understanding Poetry*, *Understanding Fiction*, and (by Brooks and Robert Heilman) *Understanding Drama*. The latter three anthologies were, in effect, extended separate versions of the poetry, prose, and drama sections of *An Approach to Literature*. In addition, Brooks and Warren produced *Modern Rhetoric* in 1949, as the preface to the third edition (1970) states, to "draw the student into a fuller participation in the actual process of learning."[28] Other anthologies would follow throughout Brooks's and Warren's careers, but all began with the efforts of two maverick English teachers who were not afraid to challenge traditional ways of teaching literature.

The *Sophomore Poetry Manual*, dated 1936 and published by Louisiana State University, has the names of Cleanth Brooks, John T. Purser, and Robert Penn Warren on its title page. Purser was a student assistant whose negative reactions to the way his courses were being taught and to the textbook in use, *The College Omnibus* (edited by John T. McCallum), may have played a role in the *Manual*'s conception. In 1985, looking back to the creation of the *Manual*, Warren wrote: "Everything was quite literally collaborative. We sat down and argued out general notions and general plans for the book—only to find as work developed that we were constantly being thrown back to revise original ideas."[29]

As one might expect, considerable attention is given to the reading of lyric poems; but again, the editors emphasize elements within poems rather than their genres. The selections in Section III might be called dramatic lyrics, in that they "deal directly with some object" and with "someone who is looking at the object."[30] Though Brooks and his circle would side later with William K. Wimsatt in forbidding the intentional fallacy, the writers of this poetry manual were not above stating that the author of such poems *wants* the "reader [to] participate in the observation." Examples range from "When Icicles Hang by the Wall" from Shakespeare's *The Tempest* and two of his son-

---

28. Cleanth Brooks and Robert Penn Warren, eds., *Modern Rhetoric* (New York: Harcourt Brace Jovanovich, 1970), vii.

29. Cutrer, *Parnassus on the Mississippi*, 180; Warren, "Brooks and Warren," 2. One of two extant copies of the *Sophomore Poetry Manual* is preserved with the Cleanth Brooks Papers at Yale.

30. Cleanth Brooks, John T. Purser, and Robert Penn Warren, eds., *Sophomore Poetry Manual* (Baton Rouge: Louisiana State University Press, 1936), 27.

nets, to Tennyson's "The Eagle." Many periods and traditions are included—even Shelley, whose "The Indian Serenade" would be the object of severe censure in *Understanding Poetry*, is represented by "Ode to the West Wind."

Overall, this modest teaching manual, with its slender commentary and carefully chosen examples, says as much by its omissions as by its inclusions. There are no examples from neoclassical poetry—not even "the sound must seem an echo to the sense" from Pope's "Essay on Criticism"—and, surprisingly, considering the New Critics' passion for the metaphysical poets, no Donne. Other than Ransom and E. A. Robinson, no American poets are included.

The Sophomore Poetry Manual set its editors on a clearly marked road to wielding much influence on the way literature would be taught. *An Approach to Literature*, first published in 1936 by LSU Press, was sold to F. S. Crofts (later Appleton-Century-Crofts) in 1939. It continued in the spirit of the poetry manual to disparage poor popular poems by Longfellow, Kilmer, and Shelley. The anthology widened its range, adding poems by Donne, Eliot, and (a total of eleven) by Frost, and, of course, it added fiction and essays to its scope. Between 1939 and 1976, the textbook went through five editions following essentially the same format.

Far more influential, however, was another offshoot, *Understanding Poetry: An Anthology for College Students*, published by Holt in 1938. *Understanding Fiction* (further discussed in Chapter 8) appeared in 1959, published by Crofts. *Understanding Drama* (Holt, 1945) was a collaboration between Cleanth Brooks and Robert Heilman, also among the "bright young men" hired during the Long era, whose area of expertise was Renaissance drama. At Yale, Brooks and Warren would collaborate on one more textbook, *American Literature: The Makers and the Making* (St. Martin's, 1973). Brooks and Warren invited the young Americanist R. W. B. Lewis to join them in the project to assist in the writing of historical commentary.[31]

A revolution had nonetheless taken place. The "approach" of Brooks and Warren would affect textbook writing up to the present. If the correspondence between Brooks and Warren during this period is any indication, their "spare" time was so dominated by the business of textbook writing that it is a wonder the two men could accomplish anything else. Randall Jarrell branded "Red's" textbook writing as a waste of his talent.[32] Certainly the activity was motivated in part by the need for financial stability when university salaries

31. Winchell, *Cleanth Brooks and the Rise of Modern Criticism*, 351–52.
32. M. Jarrell, ed., *Randall Jarrell's Letters*, 139.

were much lower, even on average, than they are today. Practically speaking, however, the textbooks were the means by which the critical theories of Cleanth Brooks were to proliferate.

While Brooks and Warren edited the *Southern Review* and engaged in textbook writing, Brooks was somehow able to write the books and articles that made him the outstanding theorist of the New Criticism. From 1935 to 1942, he had the benefit of Warren's presence to serve as sounding board for his ideas and interpretations. During the intervals when they were separated, by Warren's summers in Italy and later by his removal to Minnesota, their relationship continued by correspondence. Letters exchanged between Brooks and Warren between 1933 and 1947 discuss the practical matters connected with the textbooks as well as their own writing projects. These remarkable fourteen years, which saw the rise and fall of the *Southern Review* and the development of *Understanding Poetry* and *Understanding Fiction*, were also an astonishingly prolific period of individual creativity for both men, culminating in *All the King's Men*, Warren's masterpiece, and *The Well Wrought Urn*, Brooks's most important critical treatise.

In the same letter that invited Warren to contribute to the *Southwest Review*, Brooks set a further precedent by adding that he had "a few things [i.e., that he had written] which I should like to show you." The letters thereafter tended to follow a pattern: news of personal and literary activities was almost always followed by a request for the other's opinion on some recently completed text and, in turn, frank evaluation of the correspondent's recent submission. Not only are these letters an illuminating accompaniment to Brooks's and Warren's published texts, but they also indicate how each helped to shape the other's developing literary theories.[33]

Before Warren came to LSU, Brooks sent Warren some of his writing for evaluation, and Warren replied as follows: "At this time I want to congratulate you on the fine piece of work you have done in the thesis. I studied it very carefully, and found little to disagree with and less that I would care to take the responsibility of attacking."[34] Brooks's Tulane thesis may have been the beginnings of *Modern Poetry and the Tradition*, published in 1939. The essays for that collection were, however, gradually accumulated during Brooks's early years at LSU.

Significantly, however, Brooks chose to dedicate *Modern Poetry and the Tradition* to Allen Tate. When the manuscript was fully drafted, Brooks sent

33. Cutrer, *Parnassus on the Mississippi*, 32–33.
34. Grimshaw, ed., *Brooks and Warren*, 18.

it to Tate for his comments; afterward, in a letter of March 4, 1939, he expressed his thanks and proposed the dedication: "The notes which you had made on my manuscript were extremely helpful. Let me thank you again for having sent them. I know that you must have put in a good deal of time in going over the manuscript so carefully. Needless to say, I have adapted nearly all your suggestions; and with Red's help I have pulled the Frost section into some sort of shape." Brooks added that he "intended to dedicate the book to you if the dedication could come with no embarrassment to you." His motive was "the very simple one of gratitude, for you have undoubtedly taken more trouble with my work and have done more to help me get publication than anyone else."[35]

As usual, Tate was willing to use not only editorial skill but influence with publishers so that Brooks's crucial first book might become a reality. Tate's offices in this regard have not received their proper attention from literary historians. Frequently he played the role of Misenus/Pound for inheritors of the Fugitive legacy, but too often they returned little thanks for his efforts in their behalves. Cleanth Brooks was the exception.

Brooks defends his project—to explore only the works of those modern poets who carry on "the tradition"—by insisting that "if literature exists at all in any universal sense . . . there are qualities . . . which allow us to compare all poetry, and rank it under a permanent standard—then it is proper that we should speak of poetry as we do (i.e., as a 'total conception')."[36] For Brooks, in 1939, these were Eliot, Yeats, Frost, Archibald MacLeish, Auden—and Fugitive poets Ransom, Tate, and Warren.

The essays range from discussions of metaphysical and symbolist poetry, seen as important contributions to modernist poetics, to explorations of the eight individual poets and their poems. Modesty did not prevent Brooks from asserting his belief that the metaphysical poets were the models, Yeats was the modern-day oracle, and Keats was the problematic poet whose attention to images and metaphor, belated (or innovative) sense of irony, and "negative capability" made him comparable to Shakespeare, Donne, and Marvell. The same impulses that govern both commentary and selections of poems in Brooks and Warren's poetry manual also dominate *Modern Poetry and the Tradition*.

Brooks features the former Fugitives in only one essay, "The Modern

35. Brooks to Allen Tate, March 4, 1934, Allen Tate Papers, Firestone Library, Princeton University, Princeton, N.J.

36. Brooks, *Modern Poetry and the Tradition*, vii.

Poet and the Tradition," but as its title suggests, it is the most important one in the collection. To Brooks, the poetics of Ransom, Tate, and Warren *define* both the traditional and the modern. When Thomas Cutrer contends that *Modern Poetry and the Tradition*'s "most interesting critical pieces . . . deal with the relationship between Fugitive poets and their native region," he misses the point. Brooks says quite frankly that "the poets chosen for discussion here are Southern poets," who, in order "to hold on to a tradition," must "mediate [their] account of the Old South through a consciousness of the present"; they are not included because they are regionalists. They are, in fact, to be differentiated from modern poets like Carl Sandburg, who have cut themselves off from tradition, and, like Edgar Lee Masters, have exploited regionalism.[37] Although the word *Fugitive* is not listed in its index, the Fugitive legacy to poetry and criticism is thereby made paradigmatic in *Modern Poetry and the Tradition.*

Robert Penn Warren's response to *Modern Poetry and the Tradition* was unqualified praise. Writing from Rome in January 1940, he coyly remarked: "I receive[d] a few days ago a very handsome volume recently published by the North Carolina Press. . . . It is all that I thought it was. Certainly, nobody has done a cleaner job of getting at the very central situation in modern poetry. And the individual analyses still strike me as extraordinarily keen. And, may I say again, that I am deeply gratified by your comments on my own stuff. . . . I only hope that a little amiable perjury didn't creep into the book about that point."[38]

Well might Warren have been pleased at the ten-page section on him in "The Modern Poet and the Tradition." Brooks used Warren's first sequential poem, "Kentucky Mountain Farm," to illustrate how "items of local color are absorbed in the poem as adjuncts of the larger theme" and praised Warren's use of "ambiguity to accentuate the ironic contrast." Brooks described the "general structure of Warren's poems" as "a rich and detailed examination of the particular experience with the conclusion, which may be drawn from the experience, coming as a quietly ironical statement or as modest and guarded understatement." A prime illustration is the poem "Bearded Oaks," wherein "the resolution of the experience and the exit from it [are] made in terms—not so much of irony as—of understatement." But Brooks was scarcely less generous with Ransom's and Tate's poetry, finding elements of unity in diversity as proof of their excellence.[39]

37. Cutrer, *Parnassus on the Mississippi*, 108; Brooks, *Modern Poetry and the Tradition*, 74–76.
38. Grimshaw, ed., *Brooks and Warren*, 29–30.
39. Brooks, *Modern Poetry and the Tradition*, 77–78, 82.

In light of the multiplicity of directions now apparent in twentieth-century poetics, it is surprising that Brooks would define modernism so inclusively by reference to the poets of the Fugitive legacy. Essays on Eliot and Yeats do broaden the definition, but the former Fugitives' prominence in Brooks's first major book suggests not only his own natural biases but also the importance of these poets at the time when the Brooks and Warren textbooks were helping to make Fugitive standards the "orthodox" way of reading and analyzing poetry.

After 1939, much of the Brooks and Warren correspondence centered on textbook writing, most notably *Understanding Poetry* and *Understanding Fiction*, which would gain far wider acceptance than *An Approach to Literature*. A letter from Warren to Brooks, ca. 1941, found Warren in Chicago, where it appears that as those anthologies grew in prominence, the New Critical "method," by then attributed to Brooks rather than to Ransom, was beginning to attract attention: "Your [Brooks's] name is on every tongue here. Last night we had a radio round-table debate on 'Ethical Considerations in Criticism'—Austin Warren, Norman Foerster, myself, and three other members of the Department—Warrens against Humanists. You received high compliments over the air from Foerster, who cited you as one of the four or five stars of the New Criticism—with which, I must add, he feels ill at ease."[40]

Despite some detractors, *An Approach to Literature* and *Understanding Poetry* had begun to do quite well on the college market, being adopted by the end of 1939 at Auburn, North Dakota, Tufts, Colgate, Cornell, and St. Louis University. Most propitious for Brooks and Warren was the response of the English Department that would eventually hire them. On December 31, Warren jubilantly wrote: "I had . . . one [letter] from Professor John C. Pope, Saybrook College, Yale, asking about the *Approach*, *Understanding Poetry*, and Shakespeare's plays for the freshman work at Yale, each for one term. His questions were: What success had we had with actual use in the class room? . . . He did say that the *Understanding* had strong supporters in the department, but that the *Approach*, which was less well known, was less immediately attractive to *some* of the members. . . . It would be swell to get both books on at Yale." At the Modern Language Association meeting in New Orleans that year, when Cleanth Brooks was summoned to meet the head of Yale's English Department to discuss the textbooks, his destined departure from the South was set in motion.[41] The "new criticism" was no longer a southern phenomenon.

40. Grimshaw, ed., *Brooks and Warren*, 49–50.
41. Ibid., 27; Brooks, interview, August 7, 1991.

Meanwhile, Brooks and Warren made slow progress on their own projects. Between summers in Italy and winters at LSU, Warren worked primarily on fiction. As *All the King's Men* was undergoing its protracted gestation, Warren sent Brooks the manuscript of the play version, *Proud Flesh*, along with the request, "When you have time, please write me in detail about it, all your suggestions and criticisms." Neither *All the King's Men* nor *At Heaven's Gate*, Warren's second novel, was completed until Warren left to take a position at Minnesota in 1942. On August 31, 1943, Brooks responded to Warren's latest accomplishment with gusto: "I have read your book [*At Heaven's Gate*] with great interest—I need not tell you—and I want to say that it is truly fine. . . . It is a very rich piece of work—the characters are alive—and the integration of the characters and incidents is remarkable. (I hope that this does not sound like a cheap review)." Brooks goes on to fault the published reviews of the novel for their "wooden head[edness]," comparing the reviewer from the *Chicago Tribune* with "Fulton Oursler [*sic*] in the pulpit at a camp-meeting."[42]

Brooks meanwhile had drafted several of the essays that would appear in various journals and finally in *The Well Wrought Urn*. No less than Warren did Brooks rely on his colleague's supportive criticism. He consulted Warren (whom Ransom had dubbed a "Shakespearean") throughout his preparation of "The Naked Babe and the Cloak of Manliness" on *Macbeth*. On May 1, 1943, Warren wrote, from Minneapolis, "The outline of the Macbeth essay sounds fine. The child stuff is brilliant! I really feel that you have something by the tail. And I am anxious to see the essay." When the article was completed and sent to Warren, he shared it with his colleagues at the University of Minnesota, who were suitably impressed. Warren's letter of December 6, 1943, reported: "Well, it's a bullseye. Or I'm badly mistaken. I think that the business about the daggers is interesting and instructive, and right, but the business about the babes in the play is an eye-opener." One [unnamed] colleague was "struck dumb with admiration."[43]

Warren referred to Brooks's discovery that the clothing imagery in Act I, scene vii (where Duncan is compared to "a naked, new-born Babe"), may be joined with the image of the "daggers / unmannerly / Breeched with gore" as the basis for a New Critical reading of *Macbeth*. *Against* those critics who viewed the passages as "pure rant" or meaningless, if magnificent, fancy, Brooks asserts that not only are they instances of "characteristically Shake-

42. Grimshaw, ed., *Brooks and Warren*, 30, 77.
43. Ibid., 76, 79.

spearean poetry" but that "both . . . are far more than excrescences, mere extravagances of detail; each, it seems to me, contains a central symbol of the play, and symbols which we must understand if we are to understand either the detailed passage or the play as a whole."[44]

Warren also took a certain pleasure in Brooks's confrontation with rival critics. Caroline Spurgeon's book *Shakespeare's Imagery* was carrying the day among Shakespearean critics. In the essay's published versions, Brooks graciously (and ironically) wrote that although, for her discovery of "old clothes imagery" in *Macbeth*, "we are all in [her] debt. . . . Miss Spurgeon has hardly explored the full implications of her discovery." Perhaps Brooks's first version was less gracious and more ironic, for in his letter Warren urged his younger colleague not to be too hard on his rival: "She's like a child with a loaded machine gun, shooting off in all directions and chortling with glee. But again, it might not cost you much to take a milder tone." Warren ended his letter by remarking modestly—and sentimentally—"Well, all of my remarks are trivial. The paper is damned enlightening, and ought to stir up something. As I read it I was filled with nostalgia for all our old arguments and discussions and collaborations." Perhaps Warren frequently played the role of mediator, urging Brooks to moderate his confrontational style. It appears that on this occasion, Brooks attended to Warren's advice; for in the published version of the essay he judiciously remarked, "I began by suggesting that our reading of Donne [his use of metaphor] might contribute something to our reading of Shakespeare, though I tried to make plain the fact that I had no design of trying to turn Shakespeare into Donne, or—what I regard as nonsense—of trying to exalt Donne above Shakespeare."[45]

While Warren usually deferred to Brooks concerning poetry and criticism and Brooks regarded Warren as the authority on fiction and drama, each relied on the other's evaluation when the roles were reversed. Clearly, however, they approached the critical act with almost identical goals and assumptions. When Warren turned critic, it was Brooks's turn to act as expert critic and adviser. In the letter of December 6, 1943, quoted earlier, Warren reported that "on the side, I've worked out a new reading of the Ancient Mariner which I hope to commit to paper before too long. Boy, that thing is built like the Swiss watch, I assure you." As Brooks might have done in his place, Warren planned to turn his fascination with how coherently the poem is "built" into a masterful demonstration of thematic and metaphoric unity, that is, a

44. Brooks, *Well Wrought Urn*, 31.
45. Ibid., 32; Grimshaw, ed., *Brooks and Warren*, 80; Brooks, *Well Wrought Urn*, 27–28.

New Critical explication of the poem. Warren made some rather visceral comments in this letter about certain precursor critics, including "the allegory boys" and Earl Leslie Griggs, whose view of the poem as "a pleasant journey into a realm of imagination which means nothing," remarked Warren, "makes me want to call for the old granite slop-jar." Fortunately, in the essay, Warren alluded to them with proper courtesy.[46]

Unable to give the essay much of his attention, Warren made slow progress. On May 22, 1945, however, he could write: "I am enclosing herewith a study of Coleridge's *AM* ["The Rime of the Ancient Mariner"] for your inspection and that of Bob Heilman. I desperately want your close opinion, for I shall soon want to put the thing into final shape for publication." After his initial reading of the manuscript, Brooks wrote, on June 5 [1945], "I have gone over the A.M. paper several times and with a growing admiration. It is easily the finest thing that has ever been done on that poem—and probably the only essay on it that makes entire sense."[47]

But as usual, Brooks followed high praise with "a few quite trivial comments on the margins." He expressed some "regret . . . that you did not bring in the Industrial Revolution as you did once in conversation with me" even though to do so "might put off the reader by making him think that your argument was to prove Coleridge an Agrarian." More substantially, Brooks suggested, "I think that something might be made of the sexual imagery—the penetration of a virgin world: 'We were the first that ever burst / into that silent sea.' " He slips in, as well, a mildly proprietary reference to a possible contribution on *his* part to one of Warren's more creative points of analysis: "I noticed with interest your showing that the bird actually came to church because I thought that was a discovery of mine until I reflected that I had probably heard it from you in conversation in Washington, and then forgotten that I had." Warren's reply of June 8, 1945, reflected gratitude: "Well, you overwhelm me with your remarks on the Ancient Mariner paper. . . . It may very well be that the bird-church business was picked up from you in conversation, I just don't recall. I am going to make more the sexual business in the re-write, I think, and shall acknowledge you[r] silent sea business. I

46. Grimshaw, ed., *Brooks and Warren*, 87, 80–81. In 1944, Brooks sent Warren a poem entitled "The Maelstrom" for his opinion. Warren responded enthusiastically: "You've sure been keeping something under a bushel. Get right down and turn out a lot more of them. Quick." Although Allen Tate published the poem in the winter 1946 issue of the *Sewanee Review*, Brooks decided to hold back until he determined whether he would write more poems.

47. Ibid., 92, 93.

want to get that in insofar as it is objective."[48] Although, judging from the published version, it does not appear that Warren acted on either suggestion, he nonetheless wanted Brooks's expert opinion on the general plausibility of his interpretation before submitting it for publication. The essay would eventually appear with Coleridge's poem in an illustrated volume entitled *A Poem of Pure Imagination: An Experiment in Reading* (1946). This provocative, frequently debated essay follows Brooks—or does Brooks follow Warren?—in one of the New Criticism's most exemplary performances.

By 1945, *The Well Wrought Urn* was beginning to take shape. Among the most influential essays to be included, "The Light Symbolism in 'L'Allegro–Il Penseroso,' " provides yet another example of critical synthesis. Brooks remarked in his June 5 letter to Warren, "I do think it is interesting . . . to compare the light imagery as I have worked it out in 'L'Allegro–Il Penseroso' or in 'Wordsworth's Intimations Ode' with your brilliant handling of it in the *Ancient Mariner*." A month later Brooks sent his Milton essay on to Warren with the following comments: "I am enclosing the "L'Allegro–Il Penseroso" essay. Please make marginal comments. Since it is to be a chapter in *The Well-Wrought Urn* and is not to appear in magazine form or as a lecture as I had once intended, perhaps the style should be revised. Do not hesitate to mark what strike[s] you as repetitions."[49]

Warren replied swiftly, on July 31, with the usual mixture of praise and judicious suggestion:

The essay is very finely wrought and subtle. One of your better pieces, certainly. And that is giving it as high praise as it could ask. It really helps me with the poems—gives me a new way of considering them. As for suggestions, I have only one, and that is a matter of strategy. I don't think I'd say, at the topic of page 3, that it comes as a relief to "find a scholar who suspends his interest in literary sources long enough to . . ." It doesn't help the tone any, and in addition, it isn't phrased very tellingly. Anyway, Tillyard is a little bit better than the average in these matters.[50]

The questionable phrase does not appear in the published essay.

In the marvelous alchemy of literary synthesis, Brooks's essay on Milton is intertextually related, then, to Warren's "A Poem of Pure Imagination."

48. Ibid., 93, 95.
49. Ibid., 93, 96.
50. Ibid., 97.

Writing the essay was crucial to Warren's development because it proved to be not only one of his most influential pieces of criticism but also, as James Justus has pointed out, the catalyst for much of his fiction from *All the King's Men* onward.[51] And while these letters exchanged between Brooks and Warren do not suggest either that Warren was incapable of independent critical insight or that Brooks lacked the courage of his convictions, they do tell of a relationship that was especially close and creatively potent during and immediately after the years Brooks and Warren were together at LSU. Clearly a time of frantic and sometimes fragmentary activity, it was also an astonishingly productive period for both men. Warren's departure from LSU in 1942 necessitated the correspondence in which Brooks and Warren continued cooperative projects and preserved the close bonds that nurtured creativity. But perhaps because of their separation, each was forced to work more independently. Brooks would emerge thereafter as the foremost practitioner of the New Criticism, while Warren would develop new dimensions as writer of poetry, fiction, and social commentary.

The Well Wrought Urn achieves a much broader and more independent interpretative perspective than *Modern Poetry and the Tradition*, which, because of the prominence of former Fugitive mentors and friends, could be accused of parochialism. To counter charges of provincialism, Brooks proposes to examine several celebrated English poems, in chronological order, from the Elizabethan period to the present. These poems are to be "the concrete examples on which generalizations are to be based." Technical explanations are relegated to the appendix. Brooks's critical stance opposes two extremes, the reading of the poem "in terms of its historical context" and the "relativistic" "temper of our times." He intends to ask whether a poem can be read *sub specie aeternitatis* and whether a critic "can make normative judgments." As with almost all of Brooks's criticism, his tone is defensive in reaction to earlier critics. For Brooks those strong precursors are historicalbiographical critics who attribute the poem to events in the life of the poet (What did Wordsworth have for breakfast the day he wrote "Tintern Abbey"?). In so doing, Brooks echoes what Ransom had proclaimed in his most influential essay, "Criticism Inc." in *The World's Body*, that *criticism*, not historical scholarship, is the proper business of the English professor and the only avenue to a thorough and accurate account of the poetic process.[52]

51. James H. Justus, "The Mariner and Robert Penn Warren," in *Robert Penn Warren: Critical Perspectives*, ed. Neil Nakadate (Lexington: University Press of Kentucky, 1981), 127.

52. Brooks, *Well Wrought Urn*, x–xi; John Crowe Ransom, "Criticism Inc.," in *The World's Body* (Baton Rouge: Louisiana State University Press, 1938), 336, 349.

The critical discussions of poetry are followed by "The Heresy of Paraphrase" and his two appendixes, "Criticism, History, and Critical Relativism" and "The Problem of Belief." As early as August 1943, Brooks was at work on these theoretical essays and, as usual, soliciting Warren's response: "By the way, will you be able to look over a fairly short book MS in the next few weeks? I hope to finish up my new critical book, and I need advice badly." The essay in question is "Criticism, History, and Critical Relativism," wherein Brooks firmly reiterates his belief that although history and biography are legitimate concerns of the literary scholar, the business of the critic is to "look at the poem." As he states in the essay: "I insist that to treat the poems discussed primarily as poems is a proper emphasis, and very much worth doing. For we have gone to school to the anthropologists and the cultural historians assiduously, and we have learned their lesson almost too well." Brooks chiefly reacted to the "old historicists" who would assert that since the critic is "plainly the product of his own day and time," he cannot judge a poem in universal terms.[53]

Robert Penn Warren mentioned Brooks's latest book in a letter dated April 8, 1947: "I am anxiously waiting to see the press on the Well Wrought Urn. . . . The Sewanee has just come with your Marvell piece. I haven't read it, but I almost hate to: I have been projecting with a Marvell piece with the Ode as the central fact."[54] As Warren implied, the book was widely reviewed and discussed, and it remains the most frequently cited of Brooks's publications. The remark suggests, moreover, that Warren no longer felt competent to compete as a critic with Cleanth Brooks. With *The Well Wrought Urn*, Brooks had solidified his position as premier practitioner of the New Criticism.

After *The Well Wrought Urn*, Cleanth Brooks, no longer under Ransom's shadow and less likely to consult Warren, accepted the weighty responsibility of defending the New Criticism from more and more frequent challenges. Brooks's first important attempt to "explain" his position appeared in the *American Scholar* in 1943. "The New Criticism: A Brief for the Defense" replies to Darrell Abel, who had attacked the New Critics in a previous issue of the magazine. Abel had charged Brooks, Tate, and Ransom with writing "intellectual criticism" that turned poetry into dried up "forms" devoid of emotion, "doting on paradoxes and abstruse symbols" and displaying a

53. Grimshaw, ed., *Brooks and Warren*, 78; Brooks, interview, August 7, 1991; Brooks, *Well Wrought Urn*, 215–16.
54. Grimshaw, ed., *Brooks and Warren*, 127.

"thoroughgoing distaste for simplicity." He had dredged up Ransom's old challenge, that "any poem to which he [Brooks] gives his approval must be involved and 'ironical.' " After absolving Tate and Ransom from the general indictment, Brooks first defines such words as *irony* and *simplicity* and then demonstrates his critical method in an almost parodically "new critical" explication of Tennyson's "Tears, Idle Tears."[55] Finally, he also includes a series of "observations" about what the New Criticism is and what it is not that provide a rare and complete definition of Brooks's version of the New Criticism. By articulating these concepts, Cleanth Brooks indicated his willingness to accept the leadership role among New Critics.

Brooks's later volume, *A Shaping Joy* (1971), takes up, in a sense, where *The Well Wrought Urn* left off but from a vantage point more than twenty years later. Some of the essays, written between 1961 and 1971, were lectures; all are consistent with Brooks's time-tested method, in that they "attempt to refer a certain literary work to critical principles or to explore the principles themselves through a series of concrete illustrations." Denying that the "New Criticism" embodies an "anti-historical bias and . . . [a] fixation on 'close reading,' " Brooks demonstrates his awareness of theoretical pluralities by setting forth the "3 R's of criticism": "criticism focused on the reader, on the writing, and on the writer." Brooks warns against confusing "the genesis of a work . . . with its meaning or its value . . . (the intentional fallacy) . . . or the value of a work by its effects—such as the intensity of its impact on the reader or the fact that it achieves great popularity . . . in the realm of politics . . . (the affective fallacy)."[56]

In "A Conversation with Cleanth Brooks" (1975), Robert Penn Warren asked whether what Brooks says in this volume, as implied in its Yeatsean title, can be extended to "an underlying unity in your various books and essays." Brooks replied as follows:

> As I look back over my first fumblings at criticism, on down to my present fumblings, I see probably one constant trait: I've been obsessed for a long time with trying to define what literature is. Because our age is dominated by science and technology, the question demands an answer. What is literature? How can you distinguish it from philosophy or religion or social essays, and so on? What are its constituent prin-

55. Cleanth Brooks, "The New Criticism: A Brief for the Defense," *American Scholar* 43–44 (1943): 285–95.

56. Cleanth Brooks, *A Shaping Joy: Studies in the Writer's Craft* (New York: Harcourt Brace Jovanovich, 1971), xi, xii, xiv.

ciples? Is it simply a message, a doctrine, a philosophical or historical truth, fancied up, put in some kind of pleasant or attractive or persuasive form? Or is the unity of a piece of literature more intimate than that? Do form and content really come together?[57]

A Shaping Joy gives the student of Brooks's criticism an excellent summary of his positions on poetry, fiction, and drama, firmly based on the notion that all great literature must measure up to the Aristotelian, Coleridgean, and Brooksean standard of organic unity.

Brooks's final apologia appeared in *Community, Religion, and Literature*, published posthumously by the University of Missouri Press under the guidance of his close friend the editor Beverly Jarrett. In the introductory essay, "In Search of the New Criticism," Brooks once again attempted to explain his enterprise to those "who [have] misread *The New Criticism* or . . . just seen the movie." Another essay, simply entitled "The New Criticism," finds Brooks answering some—such as Hugh Kenner, Barbara Herrnstein Smith, Hillis Miller, and Gerald Graff—who have attacked the New Criticism. In closing, an unapologetic Brooks looks back, with supporter René Wellek, to the " 'valiant fight' " which he and others have fought, through the years, in defense of literature as "artistic transaction" and of criticism's duty to judge between "good and bad art."[58]

Cleanth Brooks's career and the New Criticism were vitally connected with the Fugitive movement. In *The Southern Connection*, Robert Heilman characterizes a mode of thought that reaches back to Nashville: "The Southern sense of the concrete takes the form of a preoccupation with the individual work and the precise means by which its author goes about his business." Recognizing the centrality of the Fugitives, Heilman adds that there is no "other group which, whatever its differences in opinion, can, because of its common background and its shared allegiances, be thought of as a group and which has so much sheer talent in all its parts as Ransom, Tate, Brooks, and Warren."[59]

Cleanth Brooks must be seen, however, as the culmination of this legacy, not merely as one of a group. René Wellek has noted that Brooks's "relation

57. Robert Penn Warren, "A Conversation with Cleanth Brooks," in *Possibilities of Order*, ed. Simpson, 6–7.

58. Cleanth Brooks, *Community, Religion, and Literature: Essays by Cleanth Brooks* (Columbia: University of Missouri Press, 1995), 1, 15, 97.

59. Robert B. Heilman, *The Southern Connection* (Baton Rouge: Louisiana State University Press, 1991), 254–55.

to the other New Critics . . . is far from simply allegiance"; that although he admires and frequently quotes Ransom, "Cleanth Brooks is clearly much more in sympathy with Allen Tate and repeatedly endorses his formula: 'Poetry is neither religion nor social engineering.' " Brooks was not exactly what Ransom ordered in his essay "Wanted: An Ontological Critic." Brooks's approach was less philosophical and more practical. Compared to the often acrimonious disputes that separate the New Criticism from contemporary theoreticians, however, the distinctions between Brooks and Ransom seem negligible. There was just enough tension between teacher and pupil, in the context of mutual respect and collegiality, to generate a rich body of criticism from Cleanth Brooks. Indeed, these "divergences" over the years between Brooks, Ransom, and Eliot seem so minor that it is not surprising that Cynthia Ozick (in a 1989 *New Yorker* essay) and others tend to see the New Critics and Eliot as emanations of a monolithic adversary. It is usually Brooks, however, who has personified the New Criticism for most contemporary critics.[60]

60. René Wellek, *A History of Modern Criticism, 1757–1950*, Vol. 6, *American Criticism, 1990–1950* (New Haven: Yale University Press, 1986), 206–7; Cynthia Ozick, "A Critic at Large: T. S. Eliot at 101," *New Yorker*, November 20, 1989, 119–54.

PART II

The Poets of the Fugitive Legacy

4 / Post-Fugitive Poetry

Allen Tate must have spoken for the rest of the former Fugitives when he questioned why the young poets at Vanderbilt did not form a "post-Fugitive group."[1] One would have expected that the four major Fugitives—Ransom, Davidson, Tate, and Warren—being poets, would have attracted a generation of disciples. They did, in fact, form a supportive network, nearly always willing to sponsor outstanding poets of the so-called middle generation. But these young poets did not achieve prominence or write their best poetry because they imitated their mentors. For them, the Fugitive aesthetic had its greatest impact in a negative sense: as a point of departure that helped to generate postmodernism.

At first the poets of the Fugitive legacy benefited from the fact that the former Fugitives were influential members of the literary establishment, editing journals, interacting with publishers, and holding teaching posts at desirable colleges and universities. But until the anxiety of influence had operated fully, none of the young poets could achieve their mature styles. When David Kalstone wrote of Elizabeth Bishop (another middle-generation poet) and Marianne Moore, he might have been describing the ambiguous relation-

1. Tate, "Young Randall," 230.

ships between Randall Jarrell, Robert Lowell, and John Berryman and their Fugitive mentors: "It was as if Bishop had in Moore both a model and a point of departure, an authority against which she could explore, even indulge, her more anarchic impulses."[2] Nevertheless, the sponsorship of the Fugitives encouraged and sustained these poets, even as they and their mentors had the good fortune to colonize a sparsely populated literary landscape. And the younger poets were only too glad to accept the older generation's assistance, although they often seemed to be oblivious both to the precariousness of their own situations in the literary world of the thirties and forties and to the importance of the elders' prestige.

The list of future poets who knew the four major Fugitives at Vanderbilt, Louisiana State University, Kenyon, and Sewanee or who made publishing debuts in their journals was extensive. For the most part, women were absent from the list, although Laura Riding once attended the Fugitive meetings and might have served as a role model. For Randall Jarrell, John Berryman, and Robert Lowell, the most prominent poets of the Fugitive legacy, relationships with the Fugitives were crucial to their entrance into and prominence in the literary arena. All three began as students and protégés of one or more of the former Fugitives; all three first bonded with and then broke away from their mentors; and all three swerved in almost identical ways from their earliest modes of composition and from their Fugitive mentors as they evolved into the first important postmodern poets.

The three poets were not initially a "group" that worked closely together. Jarrell and Lowell met at Kenyon College but soon separated when Lowell went on to Baton Rouge. Neither was acquainted with Berryman or his poetry before the 1940s; and yet, as Bruce Bawer, Stephen Matterson, and Eileen Simpson have recognized, Jarrell, Lowell, and Berryman did eventually become friends and colleagues (Mary Jarrell has called them "America's Bloomsbury group"), who interacted with and supported one another throughout their careers and, far too soon, composed one another's elegies. The habit of "networking" was another legacy from the Fugitives.[3]

2. David Kalstone, *Becoming a Poet: Elizabeth Bishop with Marianne Moore and Robert Lowell*, ed. Robert Hemenway (New York: Noonday-Farrar, 1989), 5.
3. Critics who have treated these poets as a group have searched for biographical and ideological similarities among them. Bruce Bawer has emphasized the "Turbulent Childhoods," "Alienated Adulthoods," [and] common "Dreams of Knowledge" of Randall Jarrell, Robert Lowell, John Berryman, and Delmore Schwartz (*The Middle Generation: The Lives and Poetry of Delmore Schwartz, Randall Jarrell, John Berryman, and Robert Lowell* [Hamden, Conn.: Archon Books, 1986], ix). Eileen Simpson drew on recollections of her marriage to Berryman for *Poets*

All accounts of these three poets' early careers indicate how essential were their relationships with the former Fugitives. In *The Years of Our Friendship*, William Doreski recounts the entire Lowell and Tate relationship; and in *Berryman and Lowell: The Art of Losing*, Stephen Matterson remarks that "Berryman and Lowell at first write poetry of the sort recommended by Ransom and Tate. In doing so, that poetry is informed by a comparable range of attitudes. Eventually they break from that kind of poetry, since the large range of attitudes is no longer tenable for them."[4] By passing quickly over the early careers of Jarrell, Lowell, and Berryman, however, these writers have underestimated the importance of the Fugitive legacy. Perhaps they were subtly influenced by the decline in reputation of the Fugitive–New Critical ethos or, more likely, by the poets' own denial of their roots—Lowell's less than the others'—in efforts to assert their independence. To reestablish the crucial connections between these poets and their mentors, it is desirable, first, to look into the parallel ways in which these poets began their writing careers while still in a position to benefit from Fugitive patronage, to discover what sort of poetry, from a formal standpoint, they composed.

Matterson has stated that "like all of the middle generation poets, Berryman and Lowell learnt from the New Critics and the modernists," that, as Lowell put it, "a good poem . . . was a piece of craftsmanship, an intelligible or cognitive object."[5] This common background resulted in remarkably similar apprentice poetry from many of the poets of the thirties and forties. Jarrell, Berryman, and Lowell began to write and publish poetry in the middle thirties, after the emergence, in the teens and twenties, of the Imagists, the high modernism of Pound and Eliot, and the Fugitive movement. Along with others of their generation, the three chose the formal, metric poetic style that also characterized the poetry of Ransom, most of Tate, and the early poems of Warren.

Practically speaking, American poets from the twenties onward were divided into two camps, metric and nonmetric (Lowell called it "cooked and

---

in Their Youth: A Memoir (New York: Random House, 1982), which takes up the fascinating story of the group's interrelationships after World War II, when its ties with the former Fugitives had slackened. Stephen Matterson has described the similarities between the lives and careers of Lowell and Berryman (*Berryman and Lowell: The Art of Losing* [Totowa, N.J.: Barnes & Noble, 1988]). And in *Becoming a Poet*, David Kalstone has described the role that Lowell and his circle played in the life and art of Elizabeth Bishop.

4. William Doreski, *The Years of Our Friendship: Robert Lowell and Allen Tate* (Jackson: University Press of Mississippi, 1990), 21; Matterson, *Berryman and Lowell*, 16.

5. Matterson, *Berryman and Lowell*, 15–16.

raw" poetry); but by the thirties and forties the pendulum had begun to swing back to traditional metrics. By 1951, Josephine Miles (also a formalist poet of this generation) could recognize that "the poetry [of the thirties and forties] . . . [was] . . . a poetry of pattern. It [was] devoted to the linear, tonal, and qualitative arrangement of things according to a perspective in a state of mind." Writing in 1964, Harvey Gross concluded that "the poets of the late forties and fifties have shown an almost religious devotion to iambic pentameter, intricate stanzas, and close formal arrangements."[6]

A basic distrust of nonmetrical poetry had characterized the Fugitive poets from the beginning. Tate, an Eliot apologist after 1922, wrote most of his poetry in formal stanzas; and Ransom, whose poetry had always been classically formal, remained skeptical about both the Imagists and Eliot. Poems in "experimental" free verse were allowed at the weekly meetings of the Fugitive group and later in the *Fugitive* magazine, but Davidson, Ransom, and even Tate continued to be committed to metric poetry. Harvey Gross includes Ransom among those poets who "remained largely unaffected by the prosodical revolutions of the 'teens and the twenties, and who composed the bulk of their work in syllable-stress metric."[7]

The early poetry of Jarrell, Berryman, and Lowell followed European examples in showing a marked tendency toward formal patterning. Bruce Bawer has remarked upon the "little interest, relatively speaking . . . the Middle Generation poets had in the American poetry scene during their early years."[8] The exception was, of course, their awareness of how Ransom and Tate generally composed their poetry. With such powerful pressure toward conventional prosody in their backgrounds, these poets seemed to be unaware, during their periods of apprenticeship, that nonmetric, open poetic form, such as that of Walt Whitman, William Carlos Williams, and other American precursors, was even an option.

These poets showed some interest in accentual, or, as Gross terms it, "strong-stress" prosody, following the publication of Gerard Manley Hopkins's poetry and its influence on Auden and Dylan Thomas. Randall Jarrell termed Hopkins's impact on certain poems in Lowell's first volume, *Land of*

6. Hugh B. Staples, *Robert Lowell: The First Twenty Years* (London: Faber, 1962), 13; Josephine Miles, *The Continuity of Poetic Language: Studies in English Poetry from the 1540's to the 1940's* (Berkeley: University of California Press, 1951), 384; Harvey Gross, *Sound and Form in Modern Poetry: A Study of Prosody from Thomas Hardy to Robert Lowell* (Ann Arbor: University of Michigan Press, 1964), 248.

7. Cowan, *Fugitive Group*, 69; Gross, *Sound and Form*, 42.

8. Bawer, *Middle Generation*, 124.

Unlikeness, "obvious but unimportant" in his 1945 review of the collection; but in an earlier letter to Allen Tate, Jarrell defended his own use of accentual poetry against some negative comments from Tate: "I'm sure you're right about some of the lines being limp (although I think that in the future when people are thoroughly used to reading accentual verse some of them will seem a lot stiffer)."[9] Although Hopkins was one of Berryman's early favorites, his use of Hopkins was not apparent until much later. In fact, until the fifties, most poems written by Jarrell, Berryman, and Lowell were stanzaic and in traditional accentual-syllabic meter.

Rhyming was also the rule among these poets, although there was considerable variety in their praxis. Berryman was the strictest, or "best," rhymer. Lowell was next, often composing in continuous Chaucerian couplets, and Jarrell was the most likely to resort to consonance or "sight rhyme." An overwhelming majority of their early poems are in formal, metric, rhyming stanzas, with quatrains in preponderance. They are similar not only in form but also in point of view and tone. All three poets were committed to the poetics of irony and objective detachment, in reaction to nineteenth-century subjectivity and sentimentality. None followed Whitman in "singing Myself"; most of their early poems were coldly objective lyrics wherein the "I" of the speaker is either absent or unidentified. Although Jarrell would observe in "Fifty Years of American Poetry" that the dramatic monologue had become the "norm" in modern American poetry, not even the veiled subjectivity possible through the dramatic mode initially attracted these post-Fugitive poets.[10]

During the thirties and forties, the former Fugitives—now editors—were clearly receptive to poetry from the young men whom they had mentored and who wrote their sort of poetry. Jarrell, Lowell, and Berryman owed their early publishing successes to the active sponsorship of former Fugitives. Most of their earlier poems found publication in journals edited by Warren, Tate, or Ransom.[11] Warren (with Brooks) and Ransom accepted their poems for the *Southern* and *Kenyon* reviews; Tate, first to make his presence felt in the northern literary community, was able to use his influence not only with magazine but with book publishers. Not without considerable effort, he was instrumental in the publication of *Five Young American Poets* (1940), including

9. Randall Jarrell, "Poetry in War and Peace," in *Kipling, Auden & Co.* (New York: Farrar, Straus & Giroux, 1980), 132; Jarrell to Tate, January 1941, Tate Papers.

10. Jarrell, *Poetry and the Age*, 12.

11. In the Appendix, I have provided a list of poems published by Jarrell, Berryman, and Lowell during the thirties and early forties, along with places of first publication.

Jarrell and Berryman; of Jarrell's *Blood for a Stranger* (1942); of Berryman's 1942 *Poems*; and of Lowell's *Land of Unlikeness* (1944). Without such sponsorship, these three poetic careers might have begun much later, if at all.

After their pre–World War II period of apprenticeship, the three young poets began to break away from their Fugitive mentors. The *Partisan Review*, edited by friends such as Phillip Rahv and William Phillips, in combination with the Auden influence, constituted that "Other" with which to oppose the parental presence of Warren, Tate, and Ransom. The *Partisan's* iconoclastic Marxist ideology was a major attraction to the young poets, as was the panache of the northern literary scene. Naturally, they were eager to address a national rather than a regional audience.

Perhaps the strongest trait the successful poets of the Fugitive legacy shared with their mentors was a refusal to be limited by regional boundaries. These fledgling poets continued to imitate their mentors by forming a new network and by moving out of the South. In fact, the impulse toward relocation in the North proved nearly ubiquitous among both the Fugitives and their protégés. Andrew Lytle, speaking of Tate and his wife, Caroline Gordon, put it this way: "Southerners generally did not feel uprooted. They went to New York because that was the place where writers and publishers were. They generally came home. The southerner's conscious entanglement was the family and its long cords."[12] Like and admit it or not, the Fugitives were "family" to Jarrell and Lowell and, to a lesser extent, Berryman. If the Fugitives fled the odor of magnolias, the post-Fugitives fled Agrarian regionalism and the orthodoxy—religious, political, and artistic—of the Fugitives. These acts of rebellion, often chronicled in friendly correspondence with the former Fugitives, generated the creative energy that characterizes Bloom's anxiety of influence. It is evident, therefore, that the poets of the Fugitive legacy succeeded, not *in spite of* but *because of* those exercises in letting go.

12. Andrew Lytle, Foreword to *The Southern Mandarins: Letters of Caroline Gordon to Sally Wood, 1924–1937*, ed. Sally Wood (Baton Rouge: Louisiana State University Press, 1984), 3.

5 / Randall Jarrell:
The Precocious Pupil

R andall Jarrell's relationship with all four major Fugitives began at Vanderbilt, from 1931 to 1936, when Ransom, Warren, and Davidson were his professors and he was introduced to Tate. At Kenyon, from 1937 to 1939, where, by mail, he finished his master's thesis under Davidson's direction, he was Ransom's junior colleague and a contributor to his *Kenyon Review*. Concurrently, from 1935 onward, Jarrell published regularly in the Brooks and Warren *Southern Review*. In 1939–43 and during the war years, when Jarrell was in Texas and points west, he corresponded with Tate, in effect using him as a literary agent with the New York publishers. After the war, Jarrell's publication in *Five Young American Poets* (1940) and then of his first independent volume of poetry, *Blood for a Stranger* (1942), both with Tate's help, made Jarrell independent of his mentors, although he continued to interact with Tate and Warren through correspondence, visits, and university appearances. Jarrell's career flourished until 1947 largely because of the patronage and encouragement of the former Fugitives.

The elder son of middle-class Nashville parents with both rich and poor relations, Randall Jarrell cut a wide swath at a very early age. In Suzanne Ferguson's, William Pritchard's, and Richard Flynn's accounts of Jarrell's boyhood, there are partial explanations for his precocity: posing for the statue of Ganymede for the Parthenon frieze when he was only six years old, living near movie sets with California grandparents as a young adolescent, voracious reading in solitary afternoons at Nashville's Carnegie Library, and being involved with his high school drama club and newspaper. Neither these experiences nor not uncommon childhood traumas resulting from maternal fixation and his parents' divorce can fully explain how Jarrell turned feelings of intellectual-aesthetic superiority to his family and peers into the conviction, at such an early age, that he had the creative and intellectual gifts to pursue the most tenuous of vocations: those of poet and critic. Jarrell's family background lacked even the erudition of households wherein the parents are schoolteachers or clergymen. He did not attend one of the good preparatory schools in or near Nashville, such as Montgomery Bell Academy or Battle Ground Academy, where he would have received a classical education. When his wealthy uncle Howell Campbell wisely sent him to Vanderbilt rather than into his candy business, Jarrell first majored in psychology, rather than literature, a fairly sound if unorthodox preparation for much of the poetry he would write later. It would have been unheard-of, outside Iowa, for any college student of Jarrell's generation to "major" in creative writing, and to have done so would probably have been discouraged by parents with slender means and little inclination to support his literary ambitions. He had, however, the same good luck as the other heirs to the Fugitive legacy—to be a Vanderbilt student while Ransom, Davidson, and Warren were members of the English faculty and Tate was a frequent visitor.

Jarrell's undergraduate and graduate education occurred at Vanderbilt between 1932 and 1937. His first teachers among the Fugitives were Ransom and Warren. Both reacted initially with the instinctive fear that an obviously gifted and outspoken student often excites in a teacher, although almost without reservation they believed that Jarrell was destined to be an excellent poet. Ransom recalled his first impression of Jarrell as a mixture of admiration and dis-ease: "Nobody could ignore Randall, in those years when I was seeing him daily. He was an insistent and almost overbearing talker." Robert Penn Warren freely admitted his bemused insecurity at the prospect of having among his first students in "the old standard Sophomore Survey—*Beowulf* to Thomas Hardy . . . a tall, skinny young man . . . a freshman, but since he had read everything, he didn't belong in Freshman English. . . . The tall, skinny young man was, even at the time of the Sophomore Survey, a poet."[1]

1. John Crowe Ransom, "The Rugged Way of Genius," in *Randall Jarrell*, ed. Lowell, Taylor, and Warren, 155; Robert Penn Warren, "University Tribute: Introductory Remarks on the Occasion of the University Press–Historical Book Club Tribute," in *Alumni News* 54 (University of North Carolina, Greensboro, Spring 1966), 23.

Warren, who at sixteen had struck Allen Tate as "the most gifted person [he had] ever known," was prepared, as were the other Fugitives, to entertain the possibility that creative literary genius *could* appear—at Vanderbilt—in a person hardly out of adolescence. Warren introduced Jarrell to Allen Tate, who later remembered him as a "proud and difficult young man of eighteen," who

> must even, at that early time, have been conscious of his superior gifts and chafing under the restraints imposed by youth. I remember Red leading me into another room and showing me some of boy's poems. There was one beginning "The cow wandering in the bare field" which struck me as prodigious; I still think it one of his best poems. . . . It struck all of his older friends at that time that his technical knowledge of verse must have come to him without labor: an early poem, "A Description of Some Confederate Soldiers," had formal mastery that I, nearly fifteen years older, could not have equaled.[2]

Between them, Tate and Warren apparently determined that, whenever the opportunity arose, they would do what they could to ease Jarrell's entry into the sphere of professional letters—and Jarrell not yet finished with his baccalaureate.

It appears that this "proud and difficult young man" was innocent of the dread he instilled in his teachers. Like many intellectual students, Jarrell was doubtless uncomfortably alienated both from his complacently average classmates and his professors. He had, therefore, to construct a self-protective buffer from both extremes that reinforced his diploid personality—the brazen exterior masking the vulnerable self within. Both Ransom and Warren were frequently chagrined and embarrassed by Jarrell's intimidation of less confident and knowledgeable classmates, and when they reproached him, he would profess astonishment and attempt to mend his ways.[3] But Randall was, like a character in a later poem, "the one who was different"; he could not alter his essentially exotic nature.

But not many such students perceive themselves as capable, at the age of eighteen or nineteen, of publishing poetry in a national magazine. Experience editing the Vanderbilt literary magazine the *Masquerader*, where he worked with W. R. Moses, future contributor to *Five Young American Poets*, no doubt helped build his confidence; but had Jarrell been a typical undergraduate

2. Cowan, *Fugitive Group*, 106–7; Tate, "Young Randall," 230–31.

3. William H. Pritchard, *Randall Jarrell: A Literary Life* (New York: Farrar, Straus & Giroux, 1990), 23.

writer and journalist, the likes of Ransom, Tate, and Warren would have cut
him quickly to size. They did not. Rather, they eagerly reinforced his ambitions and apparently offered no constructive criticism. They consequently
published a spate of Jarrell's poetry that compares unfavorably with his mature work, as he himself, by excluding most of it from his early collections,
was fully aware. Richard Flynn believes that Jarrell wrote so poorly at first
because he was "under the influence of his Fugitive mentors." William
Pritchard conjectures that Jarrell was "inhibited by his pronounced early success." A simpler explanation is that although Jarrell had read extensively and
written (poetry?) in adolescence, he was not, as a twenty-year-old Vanderbilt
junior, ready to publish in an arena populated by seasoned professionals. Despite the initial awkwardness of his poetry, Randall Jarrell, never a good self-
critic, was nonetheless encouraged by his mentors to see himself as a mature
writer who was ready to take on the literary establishment.[4]

In May 1934, Tate and Warren invited Jarrell, along with an impressive
list of his elders, including Ransom, John Peale Bishop, Mark Van Doren,
and Louis MacNeice, to contribute to a poetry supplement for the *American
Review*. Among them (see Appendix) was "The cow wandering in the bare
field," which Warren first showed Tate and which he termed "prodigious."
From the title, one might suppose that Jarrell had dutifully produced an
"agrarian" poem to please his mentors. Instead, the poem depicts a bleakly
surreal landscape "muffled in snow" and framed by "the starred window,"
not observed but populated by "inhabitants of the country of the mind" and
"the thirsty images of a dream." Near the conclusion, the speaker mounts a
surprisingly bold generational protest, positing himself as an "artist," whose
images are formed by authentic experience, against the "parent" (his Fugitive
mentors?), whose art has lost its vitality:

> I summon them, then, from the old darkness
> Into this wooden room, dripping and warm,
> To chorus for you their bad charm
> Because I knew their true living forms.
>
> And how shall I make you, mossy, bearded, mournful,
> A stuffed father on a Christmas night,
> Cry out in pride and blessedness: O children!

Whether or not it is a covert act of defiance, "The cow" is an impressive
poem for an undergraduate, and both Warren and Tate were impressed.

4. Richard Flynn, *Randall Jarrell and the Lost World of Childhood* (Athens: University of Georgia Press, 1990), 15; Pritchard, *Randall Jarrell*, 35.

Along with Pritchard, however, one must be "astonish[ed] that Tate and Warren chose Jarrell and used not one but five of his poems!" Just after the supplement appeared, Warren (at Vanderbilt) wrote to Cleanth Brooks (at Louisiana State University): "What did you think of the poetry issue of the *A M* [*sic*, *A R*]? Jarrell is pretty hot, isn't he? He is a sphomore [*sic*] now, the most precocious fellow I ever knew."[5]

Jarrell's letters to Robert Penn Warren between 1935 and 1941, while Warren edited the *Southern Review*, provide a witty and revealing backdrop for the period when the roles of teacher and pupil turned into those of editor and contributor. In time for the first issue of the new journal, Jarrell submitted a large group of poems, along with a letter stating confidently: "Here are the poems. . . . They haven't any title—just call any A POEM like that. The more you use the better—I'll have plenty for the group." And somewhat arrogantly he added, "If you use [John Peale] Bishop's group of poems in the second issue, I would like it a lot if you would put mine in the third."[6]

Jarrell, then a senior, became the first poet to be featured in that historic issue of the *Southern Review*, publishing two poems: "Looking Back in my Mind I see" and "And did she dwell in innocence and joy," which Pritchard takes to task for its "vagueness of . . . conception and . . . prosodic slackness." He adds that "Jarrell may have been attempting to imitate Ransom's sometimes Hardyesque ungainliness" which is "uncertain about what sort of blank verse they are trying to be, or whether and when they want to rhyme."[7] Jarrell was indeed imitating Thomas Hardy and Ransom, as well as other modern neoformalists; but even then, he was consistent—and distinctive—by substituting consonant for true rhyme in his then characteristic quatrains.

In October 1935, Jarrell wrote Warren that though other academic and athletic interests occupied his attention, he was "slowly accumulating poetry, like a stalagmite." His second series of *Southern Review* poems appeared in 1936, in a group entitled "Seven Poems," constituting his winning entry in

---

5. Pritchard, *Randall Jarrell*, 30–31; Randall Jarrell, *The Complete Poems* (New York: Farrar, Straus & Giroux, 1969), 374–75; Grimshaw, ed., *Brooks and Warren*, 18. Grimshaw identifies the abbreviation (logically) as a reference to *American Mercury*, but since Jarrell never published in that magazine, Warren must have meant to type "A. R.," for *American Review*. See Stuart Wright, *Randall Jarrell: A Descriptive Bibliography, 1929–1983* (Charlottesville: University Press of Virginia, 1986), C17–21, 217–18.

6. Portions of this discussion of the Jarrell-Warren relationship first appeared in Charlotte H. Beck, "Randall Jarrell and Robert Penn Warren: Fugitive Fugitives," *Southern Literary Journal* 17 (1984): 82–91; M. Jarrell, ed., *Randall Jarrell's Letters*, 2.

7. Pritchard, *Randall Jarrell*, 37.

the *Review*'s first poetry contest. He wrote Warren on July 27, 1936: "Here
are the poems I'm entering for your poetry prize. . . . There are about four
hundred eighty-five lines in all." The contest was judged by fellow Fugitive
Allen Tate, along with Mark Van Doren; but against charges of blatant favor-
itism toward Jarrell, it must be said that the 478 submissions to the contest
were unsigned.[8]

Jarrell continued to bombard the *Southern Review* with contributions, including reviews, essays, and many poems—most at the editors' request. A
third group of eight poems appeared in 1937 and a fourth, of six, in 1939,
along with an astonishing amount of critical prose. The opportunity to publish so much poetry in an important literary journal clearly spurred Jarrell's
creative energies as nothing else could, and Warren must have been conscious of his role as impresario to a young talent.

Even in one of his better poems of the period, "The Automaton," there
are several examples of obscure diction. When Warren was moved to object,
Jarrell replied with his usual accommodating arrogance: "You may be right
about the 'sick wind'. . . . It's a phrase that I just glide over when I'm reading
it and hardly notice it at all, for better or worse. As for 'discolored by the
gibbous moon'—*gibbous* is a perfectly neutral, scientific, colorless term to me:
a descriptive name for the shapeless sort of moon between half-and-full; so
at least to me, it would be at the other extreme from the *sick*."[9] "The Automaton" is in many ways characteristic of Jarrell in this seminal period. It com-
bines his special gift for the dramatic mode with the surreal images and ironic
tone he found not only in Auden but in his Fugitive mentors. The automaton's "powerful and lifeless head" recalls the "great head rattling like a
gourd" in Warren's "Original Sin." The formal structure and distancing
irony were Ransom's most durable effects on all his students, including Warren, although Jarrell's tonal effects are usually bitterer than either precursors'.
For his part, Jarrell nonchalantly both criticized and imitated his teachers, all
the while glorying in the first flowering of his art. Jarrell's flurry of publication in the *Southern Review* was valuable mainly in establishing his reputation
and strengthening, if strength were needed, his vocation as poet and critic.

John Crowe Ransom's relationship with Jarrell began in Ransom's advanced composition class, continued at Kenyon College, and seems to have
dissipated thereafter. Ransom's recognition of Jarrell's brilliance fortunately
outweighed his annoyance at Jarrell's frequent challenges to his authority in

8. M. Jarrell, ed., *Randall Jarrell's Letters*, 5, 6.
9. Jarrell to Warren, March 1937 (courtesy of M. Jarrell).

the classroom. Ransom later characterized Jarrell as *"enfant terrible* in my writing class at Vanderbilt," but "even then, when you came to read what he had written, you knew that he had to become of the important people in the literature of our time."[10]

Jarrell's ability to pursue an academic career undoubtedly hinged, at this point, on Ransom's encouragement, since his other professors were not prepared to overlook Jarrell's abrasive manner, as well as his unorthodox background as a psychology major, when he applied for a graduate fellowship. Writing to Warren in February 1937, he gives Ransom, not Vanderbilt, full credit: "The possibility (or probability, as it naturally seems to me) of not getting a fellowship here annoys me; I have been going to Vanderbilt for five years and have never managed to get a fellowship, scholarship, or anything else. . . . The person I am grateful to is Mr. Ransom, who got me a little NYA [National Youth Administration] job grading his papers; fortunately Vanderbilt had nothing to do with that."[11] Jarrell probably did not improve his chances at Vanderbilt when he led the undergraduate student protest against the administration for its failure to match Kenyon's offer and thus keep Ransom on the faculty. On June 2, 1937, he drafted a petition, signed by more than three hundred undergraduates, in which he called Ransom "a teacher who has faithfully and scrupulously served Vanderbilt" and "the University's most celebrated teacher." He closed with the suggestion that without Ransom students would be less likely to consider coming to Vanderbilt. The effort came to nothing, however, and, as Mary Jarrell records, Randall never forgave Vanderbilt for its indifference: "Twenty-five years after the event, an aged emeritus professor from the Ransom days called on Jarrell, who was at his mother's home on a visit to Nashville, and pathetically tried to clear himself and 'explain the other side.' Jarrell listened coldly, showed him out, and then burst forth, 'Tell me. He didn't lift a finger because he wanted Ransom to go. They all did. They were jealous, and he was, too.' Still scowling, he added, 'Wasn't that abject!' "[12]

When Jarrell did not receive a fellowship from Vanderbilt and only an offer of poorly paid editorial work from Brooks and Warren at LSU, Ransom came to the rescue by offering him a position at Kenyon College. At Kenyon, Jarrell taught composition and literature, coached tennis, and occupied an attic room in Ransom's home, where his roommates were Robert Lowell and

10. Ransom, "The Rugged Way," 155.
11. M. Jarrell, ed., *Randall Jarrell's Letters*, 7.
12. Young, *Gentleman in a Dustcoat*, 279; M. Jarrell, ed., *Randall Jarrell's Letters*, 8.

Peter Taylor. Jarrell and Ransom, as junior and senior colleagues, sustained a more problematic friendship than at Vanderbilt. Ransom wrote to Tate that at first he was pleased with Jarrell's adjustment to Kenyon, where he went "physical and collegiate with a rush," but shortly thereafter Ransom became concerned that Jarrell had such an inflated opinion of himself that "he wants just to pitch into some college department and work with the big professors," that although Jarrell's teaching was "animated when he is interested," he admitted to being bored at the prospect of a career teaching freshman composition. Pritchard believes that Ransom was troubled that "Jarrell showed insufficient seriousness about pursuing an academic literary career through the usual channel of a doctoral dissertation."[13] But neither the Fugitives nor their protégés were apt to pursue Ph.D.'s. Moreover, Ransom's teaching methods, scarcely orthodox, came in for their share of criticism from the academicians at Vanderbilt, though he had things his own way at Kenyon.

It was more likely Jarrell's open arrogance that alarmed Ransom, along with the fact that Jarrell's characteristic way of thinking differed from his own. In a letter to Tate, Ransom reported that at Kenyon, he and Jarrell "don't talk together well; I have the feeling he can't generalize though he's taken a good deal of philosophy." For his part, Jarrell had, as early as his first year as a Vanderbilt graduate student, perceived that their minds worked along different channels. During 1935, Jarrell wrote to Warren that he had "seen Mr. Ransom a good deal—he is engrossed in aesthetics. We rather argue; he wants me to do a thesis on that, but I'm afraid I could hardly make it experimental." In the same vein, Jarrell would later write to Allen Tate that "I've got a poetic and semifeminine mind, I don't put any real faith in abstractions or systems." Jarrell's nontheoretical intelligence, understandable in light of the two men's very different educational backgrounds, was therefore destined to become an increasing obstacle to future interaction with Ransom. And although Jarrell was writing "poetry constantly" at Kenyon, Ransom, as Jarrell wrote to Warren, "[was] well and wise but not writing poetry."[14] Clearly Jarrell felt some guilt that he could produce poems while Ransom could not—almost as if an invisible force had transferred the poetic power from teacher to pupil. Ransom may have feared that Jarrell's poetry was destined to outshine his at a time when Ransom's critical mind was gradually replacing his poetic.

After he left Kenyon College for a position at the University of Texas, Jar-

13. Pritchard, *Randall Jarrell*, 49.
14. Young, *Gentleman in a Dustcoat*, 327; M. Jarrell, ed., *Randall Jarrell's Letters*, 4, 19, 7.

rell's relationship with Ransom was friendly but casual. His poems were, however, well received by Ransom's *Kenyon Review*. Between 1939 and 1965, Jarrell published twenty poems in the *Kenyon*, beginning with "The Winter's Tale" and "For an Emigrant" in volumes 1 and 2, respectively, and including such mature poems as "Losses" and "The End of the Rainbow." He was to publish more poems in the journal than anyone except Josephine Miles, although he surpassed her in total lines. Like Lowell, Jarrell participated, but for only one month, in Ransom's schools of criticism.[15]

Jarrell's debt to Donald Davidson was small in comparison to that which he owed to Ransom, Warren, and Tate, but it came at a crucial juncture. During his first year of graduate work, Jarrell studied the English lyric with Davidson. Among his papers at Vanderbilt, Davidson included Jarrell's twenty-page essay "Lyric Elements in the Ballad." As an attempt to define and illustrate purely lyric components, as opposed to narrative and dramatic elements in the English ballad tradition, the paper accomplishes its purpose competently enough, although more is said about what is *not* lyric than what *is*. Its distinction lies in revealing, as might be expected, that Jarrell had apparently read and thoroughly analyzed an impressive number of ballads from the anonymous medieval examples to Thomas Hardy. Although there is almost no scholarly apparatus in the paper, a deficiency that other Vanderbilt professors might have penalized, Davidson affixed the grade of "A" to the title page without comment.[16] Davidson evidently approved of and wanted to encourage Jarrell's analytical and expressive talents.

After Ransom left Vanderbilt, Davidson was somewhat stricter when he inherited the supervision of Randall Jarrell's M.A. thesis. Jarrell changed his topic from Auden's poetry to A. E. Housman's, probably because Ransom and Davidson had different areas of expertise. After reading a preliminary draft, Davidson wrote to Jarrell at Kenyon, "I believe we shall have to ask you not to use an example from your own poems." And on the defensive against prevailing opinions in Vanderbilt's English Department, Davidson tried to dissuade Jarrell from writing a critical rather than a scholarly thesis. In the same letter, Davidson asked Jarrell whether his study of Housman was to be "about a poet or his poetry" or rather "a demonstration of a critical method." Jarrell answered all of Davidson's questions and complied with his sugges-

15. Elizabeth Browne, comp., *"Kenyon Review" Index: 25 Years Cumulative Compilation, 1939–1963* (New York: AMS Reprint Co., Arno, 1984), 147; M. Jarrell, ed., *Randall Jarrell's Letters*, 353.

16. Davidson Papers.

tions but not without hinting that he considered them rather stuffy. After finishing his revisions by April 26, 1939, Jarrell wrote: "I am sending you my thesis in a separate envelope. . . . I have made all the corrections that you and Mr. [Richmond Croom] Beatty suggested, cut out the parts you didn't like, and written between thirty-five and forty new pages. . . . I hope the tone is formal enough now; I'll be glad to make any changes you think desirable for the sake of more formality. I have cut out the chapter about my own poem, and have substituted for it the analysis of Shelley's *To the Moon*."[17] Davidson, who consistently supported criticism and agitated for the inclusion of creative writing courses in the Vanderbilt curriculum, no doubt improved Jarrell's thesis by curbing its self-assertive informality, the very qualities that made his later criticism distinctive. Almost certainly the rest of Vanderbilt's English faculty would not otherwise have supported Davidson's approval of "Implicit Generalizations in Housman," which allowed Jarrell to receive his M.A. in English late in 1939.

The friendship between Allen Tate and Randall Jarrell began on the defensive and ripened into an intimacy of mentor and pupil that nourished the young poet in his crucial maturation, only to decay and dissolve when, in that maturity, Jarrell found it essential to move beyond the anxiety of influence.[18] In 1939, Jarrell began a series of letters to Tate that chart the course of their relationship at its apex and into the beginning of its decline. Tate enjoyed a position of prominence in the world of letters which Jarrell both recognized and admired. Tate had, moreover, enough influence among publishers and editors to aid his young friend in establishing himself as a teacher, reviewer, and published poet. By 1939 the relationship had all the factors implicit in the anxiety of influence.

The first of these letters was written in April 1939, when Jarrell requested Tate's recommendation to a position at the University of Texas at Austin, to be addressed to a Professor J. B. WHAREY (written in bold capitals so that Tate would not misdirect the letter). Tate had just published his novel *The Fathers* in 1938; and in another April 1939 letter Jarrell expressed much admiration for it, saying that to read it gave him "the feel of another world." In *The Fathers*, historical and biographical elements merge in the story of two Virginia families, the Lacys and the Buchans, just before and during the Civil

17. Letters of May 4, 1938, and April 26, 1939, ibid.

18. Portions of this discussion of the Jarrell-Tate relationship first appeared in Charlotte H. Beck, "Beyond the Anxiety of Influence: Randall Jarrell and Allen Tate," in *Vanderbilt Tradition*, ed. Winchell, 71–83.

War. In a second April 1939 letter, Jarrell spoke of the "baggage of the tomb" and the "abyss you talk about," that is, the past, in tones that indicate that even though he admired Tate's work he had no desire to emulate it.[19] The theme of dissociation was to play a tense counterpoint to that of dependence and filial affection in the rest of these letters.

Letters sent from Austin to Greensboro and Princeton are dominated by the latter motif. At this time, Jarrell was given his first opportunity to publish his poems under hard cover. Tate in fact suggested to James Laughlin of New Directions that Jarrell should be included in an anthology entitled *Five Young American Poets*. After much fluster and protesting that publishing poetry was a little like throwing something down a well and getting "a few echoes if you're lucky," Jarrell, with Tate's advice and encouragement, did select twenty poems for the anthology. A letter dated November 1939 mentions "For an Emigrant" and "Christmas Roses" as new poems for Tate's perusal and comment.[20]

Jarrell's selections for the anthology reached back into his student poems for "A Description of Some Confederate Soldiers," which Tate had especially admired. Both the writing of the poem and Tate's admiration of it are obviously connected to Tate's "Ode to the Confederate Dead." Suzanne Ferguson calls Jarrell's poem a "debunking" of Tate's, but perhaps it would be more accurate to call it a mirror image. Differences in perspective begin with the titles; Tate's ode is a formal evocation of the past from the vantage point of the present, while Jarrell places his emphasis on the past but brings it dramatically into the present. Tate's speaker dwells on the "strict impunity [of] the headstones," which "yield their names to the element." Jarrell's subject, a Confederate soldier (a precursor of the dead and dying speakers who would dominate his war poetry), is captured in his last moments of life lying "beneath banks of light," among the "fatal waxworks" that were his comrades. Even as Tate's poem treats the failure of the present to come to terms with the past, except as "inscrutable infantry rising / Demons out of the earth," Jarrell's humanized speaker directly implores the soldier, Tom, to

> Tell how you were hunted by cunning death
> That night when, stumbling, soaked with blood,
> You sank there with open mouth.[21]

19. M. Jarrell, ed., *Randall Jarrell's Letters*, 17–19.
20. Ibid., 26.
21. Suzanne Ferguson, *The Poetry of Randall Jarrell* (Baton Rouge: Louisiana State University Press, 1971), 17; Jarrell, *Complete Poems*, 388.

In reliving that moment, Jarrell transforms Tate's "arrogant circumstance" into bleeding bodies, accessible to the living who can empathize with the past. And yet Jarrell's poem eventually counters Tate's overwhelming question, "What shall we ['who have knowledge carried to the heart'] say of the bones?" only with another query, "How can the grave hold, a statue name / Blood dried in that intolerable gaze?" Jarrell's partial answer is to relive the past in cinematic realism and thereby counter the "verdurous anonymity" of the graves that lie so ceremoniously still in the Confederate cemeteries. Even in this adolescent poem, Jarrell gave promise of his important war poetry but as an aspect of the living present rather than of the dead past. Here Jarrell dramatizes his divergence from the mode and direction of Fugitive poetry.

Jarrell rejected most of the poems in "The Rage for the Lost Penny" when he put together his 1955 *Selected Poems*. In fact, Jarrell seemed thoroughly unappreciative of Tate's efforts with Laughlin in his behalf. In a November 1939 letter he ridiculed Laughlin's plan for the New Directions anthology as "rather like God giving a rough account of what he would have done during the six days if he'd had a free hand." Thereafter he deprecatingly referred to the anthology as *5YAP*, and although he had yet to publish his own collection of poems, he apparently regarded the entire project with contempt, especially Laughlin's requirement that each of the poets include a "Note on Poetry." According to Mary Jarrell, "The Rage for the Lost Penny," Jarrell's title, "expresses his underlying vexation at having to comply with Laughlin's request."[22]

Jarrell's first book of poems, *Blood for a Stranger*, was in the formative stages in these last months before Jarrell enlisted in the air force and, in effect, said farewell to his early subjects and habits of composition. He solicited Tate's opinion in the selection of these poems and then disregarded the advice, finally dedicating the book to Tate in a gesture of mixed gratitude and defiance. In a 1941 letter, Jarrell wrote that he "appreciated your advice about '90 North' and feel[s] bad about not being able to show my gratitude by taking it. But if the stanza is removed the first line of the next becomes nonsense (says the opposite of what it now does)." Jarrell did not identify the stanza, but in a letter to Edmund Wilson, who had secured the poem for publication in the *New Republic*, he remarked: "I'm glad you're printing the poems. . . . I don't think Allen had read '90 North' very carefully when he suggested leaving out the fifth stanza . . . the stanza is an essential part of the argument,

22. M. Jarrell, ed., *Randall Jarrell's Letters*, 25, 29.

which compares the imaginary conclusive death at the Pole, in the child's warm bed, to the life, the inconclusive going-away, at the Real Pole."[23] Correctly defending "90 North," Jarrell placed it, uncut, in this and all succeeding collections. The disagreement seemed, however, to have caused no animosity on Tate's part.

Although Jarrell's failure to retain Tate's letters leaves no record of the latter's energetic efforts to find a publisher for Jarrell's first collections of poems, it is nonetheless clear that Tate was responsible for Harcourt Brace's eventual publication, in 1942, of *Blood for a Stranger*. In March 1939, Jarrell wrote Tate in a state of discouraged confusion: "I haven't known what to do. . . . Anyway, I'm sending you the manuscript. If Scribner's or Random House want it now, O.K., if not I can send it on to Red [Warren], as I guess I ought to anyway." Jarrell had felt sure that the LSU Press would accept the collection with Robert Penn Warren's sponsorship. Jarrell was, in fact, unable to secure a contract from the LSU Press and had therefore to rely on Tate's considerable influence with New York publishers. These letters contain no expression of gratitude from the younger poet. A brief note from Jarrell in March 1941 seemed exultant about the critics' reception of his part of the New Directions anthology, although he ruefully predicted that Malcolm Cowley's review would make him not "rich and famous," as Tate had apparently predicted, but "poor and infamous." The letter ended with a promise to send more poems soon, accompanied by a catalog of mystical look-alikes: Tate and Joyce, along with Red, for his eye sockets, and Wordsworth.[24] These friendly, bantering remarks give evidence of a friendship still in full flower.

Nonetheless, a two-year hiatus in the Tate-Jarrell correspondence occurred after 1943. As Pritchard remarks, Jarrell "removed himself from under Tate's wing" when he left for his air force assignment, but he had not relinquished his emotional attachment to his most problematic of father figures. The letter that resumed the relationship (written early in 1945 from Tucson, Arizona, Jarrell's address during his last few months in the air force) is an outpouring of the images and experiences that had held him captive during his military service. The letter began apologetically, saying that "at present you're my main debt to the world and hang over my head like Adam's fall." Uncharacteristically, the thirteen pages that follow have nothing to do with the world that included Jarrell and his mentor before the war and would bring

23. Ibid., 37, 34.

24. Mary Jarrell, interview by author, Greensboro, N.C., August 1984; M. Jarrell, ed., *Randall Jarrell's Letters*, 38; R. Jarrell to Tate, spring 1941, Tate Papers.

them together, briefly, after it. Instead, Jarrell wrote what is in effect a gloss on his amazing poetic output during the war years, his treatment, from the vantage point of a participant, of what it was like to participate in mechanized warfare, particularly as a pilot or a gunner.[25] These two volumes of war poetry (*Little Friend, Little Friend* and *Losses*) were not, despite critical acclaim, the best that Jarrell would ever write, but they did mark his coming to maturity—largely without the aid of past influences.

When he returned to civilian life, Jarrell resumed his relationship with Tate and those elder poets who occupied the literary world in the wartime absence of the younger. Tate was by this time editor of the *Sewanee Review*, and between the lines of Jarrell's next letters were Tate's requests for some of Jarrell's recent poems. In a letter dated May 10, 1945, the old and inevitable tension between editor and poet surfaced in Jarrell's remark, "I don't want you and *Poetry* cutting me up into little repugnant chunks." On Tate's criticism of his newly written poem "The Snow Leopard," Jarrell belligerently asked, "What do you mean, where did I get the caravan? It grew in me."[26] This exchange almost certainly arose from the fact that in Tate's "Ode to Our Young Proconsuls of the Air," there is also a Tibetan caravan. Tate's poem is an encomium to the "Young men, Americans . . . / With zeal proconsular"—that is, to the very pilots Jarrell wrote about from near firsthand. Despite similarities of theme and imagery, Jarrell would not admit dependency, if indeed he was aware of any.

Apologizing for not being able to send "Gunner" or "A Pilot from the Carrier," he offered for the *Review* "a long poem, almost 150 lines, named 'The Märchen' . . . the best thing I've done in months and months and months." Tate had obviously requested not only the air force poems but also something regional to fit the theme of the *Review*. Jarrell could only reply with a playful but ironic question, "Is 'She Dwelt among the Untrodden Ways' a Southern Subject?," and a bland disclaimer that "the only Southern subjects I ever thought of writing about are you, Red, and Mr. Ransom—your poems, I mean."[27]

This letter and one dated March 10, 1946, essentially ended Jarrell's personal correspondence with Allen Tate. Even as Jarrell reached out for old ties, his earlier defensiveness against any invitations to "join the club" resurged. Jarrell was ready to move to New York and take up the editorship in poetry

25. Pritchard, *Randall Jarrell*, 67; M. Jarrell, ed., *Randall Jarrell's Letters*, 119–23.
26. M. Jarrell, ed., *Randall Jarrell's Letters*, 125.
27. Ibid., 126.

for the *Nation*. Chafing under the least implication of dependency, he informed Tate that the New York literary cliques (which Tate had apparently warned him against) would "grieve and bother" him not at all. The letter closed with friendly offers of southern hospitality and "hoecakes on the hearth," should Tate visit New York.[28]

Despite such overtures, the relationship of Allen Tate and Randall Jarrell declined gradually from that time on. In his essay "Young Randall," Tate wistfully remarked that "for an inscrutable reason—I never understood Randall—he liked me very much for some years around 1940, but not much later on." Mary Jarrell calls the estrangement less than generous on Randall's part, "probably intentional," given Tate's emphasis on classicism and the tradition and Jarrell's leaning, in the fifties, toward Marxist socialism. Tate "didn't change enough" to suit the often impatient standards of Jarrell and his generation; nor did the "buddyism" of the Fugitives seem necessary to the now established poet and critic. The short paragraph that Jarrell accorded to Allen Tate in "Fifty Years of American Poetry" attributed general neglect of Tate's poems to their "lack of charm, of human appeal and human sympathy" and to their "tone of somewhat forbidding authority."[29] Tate and Jarrell apparently drifted apart because of the threat of that very "authority" which emanates both from the poems and from the presence of one who had become an irritating reminder of the expendable but never fully dispensable influence of the past.

With Robert Penn Warren, always more a colleague to Jarrell than a mentor, Jarrell remained casually friendly during the Texas and air force years. After the war he wrote a short apology: "I've meant to write and thank you for the invitation to make the records [readings of his poetry for the Library of Congress]. I've put it off so as to send my new book along with it but I'd better do it anyway." And in a most complimentary tone, Jarrell called Warren's newly published *Selected Poems* "the best book of poetry anybody's published in seven or eight years—I thought it decidedly better than [Eliot's] *Four Quartets*, for instance."[30] Both Jarrell and Warren had, in effect, loosened ties with the past and deliberately set out to forge new allegiances and new poetic styles.

Of the three poets—Jarrell, John Berryman, and Robert Lowell—Jarrell

---

28. Ibid., 157.

29. Tate, "Young Randall," 232; M. Jarrell, letter to author, January 23, 1980; Randall Jarrell, "Fifty Years of American Poetry," in *The Third Book of Criticism* (New York: Farrar, Straus & Giroux, 1969), 322.

30. R. Jarrell to Warren, 1945, courtesy of M. Jarrell.

was the least aware of or grateful for what the Fugitives contributed to his precocious entry into the world of letters. Jarrell was in every way a paradox. There was the acerbic critic and the unselfish promoter of Frost, Whitman, Lowell, and Moore. There was the sometimes boyish, sometimes witty and sophisticated letter writer who challenged his friends to follow the highest standards in their appreciation of art, especially literature, and the often impressed, therefore rather shallow consumer of and enthusiast about popular culture. And throughout there were the two voices of his poetry: distant and ironic on one hand, humanely sympathetic and empathetic on the other. These several Jarrells also emerge in his filial role to the Fugitives and, markedly, in theirs with him; for there is no mistaking the mixture of admiration and anxiety in their attitudes toward a "pupil" who seemed to have nothing—and no inclination—to learn from them.

6 / John Berryman, the *Southern Review*, and *Five Young American Poets*

To Randall Jarrell and the former Fugitives, John Berryman was an unlikely addition to the post-Fugitive network. His only personal connection with the South was his maternal great-grandfather, a Civil War general who distinguished himself during the hostilities but left the country thereafter to avoid prosecution for seditious Ku Klux Klan activities. Unlike Lowell, Berryman did not leave the North to attend a college or university where the Fugitives were a vital presence. Because of Allen Tate, first, and the *Southern Review*, second, John Berryman nonetheless became another poet who owed his early success in part to the Fugitives. Jarrell noticed Berryman, who later became a fairly good friend and valued colleague, only when *Five Young American Poets* (1940) served both as the vehicle for their arrival as published poets.

Once again it was Allen Tate, the most cosmopolitan of the Fugitives, who can be credited with producing a poet. Paul Mariani believes that Berryman spent many unproductive years trying to overcome the burden of the Fugitives' aesthetic.[1] Actually there were both bane and blessing in John Berryman's early association with the former Fugitives. Like Jarrell and Lowell,

1. Paul Mariani, *Dream Song: The Life of John Berryman* (New York: Morrow, 1990), 54.

however, Berryman not only learned from them to write poetry in a highly formal, disciplined mode but, more valuably, was able to publish his apprentice poetry on a national scale because of their friendship. Like Jarrell, Berryman began to find his own voice only after deliberately attempting to purge his style of the Fugitives' influence.

After he left the South, around 1926, to make his way among the northern literati, Allen Tate's many friends included Mark Van Doren and R. P. Blackmur, both of whom taught John Berryman at Columbia and played important roles in his early development. Cleanth Brooks once stated without qualification that Berryman formed his early poetic style from Tate alone. Berryman first became acquainted with Allen Tate through reading his poetry while an undergraduate student at Columbia. Berryman was so impressed that he burst into Mark Van Doren's office to declare, "Mr. Van Doren, you know Tate is one of the very best poets we have!"[2]

Berryman first met his idol during the summer of 1936 when Tate gave a series of lectures on modern poetry at Columbia. A personal friendship developed while Tate and Berryman took walks about the Columbia campus. Their conversations centered on the Fugitives and others closely related, including John Peale Bishop and George Marion O'Donnell, especially their poetry and aesthetic ideals. According to Mariani, Berryman was much impressed by "the Fugitives' brilliance and charm."[3] Tate gave Berryman what can only be called an indoctrination into the Fugitive and high modernist aesthetics at a very impressionable stage in the younger man's development.

Before ever meeting Tate, Berryman, who had published several poems in his college newspaper the *Columbia Review* (see Appendix), was so impressed with Tate's "Ode to the Confederate Dead" that, during the summer of 1936, he composed a similar poem, "Ritual at Arlington," for the *Southern Review*'s "long poem" contest. At the time he left for Cambridge, Berryman was calling the poem "a large smear," written at "an important personal stage," but although his poem impressed the judges, they awarded the prize to Randall Jarrell. After leaving Columbia, Tate wrote a friendly letter to Berryman complimenting his attentiveness to the lectures and explaining why he had not won the contest: "I put your poem ['Ritual at Arlington'] fifth on my list of eight; Mark [Van Doren] put it fifth on his list of twelve. [in left margin: Yours was five out of about 500 mss. . . .] If your poem had been cut down to proper length considering the form I should have placed it first. There are

2. Brooks, interview, November 15, 1991; Mariani, *Dream Song*, 52.
3. Mariani, *Dream Song*, 55–56.

very fine passages in it, the best I thought in the whole contest. But the sort of thesis-antithesis development of the theme seemed to me mechanical, not dramatic—though I felt a kind of affection for it since I used it in my Ode." Berryman replied without resentment: "Thanks very much for your letter and the criticism therein—Your use of 'form' still puzzles me a bit. I'm glad Jarrell won—he writes damn good poems."[4]

"Ritual at Arlington" was also the occasion of Berryman's first interaction with Robert Penn Warren, Cleanth Brooks, and the *Southern Review*. Warren's letter of October 7, 1936, provides another slant on why Berryman did not win the contest: "Although your poem did not receive THE SOUTHERN REVIEW prize, the judges were enormously interested in it; and so are we. We do not feel, however, that we can publish it as it stands. We think that certain sections resemble too closely even to the point of imitation, Tate's 'Ode to the Confederate Dead.' " Berryman no doubt had expected that because of its southern theme and similarity to Tate's "Ode," the poem might find favor in Baton Rouge; he had not reckoned on Tate's objection to a poem so similar to his own. Before closing, however, Warren said that he was "positive that in the near future we shall be able to arrange a large display for you in THE SOUTHERN REVIEW, if your present poem can be taken as a fair sample of your general performance." From Clare College, Cambridge, Berryman responded to Warren's letter of rejection with respectful deference: "Your criticism of 'Ritual at Arlington' is perfectly correct. Van Doren, Tate, and Rylands here say substantially the same things. I am now very glad that you did not print it, too many pleasant failures are probably floating about in ill-advised print." Enclosing his check for a two-year subscription, Berryman called the *Southern Review* "decidedly now the best literary medium in English" and added: "I've written since last summer a fair amount of verse, but have been waiting until I had a group I could respect, before sending you anything. Which looks to be never. On the chance, however, that my judgment is decaying, as friends have inferred, I'll select some poems when I have time and send them, confident in your expert opinion."[5]

4. Mariani, *Dream Song*, 58; Tate to Berryman, September 9, 1936, John Berryman Papers, University of Minnesota Libraries, St. Paul; Berryman to Tate, October 11, 1936, Tate Papers.

5. Portions of this account of Berryman's relationship with the Brooks and Warren *Southern Review* were first published as " 'Solely *The Southern Review*': A Significant Moment in the Poetic Apprenticeship of John Berryman," by Charlotte H. Beck, in *Recovering Berryman: Essays on a Poet*, ed. Richard J. Kelly and Alan K. Lathrop (Ann Arbor: University of Michigan Press, 1993), 113–24. See also Robert Penn Warren to Berryman, October 7, 1936, and Berryman to Warren, February 4, 1937, *Southern Review* Papers.

By August 1937, the editors seemed to be close to publishing a Berryman group. An excited Berryman wrote, on August 10, that he was sending "four recent poems, one an hour old." He directed that the last line in the tenth stanza in "Last Days of [later "Night and] the City" be changed to read, "The barriers were down, they fell afraid," and in the fifth stanza to change "deep" to "strict" (for "exacting").[6]

It was autumn, however, before Berryman finally received an unsigned letter in unmistakable Warren idiom: "We take a mighty long time to make up our mind some time, and this has been one of those times. We have finally decided on keeping the following poems: 'Note for a Historian,' 'Film,' 'Last Days of the City,' 'Frequently When the Night,' and 'Poem in May.' " He added, "We are planning to publish a group of your poems perhaps in the Summer issue."[7] The 1938 summer issue of the *Southern Review* did include "Night and the City," "Note for a Historian," "The Apparition," and "Toward Statement."

Although Berryman's debut was less than auspicious, he was still eager to attempt a second appearance in the *Review*. As they moved toward that issue, the relationship between John Berryman and the *Southern Review* climaxed. In a letter dated January 13, 1939, Robert Penn Warren listed the poems to be published and offered specific suggestions about "Meditation," the longest and most ambitious poem in the group: "The first five stanzas please us greatly, but the sixth stanza, which doesn't seem to advance the poem, reads almost too much like an echo from Yeats. The last line of the eighth stanza raises the same question for us. But the ninth, we believe, doesn't really bring the prom [*sic*] to focus. We do not have, of course, any specific suggestions to make for revision of the poem. That would, indeed, be a piece of presumption." Commenting on such editorial "presumption," Brooks later wrote: "We may have suggested a writer to send us something on a particular topic and then found that what he actually sent was not satisfactory. We certainly never rewrote anyone's piece. We sometimes suggested changes but in that case the author was always allowed the final say. Unless he accepted our suggestion, what he had written went to press." In the same letter of January 13, Warren added that "we are very anxious to see more of your poems so that we can fill out another and, we hope, a larger group." Like other, more famous *Southern Review* contributors, Berryman did act on such advice. On January 16, he wrote that he was "astonished and pleased to hear that you 'look

6. Berryman to Warren, August 10, 1937, *Southern Review* Papers.

7. [Warren] to Berryman, October 29, 1937, ibid.

forward to publishing a great deal more' verse by me; I thought that the *Southern Review* had given me up forever." On January 20 he sent several new poems, remarking: "Thank you for the comments on 'Meditation'; I have known for some time that it wanted revision. I will return it to you as soon as I am able to work on the poem again."[8]

Berryman's satisfaction with the final version of "Meditation" is evidenced by its subsequent appearance in *Five Young American Poets* and *New Poems*. As of May 1939, however, his relief at having survived the editorial process was mixed with irritation. Writing to the editors, he professed to be "glad you now like 'Meditation' " but surprised at rejection of the last fourteen poems, remarking testily: "I am told and know that my verse is improving, and I select with some care what I send you. I don't know what to think. If you don't like 'Winter Landscape' or 'The Disciple', I think I had better retire and try archery." Brooks's reply, on October 30, is a scarcely speedy attempt at mollification:

We have finally decided on the group with the following five poems in it, "Film," "II Song from *Cleopatra*," "Meditation," "Conversation," and "Desire of Men and Women." I think it is a fine group, and I hope that you will be pleased with it even though we are not including "Winter Landscape," and "The Disciple" [which Berryman had revised]. And please don't take up archery. Maybe we are making a mistake in ranking the poems and choosing as we do, but it is a very honest one if mistaken, and we are very happy and very much satisfied with the group which we have chosen.

Berryman shot back on November 27, "I hope the group you and Mr. Warren have selected is better than I think it is; however, since I once committed the poems and you are kind enough to want to print them, I daresay I should hold my tongue."[9]

These decisions and indecisions portended a waning relationship between John Berryman and the *Southern Review*. Although he continued to submit poems, there was never to be a third, "larger" Berryman group in that journal. On December 15, 1939, he had good reason to ask, "When do you plan to use the group of poems: I may publish a selection with New Directions

8. Warren to Berryman, January 13, 1939, and Berryman to Warren, January 20, 1939, ibid.; Cleanth Brooks, letter to author, April 12, 1986.

9. Berryman to Warren, May 1939, Brooks to Berryman, October 30, 1939, and Berryman to Brooks, November 27, 1939, all in *Southern Review* Papers.

next year, and I would want these to appear before that." Still desirous, however, of maintaining his relationship with the *Southern Review*, Berryman submitted one final poem, "A Point of Age," sometime in 1940. Not long thereafter, in the spring of 1942, the *Southern Review* would suspend operations, allegedly because of wartime austerity. John Berryman's somewhat chaotic relationship with the editors of the *Southern Review* was initially beneficial, if ultimately frustrating. As he later recalled, publication in the *Southern Review* was an "In and Out" affair, a brief but significant moment in the crucial period of his poetic apprenticeship.[10]

Tate came into Berryman's life again after his return from England in June 1938. During the summer of 1938, the Tates had rented a summer house at Falls Church, Connecticut, near the Van Dorens, whom Berryman, ill and uncomfortable in his mother's New York City apartment, was visiting at his own "invitation." By August, having struggled most of the summer to find an academic job, Berryman was overjoyed to receive a postcard from Tate, dated August 18, 1938: "Won't you come up Saturday and stay with Caroline for a week while I am away? When I get back (around 31st) we go to see Phelps Putnam, and would like to take you." Phelps Putnam was a Yale poet who had known Tate from his New York days, a sometime visitor when the Tates moved back to the South.[11] During the same visit, Berryman was able to renew his acquaintance with the *New Directions* editor James Laughlin, whom he had met in England when Laughlin sought out Berryman and got three poems for a *New Directions* annual. By reestablishing his relationship with Tate, Berryman had greatly improved his chances of gaining the attention of influential New York editors and publishers and, eventually, of getting a collection of his poems accepted for publication.

Berryman was, in fact, attempting to publish a book of his poems when the *5YAP* project began. Laughlin's concept of an anthology featuring five poets who had not yet gotten out their own books dovetailed conveniently with the demise of a much more ambitious notion on the part of Allen Tate.

10. Berryman to the *Southern Review*, December 15, 1939, ibid. In his biography of Cleanth Brooks, Mark Winchell presents a detailed account of how the *Southern Review*'s "fortunes . . . rose and fell with those of the [Huey] Long machine." According to Winchell, the *Review* fell victim to LSU's administrative "bean counters," who were at first bent on undoing what they considered the financial excesses of the Long administration and afterward used the war as an excuse to act on long-felt hostility toward the *Review* among members of both the faculty and the administration (*Cleanth Brooks and the Rise of Modern Criticism*, 190–91).

11. Postcard from Allen Tate to Berryman, August 18, 1938, Berryman Papers; Wood, ed., *Southern Mandarins*, 82–83.

After the Falls Church visit, Berryman did not write Tate again until March 5, 1939, asking him to contribute to an ill-fated Yeats collection. Tate answered that he liked the idea and would help if he could; he also apprised Berryman of his own project: "At present I am trying to get the University of North Carolina Press to get out a series of modern poets, the younger unpublished poets at first, six books a year, three in the fall, three in the spring; in uniform binding and type. The contributors to the series would be severely limited to good people, and I think we should attract the best mss. If the thing goes through, you and Marion [O'Donnell] will be among the first six." Berryman respectfully replied that he had "for some time, in fact . . . been putting together forty of my poems in a book, which probably I shall submit to the Series when you're ready for it. Meanwhile I should be very grateful indeed if you'd be willing to read it and tell me what you think; you helped me a great deal last summer." On August 15, 1939, however, Tate had to convey discouraging news: "I am sorry to tell you that the poetry series will not be published—at least by the N.C. Press. Couch, the head, wouldn't consent to pay royalties; so I withdrew. —I will now see what can be done elsewhere."[12] "Elsewhere" turned out to be *Five Young American Poets*. By December 20, Laughlin had apparently been convinced to include Berryman, Jarrell, and another of Tate's protégés, George Marion O'Donnell.

As he had with Jarrell, Tate obviously had to convince Berryman that publishing in a five-part anthology was better than nothing at all. He therefore wrote to Berryman: "I am glad you see Laughlin's anthology more favorably. But I hope you will do your own Introduction." Playing the martyr, also like Jarrell, Berryman replied in January 1940: "I have decided that my own feelings are not of much importance and I am going into the anthology, depending on you to persuade L. out of the damned Introductions and portraits— the facsimiles are silly and pretentious but less important."[13]

A former Vanderbilt student, W. R. Moses, along with O'Donnell, Jarrell, Berryman, and Mary Bernard, completed a group that, except for Bernard, seem to have been selected by Allen Tate to show off the young poets of the Fugitive legacy. Jarrell apparently participated in the selection of the female member of the quintet. In February 1940, he wrote to Laughlin that he was "right . . . about getting a girl for the anthology" but had to admit that he didn't "know any lady" they might include. There simply were no female

12. Berryman to Tate, March 5, 1939, Tate to Berryman, March 23, August 15, 1939, all in Berryman Papers; Berryman to Tate, n.d., Tate Papers.

13. Berryman to Tate, January 1940, Tate Papers.

poets in the "network," at least none whom Tate, Warren, or Ransom were willing to place on a level with the men. Laughlin's first choice was an excellent one, Elizabeth Bishop, whose poems he had published in 1936 when he edited a magazine called *New Democracy*; but when he invited her to become one of the *Five Young American Poets*, she (rightly) suspected that she was to serve as token woman and "didn't like being used for 'Sex-Appeal.' " Her replacement, Bernard, gained nothing but scornful remarks from the rest of the contributors. Jarrell ungraciously remarked to Tate, "I don't think anything in the world would help Mrs. Bernard sufficiently," but he was not much kinder to the other male poets. Apparently agreeing with Tate, Jarrell called Moses "a complete Bore"; and of the other two he had the following judgments: "I *don't* think all of him's [O'Donnell] that bad. He has real talents; for instance, he has a better feel for phrase, often, than Berryman . . . Berryman has a pretty inferior feel for language for one thing; and to talk about your old favorite, the poetic subject, he's obviously not really found his."[14]

Despite Jarrell's and Berryman's negative attitudes, the volume accomplished its goal of introducing the young poets to a much wider audience than could be reached through the literary magazines. With the exception of Bernard, all five poets had matriculated in the Fugitives' "schools" of poetry: Moses, Jarrell, and O'Donnell had not only graduated from Vanderbilt but had enjoyed the advantage of publishing in the *Southern Review*. The anthology was reasonably successful, helped along by reviews in a variety of journals. Ransom's "Constellation of Five Young Poets" appeared in the *Kenyon Review*'s spring 1941 issue. Calling *5YAP* one of "the most interesting and important book[s] of poetry in some years," he nonetheless thought that "this is perhaps enough publication for them at the moment" because "their futures will eclipse their presents." He called Jarrell "the most brilliant of the five," having "an angel's velocity and range with language" but "not a realizer of rhythms." To Ransom, the "most technically balanced and artistically satisfactory of these poets was [*sic*] Berryman and O'Donnell. . . . Berryman is more reliable, and also seems to have the bigger and wholesomer range of interest."[15]

The cover of *Five Young American Poets* bears the following commentary, presumably by Laughlin: "It is interesting, and revealing, to note that the work of these poets, although they are in no sense members of a group or school, having been chosen in open competition, shows a marked tendency

14. M. Jarrell, ed., *Randall Jarrell's Letters*, 27, 30; Kalstone, *Becoming a Poet*, 42, 77.
15. John Crowe Ransom, "Constellation of Five Poets," *Kenyon Review* 3 (1941): 377, 380.

toward a return to disciplined forms and structure."[16] Whatever the editor may have meant by "open competition," Tate had no apparent difficulty convincing Laughlin that this particular group of five poets, representing the formal, academic poets of their time, should define American poetry in the early 1940s. As for posterity's unsentimental appraisal, Laughlin and Tate batted an unimpressive .400. Only Randall Jarrell and John Berryman succeeded in rising above the average and gaining lasting reputations.

Jarrell's "Note on Poetry" turned out better than he apparently thought, although he began by proclaiming petulantly, "I don't want to write a preface," and by defying the reader's biographical interest with "I look like a bear and live in a cave; but you should worry." Near the completion of his project, an understandably weary Laughlin wrote to Tate: "Yes, I'm keen on Jarrell's preface. I don't want to make too distant promises but I should think we could do a book for him alone in time, or, at least work him into the Poet of the Month Series. . . . Now all is ready except that unspeakable Berryman. Surely he is one of the world's most difficult and trying creatures."[17]

Believing themselves destined for much better things, Jarrell and Berryman did not allow the publication of the anthology to slacken their efforts to publish their own separate books of poetry. Both divided their accumulations of poems between *5YAP* and the manuscripts they were circulating among publishers, fearing all the while that they were thereby weakening their debut volumes. Berryman's *Poems* appeared in 1942, published by New Directions. Jarrell's *Blood for a Stranger* did not find a publisher until 1945. In both cases, Allen Tate played a valuable and unappreciated role as intermediary between the two "young American poets" and the publishers who might otherwise have given them little or no notice. Tate was, however, given due credit for the part he played in the education of the third and ultimately the most renowned poet of the three: Robert Lowell.

16. James Laughlin, ed., *Five Young American Poets* (New York: New Directions, 1940), cover.

17. Jarrell, "Poetry in War and Peace," 47; Laughlin to Tate, August 21, 1941, Tate Papers.

7 / Robert Lowell: An Underlying Sense of Form

In his landmark review of Lowell's *Lord Weary's Castle*, Randall Jarrell observed that in both form and content, the poems normally move from "constriction and frustration" toward "liberation"; and in these words he foretold the shape of Lowell's entire career. In similar terms, Lowell's critics have summed up his debt to the Fugitives as a movement from subservient imitation to a redemptive escape that showed the way to freedom for an entire generation of American poets. Charles Altieri describes Lowell's early poetry as the epitome of those "basic values . . . inspired by the New Criticism in the fifties," while his *Life Studies* "interprets his break with his earlier commitment to both the poets and the theology" of the New Criticism. In *Everything to Be Endured . . .*, R. K. Meiners likewise positions Lowell as a transitional figure from the Fugitive brand of modernism, rhetorical and stoical, to a new poetics of the subjective and personal. Preferring Lowell's so-called confessional mode, most critics bestow privilege upon the poetry he produced from *Life Studies* onward. If Lowell's entire opus is carefully evaluated, however, it becomes apparent that, as Albert Gelpi has argued, Lowell's early poetry is central to any assessment of his importance among twentieth-century poets and "constitutes his principal claim

to a lasting poetic achievement."[1] Written during the years when the former
Fugitives had a crucial impact on the form and content of his work, these
poems took Lowell to a position of prominence and ensured their acceptance
in the literary marketplace. Lowell's progress toward mature expression, always accompanied by visible effort, always consciously dependent on the approval of others, makes his career an easily charted demonstration of how the
Fugitive legacy could operate in the career of a particularly talented but mal-
leable pupil.

The Fugitives' significance in Lowell's early career cannot easily be ignored, even by critics distrustful of the role played by influence. Meiners, for
example, proposed to "those critics who have roamed widely looking for ana-
logues to Lowell's explosive language that they read carefully such of Tate's
poems as 'The Wolves,' 'The Trout Map,' 'Sonnets at Christmas' . . . and the
other better-known poems." Although Tate was clearly Lowell's most important Fugitive connection, other former Fugitives were important in Lowell's
development. Without the intervention of Merrill Moore, Lowell might
never have come under the Fugitives' tutelage and patronage, for it was he
who convinced the Lowell family that their son should study with the Fugitives. At Kenyon College, Ransom was to become Lowell's surrogate father
and teacher, an encouraging and stabilizing influence operating concurrently
with Tate. Lowell's first really disciplined poems were written at Kenyon, to
appear in *Hika*, the campus literary magazine, and, constituting his professional publishing debut, in the first issue of the *Kenyon Review*. Thereafter,
when Lowell began graduate study at LSU, he came, as he said, under the
"Brooks and Warren" and "New Critical" influence, doing little composing
but devouring, along with the New Critical method of Brooks and Warren,
certain literary texts that would loom large in his mature poetry.[2] By 1942,
once again under Tate's close scrutiny, Lowell was ready to produce a substantial body of poetry that brought together all that he had by then assimilated from his Fugitive mentors. Tate's active patronage would extend

1. Jarrell, "From the Kingdom of Necessity," in *Poetry and the Age*, 189; Charles Altieri, *Enlarging the Temple: New Directions in American Poetry in the Sixties* (Lewisburg, Pa.: Bucknell University Press, 1979), 53; R. K. Meiners, *Everything to Be Endured: An Essay on Robert Lowell and
Modern Poetry* (Columbia: University of Missouri Press, 1970), 3–4; Albert Gelpi, "The Reign
of the Kingfisher: Robert Lowell's Prophetic Poetry," in *Robert Lowell: Essays on the Poetry*, ed.
Stephen Gould Axelrod and Helen Dees (New York: Cambridge University Press, 1986), 51.

2. Meiners, *Everything to Be Endured*, 22; Ian Hamilton, *Robert Lowell: A Biography* (New
York: Random House–Viking, 1982), 75.

through 1947 and facilitate the publication of Lowell's poems in the *Partisan* and *Sewanee* reviews, as well as of his slender debut volume, *Land of Unlikeness*. *Lord Weary's Castle*, which built on the first volume, followed soon afterward and won Lowell the Pulitzer Prize, in no small way because of the critical success of the former collection. Up until 1947, by which time his poetry had gained him a secure position in the world of letters, Lowell's poetics were generated and sponsored by the Fugitives.

If the Fugitive influence began to wane thereafter, the vacuum was filled in great part by Lowell's friendships with other members of the post-Fugitive generation: Randall Jarrell, Peter Taylor, and John Berryman. Lowell himself steadily confirmed that although his so-called confessional mode, which brought him his greatest prominence, seems the antithesis of the Fugitive aesthetic, he never abandoned the sense of poetic form that was his true legacy from the Fugitives.

The Fugitives' impact was strengthened by Lowell's freely admitted need not only for inspiration but for the basic elements—forms, images, plots, syntax—for his poems. Writing on Lowell's "first twenty years," Hugh Staples states that "his rejection of one tradition has often been accompanied by adherence to another. Dissatisfied with the Protestantism of his ancestors, he was not content to take up a merely agnostic position—instead he sought for spiritual values in the dogma of the Catholic Church. Finding Harvard, to which his family heritage had consigned him, something less than a nest of singing birds, he removed to Kenyon, where a new creative tradition was being developed by John Crowe Ransom." And writing later, Stephen Matterson, in *Berryman and Lowell: The Art of Losing* (1988), attributes Lowell's shifting allegiances to his (and Berryman's) search "for acceptable poetic fathers" to compensate for the "inadequacies of his real father." In *The Years of Our Friendship*, William Doreski has added that the unusually strong bond between Lowell and Tate constituted a "mock child-parent relationship," which "strained against their growing equality in literary affairs" as Lowell progressed to an equal or greater status as poet.[3] Relatively speaking, however, Lowell seemed the least of all his generation to be affected by the anxiety of influence. The same dynamics were present in nearly all relationships between members of the Fugitive legacy, but in Lowell the imprints are more easily traced because he both recognized and commented on them freely throughout his career and because he became the most prominent poet of his

3. Staples, *Robert Lowell*, 18–19; Matterson, *Berryman and Lowell*, 9; Doreski, *Years of Our Friendship*, 6.

generation. Lowell was at first a true tabula rasa for the Fugitive influence. He therefore developed more slowly, achieved more, and lived longer than his cohort of middle-generation poets.

In the beginning Lowell wrote energetically and voluminously but produced little that can even be called apprentice poetry. Against those chaotic tendencies was interposed Lowell's desire for formal discipline in his poems. He usually referred to his early free verse efforts as "slack," and even before the Fugitives became his mentors, he made visible efforts to impose structure upon himself. Lowell's attempts to forge the disparate elements of his imagination into poetry began with a collection of voluminous diaries and notebooks. In the 1935 notebooks, in the midst of a jumble of fragmentary writings, he exhibited a typically American penchant for self-improvement in the manner of Benjamin Franklin:

Practice in rhythm
             concentration
             description
             the accurate word
Don't write on the spur of the moment only for the sake of writing. If you do revise, revise. Most of these are just drafts, not poems. Control, order are essential before you have ease.

. . . .

Either: a) have something you've got to say, or
             b) have an indomitable rhythm [illegible]
And for God's sake don't be satisfied with what you've done until you've got a sense of *unity* in your poem—a progression from one thought or feeling to another.[4]

Most of Lowell's very early poems are devotional in subject matter and, though marred by misspellings, severely formal.

The tension between personal and psychic disorder and pronounced formality in his art was to drive Lowell throughout his early career, when the Fugitives were so crucial. His famous row with his father over his engagement to the socialite Ann Dick led the Lowell family to seek psychiatric treatment for their son and to encourage his ambition to become a poet. Providence intervened when the Lowell family chose to send Robert to Dr. Merrill Moore, formerly a member of the Fugitive group, who was both a psychiatrist and a practicing poet.

4. Robert Lowell Papers, bMS AM 1905 (4), by permission of the Houghton Library, Harvard University, Cambridge, Mass.

Merrill Moore graduated from Vanderbilt in 1924 and from medical school at Vanderbilt in 1928. After interning at St. Thomas Hospital in Nashville, he returned north in 1929 and worked at various Boston hospitals. By 1935 he was in private practice and had gotten his second wind as a poet. Moore published two collections of poetry during the thirties: *Six Sides to a Man* in 1935 and *M: A Thousand Sonnets* in 1938.[5] The latter was favorably reviewed in the *Kenyon Review* by John Crowe Ransom. Fortunately for Robert Lowell, Moore kept in touch with the other former Fugitives.

Moore's special professional interest was in alcohol and drug addiction among artists, an area to which he could obviously bring his own understanding of the artistic mind-set. When Lowell began to see Moore in 1937, their conversations might well have focused on the benefits to be gained by formality in the composition of poetry. But beyond any therapeutic advantages that Lowell might gain from writing poetry, Moore no doubt would have stressed the Fugitives' "group approach" to composition. Most important, if Lowell were to achieve a career as a poet, he would have to meet and work with "real" poets. The ideal route for a young man in need of formal and creative education would lie with his former friends down south. The Lowells agreed that Robert should transfer from Harvard to Vanderbilt, where John Crowe Ransom could take over the supervision of his education.

During his train trip south in the spring of 1937, Lowell first "met" his mentors by reading their poetry. He wrote to his fiancée, Ann Dick, that "reading over the 'Fugitive' poets on the train I decided Allen Tate is very topnotch, a painstaking tecnician [*sic*] and an ardent advocate of Ezra Pound."[6] Before matriculating at Vanderbilt, Lowell decided to pay a visit to Tate at his home, Benfolly, near Clarksville, Tennessee.

The engaging story of Lowell's visits with Allen Tate during the spring and summer of 1937 has been narrated, in versions that do not precisely agree, not only by Lowell's biographers but also by Lowell himself and by the others—Tate, Caroline Gordon, Ford Madox Ford—who were involved. In the final analysis, however, it matters less whether young Robert drove his car into the Tates' "agrarian mailbox" or urinated on it than that he was actually invited in and allowed to form a bond with Tate and his circle. Lowell recalled that once he was inside the Tate house, his status improved quickly

5. Henry W. Wells, *Poet and Psychiatrist: Merrill Moore, M.D.* (New York: Twayne, 1955), 113–14.
6. Hamilton, *Robert Lowell*, 43.

and dramatically from that of "a torn cat," who "was taken in when [he] needed help," to that of a potentially valuable colleague. Tate, whose teaching career began later, may have subconsciously hungered for a disciple; certainly he was always amenable to aristocratic connections. At any rate, Lowell's proud family name, coupled with his poetic ambitions, made him a desirable addition to the group. Tate immediately associated him with the New England Brahmin poets Oliver Wendell Holmes and Lowell's "renowned Uncle" James Russell Lowell, whom Lowell at once began to see as "an asset."[7] Lowell's informal education from Tate was to proceed along lines that Eliot and Pound had by then made orthodox: first, one acquired knowledge of the poetic tradition and then one should spend time practicing the craft of poetry.

So gratified was Lowell by the results of his impromptu visit in April that he decided to return to Benfolly in late May, after briefly attending classes at Vanderbilt, with the expressed intention of spending the summer. Faced with a household full of guests, including Ford Madox Ford, his mistress Janice Balliol, and her secretary, Caroline Gordon archly remarked to Lowell: "I'm sorry. There's no place to put you unless we put up a tent on the lawn." With a New Englander's ignorance of southern irony, Lowell took their "suggestion" and purchased "an olive Sears-Roebuck-Nashville umbrella tent," in which he lived and wrote for three months. There, according to Lowell, he "turned out grimly unromantic poems—organized, hard and classical as a cabinet" but "very flimsy."[8]

Undoubtedly the best of the poems Lowell crafted at Benfolly were "An Afternoon in an Umbrella Tent at Benfolly" and "A Month of Meals with Ford Madox Ford." The first, Lowell's self-effacement to the contrary, is neither grim nor "hard and classical"; except for its blank-verse packaging, it starts out as an early example of Lowell's humorously self-deprecatory idiom:

> A shaggy orange dog, large as a sheep,
> With spongy calloused pads and ponderous
> Unshaven claws, pawed on my canvas walls
> Blowsy and sagging translucent green and seamed;
> Breaking to bits a drowsy afternoon
> Of muggy fitful sleep . . .

7. Robert Lowell, "Visiting the Tates," in *Robert Lowell: Collected Prose*, ed. Robert Giroux (New York: Farrar, Straus & Giroux, 1987), 58, 60, 59; Wood, ed., *Southern Mandarins*, 209.

8. Wood, ed., *Southern Mandarins*, 210; Lowell, "Visiting the Tates," 557–59.

The Ford poem is even more amusing, its harsh caricature fulfilling Ford's prophecy "that young man will write something terrible about me some day":

> While words drooled out to me as benison,
> Harsh as the largest rotten pear on stone
> His huge inflated hand dropped on a spoon.
> Ruddy with gout and boneless as his jowl
> A plump left foot, wrapped in a turkish towel
> Slept underneath his chair, limply a prey
> To puppies tumbling avidly for play;[9]

Lowell left Benfolly more deeply committed to poetry than ever, and, although he had as yet produced no poetry fit for publication, his notebooks were growing. Most important, he had in Tate a valuable role model and counselor, who emphasized the basic elements of form and craftsmanship badly needed by a young mind, vibrant with inspiration but still in much need of focus and discipline.

Lowell arrived at Vanderbilt in the spring of 1937 to study with Ransom, who was in his last year of teaching at that institution. In May, Ransom was hired away by Kenyon College despite the efforts of loyal students Randall Jarrell and Peter Taylor and the public campaign of Allen Tate, whose open letter in the local paper obliquely referred to "the Lowell family of Boston and Harvard University" who "has just sent one of its sons to Nashville to study with Mr. Ransom." As Tate loftily predicted, Lowell did, along with Taylor and Jarrell, accompany Ransom to Kenyon. In fact, Ransom later wrote to Cleanth Brooks that Lowell "motored here with me to look the new place over, and accompanied me when I changed and lived in my home his first year."[10]

At Kenyon, Ransom was a stellar attraction for students who had literary ambitions. Peter Taylor and Robert Lowell soon discovered, like Ransom's students at Vanderbilt and elsewhere, that he did much of his teaching by example and outside the classroom. In his first essay on Ransom, Lowell tried to account for Ransom's undeniable mystique at Kenyon: "It was not the

9. Robert Lowell, 1935 notebook, bMS AM 1905 (4), by permission of the Houghton Library, Harvard University.

10. Ransom to Brooks, [1940], in *The Literary Correspondence of Allen Tate and Donald Davidson*, ed. John T. Fain and Thomas Daniel Young (Athens: University of Georgia Press, 1974), Appendix C; Ransom to Brooks, January 1, 1940, *Southern Review* Papers.

classes but the conversations that mattered. We used to endlessly memorize and repeat and mimic Ransom sentences. We learned something from that. Somehow one left him with something inside us moving toward articulation, logic, directness, and complexity." In 1974, Lowell remembered Ransom's classes as "homemade, methodical, and humdrum. For five years, he grimly taught *The Faerie Queen*; though he found Spenser's allegory without intellectual meat, it amused him like a crossword puzzle or a blueprint for his garden. . . . Sometimes a class would crackle." Lowell admitted, however, that although some of Ransom's most stimulating lectures were concerned with aesthetic theory, he was not yet intellectually mature enough to understand them: "I could not decode John's . . . metaphysical terms, ontology, catharsis, etc., with their homely Greek derivations and abstract, accurate English meaning so unlike language."[11]

By transferring to Kenyon, Lowell could not only study with Ransom but also become a part of the Fugitive network. It can be argued that the experiences of the next two academic years were as important to Lowell's career as his relationship with Tate. At Kenyon, Lowell could concentrate on academics, write for a relatively prestigious college literary magazine, and interact closely with his teachers, often as guests in their homes. For the first time, he excelled in his schoolwork and gained a measure of personal discipline, though he was still rough around the edges. Ransom wrote to Tate in October that Lowell was "sawing wood and getting out to all his college engagements in businesslike if surly manner; taking Latin and Greek and philosophy and, of course, English; wants to be really educated; and personally is about as gentle and considerate a boy as I've ever dealt with."[12]

While at Kenyon, Lowell continued to work on his poetry. In 1938, Lowell entered the Kathryn Irene Glascock Intercollegiate Poetry Contest sponsored by Mount Holyoke College and judged by a panel of experts that included the poet and critic Louise Bogan. The poems Lowell submitted included "Epitaph," "The Dandelion Girls," "The Cities' Summer Death," "Aunt Hecuba," "A Suicidal Fantasy"—based on "The Slough of Despond" in *Pilgrim's Progress*—and "The Lady." Although Lowell neither won the contest nor received honorable mention, several of the poems were later revised and published, two—"The Dandelion Girls" and "The Cities' Summer Death"—in the first issue of the *Kenyon Review*.[13]

11. Robert Lowell, "Mr. Ransom's Conversation," in *Robert Lowell*, ed. Giroux, 18; Lowell, "John Crowe Ransom: 1888–1924," ibid., 23, 20.

12. Young and Core, eds., *Selected Letters of Ransom*, 226.

13. J. Barton Rollins, "Robert Lowell's Apprenticeship and Early Poems," *American Literature* 52 (1980): 72–78.

Lowell's first two poems in the *Kenyon Review* bear witness to his desire at that time to follow the Fugitives' examples. "The Cities' Summer Death" is composed in four loosely rhyming quatrains reminiscent of Eliot's "Preludes" and Tate's "Mr. Pope." The subject is, however, Lowell's staple, the death of a family member, his grandfather:

> Cancer ossifies his features,
> The starved skeleton shows its teeth,
> Flamingo crackling embroiders
> Italian bones with shameless froth.

Clearly Lowell was trying hard to exemplify the neoclassical, modernist mode by replacing his usually violent imagery with something resembling Ransom's "elegant and unpainted" poetic idiom. There are also signs of Tate's rather stilted latinate diction ("ossified") and Ransom's ironic sense of the macabre (cf. "Captain Carpenter" or "Chills and Fever"). The obligatory classical allusion crowns the final stanza:

> But the honking untainted swans
> Float over the deathly stream
> And the aghast oarsmen of Charon's
> Ferry raise their skeleton rhythm.[14]

It is a promising poem for an undergraduate, and, unlike most of Lowell's early efforts, it avoids the baroque, often brutal religious imagery, while it successfully follows Ransom's example by tempering the quatrain's strict parameters with variations in metrics and rhyme.

Less characteristic of Lowell, but more like Ransom, was the second poem, "The Dandelion Girls." In addition to its gentle bows to various Elizabethan lyrics, "Dandelion Girls" boasts a title reminiscent of Ransom's "Blue Girls," while making Ransomian use (as in "Piazza Piece," "Antique Harvesters") of feminine tropes to personify the lowly dandelion. J. Barton Rollins's assertion that this poem was the basis for "The Drunken Fisherman," as it later appeared in *Lord Weary's Castle*, clashes with Lowell's statement that Ransom would have also published "The Drunken Fisherman" in the *Kenyon Review* had Lowell submitted it. Ransom would have scarcely accepted two versions of the same poem unless they bore little resemblance to each other, as is the case. Unlike the raucous and bawdy "Drunken Fisher-

---

14. Robert Lowell, "Two Poems," *Kenyon Review* 1 (1939): 32; Lowell, "John Crowe Ransom," 27.

man," "Dandelion Girls" is both genteel and pastoral. Like its companion, it exhibits characteristics which Lowell praised in Ransom's own poems: "structural clarity, the rightness of tone and rhythm, the brisk and effective ingenuity, the rhetorical fireworks of exposition, description, and dialogue . . . the sticking to concrete human subjects—the hardest." As much as he admired these qualities, however, they were uncharacteristic for Lowell at this stage of his development. The other poems which Lowell submitted to the *Kenyon Review* during his student days were rejected because they were, in Ransom's opinion, "forbidding and clotted."[15] It was to be five years before another Lowell poem, "Satan's Confession," would appear in the *Kenyon Review*.

The friendships that Lowell made at Kenyon proved to be of even greater value to his literary career than the poetry that he wrote and published there. Lowell formed a lifelong bond with Peter Taylor, who was his roommate first in Ransom's home and later at Douglass House and who accompanied him to graduate school at LSU. The most valuable friendship he formed was with Randall Jarrell, who also lived for a time with Ransom and later served as dormitory supervisor at Douglass House. Jarrell, already a published poet and critic, was to Lowell a source of inspiration and, because of Jarrell's broad knowledge of contemporary writers, a supplement to the classical subjects in Lowell's formal course of study. Observing Jarrell's uncommunicative conversations with Ransom, Lowell was impressed with their opposite but complementary mind-sets: "My friend Jarrell was romantic in another style than Tate or Ransom. He was educated in the preoccupations of the thirties, Marx, Auden, Empson, Kafka, plane design, anthropology since Fraser, and news of the day. He knew everything except Ransom's closed, provincial world of Greek, Latin, Aristotle, and Oxford." Lowell was attracted to Jarrell's "otherness" as much as to his erudition. In his memorial essay to Jarrell, Lowell dwells on characteristics that diametrically oppose aspects of his own nature: "His mind, unearthly in its quickness, was a little boyish, disembodied, and brittle. His body was a little ghostly in its immunity to soil, entanglements, and rebellion." Lowell also learned to live with Jarrell the critic: the acute but tactless evaluator pronouncing merciless judgment on teachers and classmates who "liked the wrong writer, the wrong poem by the right writer, or the wrong lines in the right poem!" as well as the tireless promoter who took "as much joy in rescuing the reputation of a sleeping good writer as in chlo-

---

15. Rollins, "Robert Lowell's Apprenticeship," 73; Lowell, "Interview with Frederick Seidel," in *Robert Lowell*, ed. Giroux, 239; Lowell, "Mr. Ransom's Conversation," 19.

roforming a mediocre one."[16] In Jarrell, Lowell gained a loyal friend and, more important, a competent and influential, though undeniably partisan, critic for his poetry. After Kenyon, in personal correspondence and in published reviews, Jarrell advised and encouraged Lowell, and Lowell remained unwaveringly receptive and grateful.

By the time he graduated from Kenyon, Lowell had in Ransom and his Fugitive colleagues a cohort of staunch supporters. Ransom joined Moore in interceding with Lowell's family on his behalf, and, having failed to persuade President Chalmers to hire Lowell to teach at Kenyon, Ransom was instrumental in securing for Lowell a fellowship at LSU. Ransom's letter to Cleanth Brooks, dated January 15, 1940, advertised Robert Lowell as "the last of the Lowell line bearing the name, due to give a good account of himself before he is done. He is a bit slow and thorough, but has enormous critical sense." Knowing that the *Southern Review* was in need of a secretary, Ransom added that Jean Stafford, whom Lowell had recently married, was "not only a finished typist, but she is a writer . . . ideal for a Review secretary." When summer came and the Lowells had not yet secured positions for the coming year, Ransom wrote to Charles Pipkin, then dean of the Graduate School, that Lowell had been virtually disinherited by his family and that he was "a very superlative article" who deserved a fellowship. The Fugitive network functioned as usual, and both Robert and Jean received appointments for the academic year 1940–41.[17]

From the perspective of the Baton Rouge community, neither Lowell nor Stafford, already a published novelist, cut impressive figures upon their arrival. No one knew that Stafford was not only "a writer" but a soon-to-be-famous one. Mainly interested, on behalf of the *Southern Review*, in Stafford's secretarial skills, Brooks had sent the following telegram to Ransom: "PLEASE ADVISE BY WESTERN UNION IF MRS. LOWELL KNOWS SHORTHAND." The editors were unaware until much later that Stafford did her own writing after hours on the typewriter that belonged to the *Review*. Brooks remembered Lowell as a fairly quiet student who "wandered around" and seemed more interested in his religion than in poetry.[18]

16. Lowell, "John Crowe Ransom," 24; Lowell, "Randall Jarrell," in *Randall Jarrell*, ed. Lowell, Taylor, and Warren, 91, 87.

17. Hamilton, *Robert Lowell*, 65; Charlotte Margolis Goodman, *Jean Stafford: The Savage Heart* (Austin: University of Texas Press, 1990), 114; Ransom to Brooks, January 15, 1940, *Southern Review* Papers; Cutrer, *Parnassus on the Mississippi*, 197.

18. Telegram, Brooks to Ransom, n.d., *Southern Review* Papers; Brooks, interview, November 15, 1991.

After a year at LSU, Lowell had produced very little new poetry and received no advanced degree. That year became, instead, a time for gathering
resources to be used in his later poetry. In Cleanth Brooks's classes, Lowell
extended his knowledge of Milton, especially of "Lycidas," so integral in
form and genre to his composition of "The Quaker Graveyard in Nantucket." In informal reading sessions with Robert Penn Warren, Lowell had
his first encounter with Dante's *Commedia* in the original Italian. Lowell
would meet Warren at the *Southern Review* offices, where, over lunch, they
persevered at the task for two hours at a stretch. Warren remembered that he
"had just learned enough Italian to read Dante," while Lowell "was then in
the process of learning it." Dante's *Commedia*, the "Inferno," and, particularly, the "Purgatorio" would crop up frequently in Lowell's poetry thereafter, explicitly in poems such as "The Exile's Return" ("*Voi ch'entrate*, and
your life is in your hands")," "The Holy Innocents," "Napoleon Crosses the
Berezina," and in lines like these from "The Soldier," in *Lord Weary's Castle:*

> In time of war you could not save your skin
> Where is that Ghibelline whom Dante met
> On Purgatory's doorstep, without kin
> To set chantries for his God-held debt?[19]

Lowell afterward remembered Warren as his "old master," but Warren
recalled Lowell more ambiguously, as intelligent and well-read, on one hand,
and as a "calculated naif" who was either "really mad" or "on his way" on
the other. When Lowell took Warren's seminar on Elizabethan literature,
Warren would hold forth on tyrants: Machiavelli, Cesare Borgia, and Huey
Long.[20] In the back of Warren's mind, of course, was the concatenation of
Mussolini and Huey Long, which would finally surface in *All the King's Men,*
while Lowell was forming his own mental connections between medieval and
modern instances of political oppression and heroic martyrdom, which would
dominate his first book of poems, *Land of Unlikeness.*

After LSU and an unproductive year working for a Catholic press in New
York, Lowell was more than prepared for what Doreski calls an "astonishing
outburst" of completed poetry as soon as he was once again with Allen Tate.
During the winter of 1942–43, Lowell and Stafford lived and worked side by

19. Cutrer, *Parnassus on the Mississippi*, 198; Robert Lowell, *Poems, 1938–1949* (London:
Faber, 1950), 45.
20. Robert Lowell, *Day by Day* (Baton Rouge: Louisiana State University Press, 1977), 2;
Warren interview with David Farrell, in Cutrer, *Parnassus on the Mississippi*, 199, 197.

side with the Tates at Monteagle (near Chattanooga, Tennessee). The most detailed account of this crucial period is to be found in Lowell's interview with Frederick Seidel in 1961 for the *Paris Review*: "Tate and I started to make an anthology. . . . He's a poet who writes in spurts, and he had about a third of a book. I was going to do a biography of Jonathan Edwards and he was going to write a novel, and our wives were going to write novels. Well, the wives just went humming away. 'I've just finished three pages,' they'd say at the end of the day; and their books mounted up. But ours never did." Out of a seemingly chaotic season, Lowell nonetheless forged the sixteen poems of *Land of Unlikeness* into a manuscript which, at Tate's suggestion, he sent to the Cummington Press for publication. From his research on Jonathan Edwards, Lowell also left Monteagle with the material for two of his most durable and successful poems, "After Strange Conversions" and "Mr. Edwards and the Spider," as well as "drafts or notes for 'The Quaker Graveyard in Nantucket.' "[21] Without that winter of research, discussion, and writing in Tate's creative "think tank," Lowell might never have transformed fragmentary bursts of creative energy into disciplined and powerful poems.

Lowell's poems now began to appear in literary journals, including *Chimera*, *Partisan Review*, *Sewanee Review*, and the *Kenyon*. Tate, who had just taken over the editorship of the *Sewanee Review*, would, of course, have been receptive to any work Lowell submitted. Tate was also on friendly terms with Phillip Rahv, editor of the *Partisan*, which soon became a semiofficial publishing organ for the poets of the Fugitive legacy. By 1944, Lowell had published eleven poems in these quarterlies and, at his mentor's suggestion, was ready to bring out a book.

Allen Tate's role in the eventual publication of *Land of Unlikeness* cannot be overstated. Because Lowell had almost no name recognition among editors outside the Fugitive network, Tate's location of a publisher willing to take the book on his recommendation no doubt enabled its publication. Moreover, the preface Tate wrote for the volume, in Doreski's words, "lent it the imprimatur of an established poet and instructed reviewers on how to approach these difficult, sometimes unwieldy poems." In that preface, Tate praised Lowell for his formal yet wholly individual approach to poetics: "There is no other poetry today quite like this. T. S. Eliot's recent prediction that we should soon see a return to formal and even intricate metres and stanzas was coming true, before he made it, in the verse of Robert Lowell."[22]

21. Doreski, *Years of Our Friendship*, 56, 60; Lowell, "Interview with Seidel," 240.

22. Doreski, *Years of Our Friendship*, 67; Allen Tate, preface to Robert Lowell, *Land of Unlikeness* (New York: Cummington Press, 1944), n.p.

Tate's preface, in effect, proclaims Lowell to be the true heir, in both form and content, to Fugitive modernism with all its political implications.

Land of Unlikeness was a modest accomplishment, but there is no doubt that it paved the way for its widely acclaimed successor, *Lord Weary's Castle*, only three years later. Of the sixteen poems in *Land of Unlikeness*, most are in stanzas of between eight and ten lines of metric and rhyming verse or, as in the case of the now frequently anthologized "New England" poems— "Salem," "Concord," and "Children of Light"—in single, short stanzas of ten or fourteen lines. His transplanting of Fugitive formalism to New England would make his poetry unique among poets of the Fugitive legacy. There are also plentiful remainders of the mannerisms that typified his unpublishable apprentice poems, those which critics universally condemn and which Lowell, with Jarrell's help, would soon abandon.

Not long after Lowell and Stafford left Monteagle, he would take the momentous step of declaring himself unwilling to serve in the armed forces of the United States and be sentenced to a year in prison for draft evasion. While he served his time in prisons at Danbury and Bridgeport, Connecticut, Tate acted as Lowell's literary agent. Lowell spent the greater part of his vigil editing the publisher's galleys for *Land of Unlikeness* and shoring up, against his ruins, images that would emerge in later poems such as "In the Cage" and "Memories of West Street and Lepke." Lowell emerged from imprisonment a relatively well-known poet who needed to find a better-known publisher for his second collection of poems. His friendships with Tate and Jarrell, along with several appearances in the *Partisan Review*, made it likely that Dial Press, where Phillip Rahv was also a controlling presence, would publish Lowell's next book. Finally, however, it was Harcourt, Brace that brought out *Lord Weary's Castle*, perhaps, as Mary Jarrell remarked, because "Roman Catholic Robert Giroux" brought his influence to bear.[23]

Crucial to the success of *Land of Unlikeness*, and ultimately to its evolution into *Lord Weary's Castle*, was a combination of encouraging reviews and instructive letters from Randall Jarrell, reestablishing the ties that had loosened during their four years of separation since Kenyon. Still in the air force during the winter of 1945, Jarrell reviewed *Land of Unlikeness* for *Partisan Review*, as part of an omnibus essay entitled "Poetry in War and Peace." He opened his evaluation of *Land of Unlikeness* by exclaiming that "some of Mr. Lowell's poems are so good ('The Drunken Fisherman' is the best poem in any of these books) and all are so unusual that it makes reviewing his book a plea-

23. M. Jarrell, ed., *Randall Jarrell's Letters*, 140.

sure." Jarrell's closing prediction, that "some of the best poems of the next years ought to be written by him," was not only a prophecy but also a pledge that Jarrell would personally take some responsibility for turning "ought" into "shall."[24]

Between 1954 and 1957, Jarrell and Lowell exchanged a remarkable series of letters that not only parallel the reviews but also demonstrate how great a hand Jarrell was to take, with Lowell's full acceptance, in his crucial progress from *The Land of Unlikeness* to *Lord Weary's Castle*. Not since the Pound excision of Eliot's *Waste Land* had there been such a fruitful collaboration between equals, for not only did Jarrell comment freely and constructively on which poems ought to be included and which left out of the volume, but he went to the very core of Lowell's poetry, advising him on structure of stanzas, choice of imagery, and lines to be included or omitted. As always, Jarrell failed to keep Lowell's letters; but even without his half of the correspondence, it is evident that Lowell also felt free to comment on Jarrell's poems.

In fact, it was apparently Lowell who opened the correspondence with a letter that Jarrell answered during August 1945. He began by "congratulating" Lowell on "pick[ing] out to like" the poems *he* also liked best—"Siegfried" and "The State"—and remarking enthusiastically that "I had rather read your poems than anybody else in the world is writing now" and that "if I didn't write the way I do I might or would like to write the way you do." Jarrell, who generally resented criticism of his poetry, conveyed his willingness at least to argue with Lowell's analysis of the persona who appears in Oscar Williams's anthology *The War Poets*: "What you said in the last letter about the typical protagonist of my poems is true and I am aware of it [probably that all are innocent, lacking any knowledge of what they are into] . . . there's not one out of hundred who knows enough about it to kill a fly or be stung by a fly. Talking about a slaughter of innocents!" If Lowell meant to be critical, Jarrell had no intention of changing a word. In September, Jarrell answered Lowell's reply in the same spirit:

> I enjoyed what you said about my poems and disagree only with this:
> (a) In "2nd Air Force" the rhetoric "pretty well obliterated the mother and her situation." It's a descriptive poem to show what a heavy bomber training-field was like; the mother is merely a vehicle of presentation, her situation merely a formal connection of the out-of-this-world field with the world.

24. Jarrell, "Poetry in War and Peace," 132–34.

(b) "The Emancipators" is "Brilliant lines rather than a poem." This puzzles me so much that I'm inclined to guess that it's a peculiarity of judgement coming from the fact that Western scientific, technological, industrial development isn't as natural and obsessive a thought with you as it is with me.[25]

Unlike Jarrell, Lowell was characteristically amenable to constructive criticism and apt to take Jarrell's advice literally. Jarrell took a hand, apparently at Lowell's request, in the selection of which poems from *Land of Unlikeness* to include in *Lord Weary's Castle*. He agreed with Lowell's list of suggested exclusions, adding that he would also advise leaving out "On the Eve of the Immaculate Conception" unless it could be revised. "Forest Hills Cemetery," he added, would be "better without the last stanza, which runs down like a toy." When Jarrell's furlough was unexpectedly canceled, he was forced to send all of his additional comments and suggestions in a lengthy letter dated November 1945. This time he firmly advised omission of "Immaculate Conception" because "some of the first part is too much like Allen's Short-and-Kimmel poem" ("Ode to Young Proconsuls of the Air," which, according to Lowell, Tate had composed during the winter of 1942–43 at Monteagle when he and Lowell worked together). Finding "Hooker's Statue" "still in a transitional stage rather than in the last resting-place," Jarrell advised that Lowell "leave it out of the book." Despite obvious gratitude for the advice, Lowell made up his own mind to keep "Under Hooker's Statue" while omitting "Immaculate Conception." He also wisely disregarded Jarrell's halfhearted advice to "put in 'Christ for Sale,' " "though certainly most of your readers and reviewer won't like *it*." Jarrell's approval of this controversial poem, which almost all of Lowell's critics have judged a failure, seems to be Jarrell's only lapse in judgment; truly this is "the Christ of the tabloids," but rather than condemn the poem outright, Jarrell later supplied constructive suggestions along with a heavily annotated copy of the poem.[26]

Among the new poems, Jarrell found "Mr. Edwards and the Spider" to be "tremendously effective the way it is now" and called "Colloquy in Black Rock" "an *awfully* good poem, just wonderfully done," the same for "Christmas in Black Rock." Approving changes in "A Bible House," "except the last two lines, which don't seem an effective ending to me," and in "Winter in Dunbarton," Jarrell turned his attention to "The Quaker Graveyard in Nan-

25. M. Jarrell, ed., *Randall Jarrell's Letters*, 129, 132.
26. Ibid., 135–36.

tucket" with a combination of extravagant praise—"This is your very best big poem"—and strongly worded advice—"you ought to be tremendously careful with it." He then provided Lowell with detailed directions for the poem's final revisions.[27]

Perceiving that *Lord Weary's Castle* would be proclaimed a distinct improvement over *Land of Unlikeness* and that Lowell stood on the threshold of a successful career, Jarrell took occasion to list what he saw as Lowell's major limitations at this point in his career: "(1) not putting enough about *people* in the poems—they are more about the actions of you, God, the Sea, and cemeteries than they are about the actions of men; (2) being too harsh and severe—but this is already changing, very much for the better too, I think." To no avail, Jarrell warned that *Lord Weary's Castle* is "a good private title but a bad public one: it won't convey anything to most readers" and closed as he typically ended his review essays by listing the "best" poems in the book: "The Quaker Graveyard, Colloquy in Black Rock, Where the Rainbow Ends, Mr. Edwards and the Spider, The Exile's Return, Christmas in Black Rock, The Indian Killer's Grave, The Dead in Europe, Winter in Dunbarton; Forest Hills Cemetery (2 stanzas) is almost as good; your *Partisan* Bayeux tapestry poem is easily in your first fifteen poems."[28]

Lowell followed Jarrell's advice, probably realizing not only that Jarrell was right but also that he would no doubt be called upon to review the collection. Jarrell's review of *Lord Weary's Castle* has been credited with setting the stage for Lowell's emergence as the most important poet of his generation. Not only did Jarrell call the publication of it "as much an event as Auden's first book," but, as Stephen Gould Axelrod later commented, Jarrell "brought Lowell's whole body of work into focus before that work was even written." Even more prophetically, Jarrell called Lowell's poetry "a unique fusion of modernist and traditional poetry . . . essentially a post- or anti-modernist poetry" that was "certain to be influential."[29] Therefore, like Tate's preface to *Land of Unlikeness*, Jarrell's "From the Kingdom of Necessity" instructed Lowell's other critics and readers about the importance of his poetry and how to read him. Clearly Jarrell and Lowell served each other—like Tate for Ransom, Ransom for Brooks, and Brooks for Warren—as friendly but merciless critics, who felt an awesome responsibility to refine each other's work before it faced the judgment of editors, reviewers, and ordinary readers.

27. Ibid., 136–37.
28. Ibid., 138–40.
29. Jarrell, "From the Kingdom of Necessity," 188, 195; Steven Gould Axelrod, *Life and Art* (Princeton: Princeton University Press, 1978), ix.

Surely the pattern of communication and mutual criticism that Lowell and Jarrell saw in action among their former Fugitive mentors must have suggested to them in the strongest possible way the importance of friendship to the lonely existence of the person of letters. In *Manic Power*, Jeffrey Myers has stressed the jealousy and disappointment which Jarrell naturally felt when Lowell outdid him in awards and, ultimately, in critical acclaim. Although Jarrell did covet Lowell's Pulitzer Prize, he always valued Lowell's friendship, realizing that although they did write a few poems with similar titles ("The End of the Rainbow"—"At the Rainbow's End"), their mature poetry, as Richard Flynn has persuasively argued, is thematically and tonally individual.[30] For Lowell's part, however, he never ceased to praise Jarrell or to credit him with playing a strong role in his own success as a writer.

Unlike Jarrell, Lowell maintained fairly close ties with his Fugitive mentors throughout the remainder of their lives. Lowell's relationship with Ransom became friendly but more distant. Lowell served on the faculty of Ransom's Kenyon school of criticism in 1953 and, in his two commemorative essays, gave Ransom due credit for setting him on the road to a poetic career. Both Ransom and Tate were satisfied to keep their distance from Lowell when his bouts with mania grew more frequent and violent and when his poetry began to diverge from the formality that Tate had praised in *Land of Unlikeness*.

Tate's response to *Life Studies* was to praise only one poem, "Skunk Hour," and to criticize severely "*all* the poems about your family, including the one about you and Elizabeth" ("Man and Wife") as "composed of unassimilated details, terribly intimate and coldly noted, which might well have been transferred from the notes for your autobiography without change." Tate lamented that although Lowell's earlier poems "present a formal ordering of highly intractable materials," his latest ones are "free-verse, arbitrary and without rhythm." Lowell's reply, of January 24, 1958, attempted to mediate between confidence in his own accomplishment and acknowledgment of his continuing debt to his mentor: "I am sorry you don't like my stuff because you are such a generous and good judge. I've been going to school to you for years and hope to life-long." In 1964, Lowell wrote Tate in response to Tate's praise of "A Severed Head" from *For the Union Dead*: "Thanks for liking what you like, and for being pointed and generous as always. Nothing could please me more than your picking the Severed Head. For years after reading your terza rima poems [I've] wanted to try the meter. I've always

30. Flynn, *Randall Jarrell*, 140–41.

found I could not even make sense, and somehow lacked the energy to bend the rhymes to anything. When I finally did, it nearly killed me. The poem owes a lot to you."[31]

The poem achieves the sort of assimilation of form and personal details that Tate insisted on. In a dream sequence, the speaker entertains a ghostly visitant with a "frayed mustache; too brown, too bushy" who "came toward me with a manuscript, / scratching in last revisions with a pen / that left no markings on the page, yet dripped / a red ink dribble on us." The apparition ends by tearing up the manuscript and finally "to twist / and trample on the mangle in his rage." Doreski calls the poem a "confrontation" with "a form of alter ego," and perhaps neither Lowell nor Tate recognized the visitor as Lowell's most prevalent influence and inflexible critic, Allen Tate.[32] Lowell's inability to complete Tate's authorized biography some years later was a lengthier manifestation of a relationship that could never again either be close or break apart precisely because of the anxiety of influence.

For Warren, who was never to be as close a friend to his former students as was Tate, Lowell was "crazy," unsettling to be around. From a distance, however, Warren retained a strong interest in Lowell's poetry. After reading *Lord Weary's Castle*, Warren wrote, from Minneapolis: "Your book has given the Warren household a great deal of pleasure. . . . It is real poetry, very strong and original, and doesn't bear the slightest resemblance to most of the stuff which is passing as poetry. There is nobody around any better than you are."[33]

Lowell did nothing to strengthen their friendship when, some years later, he gave Warren's first major poetic utterance in ten years, *Brother to Dragons*, a review that oscillates between praise and condemnation. Lowell began by calling the play "a brutal, perverse melodrama that makes the flesh crawl" and by characterizing Warren's "bawdy lines" as "a sort of fraternity initiation, demanded, given, to establish the writer firmly outside the genteel tradition." In an attempt at balance, Lowell praised Warren's ability to produce "the fourth remarkable long poem to have been published in the last ten or twelve years," comparable to *Four Quartets*, *Paterson*, and *The Pisan Cantos*, and proclaimed him superior to Browning in his ability to produce, in mod-

---

31. Tate to Lowell, December 3, 1957, Lowell Papers, bMS AM 1905 (1520–1681), by permission of the Houghton Library, Harvard University; Lowell to Tate, January 24, 1958, and October 9, 1964, both in Tate Papers.

32. Doreski, *Years of Our Friendship*, 101–2.

33. Warren to Lowell, December 3, 1946, Lowell Papers, bMS AM 1905 (1415–26), by permission of the Houghton Library, Harvard University.

ern times, a "metrical novel." Small wonder that Lowell would remark, in a letter to Tate: "You must have disliked my review of Red. So did he. When I read at Yale he never mentioned it. Writing it was like pulling one's teeth out."[34]

Unlike Tate, Warren, whose poetry, like Lowell's, was evolving quickly toward personal statement, did not turn away from Lowell's frankly autobiographical poems. In April 1965, Warren called *For the Union Dead* "a splendid book, truly," and in 1969, he responded to *Notebook*, which dismayed many of Lowell's most partisan readers, with the following sublime encomium: "I read it when it first came, in a rush, in gulps, as, in a way, it demands to be read, for it is a *book*, a *unit*, and it thrusts on with such furous [*sic*] energy, excitement, and *elan*. Then I had it by me all summer and got to know it in a different, deeper, and more detailed way. It is an extraordinary work, original, truly your own, with your thumbmark deep in the clay."[35]

Even before the fifties, the close-knit friendships of the middle generation poets Randall Jarrell, John Berryman, and Robert Lowell began to supplant both their need and desire for the supporting Fugitive network. By the fifties, Jarrell, Berryman, and Lowell were established as the foremost poets of their generation, or at least of its genteel, academic half. As Karl Shapiro wrote in his commemorative article for Jarrell, a "giant beast [was] slouching toward the City Lights bookstore" to publish *Howl* and to establish, in the Beat poets, a competing poetic strain with which the Fugitive–New Critics would claim no connection.[36] It is intriguing to speculate whether, without the active sponsorship and support of the former Fugitives, these three troubled and troubling poets would have played so prominent a role in the annals of twentieth-century American literature. Certainly the configurations of their careers would have been more various and their ascent less meteoric had they not first profited and then fled from the Fugitive legacy.

34. Lowell, "Robert Penn Warren's *Brother to Dragons*," in *Robert Lowell*, ed. Giroux, 66–73; Lowell to Tate, March 15, 1954, Tate Papers.

35. Warren to Lowell, April 1965 and October 12, 1969, both in Lowell Papers, bMS AM 1905 (1415–26) by permission Houghton Library, Harvard University.

36. Karl Shapiro, "The Death of Randall Jarrell," in *Randall Jarrell*, ed. Lowell, Taylor, and Warren, 210.

PART III

The Fugitive Legacy to Fiction:
Three Contemporaries

8 / The Fugitives and Fiction

An exceptionally large and talented group of fiction writers who came to prominence during the thirties and forties were, like the poets and critics, taught, sponsored, published by, even married to one or more of the four major Fugitives or to one of their protégés. The Fugitives themselves, with the important exception of Robert Penn Warren, at first laid little claim to either theoretical or practical knowledge of the craft of fiction, but their always-expanding personal and literary associations and their professional duties—as teachers, editors, and anthologers—forced them to add fiction to their areas of expertise.

John Crowe Ransom's practice, as he once wrote to Andrew Lytle, was "not to [comment] on fiction; I'd only show myself up." Robie Macauley, Ransom's student at Kenyon and his successor as editor of the *Kenyon Review*, wrote that fiction was "one of John Ransom's blind spots . . . an interesting semi-art, necessary but usually tedious and he did not read it often." Macauley added that "under Ransom's editorship, the *Review* had tended to favor southern fiction: Robert Penn Warren's, Flannery O'Connor's, or Andrew Lytle's."[1] Even though he could not theorize on the art of fiction, Ransom

1. Ransom to Andrew Lytle, October 24, Andrew Nelson Lytle Papers, Jean and Alexander Heard Library, Vanderbilt University, Nashville, Tenn.; Macauley, "*Kenyon Review*," 74.

could, through his editorship and influence, play an important role in the development of a talented young writer of fiction, especially if that young writer were a member of the post-Fugitive circle.

Donald Davidson remained at Vanderbilt, where he was instrumental in bringing a program in creative writing to the university. In this context he encouraged and influenced several generations of Vanderbilt student writers, many of them fictionists. Davidson's natural affinities for the folk tradition made him receptive not just to "mainstream" southern writers but also to fiction that the more genteel Fugitives branded as "regional" and consistently refused to publish in their journals.

When the *Southern Review* began publishing, Davidson had as student and protégé Mildred Haun, whose Appalachian-based stories were decidedly regional. He first wrote to Warren, on January 22, 1939, praising Haun as Vanderbilt's "first grad. fellow in creative writing" and adding that he "would be much pleased if the *Southern Review* would present her to the world." Davidson believed that to encourage Haun would also provide "official reasons for giving somewhat more hearty support to advanced writers here than the administration used to." When Brooks and Warren rejected Haun's stories, Davidson wrote a strong letter to Brooks expressing his disappointment, especially about their refusal to print Haun's "Pa Went A-Courtin'," which Warren "had liked." Chagrined that "his sponsorship of a young author has availed nothing in the quarter where I should have hoped it might count, at least, to the extent of . . . a 'debut,' " Davidson defiantly requested a statement of "your general line of policy in choosing stories," inquiring, "Are you interested in 'discovering' able young Southern writers?"[2]

Brooks replied on October 23, 1939, that the *Southern Review*'s first volume alone had published seven stories by first-time writers. Along with established authors Caroline Gordon and Katherine Anne Porter, the *Review* had used stories by George Abbe, Louis Moreau, S. S. Field, Elma Godchaux, Pier M. Pasinetti, K. C. Shelby, Manson Radford, Jack Boone, David Ellsworth Brown (from LSU), and "Eudora Welty, a Miss girld [*sic*] just starting out." He added, however, that the editors would "not accept a 'poor' or 'unworthy' story." Admitting that in Haun's case they "may have made a mistake," Brooks maintained that "her work was interesting" but that "none of the stories which we saw were quite competent enough to go as a story."[3]

    2. Davidson to Robert Penn Warren, January 22, 1939, and Davidson to Brooks, October 15, 1939, both in *Southern Review* Papers.
    3. Brooks to Davidson, October 23, 1939, ibid.

Neither the *Southern Review* nor the *Kenyon Review* ever published Haun's fiction because she was too "regional" for their tastes. Ransom demonstrated as much in his own letter to Haun, dated January 11, 1951: "The story [unidentified] is extremely solid, and full of pity; it's up to M. H. standards all right. But we never have done regional dialect stories; it seems wrong for us . . . we can't take the story to heart."[4] Haun produced relatively little fiction after her college days, but her collected stories were finally published under the title *The Hawk's Done Gone and Other Stories* (1968).

Unlike his three Fugitive colleagues, Robert Penn Warren wrote fiction, along with poetry, textbooks, and formal criticism, almost from the beginning of his career. His editorship of the *Southern Review* made it necessary for Warren to join Brooks in evaluating the many stories submitted to the *Review*, but it is likely that Warren had the final word on their acceptance or rejection. Except as editor of the *Southern Review*, Warren seldom advised other writers of fiction in the execution of their craft. He frequently wrote congratulatory letters, reviews, or blurbs after friends had published their novels, and his essays appear as introductions to their collections of short stories (for Jesse Stuart, Caroline Gordon, and Peter Taylor) or as retrospectives on their established careers (Katherine Anne Porter, Caroline Gordon, Andrew Lytle, and Eudora Welty). Warren did not, however, set himself up as a theorist about or authority on the writing of fiction. In fact, the editors of the *Southern Review* were often vague about their reasons for rejecting a piece of fiction, often saying lamely that they did not like it "as a story."

In subtle ways, however, Warren played an important role in shaping the fiction writers produced during the late thirties, forties, and beyond through the Brooks and Warren textbooks. After *An Approach to Literature*, in 1936, and *Understanding Poetry*, in 1938, the next logical step was *Understanding Fiction* (1943), which laid out for the next generation of would-be writers, editors, teachers, and readers a method for analyzing and teaching fiction.

When Brooks and Warren turned their mimeographed "Sophomore Poetry Manual" into a four-part introduction to literature, Warren undoubtedly had chief responsibility for the fiction section, including the introductions. The fiction section of *An Approach to Literature* takes its point of departure not from a story but a poem, "Porphyria's Lover," to illustrate how a sensational crime story could be presented as headline news, as a "sob sister

4. Ransom to Mildred Haun, January 11, 1951, *Kenyon Review* Papers.

story," and, finally, as a dramatic monologue.[5] Warren reflected that modern fiction, as well as poetry, should be governed by dramatic immediacy and objectivity. Brooks and Warren carried that emphasis forward in all their textbooks, stressing the importance of dramatic presentation over authorially controlled storytelling. Above all, they stressed the principle of organic unity, as they had always done in their discussions of poetry. The editors updated their anthology five times until 1975, each time adding new poems, stories, plays, and essays by contemporary writers.

After the success of *Understanding Poetry*, Brooks and Warren decided that taking one section of *An Approach to Literature* and expanding it into an entire textbook had potential as a source of steady, though small, income. *Understanding Fiction*, their third textbook, nonetheless took shape slowly. The work began during Warren's last academic year at LSU, 1941–42, and continued after he moved to the University of Minnesota. It was an extremely busy period for Brooks and Warren, exacerbated not only by Warren's stormy departure but also because the *Southern Review*'s days were numbered despite energetic efforts to save it. The publisher of *Understanding Fiction*, F. S. Crofts, had difficulties obtaining rights to some stories, always a limitation on anthologers, and the overburdened editors were often late in meeting deadlines.

The anthology, which finally appeared in 1943, proclaimed its loyalty to the Fugitive legacy by its dedication to Donald Davidson and the imposing presence of the Fugitives' friends and protégés. Included were "Old Red" by Caroline Gordon, "Old Mortality" by Katherine Anne Porter, and two stories, "A Piece of News" and "Old Mr. Marblehead," by Eudora Welty, all published first and therefore "owned" by the *Southern Review*. The editors included sections of interpretative commentary by the authors themselves, as well as the by now familiar list of questions to lead the student through an orderly analytical process. Warren's introductory letter to the teacher explains that the editors' and contributors' "interpretations . . . are descriptive and analytical rather than valuative." Through close reading of the stories, students would learn to value a story with structural irony, such as Chekhov's "The Kiss," over a mechanically manipulative one like O. Henry's "The Furnished Room." The teacher is warned that emphasis will be placed on "formal considerations" over "ethical, religious, philosophical, or sociological"

5. Cleanth Brooks, Robert Penn Warren, and John Thibaut Purser, eds., *An Approach to Literature: A Collection of Prose and Verse with Analyses and Discussions* (Baton Rouge: Louisiana State University Press, 1936), 1–8.

principles, which do not in themselves "indicate anything about the importance of the piece of fiction."[6] Stories that lended themselves to close reading
claimed privilege over those that did not. Brooks and Warren thereby extended the so-called New Critical method from poetry to fiction.

The former Fugitives' textbooks, their criticism, and the journals they edited provide a reasonable picture of what Fugitive, or New Critical, fiction
was like. In addition, letters exchanged among these writers, especially between Allen Tate and Lytle, Lytle and Gordon, Warren and Porter, Gordon
and Porter, Warren and Welty, Taylor and Warren, and O'Connor and Gordon, provide useful commentary on stories they were writing and submitting
to the journals and collections for which their literary friends had editorial
responsibility. These writers clearly respected each other's advice and usually
acted on the editorial commentary and informal suggestions they received.
Since the editors responded favorably to stories that resembled poems and
could be read by the New Critical method, the fictionists tended to tailor at
least some of their stories to fit these specifications, or they saved for the former Fugitive editors those stories that fit a certain broad profile.

Allen Tate, author of only a few stories and one novel, usually professed
ignorance of the craft of fiction. He had, however, the good fortune to be
married to Caroline Gordon and friendly with Andrew Lytle and Ford
Madox Ford. Tate therefore ameliorated his lack of expertise about fiction by
living with writers of stories and novels, as well as by assiduous reading. And
he always gladly assisted friends and students by using his considerable influence with editors and publishers. Tate thereby became the unofficial
promoter and adviser to some of the most important fiction writers of the
post-Fugitive generation: Andrew Lytle, Caroline Gordon, Katherine Anne
Porter, and Peter Taylor.

With Gordon, Tate published *The House of Fiction* (1950), an anthology
not unlike *Understanding Fiction*, which derived much of its narrative theory
from Henry James and codified the Jamesian standard for fiction not only by
its commentary but through stories that fit the criteria. Of all the precursors
to the fiction of the Fugitive legacy, James was the most frequently acknowledged. One of Gordon's biographers, Ann Waldron, observed that Caroline
admired James's "central intelligence," his placement of "the superior mind
. . . at the center of the action." Katherine Anne Porter also called James her
master, and Flannery O'Connor, who ridiculed all inquiries into her sources

6. Cleanth Brooks and Robert Penn Warren, eds., *Understanding Fiction* (New York: Appleton-
Century-Crofts, 1943), xiv, xv.

of inspiration, was disingenuously reported muttering, "Henry James, Henry James, Henry James," to throw researchers off the scent. All were, like Gordon, "obsessed with point of view" and fixated on objectivity. As Gordon wrote to Ward Dorrance in 1948, "One thing I have learned from James—in theory, at least—is that a character can often be rendered more dramatically when handled objectively."[7]

Fiction, traditionally a literary genre in which women have enjoyed success, was an area of significant achievement for women of the Fugitive legacy: Caroline Gordon, Katherine Anne Porter, Eudora Welty, and Flannery O'Connor. All four participated in what Sandra Gilbert and Susan Gubar have called "a flowering of feminist modernism." Although hindered somewhat by the chauvinism of the Fugitive-Agrarian brotherhood, these fiction-writing women had status—beyond that of wives, lovers, and colleagues—that no female poet or critic could claim. Although, as Rosemary Magee has written, these women "often stood on the periphery" of the Southern Renaissance, "that periphery became defined by a set of intertwining circles—communities not contained by time or space, without the comforts of a shared college campus or the hospitality of the literary establishment." One such circle was formed by the Fugitive legacy, which cut across special boundaries to embrace women who joined the academic community. Moreover, as Heather McClure has observed, the critical tenets which the former Fugitives created and to which they adhered as editors were actually advantageous to women writers. In theory, at least, because of the New Critics' "insular conception of art," "women gain the option of being judged as artists first, and overall they seem to grow in confidence and stature in this professional role." Although these women wrote fiction in the mode expected by their male cohorts, they reinterpreted those modes of narration to suit their own feminine minds and purposes. As Patricia Yaeger put it, "Women's writing employs a *useful* form of 'plagiarism' . . . adapting what has been called 'phallocentric' diction to fit the needs of 'feminocentric' expressions," so that to subvert or deconstruct this system is at once traditional and feminocentric. Women who wrote fiction therefore figured prominently in and were able to leave their imprint on the Fugitive legacy.[8]

---

7. Ann Waldron, *Close Connections: Caroline Gordon and the Southern Renaissance* (Knoxville: University of Tennessee Press, 1987), 205, 266; Sally Fitzgerald, ed., *Letters of Flannery O'Connor: The Habit of Being* (New York: Farrar, Straus & Giroux, 1970), 98.

8. Sandra Gilbert and Susan Gubar, *The War of the Words*, vol. 1, of *No Man's Land: The Place of the Woman Writer in the Twentieth Century* (New Haven: Yale University Press, 1987), xiii; Rosemary Magee, Introduction to *Friendship and Sympathy: Communities of Southern Women*

When Brooks and Warren became editors of the *Southern Review*, Tate of the *Sewanee Review*, and Ransom of the *Kenyon Review*, they relied on Caroline Gordon and Katherine Anne Porter, already established writers of fiction, to provide them with stories and, indirectly, with a standard by which to judge the stories that other writers submitted. Subsequently, these editors helped to introduce a new generation of writers of both genders to the literary world. Because these writers had access to national and better-paying magazines such as *Scribner's*, the *Atlantic Monthly*, and the *Saturday Review*, as well as to the former Fugitives' reviews, they were less beholden than poets and critics to the academic-based review, which paid very little but offered, as Warren put it, "good company between the covers." Their greater independence allowed writers of fiction to lead their Fugitive colleagues rather than to be dominated by them.

Because the number of fiction writers with connections to the Fugitive legacy is legion, it becomes necessary to focus only on those few but distinguished writers whose ties with the former Fugitives were closest. This arbitrary selection yields two groups of Fugitive-related writers, the contemporaries and peers—Andrew Lytle, Caroline Gordon, and Katherine Anne Porter—and the protégés—Peter Taylor, Eudora Welty, and Flannery O'Connor.

Writers, ed. Magee (Jackson: University Press of Mississippi, 1992), xvi; Heather McClure, Introduction to *Women Writers of the Short Story: A Collection of Critical Essays*, ed. McClure (Englewood Cliffs, N.J.: Prentice-Hall, 1980), 9; Patricia S. Yaeger, " 'Because a Fire Was in My Head': Eudora Welty and the Dialogic Imagination," in *Welty: A Life in Literature*, ed. Albert J. Devlin (Jackson: University Press of Mississippi, 1987), 140.

9 / Andrew Lytle: Fugitive Art in Agrarian Fiction

Andrew Lytle became a full-fledged peer of the former Fugitives before the publication of *I'll Take My Stand*. Because of his powerful enthusiasm for the Agrarian cause, Lytle presents his postmodern readers with a problem. Pat C. Hoy has stated that "under the heady influence of a seductive regional utopianism, the agrarian apologists skirted many of the moral problems inherent in the old order and as a result confused us about their role as Fugitives fleeing the sweet sappiness of the magnolia-and-mint-julep culture."[1] Readers of "The Hind Tit" and "The Backwoods Progression" expect naked Agrarian didacticism in Lytle's other writings, but if they can divorce the artist from the polemicist, they will find a growing commitment to excellence in Lytle's fiction. Increasingly, through strategies of indirection, Lytle dramatized rather than preached the doctrines he held to be central; those strategies—use of first person narrative and the Jamesian center of revelation—not only went far to save the fiction from its author but led him toward experimentation in those modernist modes of narration that connected the Fugitive-Agrarian legacy with the fictional avant-garde.

---

1. Pat C. Hoy, "The Wages of Sin: Terminal Considerations in Lytle's 'Jericho, Jericho, Jericho,'" *South Atlantic Review* 49 (1984): 107.

Lytle's earliest publications owe much to his participation in the Agrarian cause. After the publication in 1930 of *I'll Take My Stand*, his time was divided between farming his father's holdings in Alabama and writing Agrarian essays, broadsides, and reviews. Between 1929 and 1935, Lytle also composed his first short stories. Despite the conflicts inevitably caused by Lytle's attempt (unique among the Fugitive-Agrarians) to live out his agrarian philosophy, he became an able writer and theorist of fiction in large part because his close relationship with the former Fugitives continued after the Agrarian movement had fizzled. His stories were frequently written for and published, along with his highly polemical essays and reviews, in journals with Fugitive-Agrarian connections. As each novel underwent its long gestation, Lytle consulted with Allen Tate, Caroline Gordon, John Crowe Ransom, Katherine Anne Porter, and other members of the Fugitive circle. Robert Penn Warren would usually comment, both by letter and in published reviews, on Lytle's finished stories and novels, and he frequently called on Lytle for advice on his own writing, especially drama. As Lytle gradually developed his craft, he became, with Caroline Gordon, the major authority on fiction to the post-Fugitive circle.

The cross-fertilization so common in the Fugitive legacy is most evident in Lytle's relationship with Allen Tate. The correspondence between Tate and Lytle, edited and documented by T. D. Young and Elizabeth Sarcone, chronicles a friendship stretching over the careers of both former Agrarians and involving the most crucial matters of literary craftsmanship and promotion. As Young states in his introduction, "A closer, more personal relationship existed between Andrew Lytle and Allen Tate than between any of the other Nashville writers."[2] The letters, almost always beginning with the salutation "Brother" (or B'rer, if the writer was feeling especially southern), provide details on both men's personal and literary histories available nowhere else. Tate's weighty input into Lytle's writing, always with deference to Tate's lack of expertise about fiction, is balanced by Lytle's perceptive comments on Tate's.

The two men met at Vanderbilt in the mid-1920s when both were Ransom's students. Lytle attended one or two meetings of the Fugitive group and published a poem, "Edward Graves," in the *Fugitive*. More interested in drama than poetry, he left Vanderbilt for the Yale Drama School and a career as an actor and playwright. The Fugitive network brought Lytle and Tate together again when, in the spring of 1927, John Crowe Ransom wrote a letter

2. Thomas Daniel Young, introduction to Young and Sarcone, eds., *Tate-Lytle Letters*, vi.

to each, suggesting that they should become reacquainted. On March 15, 1935, Tate extended to Lytle the following invitation: "John Ransom happened to say in a letter the other day that you are at Yale. I was extremely glad to have some news of you, for after I left Nashville some years ago I lost track of you altogether. I should be very happy to have you call upon us here the next time you are in New York, if you have an hour or two to spare. Interesting things are, I believe, at last stirring in the South, and in that part of the South which we cannot help taking about with us forever, wherever we may go."[3] The propitious reunion occurred at the Greenwich Village apartment building on Bank Street, where the Tates were by then residing.

Almost immediately, Tate begin to play a role in Lytle's literary career by encouraging him to publish in journals in which Tate had some influence. Tate wrote from London during 1928 on a Guggenheim Fellowship, "As to the essay on the Negro theater—why not extend it to about 3,000 words, and send it to [James Southall] Wilson of the *Virginia Quarterly Review?*"[4] The essay apparently never saw publication, largely because at about this time the former Fugitives began to draw Lytle into their defense of "the South."

The process began with Tate's suggestion that he and Lytle join forces in combating a barrage of perceived attacks, from without and within, growing out of the Scopes trial and the New South movement's efforts to bring industrialism to what the former Fugitives and their friends hoped would always be an agrarian region. The twelve southerners, of whom former Fugitives Ransom, Davidson, and Tate were the nucleus, began to call themselves Agrarians and to plan, in quasi-military terms, a literary defense of their region and heritage. Writing more than fifty years later, Lytle stated that "the Twelve Southerners, the Agrarians, were not taken in by abstract political and economic theories. They by common agreement saw what was needed: to restore what was lost, if possible, and restrain further subversion of not only southern but the general well-being." For the former Fugitives, the first task was to tell the South's story from a historical perspective. It was actually Donald Davidson who enlisted Lytle to write agrarian rhetoric. The more literary Tate at first proposed a "history of the South," to which Lytle responded with great enthusiasm: "Really, the idea . . . is beyond words. And just at this time, before the final concentration of the empire, it will be a crying protest against that short-sighted greed which killed the goose that laid the egg." With this history—and with Caroline Gordon's *Penhally*, then in

3. Ibid., xx, 4–5.
4. Ibid., 13.

the works—the triumvirate would be ready to "hit the enemy front, flank, and rear, all at once, like old Forrest." Lytle was also full of ideas for his own books, a biography of John C. Calhoun, never written, and another on Nathan Bedford Forrest, not to mention plans for getting D. W. Griffith to combine Tate's Confederate biographies of Davis (in press) and Stonewall Jackson into a movie called *The Rise and Fall of the Confederacy*.[5]

For Lytle it was a defining moment. Inspired by Tate and Gordon, Lytle became, instead of a mediocre playwright, the most dedicated of southern apologists and, more important, a committed writer of fiction and essays, all having their basis in his southern roots and related fixed cultural-historical goal: to "reaffirm[ ] the history of their inherited European culture."[6] As a result, Lytle, under the Agrarian imprimatur and through close personal friendship with Tate, was propelled into the Fugitive-Agrarian network of published writers. His seminal texts, historical and polemic, became the ideological and thematic basis for the fiction that was to come. With Tate's active sponsorship, Lytle soon executed an agreement with Minton, Balch and Company, a division of G. P. Putnam's Sons, to publish a biography of Nathan Bedford Forrest; not incidentally, Earle Balch also published Tate's two Civil War biographies and for several years held his contract for the never completed biography of Robert E. Lee.

Since they were all involved in projects relating to the Civil War, members of the post-Fugitive circle undertook serious historical research in 1928–29. In addition to Lytle's and Tate's projected biographies, Warren's *John Brown: The Making of a Martyr* and Gordon's *Penhally* and *None Shall Look Back* were in gestation. The summer of 1928 saw the entire crew, including Katherine Anne Porter, heading for Virginia to visit Civil War battlefields. Porter, whom they dropped off in Pennsylvania, and Robert Penn Warren, whom they picked up along the way, traveled with Lytle and the Tates in a "secondhand Ford from New York to Alabama."[7] Lytle afterward continued without the others to follow Forrest's campaigns both geographically and through whatever written accounts he could locate.

5. Wood, ed., *Southern Mandarins*, 4; Davidson to Lytle, June 11, 1929, Lytle Papers; Young and Sarcone, eds., *Tate-Lytle Letters*, 16, 17. For Tate, Warren, Lytle, and perhaps many other writers in this era of American letters, it was necessary to write biographies, novels, and other salable volumes of prose if they were to gain publishing contracts for their poetry. A five-hundred-page book of prose would "pay for" a slender volume of poems.

6. Wood, ed., *Southern Mandarins*, 4.

7. Mark Lucas, *The Southern Vision of Andrew Lytle* (Baton Rouge: Louisiana State University Press, 1986), 6–7, quoting Lytle's "They Took Their Stand: The Agrarian View after Fifty Years," *Modern Age* 24 (1980): 115–19.

For the Tate-Gordon-Lytle enclave, Nathan Bedford Forrest was "the most typical strong man of the Agrarian South" and an appropriate symbol for the "spirit of . . . renewed fight."[8] Moreover, several members of the Fugitive circle claimed kinship to one or more of those who "rode with Forrest." He therefore dominated not only Lytle's biography but also Gordon's *None Shall Look Back* (1937). Forrest also appeared later in Robert Penn Warren's "When the Light Gets Green" and in Peter Taylor's "In the Miro District."

By 1930, Tate, Gordon, and Lytle left New York, with its useful component of writers and publishers, and returned to the South, where they could combine practical agrarianism with writing. There was at first talk of forming an agrarian community called Louisa, for Louisa County, Virginia, in the region where Caroline was born. Eventually, however, the group settled down at Benfolly, the "estate" near Clarksville, Tennessee, which Tate's brother Ben (hence the name) bought for Allen and Caroline. As their writing careers progressed, Lytle and Gordon not only wrote on similar subjects (often under the same roof) but evolved common aesthetic and technical ideas about the writing of fiction.

Lytle's Forrest biography, Agrarian essays, and early fiction were composed during this period of intimate association, when the Tates either entertained Lytle at Benfolly or were entertained by him at Cornsilk, the Lytle family farm in Alabama. Sally Wood, Gordon's close friend and correspondent and sometime visitor to Benfolly, remembered that Lytle took up residence with the Tates while he was hard at work on *Forrest*. Gordon wrote to Wood from Clarksville in November 1930: "We have no company now except Andrew Lytle who has settled down here for a long stretch—until he finishes his biography of Forrest. I am struggling with Shiloh and Missionary Ridge [in *Penhally*] and Allen is on the verge of starting Lee. Our conversations are all highly military, and are no doubt highly amusing if anybody were to overhear us." During a fall visit to Benfolly on her way to Florida, Wood often "met him [Lytle] pacing about the house with blank eyes, giving military orders. 'Then General Forrest said. . . .' Only occasionally did he become himself. Most of the time he actually was General Forrest."[9]

In a sense, Lytle's biography is his first novel. Walter Sullivan believes that *Bedford Forrest and His Critter Company*, which begins as a historical text, becomes, after one hundred pages, a work of imaginative fiction with the

8. Lucas, *Southern Vision*, 14.
9. Wood, ed., *Southern Mandarins*, 64, 65.

"structure and tone" of a "historical narrative" with Forrest as its hero and General Braxton Bragg, Forrest's nemesis, as its villain.[10] Lytle's training in drama brought immediacy to scene after scene illustrating how Forrest's unusual character and his early life in the Tennessee "wilderness" shaped him into a military genius, uniquely able to function as the nation's first guerrilla commander but certain to clash with the conventional, military school paradigm of a military leader. The Forrest project was therefore Lytle's vehicle for combining regional pieties, identification with the particular hero of Lytle's own region of birth, and training in the inclusion of dramatic elements in his first important narrative project. Tate's enlisting of Lytle in a "history of the South" thus led Lytle not only to "The Hind Tit" but also to biography and then, irrevocably, to fiction.

The literary symbiosis of the Tates and Lytle was clearly in force when he wrote his first short stories. In February 1932, Tate wrote from Nashville to ask Lytle if he "could continue any of your present work up here?" Both Tates were ill, short of money, and in need of someone to "drive in once a day to get things." Tate suggested that "if your work is so that you don't need a library, you might go ahead here without any distraction whatever—for example, your long story, which ought to be finished before it gets cold on you." The story, "Old Scratch in the Valley," was published in the *Virginia Quarterly Review* of April 1932. The *Review* was then edited by Stringfellow Barr, who was well acquainted with the Agrarians although he opposed their cause.[11] "Old Scratch," an apprentice piece that Lytle later nearly disowned, was a clear precursor to the most famous of Lytle's short stories, "Jericho, Jericho, Jericho," with which it shares characters, the Mebane family, and setting, Long Gourd plantation. Published in the *Southern Review* in the spring of 1935, "Jericho" constituted Lytle's debut as a writer of fiction and may have played a crucial role in shaping his career.

Robert Penn Warren, already an acquaintance since Vanderbilt days, turned to Lytle for contributions to the *Southern Review*. Warren asked Lytle, first, for a review of Zora Neal Hurston's *Mules and Men* and then for a story. Upon receiving "Jericho," however, Warren did not hesitate to make editorial comments. Writing on January 28, 1936, he called the story "essentially

---

10. Walter Sullivan, preface to Andrew Lytle, *Bedford Forrest and His Critter Company* (1931; rpt. Nashville: Sanders, 1992), xvi–xvii.

11. Young and Sarcone, eds., *Tate-Lytle Letters*, 51; Waldron, *Close Connections*, 102. Stringfellow Barr represented the progressive, or "New South," point of view in a debate with John Crowe Ransom that took place in the Richmond, Virginia, city auditorium on November 14, 1930. Tate believed that Ransom won the debate because Barr "was an Agrarian at heart."

magnificent—and we use the word 'magnificent' advisedly," but he followed up the compliment by objecting to "some vagueness about the question of the woman's sin; is it a specific act or her 'worldliness' "? Warren then suggested that details of recollection be "cut to sharpen basic issue," that the last sentence about "end" was unnecessary, and that the story should close, instead, with the last line in the spiritual, "Joshua fit de battle of Jericho, Jericho, Jericho, and de walls come a-tumblin down."[12] Lytle followed these suggestions to the letter.

The personal relationship of Warren and Lytle continued through frequent visits, as Red and his wife, Cinina, spent holidays and vacations in Tennessee and Alabama, taking what Tate called a "Warren journey—practically nonstop except at bathrooms."[13] Warren faithfully read and responded to each of Lytle's novels after its publication but did not take an active part, as Tate and Gordon did, in their creation. Warren's ambivalence toward the Agrarian sentiments which Lytle so insistently defended, in his writing as well as in his way of life, no doubt limited Warren's relationship with Andrew Lytle to casual or purely professional contacts.

Lytle's relationship with John Crowe Ransom began in Ransom's classes at Vanderbilt and continued, though not intimately, through the various activities of the post-Fugitive network. It was Ransom who recommended Cleanth Brooks to Lytle as "a first-rate full grown and fair-sized Agrarian: all ready for the ceremonies when we can get him in Nashville to hear his profession of faith and take his pledge."[14] Later, when Ransom's *Kenyon Review* replaced the *Southern* as the major organ of post-Fugitive and Agrarian publication, Ransom enthusiastically published Lytle's short fiction and judiciously reviewed his novels. Lytle became, for Ransom, a source of authority on fiction. Their relationship was crowned in 1956, when Lytle won the *Kenyon Review*'s Fellowship in Fiction, allowing him to complete *The Velvet Horn*, which he dedicated to Ransom.

Andrew Lytle's contribution to fiction can therefore be called one of the first and finest fruits of the Fugitive legacy. Not only did his involvement with agrarianism and his intense connection with the South give him his subject, but the continued support of the former Fugitives and their personal and professional associates nurtured his writing of and essays about fiction.

12. Warren to Lytle, November 12, 1935, Lytle Papers; Warren to Lytle, January 28, 1936, *Southern Review* Papers.

13. Young and Sarcone, eds., *Tate-Lytle Letters*, 144.

14. Ransom to Lytle, January 20, 1932, Lytle Papers.

From the beginning, Lytle's fiction was an intensive experiment in point of view, operating on the principle that an impersonal distance existed between author and narrator. Typical for this group of storytellers, Lytle at first favored first person narration and then gradually came to prefer the more flexible Jamesian center of revelation, which he later called the "roving." In general, Lytle succeeded in this strategy, which kept his fiction from lapsing into the rhetorical stridency that almost certainly alienated readers unsympathetic to "the cause." In Lytle's earliest stories and first novel he was committed to but chafing under the restraints of tightly focused points of view. "Old Scratch in the Valley" had, in Mark Lucas's opinion, two major defects: its somewhat "clumsy" point of view and the fact that it "strains . . . under the contrary demands of Agrarian polemics and the Muse."[15] "Jericho, Jericho, Jericho" is, however, an outstanding example of a deliberately straitened perspective. Almost stream of consciousness, the narrative emerges entirely from Kate McGowan's sequence of thoughts and impressions on the evening of her death, a reverie broken only by dialogue, real and remembered, with her dead husband, her grandson Edwin, and his fiancée Eva Callahan.

When each of his novels was in process, Lytle was supported and challenged by Tate's and Gordon's comments on point of view. On May 3, 1935, Lytle wrote to inform "General" Tate that he was presently "getting shet of an essay [either a review of *Follow the Furies* by Eleanor Carroll Chilton or *R. E. Lee* by D. S. Freeman for the *Southern Review*] before I begin the novel [*The Long Night*] and research."[16]

Lytle's donnée was given him in 1933 by fellow Agrarian Frank Owsley, a true account of how Owsley's great-uncle Dink laid upon Owsley's father (not Owsley, as Robert Penn Warren later erroneously reported) the task of completing a vendetta against the men who killed Dink's father. The Owsley saga begins shortly before the Civil War and continues until the death of Uncle Dink and his passing of the torch to his relative. Lytle at first intended to turn the Owsley material into a "fictionalized biography" similar to *Forrest*, but as the work progressed, he gradually came to realize that the facts should be instead the raw material for a novel.[17]

As a series of letters from Owsley to Lytle makes evident, Lytle's change of mind led to a rather serious misunderstanding with Owsley, who thought

15. Lucas, *Southern Vision*, 52–53.

16. Young and Sarcone, eds., *Tate-Lytle Letters*, 97.

17. Ibid., 4. Frank Owsley was the author of "The Irrespressible Conflict" in *I'll Take My Stand*.

the project was to be a collaboration. During the fall of 1935, after reading Lytle's manuscript version, Owsley wrote a detailed commentary, mixing lavish praise with constructive criticism. His letter of November 25 calls "the first 41 pages . . . perfect," the next few pages "strained," the "section which develops the neighborhood about Four Corners . . . much better," and the rest "mighty good." Like almost everyone who later commented on the novel, Owsley was enthusiastic about Lytle's depiction of the "wake" of Mr. Weaver—Lytle proved to be particularly skillful in "wake" stories— especially the part about the washing of Brother Macon's corpse; but Owsley warned Lytle against too much "comedy relief" in an otherwise serious tale. Owsley finished the letter with promises of more material, including accounts of Pleasant McIvor's funeral and of "the assumption of leadership by *Dink*," neither of which turned out to suit Lytle's eventual design.[18]

No doubt sensing that Owsley would resent his assumption of control in the cause of imaginative license, Lytle apparently avoided further consultation with his "collaborator" from spring of 1936 on, offending Owsley, who, as he wrote on November 25, 1935, had actually attempted twice to write the story himself some years earlier but abandoned the task when "both efforts were a flop." In the fall of 1936, when the novel was near publication, Owsley had outlined in detail his understanding of their agreement, including his early desire to write "two or three chapters—dealing with matters which I considered myself fairly well acquainted with." A second letter of October 3, 1936, poignantly conveys Owsley's distress and embarrassment upon realizing that, contrary to what he had planned and announced to friends and family, he had been left out of the project entirely until the book was in press.[19]

Eventually, Lytle patched up the quarrel with a letter dated August 1936 and published with the novel on September 5 of the same year. It not only expresses gratitude to Owsley for his "help and suggestions" but also states how Lytle decided to write a historical novel rather than a fictionalized history. When life is transmuted into art, says Lytle, "it is impossible, I believe, even if it is desirable, to make a fiction adhere too strictly to life." Thus the "long night" of Pleasant McIvor "does not follow as closely as we had intended the performance of the original character." His contribution reduced from that of coauthor to informal source, Owsley could do nothing but express his "satisfaction" with the "fine and Lytlesque" spirit of the letter and his intention to "treat the matter as one of those things we hide and try to

18. Owsley to Lytle, October 3, 1936, November 25, [1935], Lytle Papers.
19. Owsley to Lytle, November 25, [1935], October 3, 1936, Lytle Papers.

forget." Apparently unaware of the novel's factual basis, John Crowe Ransom, in his *Southern Review* article "Fiction Harvest," faults the "prefatory letter at the front of the book" as a device better left for such "notoriously technical writers" as Henry James.[20]

The Tate-Gordon circle responded enthusiastically to Lytle's first novel. Writing to Lytle's publisher, D. L. Chambers of Bobbs-Merrill, Tate "blurbed" *The Long Night* as "at once the most powerful and the richest in substance of all contemporary novels about the South. There is in the book enough material for twenty novels." He offered to "review the book in a New York journal," in which case the blurb should not appear. Along with Lytle's *Forrest* and Gordon's *None Shall Look Back*, *The Long Night* constituted yet another product of the group's informally collaborative project, to write of the tragic and heroic war in which, as Gordon wrote Maxwell Perkins, "all the good people in the South were killed off." Ransom hailed it as "an original and amazing book" despite its "technical blunders." Both novels had, however, the bad luck to be published at about the same time as *Gone with the Wind*, dooming them to virtual obscurity in the public's consciousness. In Lytle's words, "I got the reviews and Margaret Mitchell got the jack."[21]

The Long Night followed "Jericho, Jericho, Jericho" as Lytle's next experiment in point of view. Realizing the need for more than one perspective, he framed the narrative in the contemporaneous, first person account of Lawrence McIvor, a recent graduate of "an Arkansas college" about to return home, marry, and "take up those responsibilities which a young man is eager to assume."[22] In chapter 2, the narrator becomes Pleasant McIvor, Lawrence's uncle, initiating a double frame as he begins his account—no mere entertainment but a purposeful message that will end in an urgent command: "Finish my task of revenge." Realizing the need for more narrative immediacy as well as for multiple perspectives, Lytle shifts once more, in part 3, into a third person point of view that can move freely from scene to scene and mind to mind.

It was Lytle's first experiment with the "roving" point of view, which he defined in "The Working Novelist and the Myth-making Process": "In the roving point of view it is only necessary, I feel, for one mind to dominate throughout the story, so that no matter where the view shifts, it might seem

20. Lytle to Owsley, August 1936, Owsley to Lytle, November 3, 1936, both in Lytle Papers; John Crowe Ransom, "Fiction Harvest," *Southern Review* 2 (Autumn 1936): 405.

21. Young and Sarcone, eds., *Tate-Lytle Letters*, 375; Waldron, *Close Connections*, 163; Ransom, "Fiction Harvest," 403.

22. Andrew Lytle, *The Long Night* (Indianapolis: Bobbs-Merrill, 1936), 14.

to belong to one central intelligence, that intelligence and sensibility alone equal to the fullest knowledge. The success of this depends upon how you write it, and especially upon the transitions from section to section. (The roving is no good written in chapters.)" In crafting his first novel, however, Lytle did not know how to accomplish that smooth elision from mind to mind; therefore the text "forgets about" its ingenious framework of narrators and narratee. For Ransom, who reviewed the novel for the *Southern Review*, the use of the double frame, or "fictional envelope around the story," is "not only impossible . . . [but] undesirable." The second narrator, who is "not of the author's mental stature," *must* be abandoned because he is "cramping the author's style."[23] Undeterred by Ransom's objection, Lytle was to continue experimenting with narrative "envelopes" throughout his fiction-writing career, with an increasing determination to emulate the "notoriously technical" James.

Gordon, Davidson, and Warren later agreed on the "power" of the novel and praised its rich detail. On May 23, 1943, Donald Davidson wrote the following encomium: "I was reading *The Long Night* once more with my students in advanced writing, and became again aware for the 100th, perhaps nth time, how you in this and other books, have brought a strength and fire to prose narrative that nobody else in our time has given it." And in his 1971 "Rediscovery" of *The Long Night*, Robert Penn Warren stated that despite Owsley's personal involvement in the story, Lytle was the perfect teller for the tale because he "knew the world of the plantation and of the deeper backcountry in the hills beyond the plantations. He knew the language, every shade of it by tone and phrase, every inflection, every hint of pain or poetry."[24]

Lytle's next novel, *At the Moon's Inn* (1941), was his longest and most frustrating project; without friends' encouragement, he might never have completed this most unusual story. One frustrating factor was the scope of Lytle's original plan: in January 1938, he wrote to D. L. Chambers his intention to compose a "series of novels which would be progressive in time," centered around the conquests of Hernando De Soto and unified by a common theme: "The new world will be seen as the old world's sin, even its destruction." Lytle's epic was to be another expression of his historical thesis that the ad-

23. Andrew Lytle, *The Hero with the Private Parts* (Baton Rouge: Louisiana State University Press, 1966), 190; Ransom, "Fiction Harvest," 405.

24. Davidson to Lytle, May 23, 1943, Lytle Papers; Robert Penn Warren, "Andrew Lytle's *The Long Night*: A Rediscovery," *Southern Review* n.s., 7 (1971): 133.

vance of greed-motivated expansion in the New World accompanied and par-
tially explained what he termed "the breakdown of Christendom." Lytle first
drafted a prefatory narrative, set in Peru, with De Soto as second in command
to Pizarro, and treating the Spanish conquest of the easily conquered, simple
"agrarian" Incas. De Soto, the able and virtuous young general (a sort of
Spanish version of Forrest) becomes wealthy, "corrupted by avarice," and
"accustomed to cruelty." The proposed "introductory novel" never grew beyond novella length and was eventually published as "Alchemy" in Ransom's
Kenyon Review in 1942, after having been rejected in 1941 because of its
length by Warren at the *Southern Review*.[25] *At the Moon's Inn* eventually appeared as a single volume, preceded by the publication in 1939 of "Fragment:
How Nuno de Tovar Came to Cross the Ocean Sea," in Kenyon College's
Hika.

At the Moon's Inn concerns De Soto's ill-fated invasion of what is now the
southeastern United States in 1539. The Spaniards find no gold and are eventually demoralized by their efforts to subdue a proud and noble Indian civili-
zation. Despite what appears to be a radical shift in subject matter, the novel
is cut from the same pattern as Lytle's southern novels. Nuno de Tovar, de
Soto's second in command, is the novel's principal narrator, in roughly the
same relationship to the heroic commander de Soto as Pleasant McIvor is to
Albert Sidney Johnson in part 4 of *The Long Night*. In his letter to D. L.
Chambers, Lytle defined his title: "It is a Spanish phrase, an old one, meaning literally to sleep out in the open. But it also has meaning for the book.
First, the moon is false; also it governs the tides which brought the Spaniards
to the new world; its goddess, Diana controls the fields and streams and for-
ests and all who violate her domain. This fits de Soto's career well." Lytle
tropes on the similarity between the Spaniards' quest for riches and the Western world's spiritual suicide.[26]

Lytle's letter to Tate on October 14, 1937, stated that he was planning to
"get down to it" as soon as his sister Polly's wedding festivities were over; but
the novel did not appear until 1941. By spring of 1938, Lytle was still deep
in his research. A letter to Tate speaks of a hurried trip through Arkansas,
Texas, and Louisiana to follow "De Soto's route" and of his plans to interview "Swanton of the Smithsonian" to "pick his brains" on this complicated

25. Lytle to D. L. Chambers, in Neal Polk, "Andrew Nelson Lytle: A Bibliography of His
Writings," *Mississippi Quarterly* 23 (1970): 453–54; Warren to Lytle, November 3, 1941, *Southern Review* Papers.

26. Polk, "Andrew Nelson Lytle," 456.

historical subject.[27] It was a hectic period that included his father's serious illness, his sister Polly's marriage, and, in June 1938, his own marriage to Edna Barker of Memphis.

The preliminary drafting of the novel went very slowly. At one point in 1940, Edna Lytle became so concerned about her husband's creative impasse that she wrote asking Tate to "write him if you think it's a good idea, you're anxious to see what he's done . . . or whatever's appropriate." Lytle's circle of friends offered the best encouragement they could. On March 30, 1939, Warren wrote from Baton Rouge, "I'm happy to hear also, from other sources, people who've heard part of De Soty [sic], that it's pretty damned good. But that, in my mind, is to be expected. I can't imagine what the book will be like, but I know it'll be good." In an undated letter, Gordon wrote, "I do hope . . . that De Soto doesn't ride you too hard"; and in January 1940, Tate wrote to "hope De Soto is going well" and to propose that Lytle apply to succeed him as teacher of creative writing at Princeton "after the publication of De Soto."[28]

The members of the Fugitive circle were prompt in their responses to the long-awaited novel. Writing on December 15, 1941, Ransom called *At the Moon's Inn* "brilliant" but wished Lytle had written up De Soto's entire military campaign "on the minutest scale possible," making it "a regular War and Peace." He also would have liked "a lot more reflection, philosophy, of his characteristic kind, as he goes along, a sense of the *whole time* in the intensive way." Davidson, on November 20, 1941, praised *At the Moon's Inn* as "wonderful piece of work . . . the best piece of historical fiction . . . that I have read" and "a work of art full of profound meaning as well as art in the more limited sense of craft." Always generous but judicial, Caroline Gordon used her second perusal of the novel to take both a forward and a backward look at Lytle's fiction: "I re-read The Long Night before reading At The Moon's Inn. It [*Night*] is even better than I had thought it. . . . But this second one is a much more powerful book." The same letter goes on to apprise Lytle of the book's flaws: "My chief criticism of your book is that it lacks organization. In some places you cannot see the forest for the trees. . . . That is partly because you have a lot more in your head that you want to get out than the average novelist has."[29]

27. Young and Sarcone, eds., *Tate-Lytle Letters*, 115–16, 119.

28. Young and Sarcone, eds., *Tate-Lytle Letters*, 157, 152–53; Warren to Lytle, March 30, 1939, Lytle Papers; Gordon to Lytle, [1942?], Lytle Papers.

29. Young and Core, eds., *Selected Letters of Ransom*, 288; Davidson to Lytle, November 20, 1941, and Gordon to Lytle, [1941?], both in Lytle Papers.

At the Moon's Inn was neither a critical nor a popular success. Most who read it were surprised to find Lytle abandoning his southern subject, and only years later did students of Lytle's fiction realize that the novel was a logical extension of his habitual jeremiad against the rape of an Agrarian culture. After this attempt at a didactic epic of "the new world . . . as the old world's sin" and experiencing such formidable problems of organization, Lytle wisely opted, in later novels, for tighter control using a single operative symbol to embody his myth; he chose the New Critical solution and the Jamesian-Flaubertian example that his circle of post-Fugitive fiction writers had, by then, more or less adopted as their own.

Their common fascination with point of view became, for Lytle, slightly more compelling than the Agrarian message, or at least a more artistic way to express it. The full force of his success was indicated by Ransom's decision to print "Alchemy" in the *Kenyon Review*. As Ransom wrote on August 29, 1942: "The story is tremendously good; everybody has said so. And much, much longer than anything we've ever printed. But we are enlarging, to a point nearly midway probably between the Southern's size and our old size. So we will just print your story as a sign of our picking up speed."[30]

Perhaps Lytle's most problematic, and therefore interesting, encounter with his characteristic theme is found in *A Name for Evil*, where the demonic desire to conquer and control, the Faustian spirit, is split between the narrator, a writer of essays and reviews like Lytle, and the ghost of Major Brent. Mark Lucas describes it as "an unflinching look at the ambiguities of a southern allegiance that craves the past," the same theme as Tate's "Ode to the Confederate Dead" and *The Fathers*. The narrator goes mad and eventually destroys—first psychically and then physically—his innocent bride, whom he sees as a pawn in his struggle with Major Brent for control of The Grove, a corrupted Eden which becomes their battleground. Perhaps unwittingly, Lytle made his first person narrator, Henry Brent, an alter ego for himself. As Lucas points out, Lytle was at the same time attempting to act out his Agrarian philosophy by rebuilding a farm near Portland, Tennessee, a venture that nearly drove his wife insane, as in the novel, and ended in failure. Seeing the connection, Ransom teasingly labeled the protagonist "an agrarian."[31] More important, he is a writer, like Lytle, who closes himself off in his study to write essays and reviews.

The composition of *A Name for Evil* was characterized by an unusual de-

30. Young and Core, eds., *Selected Letters of Ransom*, 299.
31. Lucas, *Southern Vision*, 90, 97–98; Young and Core, eds., *Selected Letters of Ransom*, 336.

gree of interaction between Lytle and his Fugitive friends, especially Tate. Lytle's planning for the book came soon after a short story, "The Guide" (later, at Tate's suggestion, "The Mahogany Frame"), was published by the *Sewanee Review* under Tate's editorship. Lytle took Tate's editorial counsel about reducing the "obscenity" in one aspect of the story and about clarifying its ending. As a letter of June 20, 1945, makes plain, Lytle had originally meant to center on a secondary subject, "the boy's inheritance, his romantic image of the ancestor," but decided instead to focus on the aspect of the young boy narrator's passage into manhood, as in Faulkner's "The Bear," through a hunting expedition with his uncle. As the letter continued, Lytle remarked, "The story I originally started has spent itself in this one. I will use the material probably in a book. I've got a short novel in mind and I will probably get on it this summer."[32]

As he progressed on the novel, Lytle tried out his ideas on Tate and received extensive and helpful advice. Lytle's letter of July 7, 1947, outlines the novel's thematic and technical dimensions: "I experimented with this: how far can you take the form of a certain book (*The Turn of the Screw*), deliberately take it and make something else . . . without having it said it is derivative, 'it is just another. . . .' " By July 29, 1947, Tate had read the manuscript and commented that he *was* "a little too conscious of the close parallel to *The Turn of the Screw*—even down to the last word, 'alone,' in the book. The story has very considerable power, and the tone is maintained throughout." Pronouncing the novel "powerful" and "morally convincing," Tate added that "it is nothing less than a triumph to have written it under the circumstances. What next?"[33]

Tate's comments came too late to affect revisions—the novel was published August 11, 1947, by Henry Holt—but were essentially echoed by Lytle's other knowledgeable readers. Ransom (in a previously cited letter) called *A Name for Evil* "a very big achievement" but objected that "the style and intention are not decided. . . . The speaker . . . is a bit garrulous, has a lot of *genera* commentary about things. . . . But slowly the book got hold of me. The latter half of it is cumulative & powerful." Ransom finally pronounced *A Name for Evil* "a great book with one reservation: I wish it could have sat and got one more revision." Also on September 8, 1947, Robert Penn Warren wrote to express his "many thanks for the book. . . . It is a brilliant conception and in the second half of the book seems to be brilliantly

32. Young and Sarcone, eds., *Tate-Lytle Letters*, 205–8.
33. Ibid., 211–13.

carried out." Warren found, however, that "the first part of the book disturbed me somewhat. I don't know that I cold [*sic*] document this by chapter and verse, but I feel that it is somewhat ambiguous stylistically." Warren tactfully added that "there is enough in the bank [i.e., the book] for me to afford the reservations" and wanted to know what Lytle was "up to next"—he hoped a "populous book . . . with lots of space to develop and turn around in," more in the "true line" of *The Long Night*.[34] Lytle allowed himself such scope in *The Velvet Horn*.

Lytle's last and, by unanimous agreement, best novel was an exemplar extraordinary of how the Fugitive legacy could create a literary masterpiece out of the symbiosis of creative like minds. Tate's contribution to the novel is as crucial as Pound's input into Eliot's *Waste Land*.

By 1952, Tate was in the midst of composing his answer to *Four Quartets*, the long poem entitled *The Swimmers*. On November 17, Lytle sent Tate a long analysis of "The Buried Lake," commenting that the images, despite the "stiffness" of mere words—"in life they are nothing but counters"—are "fine," especially the "light-dark images" and the "sound-silence" ones, making "the reader specify as the Master [James] said to do." Lytle mentioned that he was working on "The Water Witch," a key incident with similar imagery, for *The Velvet Horn*. By 1953 he was "trying to get my central intelligence into the realm of the dead, in this instance history preceding the present action." After rereading Tate's essay "The Symbolic Imagination," on Dante's "Paradiso," Lytle thought he had "happened on something which might become a technical device able to obviate the clumsiness of backward-looking, the flashback etc."[35]

It was late in 1954 before Lytle was ready to send a portion of the manuscript for Tate's opinion. After two readings, Tate complained of "difficulty following the action and the relation of characters" but called the "water-witching and hunt-seduction-knifing" episodes "wonderful." To handle complicated "continuity," Tate advised Lytle to make "all the complicated family relationships perfectly plain at the outset . . . [by using] an extension of Faulkner's method in *As I Lay Dying*." Tate objected to Lytle's use of "extreme rural Southern idiom," with which "you and Red have gone rather wild" and not done as well as Elizabeth M. Roberts, Caroline Gordon, and Flannery O'Connor, who, though young, is "a master of it." Although Tate considered Jack

34. Young and Core, eds., *Selected Letters of Ransom*, 336; Warren to Lytle, September 8, 1947, Lytle Papers.

35. Young and Sarcone, eds., *Tate-Lytle Letters*, 229–30, 232.

Cropleigh's "flights of idiom, in the midst of 'educated' language . . . highly effective," he warned that "when you are in the mind of a character . . . or rather in whatever idiom he may conduct his interior monologue, I am sure that it should be represented on the page as straight prose, with only an occasional exception which one's sense of fitness alone can justify."[36]

Lytle retained the Sol Leatherbury monologues, the source of Tate's objection to dialect, which frame the entire novel, as well as Jack Cropleigh's "flights of idiom," but he apparently simplified the dialect and made the interior monologues less orthographically quirky, as Tate suggested. On December 11, 1954, Lytle wrote a lengthy reply to Tate's comments, summarizing the method that he sets forth more formally in his noted essay "The Working Novelist and the Mythmaking Process." In the writing process, Lytle reported that his need to keep the central revelation of the novel hidden had resulted in a structural dilemma, a "monologue within a monologue within a monologue" that took "a year to break down." He had been unwilling, however, to avoid the problem by resorting to the "dull[ness]" of straight chronological order."[37]

Late in 1954, Lytle was still in the throes of his Olympian struggle with point of view. On December 23, Tate suggested that Lytle's "practical problem" was still "the matter of the 'envelope,' the narrative within a narrative, even to three stages beyond the first narrator." He surmised that Lytle's "*pudeur*" had led him into "the snare of the first-person narrator, or a series of them. You let these various Masks speak for themselves because you feel that you ought not to take charge of them." Having good reasons for avoiding such authorial intrusion, Lytle expressed surprise, in his January 5, 1955, letter, that Tate would call the segments "envelopes": "I had thought to begin on the periphery and move towards the center increasing the tension until it narrowed toward the climax. Surely didn't get the feeling they were envelopes. Each segment is separate, whether it is an action or not." Tate had also faulted the novel for its "absence of a plot structure; and as our old friend Aristotle said, a plot is an action, not a quality. You seem to me to have a group of 'confessions,' each character exhibiting his inner quality, but this quality is not being moved toward a resolution." On January 5, Lytle retorted that "our old friend Aristotle" was "talking about plays" and of plots already known by the audience.[38]

Lytle was not thinking, as Tate was, of an envelope, an enclosing structure,

36. Ibid., 238–39.
37. Ibid., 240.
38. Ibid., 243–45.

but of a horn, a conical, spiraling, opening form. Perhaps a little ahead of his time—and certainly more sophisticated about a narrative strategy than Tate—Lytle finally completed his masterpiece. By partly acting upon and partly disregarding Tate's advice, Lytle brought his use of the "roving" to a high level of skill.

Perhaps because of its innovative qualities, *The Velvet Horn* did not bring forth the usual show of support from the Fugitive network. Lytle at this time had such high hopes for the commercial success of the novel that he dared to sever his long-standing connection with Bobbs-Merrill and gave the book to David McDowell, a Vanderbilt graduate who was energetically functioning as managing editor of Obolensky Press. McDowell, who traveled from city to city peddling his wares at local bookstores and eliciting as many supportive recommendations as possible for his publications, subsequently asked Robert Penn Warren to provide a friendly review of the novel. He was astonished when Warren refused, explaining that after "meditating, off and on, on my relation to it . . . as a novel by an old and intimate friend and a fellow South-erner," he concluded that "either a blurb or a review from me would, in the long run, do more harm than good." He and "Eudora" had "blurbed" Eliza-beth Spencer's *A Voice at the Back Door* and been referred to as "the 'Southern gang' " or " 'southern clique.' " Convinced that "if Andrew's book is backed in the same way, the reaction will be even more violent for a good many rea-sons," he advised McDowell to "get some non-Southern backing." More-over, as Lytle wrote to Tate on June 5, 1957, Donald Davidson also refused McDowell's request for a blurb or review; Lytle later informed Tate that Da-vidson "hated" the book. The ever-loyal Tate apparently *did* supply McDow-ell with a blurb, a copy of which he sent to Lytle on May 28, 1957, with a note that "it says only 1/10 of what I think about *The Velvet Horn.*" After a couple of readings, Tate wrote that he hoped the book was "still selling" and believed that despite his friends' reluctance, it had received "the right kind of reviews for the purpose." In his opinion, "there [was] nothing like it in Southern writing." *The Velvet Horn* was to be Lytle's last novel.

Lytle continued to function as an able editor, serving both before and after Allen Tate as editor of the *Sewanee Review*. He went on to distinguish himself in the area of criticism but not in the manner of Ransom, Warren, or Brooks. In his preface to *The Hero with the Private Parts*, Allen Tate called him a reader and a translator rather than a critic.[39] Lytle's essays have nevertheless greatly expanded his impact on fiction writing in the last half of the century.

39. Warren to David McDowell, May 27, 1957, Lytle Papers; Young and Sarcone, eds., *Tate-Lytle Letters*, 263, 282, 262, 265–66; Tate, Preface to Lytle, *The Hero with the Private Parts*, xv.

Andrew Lytle left his mark on modern American fiction as much through his teaching as through the novels and stories he produced. He served as an active proliferator of the kind of fiction that the former Fugitives approved of and, more important, were willing to publish in the journals they edited. While at Florida, Lytle received a letter from Ransom, at the *Kenyon*, urging him, "Don't hesitate to ask the good young writers you have there, for me, to send us stories. We have a hard time finding fiction of any distinction."[40] Unfortunately, the historical novel, métier of Lytle and Caroline Gordon, had fallen from popularity among common readers and acclaim from critics—both of whom were weary of plantation and Civil War plots in the wake of the more popular novel by the lady from Atlanta, Margaret Mitchell. It would, however, be unfortunate if the name of Andrew Lytle and his masterpiece *The Velvet Horn* should disappear from view and be denied places of honor in the literary annals of this century.

40. Ransom to Lytle, March 25, 1957, Lytle Papers.

10 / Caroline Gordon: Fiction in the Family

Because of his close personal and literary relationship with Caroline Gordon, Andrew Lytle has been one of the best commentators on her beginnings as a writer of fiction. In his foreword to Sally Wood's *Southern Mandarins*, Lytle summarized the formidable conflicts that Gordon faced, even accepted, in her attempt to succeed as a writer: "A woman who writes either fiction or verse, particularly if she is married, has problems a man doesn't have. Keeping a house makes daily demands. If she has a child, her responsibilities obviously increase. Neglect of her work or child can make her wretched, and the demands of each usually conflict." Lytle's apparent condescension actually indicates his admiration for a contemporary whose eleven-year apprenticeship took place, like his, during the Great Depression, when struggling writers were forced to band together to survive. Under those circumstances, it was natural that Allen Tate, as a former Fugitive, should gather around him a "family" of writers who had been born and educated in the South. At a 1985 symposium in Clarksville, Tennessee, Lytle recalled that there were advantages to the group approach to creative writing: "We were becoming artists. . . . We had a very fine accidental community. We had a common background and inheritance; we understood things the same way."[1]

1. Andrew Lytle, foreword to Wood, ed., *Southern Mandarins*, 5; Waldron, *Close Connections*, 85.

A thorough evaluation of Gordon's work necessitates separating her from her role as Allen Tate's wife. In this attempt, Gordon herself was a formidable hindrance. Her authorized biographer, Veronica A. Makowsky, theorizes that Gordon became the "good artist she was and was prevented . . . from becoming the great artist she might have been" in large part by her deep-seated belief that in the universe into which she was born, "men were the creators" and "the woman artist is an anomaly." Makowsky has admitted that Gordon grew up, became a writer, and functioned in the literary world harboring a "lifelong distrust of the quality of women mentors, and women's abilities in general" and a reliance on a "succession of male mentors"—her father, Professor Frank Roy Gay at Bethany College, Tate, and Ford Madox Ford—who "at once enabled her and yet crippled her by her dependence on their opinion."[2]

As Gordon matured and enjoyed success as an artist in her own right, however, she enjoyed the status of peer and, in her fiction, superiority to most of the former Fugitives. Ann Waldron, another biographer, titled the first chapter of *Close Connections: Caroline Gordon and the Southern Renaissance* "Benfolly, the Summer of 1937"—the summer of Ford, Robert Lowell, the dewpond, and the tent—and devoted her second to an account of how Gordon was introduced to the Fugitives and, subsequently, to the literary world as "one of their reviewers." Rose Ann C. Freistat has argued that Gordon may be called a "woman of letters" because she, like the four major Fugitives, was "devoted to scholarly, critical, and 'creative' or fictive writing" and because "her sense of vocation was reinforced by her close associations with the leaders of the Fugitives and Agrarian groups, by her friendship with Ford Madox Ford, and by Tate's belief in the importance of the realm of letters."[3]

There can be no doubt that Caroline Gordon's career was both enabled and inhibited by her participation in the Fugitive legacy. Waldron remarks that "she acted like a feminist, [but] talked like a southern ninny"—as rabid a southern conservative and apologist as Lytle and as thoroughly conditioned by southern traditions as any member of her maternal Meriwether dynasty.[4] Yet one discovers in her letters to fellow writers and her essays about the art of fiction a confident, adamant sense of self and artistic worth and a well-thought-out, if inherited, theory of fiction. More than any other person in

2. Veronica A. Makowsky, *Caroline Gordon: A Biography* (New York: Oxford University Press, 1989), 3–4, 33, 88.

3. Waldron, *Close Connections*, 26; Rose Ann C. Freistat, *Caroline Gordon as Novelist and Woman of Letters* (Baton Rouge: Louisiana State University Press, 1984), 1.

4. Waldron, *Close Connections*, 357.

the post-Fugitive network, Gordon became an influential teacher of creative writing and mentor to young writers.

Though her novels have their undeniable weaknesses as well as strengths, she wrote nine of them, and she got them published, circulated, and reviewed on a national level. Like every other writer of the Fugitive legacy, her publication and reception owed much to sponsorship by the former Fugitives and their contacts in the literary world. Gordon perhaps did her best work as a short story writer, despite her frustration with the form, and, partly because of her membership in the network, her stories were published in the former Fugitives' literary magazines and anthologized in their textbooks, assuring a longer life for her stories than her novels.

Like Lytle, Gordon was a student of the Jamesian-Flaubertian school of fiction. Like Henry James, she soon became, as Waldron says, "almost obsessed with point of view." She admired James's "central intelligence," the superior mind placed at the center of action. "The central intelligence, she told her classes, combined all the advantages of the other three possible points of view—the omniscient narrator, the first-person narrator, and the author identifying with one character." Along with Porter and Lytle, Gordon made the Jamesian novel of experience and the use of the Jamesian restricted method of revelation the hallmark of post-Fugitive fiction. As Lytle later put it, "It was . . . Henry James, to whom Caroline looked as master."[5]

Gordon's introduction to the Fugitive group and thereby to her future husband and mentor has the quality of a romantic novel. As a very young writer for the *Chattanooga News*, Gordon had written an article entitled "U.S. Best Poets Here in Tennessee," which surveyed several little literary magazines then springing up in the South. In preparation, she had written to John Crowe Ransom requesting information on the Fugitive poets, and in the article, she rated them the best of the lot. Ransom wrote Allen Tate on February 23, 1923, that "when I get copies tomorrow I'll send you one of the Saturday's Chattanooga News containing a Fugitive story in the magazine supplement. Written by one Miss Gordon, who has developed quite a fondness for us, and incidentally is kin to some of my kinfolks in Chattanooga."[6] The following summer, she just happened to be visiting her parents in Guthrie, Kentucky, where her father was occupying a Campbellite Church pulpit, at the

5. Ibid., 250–51; Lytle, introduction to Wood, ed., *Southern Mandarins*, 7.
6. Cowan, *Fugitive Group*, 98. Gordon's early career as a journalist is discussed at length in Nancylee Jonza's biography, *The Underground Stream: The Life and Art of Caroline Gordon* (Athens: University of Georgia Press, 1995).

same time Allen Tate was visiting Robert Penn Warren at his parents' home. A friendship between Tate and Gordon flourished, no doubt in part because of her knowledge of and interest in the Fugitives as new men on the literary scene. By the time of their marriage in 1924, Gordon had fastened on what Waldron calls her two lifelong "obsessions": Allen Tate and the writing of fiction.

Gordon's determination to become a writer, however, predated her relationship with Allen Tate. By 1929, she had produced two unpublishable manuscripts. One she destroyed after Allen responded negatively, and the other's fate is uncertain.[7] Gordon first gained attention by publishing two short stories, "Summer Dust" and "The Long Day." Significantly, these all-important acceptances came not from the Fugitive-run reviews but from *Gyroscope*, a little magazine published in California by Yvor Winters. Thereafter, because she was a published writer of fiction, she could assume a position of greater authority within the male-dominated Fugitive network than if her métier had been poetry or criticism.

It was also beneficial for the Tates and Lytle to buy Benfolly and move south to the source of Caroline's fictional material. The change in venue isolated Gordon from many of the distractions that had limited her in New York and Paris and with a smaller, more homogeneous literary community that would be implemental to her writing in what Makowsky calls her "most productive decade."[8] Here in the Tennessee-Kentucky border country where she grew up and where Benfolly is located were the settings for her first four novels. And although she later resided mostly in the North, her stories and novels, particularly *The Women on the Porch* (1944), *The Strange Children* (1951), and *The Malefactors* (1956), owed their settings and situations to the period in Gordon's life when she lived and wrote in her home country.

During 1930 and 1931, Gordon completed two more stories and, with Ford Madox Ford's encouragement, the novel *Penhally*. The stories, "Mr. Powers" and "The Ice House," constitute for Makowsky Gordon's "own analysis of postbellum South, perhaps her fictive counterpart to *I'll Take My Stand*" in that they deal with racial and class conflict.[9] Maxwell Perkins published "Mr. Powers" for *Scribner's*, in November 1931. By then Gordon had found in Perkins her own publisher—without depending on Allen's friends—and a very practical-minded mentor. Moreover, after Perkins came through

---

7. Makowsky, *Caroline Gordon*, 71.
8. Ibid., 88.
9. Ibid., 99.

with a $500 advance on *Penhally*, Gordon was forced to meet his deadline for completion of the novel. In July 1931, after three years in making, *Penhally* was sent to the publisher.

When the novel was near completion, Gordon allowed her husband and friends to pass on the final version. Tate and others objected to the title, but Gordon stood firm, citing such formidable precursors as Austen, Dickens, and Scott. When they warned her that the comparisons were unflattering to her and suggested *Llewellyn's Choice*, Perkins sided with Gordon and took over the job of mentoring in the final stages. As always, Allen Tate clearly played a part, albeit that of inspiring nuisance. In a letter to Sally Wood on May 30, 1931, Gordon described how they "worked together" on the final chapter: "I went to pieces pretty badly the other night. I got frightened when Allen told me plainly that the last chapter, the climax that I had built up so fondly simply would not do. My hands got to shaking so I couldn't even hit the keys. Finally I told Allen he had to write it then if it didn't suit him. He wrote a few pages and I got interested trying to fix up what he had written—it seemed to me so impossible—that I worked out of the fit." This incident could serve as a paradigm of what living with Tate and his circle did to and for Caroline Gordon. As was the custom in the Fugitive circle, one submitted one's writing to the rough scrutiny of the group. The only trouble was that they were less knowledgeable than she in the writing of fiction. Not even Lytle, still five years away from his first novel, would be much help. Therefore, at Benfolly, without Ford at her elbow, Caroline had to trust her own genius, spurred on negatively by their inexpert advice and the need to fulfill her commitment to her publisher and to herself. But conversely, an honest reader of Gordon's fiction surely must admit that endings were never her long suite. Allen Tate, *il miglior critico*, astutely detected the weakness and caused Caroline Gordon to make revisions that were probably beneficial. Obviously proud of the final result, Tate wrote to Lytle on July 28, 1931: "Miss Carrie's page proofs are done, and we expect the book soon. I read it consecutively for the first time. My God, but it's grand!"[10] Despite proofreading by Tate and a friend, Marion Henry, however, there were enough errors in the published version to cause Caroline considerable distress.

Whatever its weaknesses, *Penhally* shows the careful attention to structure and point of view that were typical for the fiction writers of the Fugitive legacy. From Ford, Gordon derived the idea of using time shifts as structural

10. Makowsky, *Caroline Gordon*, 102; Wood, ed., *Southern Mandarins*, 78; Young and Sarcone, eds., *Tate-Lytle Letters*, 48.

devices. Naturally, Ford would and did praise the episodic structure of *Penhally*, how it "progresses forward in action and back in memory so that the sort of shimmer that attaches to life attaches also to the life of the book." As Freistat points out, "The episodic structure, by creating an interplay of time, makes history ever present." Small wonder that *Penhally* did not sell like *Gone with the Wind*, a novel that dramatizes the same forces but along more Darwinian lines, wherein the toughest-minded characters survive. *Penhally*, ends, as Gordon wrote to Katherine Anne Porter, with catastrophe, including "two suicides, fratricide and one man shot from ambush by the Yankees." Porter replied that *Penhally* was "a monstrous fine book. An impossible kind of book to write but she did it! . . . Such knowledgeable scenes, one episode going on to the next so decisively. I'm interested in the technical things because I'm finding it almost an impossible problem."[11]

As a not entirely successful experiment with point of view, as well as a deliberately fragmented plot structure, *Penhally* is a true example of the modernist novel. Lytle wrote that "the central meaning of the book is its complexity, striking like alternating current, back and forth among the characters, the situation, the historic changes." Writing at a time when authorial objectivity was highly valued, Gordon would not elect what she would later call the "panoramic technique" of the omniscient narrator; to do so would "tempt" her, as author, to "tell the reader what happened and to leave the actual happening vague."[12] Like Lytle, she would most often choose the "roving narrator" (omniscient narrator concealed).

After *Penhally*, Gordon felt "pregnant," having conceived the basic idea for *The Garden of Adonis*. The gestation was long and complicated, and in the interim she wrote another unique sort of novel, the semiautobiographical *Aleck Maury, Sportsman*, and several stories. One, "Mr. Powers," is closely related to *Adonis* in plot and character; another, "The Captive," is based on the journals of Jinny Wiley, who was captured and held for some time by Indians (Gordon would return to the frontier and the subject of Indian captivity in *Green Centuries*). In both texts, savages brutally murder the woman's children while the husband and father are off on unnecessary expeditions. Makowsky draws an analogy between Jinny Wiley and Gordon, "lost in a forest of self-

---

11. Ford Madox Ford, "A Stage in American Literature," *Bookman* 74 (1931): 375; Freistat, *Caroline Gordon*, 56; Waldron, *Close Connections*, 93; Isabel Bayley, ed., *Letters of Katherine Anne Porter* (New York: Atlantic Monthly Press, 1990), 72–73.

12. Andrew Lytle, "Caroline Gordon and the Historical Image," in *The Hero with the Private Parts*, 162; Caroline Gordon and Allen Tate, eds., *The House of Fiction: An Anthology of the Short Story with Commentary* (New York: Scribner's, 1950), 621–22.

doubt" about her acceptance and status in the world of letters that so readily accepted her husband and his male colleagues.[13]

"The Captive" had a troubled writing and publication history. In 1932, Perkins rejected the story on the grounds that it lacked "enough regular story interest." Tate wrote a letter of strong protest to Perkins, to which Gordon signed her name. In her name, he wrote, " 'I am not a talented amateur; I am as mature as I shall ever be. . . . I am not only at my best right now; I am at my best because I am one of the few writers in this generation who have something to write about.' " But Gordon was only briefly unable to defend herself to Perkins. As Waldron records, Gordon quickly replied to his molli- fying letters asserting that "The Captive" was "the best writing I can do," after which she nonetheless revised the story, using Perkins's comments, and published it in the *Hound and Horn*. It became the lead story in her first col- lection.[14]

Once again, the advantages of being married to Allen Tate came into play, however, for as a letter from Tate to Lytle clearly indicates, Lincoln Kirstein, editor of the *Hound and Horn*, was a Tate intimate who readily published Agrarian writing.[15] Without the opportunities to submit her work to editors who were inclined, because of her connections, to look seriously at what she submitted, the disadvantages of sponsorship would be moot.

In 1971, nearly thirty years later, Gordon discussed her writing of "The Captive" with Catherine Baum and Floyd Watkins. She reported that her in- spiration had come not only from reading William Essley Connelley's "won- derful" book (*The Founding of Harman's Station with an Account of the Indian Captivity of Mrs. Jinny Wiley. . . .*) but also from other captivity narratives. Among them was the real-life story of how Donald Davidson's great-great- grandfather's first wife was captured by Indians and taken to Canada, where her husband found her working in a boardinghouse.[16] Gordon and her inter- viewers wondered why Davidson had never used this material in his own writing, but given the Fugitives' resistance to regional frontier material, it is not so surprising. Ironically, she actually found her source in the Vanderbilt library. Andrew Lytle's "Jericho, Jericho, Jericho" was her source for the game "Hog-Drovers," which Jinny's children play to take their mind off the

---

13. Makowsky, *Caroline Gordon*, 107.

14. Ibid., 108; Waldron, *Close Connections*, 98–99.

15. Young and Sarcone, eds., *Tate-Lytle Letters*, 80.

16. Catherine Baum and Floyd Watkins, "Caroline Gordon and the Captive," *Southern Re- view* n.s., 7 (1971): 448.

Indians; it might also have contributed to her depiction of a woman who, abandoned or tortured by males, is both physically and psychically a survivor.

Gordon remembered that she "suffered more writing it than any story I ever wrote," that after finishing it she had to "coddle herself" by making doll dresses for her daughter Nancy. The story grips the reader with its contrast between the laconic narrator and the horror of her account, which gives the story the objective tone of a documentary (she remembers the captivity narrative as "nearly finished" before she began her shaping of it). Jinny's account of how, on their trek to the Indian village, an Indian bashes her baby's brains out against a tree, is told with remarkable *sang froid*. Gordon's intent to make Jinny a simple but stoic character is made clear in two of Wiley's remarks: "I ain't too young to know my own mind" and "I'm a white woman, but I can't do nothing"—both directed to white men less heroic than she.[17]

For many readers the device backfires, however, when after her courageous escape, Jinny's first remark is "Lord God . . . I was lucky to git away from them Indians!" When Watkins (whose daughter had been highly amused by the ending) questioned Gordon about it, she recalled that Phelps Putnam, one of Allen's friends and a visitor to Benfolly during the summer of 1931, had advised her to cut it and end the story as soon as the narrator is inside the fort. Gordon replied to Watkins and Baum (at least one of whom liked the ending) that the remark is "characteristic" and "necessary to round it [the story] off." Jill Fitz-Piggott asserts that "Jinny's understatement . . . says less about her savior than it does about her style. Jinny doesn't need the bolster of boasts any more than Davy Crockett needs frills to fill out his tales."[18]

Like most of Gordon's stories, "The Captive" has held up well, being the first of her stories to be chosen for *Best Short Stories* and Linda Burton's choice for *Stories from Tennessee* (1983).[19]

While she was still struggling with *The Garden of Adonis*, Gordon's success thus far and future promise were rewarded by her receipt of a Guggenheim Fellowship in 1932, which enabled the Tates to live once more in France.

17. Ibid., 449; Caroline Gordon, *The Collected Short Stories of Caroline Gordon* (New York: Farrar, Straus & Giroux, 1981), 191, 196.

18. Waldron, *Close Connections*, 88; Baum and Watkins, "Caroline Gordon and the Captive," 458; Jill Fitz-Piggott, "The Dominant Chord and the Different Voice: The Sexes in Gordon's Stories," in *The Female Tradition in Southern Literature*, ed. Carol S. Manning (Chicago: University of Illinois Press, 1993), 211.

19. Wood, ed., *Southern Mandarins*, 133; Linda Burton, ed., *Stories from Tennessee* (Knoxville: University of Tennessee Press, 1983).

After a horrible January in a cold Paris flat, during which both Allen and Caroline endured bouts of illness, she wrote her most famous and most frequently anthologized story, "Old Red." In late January 1933, Gordon wrote to Wood, "I finished my story about Allen and Dad. I'll enclose a copy if I can get around to correcting it up enough to have it make sense. It's not one of my best, just a kind of trick."[20] Based on her father's life as a nomadic sportsman, the story led to a spate of others on the same subject, as well as to *Aleck Maury, Sportsman*. It was, as well, a first attempt to produce fiction out of the conflict between her two polar attractions: her southern home and family on one side and her husband and the literary world on the other.

Although in Paris Gordon was discouraged about her work—writing stories never brought her much feeling of accomplishment—and although a flurry of writing projects got in one another's way, the Aleck Maury pieces brought Gordon much-deserved success. On January 22, 1933, she wrote to Sally Wood, " 'Old Red' is in Sept. *Criterion* and will be in December Scribner's—two versions. Take your choice. In the Scribner version I lopped off the ending, finishing it up with the fox taking to earth. You won't like it but I always was worried for fear I had an anticlimax there."[21] Though she preferred to be known as a novelist, getting published in a respected English journal was still nothing to sneeze at. In America, "Old Red" was reprinted in the prestigious *O. Henry Prize Winning Stories of 1934* and was awarded second honors for that year. Despite Gordon's initial misgivings about this project, it became her representative in *Understanding Fiction*.

By the time she began *Aleck Maury, Sportsman*, Gordon was almost prepared to turn it into a memoir, but her instinct for objectivity caused her to make the novel quite different from the story. While most of the Aleck Maury stories concern an aging protagonist, the novel that bears his name begins in his youth. While the story sets up strong tension between Maury and the family who would restrict his freedom, the novel moves in a different ironic continuum, a restrained, Horatian sort that exists within Maury, between the Appollonian element of classical study and accompanying responsibilities and the Dionysian urge to range free, to fish and hunt and thus cheat time—*Carpe diem* both literal and figurative. The father who in "Old Red" bores his children by reciting either his own poetry or Shakespeare's at the dinner table is a classical scholar in the novel, who marches along to the beat of "Arma virumque cano" and believes that teaching his son the classics is

---

20. Wood, ed., *Southern Mandarins*, 133.
21. Ibid., 153.

"doing the boy a favor."[22] Old Red's demise is not mentioned in the story. Aleck's wife, Molly, unlike the Mary of "Old Red," shows little tendency to restrain him; his daughter Sara (or Sally)—Gordon was to use the same name and nickname in *Green Centuries*—adores him and wants to take care of him. In the novel she *is* a newspaperwoman, like Gordon before the Fugitives; but in the later Aleck Maury stories, she merely paints a little and leaves the celebration to her husband, Steven.

In many respects, *Aleck Maury, Sportsman*—the novel she did not mean to write—is the central text for Gordon, a source not just for the four Aleck Maury stories but for other stories such as "Those Burning Eyes" and for bits and pieces of *Green Centuries*, *The Strange Children*, and, indirectly, *The Glories of Hera* and *The Malefactors* as well. In "Old Red," Gordon created her fictional family, all based on her own—her father, herself, Allen, Nancy—objectified, as a good New Critic would demand, but deeply personal and profoundly interrelated in ultimate concerns. In the end, it is a much lighter story than either "Old Red" or the other short stories about Maury.

In a most remarkable cooperative effort, Gordon worked on the novel not only with her father, who was persuaded to dictate from memory, but with her husband and whatever friends were around during that autumn of 1933. Gordon's father, James Maury Morris Gordon, at first refused to take part in the project, not wishing to be tied down as he had been during his years as a preacher. But Caroline tricked him into cooperating by pursuing him to the Hill Side Inn at Walling, Tennessee, on the Caney Fork River, where she "got him to talking" about himself while she listened. Once he awakened in the early morning, jumped up, and yelled "Caroline! This is good, take it down." Early in 1934 she wrote to Lytle to report that "this place was a regular book factory the last two days. Cath [Wilds] and Allen and I went down to Caney Fork a few days ago and Dad read the manuscript while I wrote some sections that hadn't been tackled yet and Allen revised and Cath copied. I think the inmates of the hillside inn thought we were crazy, shouting at each other 'My God, you can't have that,' and 'Don't you know you tie the fly on the hook?' "[23]

Aleck Maury, Sportsman was published in October 1934, dedicated to Ford Madox Ford, and defended, in a letter to him, as follows: "I'm a little sorry now because you will not enjoy reading it. It marches but is flimsy in spots and you will see how I could have made a really good book out of it if I hadn't

22. Caroline Gordon, *Aleck Maury, Sportsman* (New York: Scribner's, 1934), 15.

23. Makowsky, *Caroline Gordon*, 121–22; Gordon to Lytle, [1934], Lytle Papers.

been so harried." Katherine Anne Porter called it "magnificent," saying that it "read 'as if a gentleman of the Old South who knows not only Latin and Greek but English had sat down and written his memoirs' "; Howard Baker said that, contrary to his reservations, Caroline Gordon was competent to write from a masculine point of view.[24]

In the spring 1935 issue of the *Southwest Review* (not long before it merged with the *Southern Review*), Robert Penn Warren wrote a review of *Aleck Maury, Sportsman*, with the general title "The Fiction of Caroline Gordon." Calling her talent *"intensive* rather than *extensive,"* he compared her most favorably with Sinclair Lewis and Evelyn Scott. Summarizing her achievement from *Penhally* to *Aleck Maury*, Warren praised the "special power" that through "sudden and illuminating perception . . . can re-order a body of experience." Predictably Warren favored her adoption of a "discipline of composition on a more objective basis" (unlike Ernest Hemingway, for example), so that "the success of the book is that it is not Caroline Gordon's novel, but, after all, the autobiography of Aleck Maury." Years later, in introducing her *Collected Short Stories*, Warren still called it "her finest novel."[25]

The same year, living in Memphis, where Allen taught at Southwestern College, Gordon followed up *Aleck Maury, Sportsman* with "B from Bullsfoot," published in *Scribner's*, and three more Aleck Maury stories: "One More Time," "To Thy Chamber, Sweet," and "The Last Day in the Field."

In 1935, Robert Penn Warren convened a conference in Baton Rouge that was attended by "forty men and women of letters"—including Tate, Gordon, John Gould Fletcher, John Peale Bishop, John Donald Wade, and Frank Owsley—along with such editors as Lambert Davis of the *Virginia Quarterly Review*, Ford Madox Ford, and lesser known figures in the publishing world. The recorded proceedings of a session on the publication of books by southern writers included mention of Caroline Gordon and her recently published but commercially unprofitable novel. Fletcher emphasized the need for a press that would be willing to "publish regional books" such as Stark Young's *So Red the Rose* and *Aleck Maury, Sportsman*, which "deals with a way of life in a milieu" that is little known and thus not likely to attract a commercial publisher. Gordon's only remark, "The Southern writer has no chance in New York for such contact with fellows of his craft," came later in the discussion

24. Waldron, *Close Connections*, 140, 14; Porter to Gordon, spring 1934, Papers of Katherine Anne Porter, Special Collections, University of Maryland Libraries, College Park, Md.

25. Robert Penn Warren, "The Fiction of Caroline Gordon," *Southwest Review* 20 (1935): 6–7, 10; Warren, introduction to Gordon, *Collected Short Stories*, xx.

and reflected her intense frustration at what she regarded as the dismal failure of *Maury*, as well, perhaps, as a feeling that as a woman writer she had little impact. A letter to Sally Wood called the conference an encounter of "two armed camps," "the Agrarians and those who thought there were too many Agrarians present."[26] By the summer of 1935, Caroline Gordon had achieved recognition as a professional writer—but not the fame and fortune she so desired.

One permanent contribution of the Baton Rouge conference was that it launched the *Southern Review*, with which Gordon would have a relationship that would bring her mixed blessings. Her first story in the *Review*, "A Morning's Favor," appeared in the second issue and concerned a rural preacher, like her father, who bore the familiar name of Mr. Ransom. In the short, seven-year life of the *Southern Review*'s first series under Brooks and Warren, Gordon would publish four stories and one review and have one of her novels (*None Shall Look Back*) reviewed.

By no means were all of her experiences with the editors happy. After her debut with "A Morning's Favor," Gordon sent "At the Cannon's Mouth," only to have it returned because, as Robert Penn Warren wrote on May 29, 1936, "a reader would find no substantial center of a story." Her second acceptance was for "The Women on the Battlefield," published in volume 2, number 3, for winter 1937; but before it was finally ready for publication, she went through a round of editorial changes. Warren wrote to Gordon on November 17, 1936, asking her to take out the first three and one-half pages, which, in his judgment, were "not well coordinated with the rest, and are out of scale." In sharp reply, Gordon informed Warren that she was "used to editors saying 'cut out five pages and I'll take it.' " In comparison, the *Southern Review* editors were at least "soft-spoken" in their arbitrary directives. She added that she would soon be sending "The Brilliant Leaves," calling it "the last story I shall ever write." She could "face a lifetime of incessant toil at writing novels but a short story takes as much out of . . . me . . . as a novel and then [I] have to start again."[27]

Warren also rejected "The Brilliant Leaves" (which was later published by *Mademoiselle* in November 1937). On May 3, 1937, he wrote to say, lamely, that he and his fellow editors did not like the story but "can't define

26. "Conference on Literature and Reading in the South and Southwest, 1935," in Simpson, Olney, and Gulledge, eds., *The Southern Review and Modern Literature*, 49, 77; Wood, ed., *Southern Mandarins*, 185.

27. Warren to Gordon, May 29, November 17, 1936, Gordon to Warren, n.d. [1936], *Southern Review* Papers.

the basis of our dissatisfaction . . . [it] doesn't strike a satisfactory focus." He did, however, want to use "Old Red" or "Tom Rivers" in a projected collection of stories from the *Southern Review*. Warren wrote to Gordon on October 18, 1937, to say that they were keeping "Two Strong Men"; for some reason, the story never appeared.[28]

In June 1940, Brooks wrote to Warren concerning a story just received from Gordon: "Caroline's is obviously a piece out of her next novel. I think it's got some good stuff, though I think that the last detail of the torture doesn't get itself integrated, as least in terms of this context." Small wonder that Gordon found short stories so frustrating. Not only were they time-consuming and creatively exhausting, but they could quickly be rejected by editors who, though friendly, were apt to base their opinions on gut reactions rather than on firm critical principles. A despairing letter to Lytle chronicles the end of Gordon's relationship with the *Southern Review*: "I hurt Cleanth's feelings when he was here. I jumped on him about the way they have been turning my stuff down lately, with letters that might have been written by the editor of the Atlantic Monthly. 'This isn't quite it' or 'It doesn't quite jell' are the expressions that particularly infuriate me. . . . It doesn't really matter, except for the personal side, as I am not going to write any more stories." Fortunately, Gordon did not carry out this threat, and Warren was to include at least one of her stories in all of his and Brooks's anthologies. Warren's introduction to Gordon's *Collected Short Stories* (1981) calls her stories "dramatic examples of man in contact with man, and man in contact with nature; of living sympathy; of a disciplined style as unpretentious and clear as running water, but shot through with glints of wit, humor, pity, and poetry."[29]

The way Gordon wrote *None Shall Look Back* (1937) illustrates how proximity to those actively writing was much more energizing than privacy in a "room of her own." Still in Memphis on June 2, 1935, she informed Sally Wood that she had "written three chapters of The Cup of Fury. It doesn't seem to go very well when you examine it in detail. I can only hope it will be impressive in the mass. Anyhow I am going to barge through, paying very little attention to the writing of it." By July, however, she and Allen were at Cornsilk, the Lytle family farm in Alabama. Her enthusiastic letter to Wood attributed the spirit of the place to Lytle's father, who was the proprietor of "half a dozen farms" and also "specializes in making fancy desserts for din-

<hr />

28. Warren to Gordon, May 3, October 18, 1937, ibid.

29. Brooks to Warren, June 1940, ibid.; Gordon to Lytle, n.d., Lytle Papers; Warren, introduction to Gordon, *Collected Short Stories*, xiii.

ner" (at noon), coming in from the farm at 11:00 with two field hands and "shout[ing] for a quart of whipped cream." But more important for Gordon, she "never saw such a place for work as Cornsilk. The first morning I was there I walked as in a trance into a secluded corner of the dining room. I dug myself out a spot by removing several bushels of peanuts, medieval cuirass, three or four demijohns of cherry bounce etc., set up a card table in the spot thus cleared and almost without thinking began to write steadily. . . . Well, God moves in a mysterious way. . . . Writing there I produced fifteen thousand words in one week."[30] She added that she was "lifting sentences from . . . every place that I can find them," including John Wyeth's *Life of Forrest*; but her inspiration came from Andrew Lytle, involved at the same time with *The Long Night*, his Civil War novel. She fell in with Lytle's writing "routine": "breakfast, work, lunch, short nap, work, swim from five to six thirty, cocktail (one), supper, bed. Sleep like hell. Get up and go at it again." She was able to maintain that pace when they returned to Memphis that fall. By January 8, 1936, Gordon had "read half of Andrew's novel" and was ready to admit that "everything he's done I'd have said couldn't be pulled off . . . but somehow he's contrived to turn out some tremendous stuff."[31]

There are many parallels between the two novels by Lytle and Gordon. Both make the battles of the western war theater, particularly in Tennessee, the central stage for their dramas; both combine detailed dramatic depictions of Civil War battles and close physical and psychological profiles of historical figures with invented or half-invented characters. Surely a sense of common purpose encouraged both Gordon and Lytle as they composed their novels, but no doubt without Lytle's previous work on Nathan Bedford Forrest, Gordon's *None Shall Look Back* would have been a very different book. Forrest would almost have to have been Gordon's heroic paradigm because several of her relatives actually served in his "critter company" at Shiloh and Chickamauga and the battles around Clarksville and southern Kentucky were a part of her family saga.[32]

It is remarkable how much intertextual relationship exists between *Bedford Forrest and His Critter Company*, published in 1931 and partly written at Benfolly, and *None Shall Look Back*. Though nowhere does Gordon speak of actually using the biography, she most certainly read it closely, and she would

30. Wood, ed., *Southern Mandarins*, 188, 191–92.

31. Makowsky, *Caroline Gordon*, 130, paraphrasing Wood, ed., *Southern Mandarins*, 192–93; Wood, ed., *Southern Mandarins*, 199.

32. Makowsky, *Caroline Gordon*, 14, 16–18.

have to have been both blind and deaf not to have soaked up considerable factual information about Forrest when Lytle was in the process of writing about him. Makowsky records that Gordon's publisher received several letters chiding Gordon and Scribner's for using not only Lytle's *Forrest* but *Battles and Leaders of the Civil War* without attribution, adding that Gordon was probably "ignorant of the need for correct citation in fiction" and that she "tended to rely too heavily on her research and factual materials because she lacked confidence in her imagination and found the research much more pleasant than the actual writing."[33] Since Lytle seems not to have complained, it appears that in the post–Fugitive-Agrarian group, writing was a shared activity as long as history and fiction were regarded as separate genres with different rules and requirements.

Gordon's plot is consistent with Lytle's account of Lieutenant Colonel Forrest's march from Louisville to Brandenburg, Kentucky, and with his company of rangers, to Clarksville, Tennessee, "by way of Bowling Green." Gordon's depiction of the siege and eventual loss of Fort Donelson may be closely correlated with Lytle's, notably in their transmission of Forrest's remark, when asked to lead a charge of Kentucky cavalry against the Federal forces at Wynn's Ferry: Lytle's quotation is "I can try it," while Gordon's reads "I'll try it." Both Lytle and Gordon portray the fateful conference between Confederate commanders Floyd, Pillow, and Buckner—with Colonel Forrest standing by—that resulted in the surrender of Fort Donelson. It was on this occasion that Forrest refused to surrender his company, pleading his obligations to the families who had trusted him with their sons. Lytle's Forrest proclaims to his superiors that he had not come out to surrender, that he had promised the parents of his boys to look after them, that he did not intend to see them die that winter in prison camps in the North, that he would not surrender if they would follow him out, and that, in fact, he was going out if only one man followed. Gordon's hero asserts, "I didn't come out to surrender. . . . I came out to fight. I promised the parents of my boys that I'd take care of them, and I'm not going to have them rot in Yankee prison camps." After kicking over a table and overturning glasses and decanters, Forrest strides from the room, shouting back, "You can surrender the infantry. . . . But you can't surrender my cavalry. I'll take 'em out if it's the last thing I do."[34]

33. Ibid., 139–40.

34. Lytle, *Bedford Forrest*, 37, 76; Caroline Gordon, *None Shall Look Back* (1937; rpt. Nashville: Sanders, 1992), 113.

Both Lytle and Gordon make effective use of contemporary accounts of Forrest's early triumphs in Tennessee. In the novel, Rives and Ned Allard are among those who escape from Fort Donelson with Forrest, first to Nashville, where they witness how Forrest restores order to a dispirited city that has fallen to mob violence. Gordon also makes Rives one of the prisoners of war, soon to be shot, at Clarksville on the day when Forrest stormed and captured the town, an event Lytle had described in vivid detail in his biography. Both include, as an illustration of how the citizens adored their rescuer, the account of a woman who approached Forrest with an unusual request:

Lytle:

As she swept her skirt along the red brick walk, she held in one of her thin white hands a small lace handkerchief and, in the other a silver spoon.

"General Forrest," she asked, "will you back your horse for me?"

Bedford lifted his hat, and, with his heavy black hair falling down his shoulders, bowed; then pulled on the reins.

Leaning over, she scooped up a spoon of dust from the ground where the horse had been pawing and poured it carefully into the folds of the handkerchief.

Gordon:

Rives looked and saw that the door of one of the red-brick houses on the square had opened. A slender woman dressed in black was coming down the path. She had a handkerchief in one hand. A silver spoon glinted in the other. She was coming straight up to the General. Rives heard her voice, low but distinct: "General Forrest, will you back your horse for me?"

The cavalry commander looked down, startled, then lifted his hat and obediently pulled on the reins. The horse, a powerful gray, took two steps backward. The woman bent over and with the silver spoon scooped up some of the earth on which the charger's hoof had rested and put it in the handkerchief.[35]

Gordon's novel climaxes when, before the battles of Missionary Ridge and Chickamauga, Rives Allard senses that the Confederate cause must fail and that his own life will be lost. The denouement is accomplished with Forrest being inexplicably relieved of his command after Chickamauga and with

35. Lytle, *Bedford Forrest*, 82, 92–102; Gordon, *None Shall Look Back*, 139, 200–211.

Rives's death in the fighting near Memphis. Lytle's account carries Forrest through the end of the war and beyond.

When *None Shall Look Back* was at last completed, Gordon once again ran into difficulties with the title. From the beginning, she had intended to call it "The Cup of Fury"; but Maxwell Perkins wrote her in November that someone else had used her title. With the help of a Bible, she and Tate looked for a new title. Perkins suggested several, including *Grapes of Wrath* or *Terrible Swift Sword*, but Tate and Gordon ruled out any allusion to "The Battle Hymn of the Republic."[36] Finally, they settled on the phrase "None Shall Look Back" from Nahum 2:8. Once again Gordon called on the erudition and creativity of Allen Tate to assist her in bringing an important project to fruition.

Responses from Gordon's circle to *None Shall Look Back* were complimentary. The most eloquent of her reviews was Katherine Anne Porter's "Dulce et Decorum Est" in the *New Republic* of March 31, 1937. Taking both title and tone from Horace, not Wilfred Owen, Porter asserted that for Gordon's characters "to live beyond or to acknowledge defeat is to die twice, and shamefully." Approving Gordon's handling of narrative perspective, Porter observed that "having chosen to observe from all points of view, rather than to stand on a knoll above the battle and watch a set procession of events through a field glass, she makes her scenes move rapidly from Federal lines to Confederate, from hospitals to prisons, to the plantations." Porter closed by proclaiming *None Shall Look Back* to be "in a great many ways a better book than 'Penhally' or 'Aleck Maury, Sportsman,' Miss Gordon's other two novels."[37]

In May 1937, just as *None Shall Look Back* was enjoying modest success in the bookstores, Gordon wrote to Sally Wood, "We are back at Benfolly after two years' absence." This was Lowell's tent summer, the last and best at Benfolly. In October she wrote that Katherine Anne Porter had "stayed with us five weeks but went to New Orleans about a month ago. She couldn't write here—life was so distracting, what with the cats and all the fruits of the earth needing to be preserved, pickled or made into wine." In the midst of it all, as usual, Gordon tried to write, encouraged by Perkins to "finish a novel called 'The Garden of Adonis' (see The Golden Bough) in time for fall publication." She thought it "absurd" to be rushing the novel to publication, but Scribner's insisted that "the iron is hot and must be struck quickly. *NSLB* has

36. Waldron, *Close Connections*, 164.
37. Katherine Anne Porter, "Dulce et Decorum Est," *New Republic*, March 31, 1937, 245.

sold about ten thousand." On July 11, Andrew Lytle wrote Tate that if he were Gordon, he would not "feel impelled to hurry her novel" (*The Garden of Adonis*) because Maxwell Perkins had not sent promised money. Her scheme, conceived after completing *Penhally*, was to write about two families, "white and poor white, living on the same farm."[38] Like "Mr. Powers," published six years earlier, the novel explores the delicate relationships between landowners and their (often happier and more resilient) tenant farmer families, a subject with which the Tates became familiar as absentee owners of Benfolly.

There seems to have been virtual silence about *The Garden of Adonis* among the former Fugitive-Agrarians, although Gordon clearly intended that the novel would advance their favorite thesis: that industrial and commercial forces would eventually defeat agrarianism and the southern way of life. As it came out in the novel, however, Mother Nature is the real culprit. A harsh drought is as responsible as a failed bank for Ben Allard's financial ruin. Because he cannot come to Ote Mortimer's aid with a few dollars for a marriage license, Ote cannot marry Idelle, who carries his child, forcing a fatal confrontation with Ben over the hay which Ote had been forbidden to harvest. As in her three previous novels, Gordon is an uncompromising realist who has no truck with Pollyanna endings. *The Garden of Adonis* ends with the almost total destruction of life and hope.

By the end of the 1930s, Caroline Gordon had published four novels and fifteen stories, and *Green Centuries*, her last historical novel, was in progress. She had a continuing if sometimes hectic relationship with Maxwell Perkins at Scribner's for as long as she wanted it. In short, she was an established author and, for a short time at the Women's College at Greensboro, North Carolina, a full professor of creative writing. Despite heavy involvement with students in and out of class, she found time to pursue research toward her novel in the college library, where she read travel books; diaries; historical records from Tennessee, Virginia, and North Carolina; and various accounts of the relationships between settlers and Indians on the Tennessee-Carolina frontier.

Gordon delighted in historical research and wanted to get the facts exactly right. In addition to letters to various knowledgeable persons for information to use in the book, Gordon wrote to her compatriot Lytle, who was also writing his historical novel, *At the Moon's Inn*: "I have my novel planned out pretty well and have seven chapters outlined in detail." She closed with a

---

38. Wood, ed., *Southern Mandarins*, 205, 214, 206; Young and Sarcone, eds., *Tate-Lytle Letters*, 113; Makowsky, *Caroline Gordon*, 106.

postscript, "Allen says tell you he has seventy thousand words written" on his novel *The Fathers*. Struggling with a novel gave Tate an appreciation for how hard it was to produce a novel and additional respect for Caroline as a writer.[39] Perhaps because it has almost nothing to do either with Gordon's family history or with the Agrarian theme, *Green Centuries* marked a coming of age for Caroline Gordon.

In the fall of 1939, Tate accepted an appointment at Princeton, causing Caroline to give up her professorship at Greensboro and the parity with her husband that it had brought her. As she wrote to Murial (Mrs. Malcolm) Cowley, she divided her time between her writing and faculty wives' social affairs: "Must get back to my Indians. I plan to kill off twenty six of them today but alas, I will have stop the bloody work at four o'clock to go and pour tea at a ladies' gathering." To Katherine Anne Porter, she wrote in the spring that she had just "killed off Dragging Canoe [historic Indian character in the novel] and Archy [Orion's brother, who joins the Cherokee nation and dies at the settlers' hands]. Tomorrow I write Cassy's death scene, Deo volente." Once again, Gordon had difficulty ending her book, and, as she confessed in a letter to Edna Lytle, "Allen helped manfully towards the last. . . . In fact he practically wrote the last chapter. I was off on the wrong foot, striking the folksy note, using too much clinical detail—Cassy dies of pneumonia. Allen stepped in, took a look and pulled the whole thing together with a passage that works in the symbolism of the constellation Orion—very boldly and I think successfully." She went on to report that Allen had also proofread the manuscript, "taking out the 'thens,' 'theres,' and 'nows' " that were "thick as fleas on a dog's back. He also made me take out some of the dialect." She chose her title from a poem by friend of the Fugitives John Peale Bishop. The novel was completed in June and published late in 1941; unfortunately, it was, in her words, "a complete failure" because of "poor timing . . . people are tired of pioneer novels."[40]

Most of Gordon's critics separate her five "early novels," through *Green Centuries*, from her four "late novels." From some point in the late 1930s her relationship with Allen Tate had begun to deteriorate and with it her loyalty to the former Fugitive-Agrarian confederation. She was moving toward a strong commitment to Roman Catholicism. All of these changes are reflected in the later novels, but in the context of the Fugitive legacy, she had also reached a stage in her writing when she needed to relinquish dependency on

---

39. Gordon to Lytle, [1938], Lytle Papers; Makowsky, *Caroline Gordon*, 178.
40. Makowsky, *Caroline Gordon*, 153, 157; Waldron, *Close Connections*, 199, 200.

her friends in the network. As a result, in *The Women on the Porch* (1944), *The Strange Children* (1951), and *The Malefactors* (1956), Gordon uses her twenty-odd years as a coterie writer as the basis for a critique of the group and their literary lives. The anxiety of influence would take the shape, then, of fiction that presents her former self and her allegiances in a harsh light.

Gordon's idea for *The Women on the Porch* had come as early as Christmas of 1936, when she stayed at Merry Mont to work on proofs for *None Shall Look Back*. According to Waldron, spending time with her grandmother, (Aunt) Loulie, and crazy cousin Kitty inspired a "pretty Russian" novel. The seed began to bear fruit in the spring of 1942. By then Tate knew that he would not be returning to Princeton, and, though he seriously considered joining the armed forces, they decided to move to Monteagle, where they would be near Andrew Lytle and writing as a group again. Allen had "a novel in his head" (quoting letter to Van Doren), and Caroline was ready, after the poor reception of *Green Centuries*, to think about a new project. In a letter to Ward Dorrance, she wrote, "I'm calling it The Women on the Porch. The porch is affixed to an old house like Merry Mont."[41]

As she gained her writing stride, Caroline Gordon found herself in the work situation she liked best. It was the winter when Robert Lowell and Jean Stafford shared a cottage with the Tates, and Stafford, deep in the writing of *Boston Adventure*, would spur Gordon to productive days at the typewriter. Peter Taylor spent a military furlough at the cottage. Lowell completed several poems for *Land of Unlikeness* (see Chapter 7), and Tate translated the *Pervigilium Veneris* (*The Vigil of Venus*, anon.). Radcliff Squires commented, "We may be sure that literary theory and passionate argument thickened the air at Monteagle, even though the brilliant creativity and bright strife nested secretly, like crystals in a geode." The creative electricity at Monteagle may have energized Gordon, but the novel that emerged, *The Women on the Porch*, is in shocking contrast to her earlier pastorals. As Squires put it: "Instead of treating an environment of social slippage and decline, Miss Gordon decided to deal with an environment where the decline has been perfected. That is to say, we have an environment of decadence, just as we have in Tate's and Lowell's poetry."[42] Borrowing from Dante and Greek mythology, Gordon makes Swan Quarter an inferno where the women sit, like three weird sisters, on "the stoa of hell." Against the context of World War II, Gordon registered

41. Waldron, *Close Connections*, 164; Makowsky, *Caroline Gordon*, 159.

42. Radcliffe Squires, "The Underground Stream: A Note on Caroline Gordon's Fiction," *Southern Review* n.s., 7 (1971): 470.

for the first time her distrust in the artists' existence, which could emerge only in a malediction on all their houses.

The protagonist, Catherine Chapman, flees New York City and her husband, Jim, and takes refuge with her grandmother, Aunt Willy, and Cousin Daphne. While Jim is a history teacher and former poet, Catherine has no interest in literature. During her long visit to Swan Quarter, Catherine reverts to agrarianism: she gathers vegetables, rides horses, and has an affair with Tom Manigault, who shares her love for the land. The Chapmans' estrangement lasts until the final pages of the novel, when, after nearly strangling Catherine, Jim experiences a moment of recognition that is followed by a tentative renewal of their relationship.

The Women on the Porch really was Gordon's final experience writing, as she had begun, surrounded by the members of the circle. Once more, however, she called on Andrew Lytle for help in completing one sequence in the novel, a bar scene that recalls Eliot's *Waste Land*, when one of Jim's literary friends recounts tales of his schooldays in Tennessee. According to her March 15, 1943, letter to Lytle, Lytle's father came to her assistance by solving "a technical problem that might have held me up for days, weeks. . . . Mr. Lytle's stories about Sawney Webb did the trick better than anything I could ever have thought up for myself and I have felt very grateful to him for supplying them just when they were needed." The Tates had quarreled with Lytle, partly over the editorship of the *Sewanee Review*, partly over Mrs. Lytle's brief affair with a Sewanee student (Caroline was so sensitive about marital fidelity, partly because of her husband's peccadillos, that she wanted Lytle to have the student horsewhipped). In the same letter, Gordon proceeded to suggest that it would be best to close off their relationship, saying that further visits between them would be futile and that since he had stated his desire to "stand on your own two feet" as an artist, it was time to say "ave atque vale." She charged him to remember that his talent was "the great thing in your life, the thing to which everything else must be subordinated if you are not to rot— and lilies that fester smell far worse than weeds, you know." The breach between the Tates and Lytles was mended, only to become permanent, as Walter Sullivan records, near the end of Tate's life.[43]

Apparently harboring no resentment against either of the Tates, Lytle was the one who mentioned, in a May 6, 1948, letter to Tate, that he had been "thinking for some time that a serious criticism ought to be done on Caro-

43. Waldron, *Close Connections*, 212; Walter Sullivan, *Allen Tate: A Recollection* (Baton Rouge: Louisiana State University Press, 1988), 69–82, 98.

line's work. I have thought Red was the person to do it. I've been turning it over in my mind for a year or so[;] if she has no objections I would like to try my hand at it." The result was "Caroline Gordon and the Historical Image," first published in the *Sewanee Review* of autumn 1949. Indeed, Lytle tells us more about himself than about Gordon in that his obvious reason for approving of her work was its similarity to his own. Both, in his estimation, were essentially historical novelists but not in the popular sense: "the costume piece" wherein "historic personages, when they appear, appear; not as men or women but in a quasi-mythical clothing." What he means by "image" is a comprehension of the whole in its private and public dimensions, along with "a long range of vision," whereby the author "makes of the period at once the setting and the choral comment." Always the author remains removed at her or his "post of observation," providing the reader with the means to grasp with the author the "essential meaning" of history through a lens corrected by the sense of the whole but colored by "literary irony at a high level."[44]

On October 22, Tate wrote that he and Caroline did like the essay and that "after a third reading I am at a loss to find any fault in it." In his reply on the twenty-seventh, Lytle explained, "You know you read and like things, but you don't really read them until you do something like this. . . . In the end all I did was try to understand why I like Caroline's work, and in the process I developed a vague feeling I had about historical writing."[45] Lytle's essay on Gordon is testimony of the parallel direction their careers had taken from Agrarian days until, after twenty years of writing fiction, their craft had begun to matter more than their message.

After *Green Centuries*, Gordon decided to write no more historical novels. *The Women on the Porch* would be the first of three novels set in a contemporary context and in which Allen Tate would form the prototype for the artist *manqué*. Jim Chapman teaches history because he must support a wife, although he once published a book of poems. He is constantly reproached by memories of Hart Crane, who committed suicide just as his poetry was becoming successful. (Another version of Crane appears in *The Malefactors*, where he is Horne Watts, Tom Claiborne's "first literary friend.") Tom is a poet, unable to write even when his wife's secure finances make other work unnecessary. Steven Lewis, in *The Strange Children*, writes essays and talks incessantly about Civil War history. Taken together, *The Women on the Porch*,

44. Young and Sarcone, eds., *Tate-Lytle Letters*, 213–14; Lytle, "Caroline Gordon and the Historical Image," 155–56.
45. Young and Sarcone, eds., *Tate-Lytle Letters*, 216–17.

The Strange Children, and *The Malefactors* present the New York and Benfolly communities, and Allen Tate in particular, as objects of bitter satire. In the latter two novels, written after Gordon's religious conversion, the characters' only route to clear vision, artistic and otherwise, is an epiphanic religious experience.

Andrew Lytle had been Gordon's strongest ally in the post-Fugitive and Agrarian group. It is therefore astonishing but indicative of her desire for separation from her former ties that she would inform him, in a letter written years later, that because "our literary paths diverge too widely," she "could not appear in any anthology of fiction edited by you."[46] Since there were no two writers of this literary group who were more alike in purpose, material, and techniques, Gordon was partly deluding herself, partly defensive in her own desire for artistic independence.

When writing or lecturing on the art of fiction, Gordon did not entirely trust her own knowledge, experience, and reputation to lead her to any truly original theory of fiction. According to Waldron, Gordon's and Tate's *House of Fiction* began with Gordon wanting to write "a book on the novel." Tom Walsh, of Scribner's textbook division, thought that both their names should appear on the title page of "an anthology of short stories . . . 'with suitable annotations and introduction, for the education market.' " Tate therefore planned the anthology, wrote "three of the commentaries, and left the rest to Caroline." Her introduction, with its extensive, diagrammed discussion of point of view, has been helpful to many teachers and even to young writers. David Madden even called it his "bible." As for the short stories that appear therein, Makowsky remarked that "half of the writers were American, and almost half of those Americans were southern friends of the Tates such as William Faulkner, Katherine Anne Porter, Robert Penn Warren, Andrew Lytle, Eudora Welty, and Peter Taylor."[47] Except for Faulkner, all were of the Fugitive legacy. Still a believer in objectivity, however, Gordon used no story of hers in the anthology.

How to Read a Novel was Gordon's own independent project. Reviewers who looked in it for theoretical breakthroughs were, however, disappointed. A major source of Gordon's theory of fiction must have been Brooks and Warren's *Understanding Fiction*. Writing on the assumption that while no one can teach writing (she hated creative writing courses though she taught them

---

46. Waldron, *Close Connections*, 271.

47. Ibid., 255; David Madden, interview by author, Baton Rouge, La., July 16, 1985; Makowsky, *Caroline Gordon*, 187.

for years), it *is* possible to teach a student to read. In that regard, Caroline Gordon indicated her concurrence with Brooks and Warren, indeed with all the writers of the Fugitive legacy, which first and foremost taught techniques of reading and, through reading, of writing.

Despite all she accomplished, Gordon would still write, in 1970, to Tate, no longer her husband, "You are the only editor I have ever been dependent on, for criticism as well as encouragement. You taught me practically everything I know about writing." This statement is testimony to the conservatism that led her to choose as epigraph to *The Malefactors* Jacques Maritain's remark, "It is for Adam to interpret the voices that Eve hears."[48] Clearly Caroline Gordon's debt to her husband and, by extension, to the Fugitive legacy was as basic to her literary as to her personal life. Her own independent contributions cannot, however, be ignored.

Caroline Gordon's stock has remained high among critics, but the general public has failed to acknowledge her achievement. Freistat believes that the religious dogmatism of her later novels puts readers off, but a more likely culprit is her style, difficult and uncompromising, learned as a member of the Fugitive circle. The problem of closure may also have cost her both critical and popular acclaim. As Larry Allums pointed out, Gordon changed from the tragic to the (classically) comic mode in her fiction, which, of course, affected her endings.[49] In the first five novels, through *Green Centuries*, the endings are implacably stark and tragic; in the latter four, they rush to improbable epiphanies. Throughout, as she grudgingly admitted, she was, like the other figures in the Fugitive legacy, always a writer's writer.

48. Waldron, *Close Connections*, 356, 336.
49. Freistat, *Caroline Gordon as Novelist*, 25; Larry Allums, "From Classical to Christian: Versions of the Hero in the Novels of Caroline Gordon," *Southern Review* n.s., 28 (1990): 63.

11 / Katherine Anne Porter: A Gift for Friendship

In her biography of Caroline Gordon, Veronica Makowsky compares the first two important women fiction writers of the Fugitive legacy: "Caroline seemed to regard [Katherine Anne] Porter and herself as the grasshopper and the ant, both in literary productivity and the duties of domesticity." The two women were destined, from the beginnings of their literary careers, to be both rivals and close friends. In time, Gordon could not help envying Porter, who wrote so much less but enjoyed so much more fame than she. In a letter to Jean Stafford in 1944, Gordon called Porter "an actress who happens to have a talent for setting down her emotions in felicitous prose."[1] Surely Katherine Anne Porter used her many gifts—histrionic, creative, aesthetic but foremost her gift for friendship—to the fullest. The Fugitive circle was only one of many orbits in which she moved, and therefore her debt to the Fugitive legacy was concentrated in brief but crucial moments in her long career.

While Joan Givner's *Katherine Anne Porter: A Life* contains valuable information about Porter's background, Jan Nordby Gretlund correctly observes that the biography gives a "faulty view of Porter's ability as a letter writer and

1. Makowsky, *Caroline Gordon*, 167.

... the [incorrect] impression that she had little contact with literary circles."[2] Although others had recognized Porter's talent before she met Allen Tate, Gordon, and Andrew Lytle in New York around 1927, the stories that solidified her reputation were products of the thirties to early forties, when she interacted with these fellow southerners. The impact of the Fugitive legacy on Porter, though not all-important, was therefore a major factor in her literary career, a matter of mutual support and shared attitudes about literature expressed in letters, essays, and, most important, in her fiction.

Porter's earliest relationships with the group are veiled in mystery. We first catch sight of her in the summer of 1927 living in the same Greenwich Village apartment building, at 561 Hudson Street, as Caroline and Allen Tate. One day when a visitor asked for Porter at that address, he was informed that "the ladies of the house [including Porter] are at the riot in Union Square" protesting the disposition of the Sacco and Vanzetti case. And in 1928, when Sally Wood came to visit, Caroline Gordon directed her to "get hold of Katherine Anne Porter, either by telephoning or standing in the hall and shouting her name. She will have our key and she will introduce you to the ways of Caligari."[3] In that setting, Gordon, Porter, and Porter's lifelong friend Josephine Herbst formed a mutually supportive subgroup of women writers who offered one another the feedback and encouragement which the male writers in their circle already enjoyed and from which the women were often excluded.

Porter also enjoyed complimentary personal attention from those same men—Tate, Lytle, and Robert Penn Warren—because she possessed both physical attractiveness and literary talent. When Tate was in Paris on a Guggenheim Fellowship, he remarked in a letter to Lytle, "If I would have three wives, and were privileged to *take* them [to Europe, we presume], they would be Carolyn, Katherine Anne, and Léonie [Adams]"; and on March 14, 1929, Tate wrote, "I am certainly glad you kept after K. A. She is one of the bright spots in a dingy world, and we must keep her shining." Tate acted in his usual role of sponsor and advocate for the publications that established Porter's reputation. In 1929, along with other literary acquaintances, Tate encouraged her to publish a collection of her early fiction entitled *Flowering Judas and Other Stories*. Matthew Josephson wrote to Harcourt, Brace, in June 1929 that "it would be a good idea to get Katherine Anne Porter authoring for you. . . .

2. Jan Nordby Gretlund, "Three on Katherine Anne Porter," *Mississippi Quarterly* 36 (1983): 123.

3. Waldron, *Close Connections*, 59; Wood, ed., *Southern Mandarins*, 35.

Many people who know her, like Cowley and Allen Tate, have a great respect," but it was Tate who received the credit.[4]

In an exchange of letters with Porter in January 1962, Tate attempted to clarify the circumstances surrounding that publication. On January 10 he wrote: "I have just read Matty Josephson's *Life among the Surrealists*. On pages 352–54 he says he got *Flowering Judas* published. Did he? I thought it happened otherwise. Please tell me." On January 18, Porter hotly replied that "Matthew Josephson never helped me get *Flowering Judas* or anything else published. . . . You see, Allen, all these years I had thought it was *you* who, if you did not do it single handed, was the moving spirit of getting Flowering Judas published." Her reply, said Tate, "only confirms my memory of that time. I didn't get F.J. published all by myself."[5]

After the collection appeared, Tate did his part by giving it a rave review in the *Nation* magazine, calling *Flowering Judas* "not a promising book . . . it is a fully matured art." He also used his influence in regard to "Hacienda." When in 1934 Scribner's rejected the forty-five-hundred-word story, Porter sent it to the *Virginia Quarterly Review*, to which Tate was a contributing editor. Caroline Gordon wrote to Porter, "Stringfellow Barr probably accepted your story because we told him when we were in Charlottesville that he ought to be ashamed of himself and would bring lasting obloquy [*sic*] on the magazine if he never printed any of your stuff."[6]

Clearly, the Fugitive circle remained unbroken even when its members ventured far afield, to California, to New York, or to France, as well as back to Tennessee, Alabama, and Kentucky. Even so, the Tates and Lytle found the somewhat reclusive, always traveling Katherine Anne Porter an intriguing anomaly. By the time the Tates and Lytle moved south, Porter was obviously one of the group. She even considered joining them in the establishment of a literary community in Virginia. In 1929, moreover, when Tate, Lytle, and Warren were writing their Civil War biographies, Porter also

4. Young and Sarcone, eds., *Tate-Lytle Letters*, 15, 18; Joan Givner, *Katherine Anne Porter: A Life* (Athens: University of Georgia Press, 1991), 220. In a letter to Porter written on October 22, 1932, Tate alludes to his ocean passage home from Europe, a poem just written, and a secret shared with Porter alone: "My beautiful escapade is over. Alas, I wish I could resign myself to *that*. I'm afraid—no, grateful—that it will last the rest of my life. Always my love, Allen. P.S. In case I forget when I see you, you can always write with absolute freely [*sic*] to my University address (Porter Papers).

5. Tate to Porter, January 10, 1962; Porter to Tate, January 18, 1962; Tate to Porter, January 21, 1962, all in Porter Papers.

6. Allen Tate, "A New Star," *Nation* 131 (1930): 353; Caroline Gordon to Porter, n.d., Porter Papers.

turned to biography. All four were under pressure from publishers to produce a novel or a biography. Porter's subject was, however, anything but southern: the New England Puritan intellectual and divine Cotton Mather, an interest that Givner traces back to Porter's childhood fascination with a book that erroneously connected Mather with witch-burning in colonial Massachusetts.[7] It was an unfortunate choice for Porter, who, despite her publishers' patient financial and motivational support, never completed the biography. Instead, she returned to the writing of short fiction and, unlike Tate and Lytle, did not seem to be damaged in the eyes of her publisher because she did not produce the biography; on the contrary, the advances she received from the long-suffering Donald Brace at Harcourt sustained Porter and allowed her to write her fiction.

On August 18, 1932, in his inimitable cornpone argot, Lytle wrote to Tate, "Have you all seen that beautiful, soft-talking tiger-wandering woman, Katherine Anne? I hear she got a Prize outarn the Scribners? Was it all the first prize? I hope to our Saviour hit was." Although Lytle's admiration for Porter's personal qualities was unqualified, he nevertheless found Porter's earliest stories inferior to Caroline Gordon's in respect to the objectivity that these Jamesians considered all-important. In a revealing letter to Tate, he remarked: "I've been looking into *Flowering Judas* recently. As fine as it is, it is not as tough as Caroline's work. There is a certain female impurity which Caroline lacks, and I believe this is the thing a woman writer will naturally find the greatest hazard. With a man it is easier to obliterate himself."[8]

One may conclude, as Lytle did, that Gordon either deliberately or accidentally androgynized her fiction, while Porter, although she followed the same aesthetic standards, consistently told her stories from a feminist perspective. Louise Westling argues that female writers whose literary models are "predominantly masculine" suffer from a "problem of persona" that may complicate the formation of their own fictional voices.[9] But neither Porter nor Gordon found the lack of female role models problematic, either personally or artistically; both took what they believed to be a gender-neutral approach to reading and to writing—when they were not consciously using their femininity to manipulate the men! Porter used her personal and professional relationships with men to her advantage, all the while carefully retaining her autonomy and independence.

7. Givner, *Katherine Anne Porter: A Life*, 185.

8. Young and Sarcone, eds., *Tate-Lytle Letters*, 61–62, 171.

9. Louise H. Westling, *Sacred Groves and Ravaged Gardens: The Fiction of Eudora Welty, Carson McCullers, and Flannery O'Connor* (Athens: University of Georgia Press, 1985), 57.

Porter differed from the smaller Tate circle in her work habits. Tate, Gordon, and Lytle had found the concept of an informal writers' colony at Benfolly stimulating. Although Porter considered joining them and later paid at least one visit to Benfolly, she did not find communal writing productive but needed solitude to create. She had other ports of call during the early thirties and forties: Bermuda, Mexico, and Europe, where she would live and try to write while married to Eugene Pressly.

Visiting and letter writing were Porter's means of keeping alive her ties with the Fugitive legacy. On February 21, 1931, Caroline Gordon wrote to Sally Wood: "About Katherine Anne. She seems to be set on coming here, and I should certainly be pleased to see you two hooked up, as it were. . . . I believe that she will get a Guggenheim fellowship, though, which will mean that she will go abroad. She could stay in Mexico, but I detect signs in our friend of being tired of Mexico, so I fear she will make tracks for France." The proposed 1931 visit did not take place, but, indeed tired of Mexico, Porter left for Europe in August 1931, sailing from Vera Cruz on a German ship called the *Werra*. Thirty years afterward, Porter told James Ruoff that "when we arrived at Bremerhaven I sent my ship's log to Caroline Gordon . . . in the form of a long letter. . . . A few years after I left Germany, Caroline Gordon returned my letter because she thought I might find use for it in my writing." The letter to which Porter referred, dated August 28, 1931, turned up during the early seventies among the Caroline Gordon Papers at Princeton. As Givner has established, it was truly "the genesis of *Ship of Fools* and more than any other document provides information about Porter's fictional method. It supports her statement that few of the names, characters and events in the novel were invented."[10]

Although many details were transported directly from letter to novel, any reader of both texts is aware of crucial differences. Most noticeable, of course, is the difference in length: from a twenty-page letter, more or less, came a novel of some five hundred pages. Moreover, as Robert Brinkmeyer has observed, Porter's letter to Gordon is much more "upbeat," punctuated with indications of how much Porter enjoyed the crossing, while the novel grew into a rather grim, ponderous reflection of a "radical hardening and harshening of Porter's views" in the years afterward, which Brinkmeyer attributes to her "obsession with totalitarianism." Porter's title, mutating from "Promised

---

10. Wood, ed., *Southern Mandarins*, 72; Joan Givner, ed. *Katherine Anne Porter: Conversations* (Jackson: University Press of Mississippi, 1987), 66–67; Givner, "The Genesis of Ship of Fools," *Southern Literary Journal* 9 (1970): 15.

Land" to "No Safe Harbour," to *Ship of Fools*, is evidence as well of how the medieval allegory *Das Narrenschiff* invaded the text and transformed it from realism to heavy symbolism. The all-important details that constitute the concrete component of the novel depended, however, on Gordon's preservation of the letter. It is clear that writing the letter served to focus and systematize Porter's perceptions. She commented that "if I were not keeping this kind of journal for you I could never believe it has been so long." When near the end of the voyage, Porter affixed a premature closure—"Here ends this foolish note-book, made to amuse you a little and to remember my first Atlantic crossing by"—the details of voyage had already begun to blur, leaving her "like one of these tourists who rush through the world with eyes tightly closed, gaining momentum by the hour, counting on his fingers the lands he has travelled through . . . getting home with a souvenir spoon from each."[11]

That Porter chose this particular method of preserving her observations on that voyage may well explain why, after such a long and agonizing gestation, *Ship of Fools* finally saw the light of day on April 1, 1962. Writers typically find it embarrassing to abandon a project once they have revealed it to and been encouraged by their closest professional colleagues. Porter's letter therefore set the stage for what amounted to a contract between two writers who were simultaneously supporters and rivals. The force of Porter's commitment emerges from a 1948 letter to Gordon, written near the end of the decade during which Porter made her strongest effort to make progress on the novel: "It has never in most disheartened moments occurred to me that the novel was not, in some way, at some time, going to get finished. . . . I would as soon thinking [*sic*] of throwing myself into the ash-can as discarding even a page of it."[12]

Ship of Fools, when completed, was exactly the kind of novel that the Fugitive legacy prized, thematically unified and a tour de force in what Andrew Lytle called the "roving" point of view. One center of revelation replaces another by a variety of transitions, sometimes after passages of dialogue, sometimes abruptly after the interruption of white space. The technique is espe-

---

11. Robert H. Brinkmeyer, Jr., *Katherine Anne Porter's Artistic Development: Primitivism, Traditionalism, and Totalitarianism* (Baton Rouge: Louisiana State University Press, 1993), 219; Bayley, ed., *Letters of Katherine Anne Porter*, 57. M. M. Liberman's discussion of another post-cruise letter, to Malcolm Cowley, reveals, however, that for Porter the voyage was a "purgatorial" experience, similar in spirit to *Das Narrenschiff*, the source of her title ("Some Observations on the Genesis of *Ship of Fools*: A Letter from Katherine Anne Porter," *PMLA* 84 [1936]: 135–37).

12. Porter to Gordon, July 18, 1948, Porter Papers.

cially appropriate when the narrative jumps into the mind of one of the more isolated characters such as the hunchback, Herr Glocken, sometimes without any apparent rupture. More than any other character in *Ship of Fools*, Jenny Brown mirrors Porter's own ambivalence toward writing, as well as toward the possibility of sustaining it in tandem with an affair of the heart. Not until Porter had decided on her priorities could her best writing, including her novel, be completed.

In the eventful year that followed her voyage, Porter was reunited, in France, first with Ford Madox Ford and then with the Tates. At that time, when both Porter and Gordon were writing some of their most important short fiction, some cross-fertilization no doubt occurred. In November, in Basle, Switzerland, Porter began preliminary work on "Old Mortality" and on the violent climax of "Noon Wine." Gordon, having published *Penhally*, was writing a second novel, already outlined, and several stories, including "Tom Rivers." Such a close-knit group of like-minded writers must have been aware of what each was working on. Perhaps as a result, Porter's stories began to show superficial similarities—in setting, characterization, even plot—to Gordon's. Ford had advised both women to center their fiction in their native South, but it was Gordon who, writing to Porter, encouraged her to mine the treasure trove of family experience: "I am glad you are wallowing in family after years of exile . . . I, of course get right down among mine, pick up the gems—and gems do fall from their lips—as said gems fall, I am really a sort of reporter of my family."[13]

Although Porter, like Gordon, was excluded from active participation in the Agrarian movement, Mary Titus calls Porter's stories "a gender-inflected response to the Agrarian pursuit."[14] Like Gordon, Porter recognized that not only were their *real* family sagas as freighted with poverty and suffering as with the serenity and order so celebrated by the male Agrarians but also that the ensurers of that order were not Confederate generals and patriarchs but the strong women who actually ruled and stabilized their families. The memorable scenes in *None Shall Look Back* in which Charlotte Allard commands the preparation of breakfast for Forrest's brigade and Susan Allard produces out of severely straitened resources a party for the haggard troops resemble Porter's flashback portrait of Sophia Jane as capable manager of the family's

13. Givner, *Katherine Anne Porter: A Life*, 278–79; Waldron, *Close Connections*, 90.

14. Mary Titus, "Katherine Anne Porter's Miranda: The Agrarian Myth and Southern Womanhood," in *Redefining Autobiography in Twentieth-Century Women's Fiction*, ed. Janice Morgan and Colette T. Hall (New York: Garland, 1991), 195.

depleted resources in "The Old Order." By fictional renderings of grand-mothers who had grown mythic in their memories, both Gordon and Porter were, at about the same time, creating examples of women who ruled their families because they were much more competent managers than their im-practically idealistic husbands and sons.

There are even more striking resemblances between "Old Mortality," which appeared in the *Southern Review* in the spring of 1938, and Gordon's two Allard novels. "Old Mortality" is a tour de force of Jamesian point of view narrated entirely by Miranda, Porter's semiautobiographical character. The portrait of Aunt Amy that opens the narrative is but the first of a series of conflicting texts from which Miranda must construct her own family history. Miranda's gradual realization that self-knowledge can come only through physical and intellectual autonomy forms the principal movement of the plot.

Both *Penhally* and "Old Mortality" are highly self-referential texts in which the true subject, how to write a family story, is managed through shifts in point of view, conflicting recollections, and abrupt leaps in time. "Old Mortality" was written in 1936 (though she reports beginning it earlier) and published approximately one year after Porter had reviewed Gordon's *None Shall Look Back* for the March 31, 1937, issue of the *New Republic*. Porter's manipulation of conflicting texts in "Old Mortality" is similarly complicated by the unreliability and resulting inconsistency of family storytelling, and Mi-randa's fix on what actually happened comes only as she compares these vary-ing renditions. Both Porter and Gordon ironically employ authoritative but unreliable internal narrators. Gordon's Cousin Nanny is presented as the "perfect repository of knowledge of all the marriages of the whole Llewellyn-Crenfrew connection and their issue," while Porter's chinless Cousin Eva and grandmother supply equally confident but radically different versions of the story of Aunt Amy and Uncle Gabriel.[15]

Gordon's harshly fatalistic Civil War novel may have helped to shape Por-ter's disillusioned perspective on her southern upbringing. The two party scenes in Gordon's Civil War novel—the ball at Music Hall in part 1 and Susan Allard's "one last dance for the soldiers" in part 4—are comparable to the two dancing scenes of "Old Mortality," described first by the grand-mother and second by Cousin Eva. In sharp contrast to such gala, romantic settings in a magnolia novel such as the contemporary and rival *Gone with the Wind*, the Gordon and Porter treatments are macabre foreshadowings of imminent death.

15. Caroline Gordon, *Penhally* (1931; rpt. Nashville: J. S. Sanders, 1991), 14.

Porter was almost certainly reinforced, if not actually influenced, by Gordon's almost sociological treatment of impoverished southern agrarianism. In an undated letter, Gordon told Porter of her "research" for *The Garden of Adonis*: "I don't know how in the hell I am going to get the second novel written. It is about poor white people. I know that it is praiseworthy to write about poor white people but it is a damned sight harder than people think. You have to skulk about so. . . . Mister Norman and his friend, Mister Suiter [are] a distant kinsman of Mister Powers."[16] The characters in Porter's "Noon Wine" are other "distant relatives" of Mr. Powers. In both stories, a southern farm is invaded by an intruder with a history of violence. In both stories, downtrodden women become remarkably assertive. The Powers family moves away because Mrs. Powers is dissatisfied with their living quarters, and the sickly Mrs. Thompson is the conscience that drives her husband, after an unsuccessful attempt to atone for killing Mr. Hatch, to take his life.

Aware of the interrelatedness of their fiction, Porter wrote Gordon on "the first day of Spring, 1935": "It's odd in a way how our development runs along neck to neck." Porter was challenged not only by Gordon's confident use of personal experience in her fiction but also by her ability to write both stories and novels. Encouraged by Gordon's example, Porter would now direct her energies to a new form, longer than the short stories but not nearly so long as Gordon's novels. In the same spring 1935 letter, Porter commented on the projected change in her artistic parameters: "I have come to the time when I simply must take my own advice and sprawl. I began it, a very discreet sprawl indeed, when I started the long stories. The one I am trying to finish now is called Pale Horse and Pale Rider, and it should be about twenty thousand words."[17] The three short novels which Porter subsequently completed are her chief contribution to modern fiction: *Noon Wine*, *Old Mortality*, and *Pale Horse, Pale Rider*. All were written in close contact with and encouraged by Porter's post-Fugitive colleagues.

In the mid-1930s, Robert Penn Warren became an editor and chief fiction selector for, first, the *Southwest Review* and then, with Cleanth Brooks, of the *Southern Review*, while Allen Tate was connected with the *Virginia Quarterly Review*. All three were highly desirous of exploiting their contacts with Katherine Anne Porter. In the spring of 1937, Warren wrote that he was "green with envy when I found 'Noon Wine' in STORY." "Circus" appeared in the very first issue of the Brooks and Warren *Southern Review*, and "The Grave,"

16. Gordon to Porter, n.d., Porter Papers.
17. Porter to Gordon, spring 1935, ibid.

"That Tree," and "Two Plantation Portraits" soon appeared in the *Virginia Quarterly*. Givner believes that Porter gave these "little magazines" her stories because she was "disappointed that she could not make more money by selling her work to well-paying magazines like *Harper's*," but Porter's letters to Warren suggest that she was anxious not only to have her work readily accepted and published but to support the efforts of the southern writers with whom she had by then come to identify.[18]

Porter's correspondence with the *Southern Review* editors provides a colorful commentary on her most productive period. On February 24, 1935, when Warren asked her to contribute to the *Southwest Review*, she replied from 70 Rue Notre-Dame-des-Champs, Paris:

> If I had known in time I could have sent you the section from my novel, *Midway in This Mortal Life*, called *Legend and Memory*. But the Virginia Quarterly published two portraits from it, and have accepted for April a fragment called *The Grave*. That leaves only three other fragments, *The Grandmother*, a short portrait; *The Circus*, which might not stand by itself, I don't know; and a very long middle section called *The Old Order*. I am sending you a copy of this anyhow, for I should like for you to read it, whether you wish to use any of it or not.

She added, "Otherwise I have on hand, trying hard to finish it, a fairly long story which I call *Pale Horse and Pale Rider*, though I may find another title. What are your limits as to space for a short story?" On April 4, upon hearing that Brooks and Warren were to establish a new journal, Porter wrote enthusiastically, "I'm so glad there is to be a really substantial review published in the south, and even more glad that you have some authority in it. . . . If I get *Pale Horse and Pale Rider* to you by the end of this month, will there be time enough for you to read and decide?"[19]

True to her word, Porter dispatched manuscripts as quickly as she could produce them, depending on the judgment of the *Southern Review* editors to determine their state of readiness and suitability for publication. The editors, who as in the case of Caroline Gordon did not hesitate to ask for extensive revisions, were eager to take whatever Porter sent them. There is, in fact, no record that they even suggested revisions, much less that they ever considered rejecting one of Porter's stories.

18. Robert Penn Warren to Porter, May 26, 1937, ibid.; Givner, *Katherine Anne Porter: A Life*, 287–88, 306.

19. Porter to Warren, February 24, April 4, 1935, both in Robert Penn Warren Papers, Beinecke Rare Book and Manuscript Library, Yale University, New Haven, Conn.

The *Southern Review* editors eagerly accepted "The Circus," for the same issue (spring 1935) that included Howard Baker's review of *Hacienda*. After Warren wrote, on December 6, "We can't let *The Old Order* go," the story appeared in volume 1, number 3, winter 1936. "Old Mortality," which most authorities consider a short novel, was selected for volume 2, number 4, spring 1937, proving that for Porter, the editors were prepared to exceed their usual word limitations. Finally, the long-awaited *Pale Horse, Pale Rider* constituted the entire fiction section of volume 3, number 3, winter 1938. On June 9, 1941, Warren wrote, "I am hoping to find the novelette you spoke of waiting in Baton Rouge, when we arrive there next week."[20] The "novelette" in question, "The Leaning Tower," appeared in volume 7, number 2, autumn 1941, and was the last story Porter would publish in the *Southern Review*.

Although Porter's privileged position with the *Review* was assured through her connection with Warren and Brooks, it initially fell to Albert Erskine to correspond with her on *Southern Review* business. Erskine met Robert Penn Warren in 1930 when he was an undergraduate at Southwestern College at Memphis (now Rhodes College) and followed him first to Vanderbilt and then to LSU for graduate study. He became associate editor of the LSU-SMU *Southwest Review* and, later, business manager of the *Southern Review*. In that capacity, he became acquainted with Katherine Anne Porter through reading her manuscripts. Porter and Erskine exchanged a series of intriguing letters, beginning in Paris and continuing when she took up residence in New Orleans, while he balanced graduate work with editorial duties in nearby Baton Rouge.[21]

Crucial to Porter's continuing relationship with the former Fugitives and their friends were the events of summer 1937. At Allen Tate's suggestion, Porter was invited in July to fill a vacancy at the Olivet writers' conference in which the Tates and Ford participated and to which Robert Lowell tagged along. It was the first of many such enjoyable and professionally important invitations for Porter. After the conference, Porter finally visited Benfolly. As fate would have it, Erskine also visited the Tates that summer. After a night of talk on the moonlit porch of Benfolly, they began a relationship that led to their ill-fated marriage.[22] With Porter in her late forties to Erskine's late

20. Warren to Porter, December 6, 1935, June 9, 1941, Porter Papers.

21. Albert Erskine, editor's note, *A Robert Penn Warren Reader* (New York: Random House, 1989), xi–xii; Winchell, *Cleanth Brooks and the Rise of Modern Criticism*, 91.

22. Givner, *Katherine Anne Porter: A Life*, 305.

twenties, the two made an improbable match that centered in her literary relationship with the *Southern Review*.

Porter's romance took some members of the Tennessee group by surprise. As late as March 19, 1938, Tate wrote to inform Lytle that "Katherine Anne and Albert Erskine have announced their intention of getting married. [¶] Let it sink in." In his spring 1938 reply, Lytle referred to the couple as "Paris and Helen" and declared that he "foresaw all when they sat up all night together at Benfolly. But must Troy fall again? Will the forty fruit trees be uprooted to make another horse?" Stretching the conceit, he rhetorically inquired, "How many times . . . can the sound of war be bruited about the embattlements surrounding her ladyship's power?" In a letter to Gordon, Porter regaled her friends with an account of the nuptial event, which took place on April 19, 1938:

> The actual wedding was one of those highly secular affairs beginning at eleven o'clock A.M. with drinks—Planters Punches, three all around, in the St. Charles Bar, now a wreck of its former self with Surrealist decorations—a bar quelconque, en effet—Red was best man, of course, and so of course by logical sequence, C[inina Warren]. was best woman or whatever that role is called; Wedding party, decorated with lilies of the valley to which was added three pink roses to the shoulder knot of the bride, erupted out of dusty cars before the Court house . . . on Royal Street.[23]

The Erskines never completed "The Cares," their elaborately planned house, and their marriage was doomed, like the literary journal that fostered it, to an early dissolution.

In its seven-year existence, the *Southern Review* was, however, privileged to publish, in addition to her five works of fiction, Porter's first literary criticism, an essay on Katherine Mansfield (in 1937), and her contribution to the Hardy volume of summer 1940. Of the latter she wrote Warren, two years later, that having to meet the *Review*'s deadline gave her the impetus to complete the essay in an interval which for Porter amounted to dispatch: "You remember the time, Christmas in Baton Rouge, when you and Albert were talking about the Southern Review and you suddenly thought up the Thomas Hardy number, invited me then and there to contribute, and gave me in effect a year and a half notice?" Just before the *Review* ceased operations, she

23. Young and Sarcone, eds., *Tate-Lytle Letters*, 118–20; Porter to Gordon, May 7, 1938, Caroline Gordon Papers, Firestone Library, Princeton University, Princeton, N.J.

had written to Warren: "I know that you and Cleanth did the work of an army in defending the Southern Review. . . . As John Crowe Ransom says in his notice in the latest Kenyon Review, the SR was one of the casualties of the war. But I think, a casualty planned by the enemies in our own house. . . . Well, it is done, and there is one thing they can't destroy: the record of seven years superb work. That stands. And that is where they fail, always. They can't destroy the record."[24] Neither could "they" destroy the ties that the review strengthened between old and new beneficiaries of the Fugitive legacy.

During the New Orleans and Baton Rouge years, Porter formed a close personal friendship with the Brookses, particularly with Mrs. Brooks (Tinkum), that was to endure for their lifetimes. In "The Woman and Artist I Knew," Cleanth Brooks reminisced about their friendship, which began in Baton Rouge when the Brookses lived in an apartment "just across a narrow corridor" from Katherine Anne, and continued through correspondence. These letters, Brooks commented, "display her wit, her sense of humor, her pride in her own abilities, her gift for friendship, and other aspects of this very complex, and in many respects most delightful, woman."[25]

Not surprisingly, Brooks later demonstrated his allegiance by astutely praising Porter's writing. His essay "On 'The Grave,' " first published in the *Yale Review* in 1966, demonstrated why that particular story, already promised to the *Virginia Quarterly Review* before he and Warren could claim it, was just the kind of fiction the *Southern Review* liked best. Brooks began by describing Porter's style as "rich, not thin, full of subtleties and sensitive insights . . . compact and almost unbelievably economical." In Cleanth Brooks's papers at Yale's Beinecke Library, there is another assessment of Katherine Anne Porter's life and literary achievement, written sometime shortly after her death. Brooks lists her best stories: "Noon Wine," "Old Mortality," "The Grave," and "The Circus"—all but one of which appeared in his *Southern Review*— and a catalog of the qualities that marked her style: "symmetry and proportion and an almost perfect management of tone" and "emotion shaped and controlled and directed," resulting in stories that are "classic" but never "bloodless or dry."[26]

24. Porter to Warren, October 8, April 15, 1942, both in Warren Papers.

25. Cleanth Brooks, "The Woman and Artist I Knew," in *Katherine Anne Porter and Texas: An Uneasy Relationship*, ed. Clinton Machann and William Bedford Clark (College Station: Texas A & M University Press, 1990), 13, 15.

26. Cleanth Brooks, "On 'The Grave,' " in *Katherine Anne Porter: A Collection of Critical Essays*, ed. Robert Penn Warren (Englewood Cliffs, N.J.: Prentice-Hall, 1979), 112; Brooks, unpublished essay on Katherine Anne Porter, Brooks Papers.

Robert Penn Warren, who also remained Porter's lifelong personal friend, became her wisest critic. His most perceptive comments are to be found in an essay entitled "Irony with a Center," first published in 1941. Before the essay was published, he wrote to Porter, "I have tried to define the basic attitude (not specifically *literary*) which underlies the stories and have tried to see how this finds its special technical manifestations in structure and style." In his essay, Warren was ready to place her among the "relatively small group of writers—extraordinarily small . . . who have done serious, consistent, original, and vital work in the form of short fiction." He accounts for apparent contradictions, paradoxes, and tonal inconsistencies, in typical New Critical strategy, under the broad umbrella of irony. He argues, however, that Porter's is "an irony with a center, never an irony for irony's sake."[27]

Despite mutual admiration, expressed in frequent exchanges of letters, there seem to be few commonalities linking Warren's fiction with Porter's. Porter was far more generous in her praise of Warren's poetry than of his fiction. She even stated in an interview that she would have preferred that Warren stick to poetry (perhaps so as not to compete with her): " 'I've told Red a hundred times to leave fiction alone and go on with his poetry, but he won't listen to me.' " Of his 1942 *Selected Poems*, she remarked, "Your collection of poems is so fine I would feel impertinent to praise it. Every poem, every line, is splendid." But it was *Promises*, with its lyrical celebration of her goddaughter Rosanna, that brought forth Porter's most eloquent praise: "Rosanna's short series is divine all the way through, like a prelude in music that introduces the main theme, preparing the ear for everything that is to come."[28]

Warren often discussed the arduous travail of his fiction writing with Porter, but he seemed never to have asked her advice on any technical problem. In the middle of writing *All the King's Men*, Warren wrote somewhat dejectedly: "Things here drift along. I am revising my novel, and have the dumps over it and over everything else I've ever done. Very badly. It must be nice to feel that you must feel—you've been told it often enough anyway—that some of the things you've done are just as they ought to be."[29] In the same letter, Warren described Eleanor Clark, Porter's friend since Yaddo and Warren's

27. Warren to Porter, June 9, 1941, Porter Papers; Robert Penn Warren, "Irony with a Center," in *Katherine Anne Porter*, ed. Warren, 93, 107.

28. Givner, ed., *Katherine Anne Porter: Conversations*, 62; Porter to Warren, September 26, 1957, Warren Papers.

29. Warren to Porter, June 30, 1945, Porter Papers.

new acquaintance, as a "fine, intelligent, gifted girl." Porter may actually have introduced Warren to the woman who would become his second wife.

Porter preferred Warren's "Cass Mastern's Wedding Ring," a portion of *All the King's Men* which he published in the fall of 1944 in the *Partisan Review*, to any of his short stories. On December 22, 1946, she wrote *"Blackberry Summer [sic]*, is such a superb story it almost threw me off my first love, *Cass Mastern's Wedding Ring*. But the whole fine breathing manuscript gave me a beautiful day and also threw me into momentary confusions."[30]

For his part, Warren always included Porter when planning an anthology of fiction. On May 26, 1937, Warren wrote, with his "more amiable impulses . . . fortified by a small piece of brutal self interest," that "Houghton Mifflin has asked me to prepare a collection of short stories by Southern writers. Naturally, I want to include something of yours, and something that will make as big a showing as possible—probably 'Noon Wine' or 'Old Mortality.' " As always, such arrangements depended on permissions from and fees paid to the publishers who owned the material, and they were not always either generous or forthcoming. For whatever reason, it was "He" that actually did appear in *A Southern Harvest*. Writing on November 5, 1941, Warren asked Porter's permission to include "Old Mortality" in a companion book to *Understanding Poetry*. They "already have an analysis of *Old Mortality*, which we shall include if our budget which Crofts allows us is big enough. If the budget doesn't permit, we shall have to use a shorter, and therefore cheaper, story." Porter fervently replied that she indeed wanted Warren to "have *Old Mortality* for the other book of fiction. . . . I will see that you get it for . . . $200, same as Harcourt had charged another anthologer for *PH, PR*, or less if I can persuade them."[31] This "other book" was *Understanding Fiction*, Brooks and Warren's most influential collection of and commentary on short fiction.

On March 15, 1958, elated at having just received the National Book Award for *Promises*, Warren sent some recently written poems for Porter's opinion. These typed pages, signed "La Rocca, September 22, 1958," include the following poems: "Garland for You, Poem," "Debate: Question, Quarry, Dream," "Fatal Interview: Penthesileia and Achilles," "Equinox on Mediterranean Beach," "Switzerland," and, in a group entitled *Some Quiet Plain Poems*, "Ornithology in a World of Flux," "Holly and Hickory," "In Moon-

30. Porter to Warren, December 22, 1946, Warren Papers.

31. Warren to Porter, May 26, 1937, November 5, 1941, both in Porter Papers; Porter to Warren, November 9, 1941, Warren Papers.

light, Somewhere, They Are Singing," "The Well-House," and "In Italian They Call the Creature *Civetta*." He directed her, "Don't return them—throw into waste basket," and closes, in all caps, with "AND FOR GOD'S SAKE FINISH YOU KNOW WHAT SO I CAN READ IT!"[32]

He alluded, of course, to *Ship of Fools*, still four years away from publication. When the novel appeared in 1962, it drew reviews ranging from encomium to diatribe, but the post-Fugitive circle was warmly supportive. Warren later wrote: "For what it is worth, I'll submit the fact that the first time I picked up a copy of *Ship of Fools*, I expected to read through breakfast and then go to work. I did not lay the book aside until after midnight, and not once did I worry about method, point of view, thematic concerns, or the relation of this or that episode to the entire work. I was simply caught in its toils."[33] Warren considered Porter an authority on fiction and never presumed to advise her, although his output of fiction far outdid hers. Porter's impact on Warren's fiction is, however, demonstrated by the fact that while both were in residence at the Library of Congress in 1944, she provided him with the donnée for *World Enough and Time*, which some consider his greatest novel.

Although it is difficult to gauge how her association with the Fugitives and their circle actually affected Porter's writing, their collective impact, as productive writers who expected a lot of their writer friends, cannot be discounted. The stories which Porter, Gordon, and Lytle wrote have strong similarities. Lytle's "Jericho, Jericho, Jericho" (1935) has more than superficial similarities both to "The Jilting of Granny Weatherall" (1929) and to *Pale Horse, Pale Rider* (1938). Intertextual relationships in the literary careers of Katherine Anne Porter and Caroline Gordon are more likely.

The friendship between the grasshopper and the ant was to endure through the years, though not without its stormy episodes. Shortly after Caroline and Allen decided to divorce in 1945, Porter wrote to Andrew Lytle in a spiteful tone: "I think of the marriages they [Tate and Gordon] tried to break up—I know of three, myself—it isn't irony at all but just exactly the slow overtaking of poetic justice that it was their own marriage they were breaking up all that time." Nevertheless, Gordon remained constant in her admiration of Porter's accomplishment. In 1963, when Gordon reviewed William Nance's book *Katherine Anne Porter and the Art of Rejection*, she hotly attacked Nance for reductively subjecting all of Porter's work to his "interna-

32. Warren to Porter, September [1958?], Porter Papers.
33. Warren, introduction to *Katherine Anne Porter*, ed. Warren, 19.

tional critical machine" of Freudian psychological analysis. Porter's grateful reply, in a letter to Gordon, attested to the unity, against outside threats, among the writers of the Fugitive legacy: "It was a heroic act of friendship for you to take the immense trouble to smack that hovering insect, and I am grateful, for I have had a swarm of them."[34]

To her contacts within the Fugitive legacy Porter owed much; and in her own harum-scarum way, she carried on the tradition, lending a share of her own confidence and her imprimatur to those young writers, whose fiction, as well as personalities, was congenial with her own. In one of her most famous interviews, in 1965 with Hank Lopez, Porter was asked, "Who of this newer generation of writers do you like most?" In addition to Eudora Welty, who became "spectacularly famous," Porter invoked the names of several who were then relatively unknown, including Peter Taylor, "one of the best writers we have. . . . [He] has published three books and the latest one, *Miss Leonora When Last Seen*, is a collection of splendid short stories," and Caroline Gordon, whose *None Shall Look Back* is "the best novel I know set in the South during the Civil War." But to Lopez's comment on the similarity to and possible influence of "Noon Wine" on Flannery O'Connor's "The Displaced Person," Porter shot back that she "cannot see it" although O'Connor herself had acknowledged the influence.[35] Despite the multitude of literary friends and pupils Porter claimed in her career, the mantle she passed was in essence a bequest to the most talented young fiction writers of the Fugitive legacy.

34. Porter to Lytle, n.d. [1945], Lytle Papers; Caroline Gordon, "Katherine Anne Porter and the ICM," *Harper's* November 1964, 146; Porter to Gordon, November 5, 1964, Gordon Papers.

35. Givner, ed., *Katherine Anne Porter: Conversations*, 131–32.

PART IV

The Fugitive Legacy to Fiction:
Three Protégés

> It happened for me that the strangers—the first readers of my first stories—included Robert Penn Warren and Cleanth Brooks, the editors of the *Southern Review*. This distinguished quarterly, between 1937 and 1939, gave space to six stories of mine. Katherine Anne Porter, when she read some of them there, sat down and wrote me a letter of encouragement. The generosity of these writers' openness to me, their critical regard when it mattered most, not to mention the long friendships that began by letter in those days, have nourished my life.
>
> —Eudora Welty, Introduction to *The Collected Stories of Eudora Welty*

Along with Peter Taylor, Eudora Welty and Flannery O'Connor belong to a second, somewhat younger generation of fiction writers whose careers benefited from association with one or more of the former Fugitives. Welty and Taylor were especially fortunate in having entrées with the editors of the *Southern Review*, Cleanth Brooks and Robert Penn Warren; and Brooks and Warren, in turn, were fortunate to have access to the short stories of two young fiction writers of immense potential. Unlike all the other heirs to the Fugitive legacy, Eudora Welty was never at Vanderbilt, Kenyon, or Sewanee; nor did she visit the Tates in New York City or at Benfolly. Welty's introduction to the circle was her writing, and it was some time before she exchanged the status of a faceless contributor to the *Southern Review* for that of a valued colleague within the Fugitive legacy's widening circle. For Welty, the Fugitive legacy, though not essential to her career, became a source of support through valuable literary relationships, two of which, with Robert Penn Warren and Katherine Anne Porter, remained strong throughout the most productive years of her writing.

After Welty had published five stories—"Death of a Traveling Salesman" (*Manuscript* 3 [May–June 1936]), "The Doll" (*Tanager* 11 [June 1936]), "Magic" (*Manuscript* [1936]), "Lily Daw and the Three Ladies" (*Prairie*

Schooner 11 [Winter 1937]), and "Retreat" (*River* 1 [March 1937])—for the "honor" of seeing her work in print, she finally received payment in 1937, when "A Piece of News" was accepted by the *Southern Review*. Between 1937 and the final issue in 1942, the Brooks-Warren *Review* published seven of her stories (see Appendix), making Welty one of the *Review*'s most frequent contributors.

As an unknown, almost unpublished writer, Welty did not enjoy anything like Porter's automatic success with the *Southern Review*. Her first submissions, not fiction but poetry, elicited a polite rejection from Robert Penn Warren: "We find much to interest us in your verse, but have decided against immediate publication. May we see more of your work?" When Welty began to send stories, however, the editors warmed up rapidly and, as Warren later recalled, greeted with eager anticipation anything postmarked "Jackson, Mississippi": "I'll never forget the morning of the first envelope from Mississippi . . . a special piece of good luck had come our way. . . . Everything is recognizable, but illuminated by a strange, unique glow. . . . Once you seemed to me a sudden comet shooting across . . . darkness and stars, but now you and your work—seem a fixed star, shedding steadily your peculiar transmuting light."[1]

It was some time, however, before Brooks and Warren could decide just which of Welty's stories to publish. On January 13, 1937, Warren wrote: "We have been extremely interested in these stories and several times have been on the verge of publishing two of them[,] 'Petrified Man' and 'Flowers for Marjorie.' We thank [*sic*] that both of them are extremely well done." Warren nonetheless rejected "Flowers for Marjorie" as being "somewhat conventional in subject matter" and "Petrified Man" because "we were not quite satisfied in the way it held together as a story." (According to Mark Winchell, however, it was actually Charles Pipkin, nominal editor of the *Review*, who insisted that the story be rejected on first submission.) Warren added that "we are absolutely confident that if you are good enough to submit other work to us, we can publish your things in THE SOUTHERN REVIEW." On February 4, however, the editors were still waffling: "We do not like the present story—as a story—as much as we liked your previous one. But there is certainly a touch of distinction in the writing of the present piece. We are beginning to regret that we rejected 'The Petrified Man' [*sic*], and we might like to

1. Robert Penn Warren to Eudora Welty, September 23, 1936, Eudora Welty Papers, Mississippi Department of Archives and History, Jackson, Mississippi; Warren to Welty, 1984, Warren Papers.

reopen the question of publication some time in the near future." On May 17, 1937, Warren finally informed Welty that the editors had come to a decision: "We are going to use your story, 'A Piece of News,' probably in the Summer issue. The other one is here enclosed. May we see more of your work soon?"[2]

Nor was it to be smooth sailing thereafter for Welty and the *Southern Review* editors. On August 17, 1937, Cleanth Brooks wrote: "We have kept your stories perhaps longer than we should have, but the delay has been prompted by a very genuine interest in them. I think that your story which we published is very fine indeed, and I think that the writing in the two stories, which we regret to be returning, is uniformly good. . . . At any rate, we certainly want to see more of your work and all of your work that you will send to us." On September 23, Warren conveyed another acceptance—"I am happy to say that we are using your story 'A Memory' in the Fall issue, which will be out soon"—and asked to see "other pieces." On February 22, 1938, he accepted "Old Mr. Grenada" and characteristically added: "Here is the other story, which we should have sent back to you before this. But have you any more handy?" On March 23, 1938, Warren wrote to Welty, "Mr. Paul Brooks, of Houghton Mifflin, has sent me the enclosed material with the suggestion that we ask you to compete for their fiction award this year. If you are interested in doing this, THE SOUTHERN REVIEW will certainly do everything it can to push your case." Welty did not receive that award; but in closing his letter of March 23, 1938, Warren remarked that "Old Mr. Grenada" would appear in the spring issue and added: "I like it better all the time. Have you any more stories on hand? And may we give another look at 'The Petrified Man' at some time?"[3]

Like other contributors, Welty was willing to revise her stories to enhance their attractiveness to the *Southern Review* editors. On September 9, 1938, Warren reacted to one such effort by writing that "we are very much interested in 'A Curtain of Green,' but want to have the revision which you mentioned in your letter of August 16, before making a final decision." Before Warren requested another look at "Petrified Man," Welty had burned the story but was able to reconstruct it. She was afraid, however, that she "might

2. Warren to Welty, January 13, February 4, May 17, 1937, all in Welty Papers; Winchell, *Cleanth Brooks and the Rise of Modern Criticism*, 106.

3. Cleanth Brooks to Welty, August 17, 1937; Warren to Welty, September 23, 1937, February 22, March 23, 1938, all in Welty Papers.

have done something wrong—this couldn't be exactly the story they thought they'd bought."[4] "Petrified Man," one of Welty's most popular stories, appeared in the spring 1939 issue.

Although Welty was bolstered by her successes in Baton Rouge, the relationship had its frustrations. In *Author and Agent: Eudora Welty and Diarmuid Russell*, Michael Kreyling has made Welty's correspondence with Diarmuid Russell available, revealing the other side of her relationship with the *Southern Review*. When she wrote on May 31, 1940, to accept Russell's offer of agency, Welty was beginning to look elsewhere for a place to publish: "It will take some desk-clearing on the part of certain editors for me to get the stories back to send you. The Southern Review, a quarterly, which has helped me very much by being interested in and publishing my stories, likes to see them first, and I try to let them have their choice. . . . The fact is, they already have enough of my stuff on hand to read, without this. I am hoping that you can get my stories in other magazines." When both the *Southern Review* and *Story* rejected "Keela, the Outcast Indian Maiden," she finally wrote to Russell on November 5, 1940, in a rare display of disgust and anger: "The Southern Review people, while they were nice and friendly, and helped me greatly by starting me out and printing what I wrote, still never made any remarks or comments at all, and it was just like being kept in the dark. They stayed like that, after all they had done for me, up to the last story I sent, Powerhouse, which they returned without a word about it. . . . They were a little sultanic, don't you think? An acceptance was equally baffling—they would just send me up a proof-sheet to correct." Russell's reply was sympathetic but frank: "The way the Southern Review sends back stories to you is in a way a reflection of their opinion about you. When there is something wrong about your stories it is impossible to pin it on anything definite."[5]

Welty was fortunate that her agent and publishers were not working at cross purposes and could supplement each other's editorial commentary. The editors' problem was, in part, their lack of critical expertise about the craft of fiction and their subsequent preference for stories that resembled lyric poetry. Welty's early stories fall into two basic types: satiric and realistic or mythic and lyrical. Brooks and Warren, New Critics ever, had a strong bias not only toward stories that satisfied their requirement for "organic unity"

---

4. Warren to Welty, September 9, 1938, Welty Papers; Cutrer, *Parnassus on the Mississippi*, 93.

5. Michael Kreyling, *Author and Agent: Eudora Welty and Diarmuid Russell* (New York: Farrar, Straus & Giroux, 1991), 23, 48–50.

but also toward those in which lyrical qualities and linguistic dexterity were as important as plot or characters. When they were vaguely dissatisfied with a piece of fiction, they most likely thought that the story did not cohere in all aspects of content and style and therefore did not lend itself readily to New Critical analysis. Like other young contributors, Welty was almost certainly encouraged to develop qualities in her fiction that would make it attractive to Brooks and Warren. Consequently, the stories Welty published in the *Wide Net* were so uniformly of the second type that even Robert Penn Warren complained when he reviewed the collection.

Welty's publications in the *Southern Review* brought her the unexpected pleasure and the benefit of a close personal and professional relationship with Katherine Anne Porter, who was at the time of Welty's debut living in Baton Rouge during her marriage to Albert Erskine. Welty later recalled that she was both surprised that a writer of Porter's caliber had deigned to write to her and well aware that it had happened because of her connections with the Baton Rouge community: "When in 1937 Robert Penn Warren, Cleanth Brooks, and Albert Erskine, editors of the *Southern Review*, had decided to use two of my stories, the significance of that acceptance was not lost on me. They had thought my work good enough to take a chance on, to encourage. Still I had not been prepared for a letter, out of the blue, from Katherine Anne Porter after the stories appeared. She was not an editor, but a *writer*, a writer of short stories; she was out in the world, at Baton Rouge."[6] That Baton Rouge was Welty's idea of "out in the world" is humorous, but her reaction was nonetheless appropriate; Porter, whose reputation was well established, had recognized affinities with Welty that would solidify their personal and professional relationship.

Porter was not only a successful writer but also a woman. As Peter Schmidt has pointed out, both Porter and Welty "came of age during some of the most severe attacks against the New Woman."[7] Women who wrote for publication had to appeal to the men who for the most part wrote, edited, and published the nation's books and magazines; nor did Welty and her contemporaries appear to question that arrangement. Despite their differing attitudes and priorities, these women writers of the Fugitive legacy felt strong allegiance to its essentially patriarchal structure. Since the Fugitive legacy to

6. Eudora Welty, "My Introduction to Katherine Anne Porter," in Rosemary M. Magee, ed., *Friendship and Sympathy: Communities of Southern Women Writers* (Jackson: University Press of Mississippi, 1992), 120.

7. Peter Schmidt, *The Heart of the Story: Eudora Welty's Short Fiction* (Jackson: University Press of Mississippi, 1991), 265.

fiction foregrounded women writers from the beginning, however, Welty, like Porter and Gordon, quickly attained peerage with members of the male contingent who did not specialize in fiction. For Welty, who was temperamentally unlikely either to rebel against the male literary establishment or to seek out a supportive female precursor, bonding with Porter was an unexpected sign that she could indeed succeed as a writer.

In 1940–41, after several of her stories had appeared in journals and popular magazines, Welty had naturally begun to explore possibilities for the publication of a collection. To do so not only would place her stories within the relatively permanent protection of hard covers but also would authenticate her status in the literary world. She was, however, laying herself open to another round of disappointing rejections. In an undated letter that gives what Kreyling calls "a condensed history of her frustrations in the literary marketplace," Welty dejectedly remarked that, in the autumn of 1940, she was not sure who had already seen and rejected her stories. She had heard that Ford Madox Ford, at the instigation of Katherine Anne Porter, was sending a collection of them "round among his friends, but from his notes I could not ever be sure just who saw it."[8]

Through the efforts of Russell with John Woodburn at Doubleday Doran, Welty's book, eventually entitled *A Curtain of Green and Other Stories*, was finally contracted as of January 21, 1941. Although Porter had expressed interest in Welty's stories, Welty was even more surprised and delighted when, at Russell's suggestion, Porter consented to write an introduction. The next step was for Welty to provide Russell with a fair copy of the stories to be included, which he would subsequently place in Porter's hands. On February 22, 1941, having "this minute finished typing up the stories," Welty wrote to Porter at Yaddo, the writers' colony at Saratoga, New York. Her growing excitement about the collection was mixed with polite concern for any burden the introduction might place on a busy, successful author: "I stay a little overwhelmed from day to day, that all this is happening. Of course you're not to give a thought to my stories until the novel is good and finished." Asked for a little background material, Welty replied: "I'll set down the little things you asked and you can have them when the time comes. No, I didn't have my first story in the Southern Review, or even submit it there—who would have thought I would get paid for things—John Rood of Manuscript printed the first, 'Death of a Traveling Salesman' in 1936. . . . The S.R. gave me money

8. Kreyling, *Author and Agent*, 34.

first though, soon after, the next year, for 'A Piece of News.' They've published 6, Atlantic will have had 3, Harper's Bazaar 1. That's the story."[9]

On May 1, 1941, Welty thanked Porter for getting her an invitation to Yaddo for the following summer: "Mrs. Ames wrote that I was invited to come to Yaddo, which is grand, delightful news—and thanks for handing in my name and saying I would work hard, for she told me she had that report." At Yaddo, Porter and Welty actually got to know each other in a personal way—but not because of any close collaboration on Welty's book. In "My Introduction to Katherine Anne Porter," Welty related how, after quickly reading proof for *A Curtain of Green*, she spent the rest of her time at Yaddo sight-seeing and listening at Porter's door for signs that she was at work, perhaps on the introduction. By March 16, 1941, Porter's introduction was finally in the hands of the Doubleday establishment. Later the same year, Welty conveyed her delight and gratitude for Porter's help on a job well done: "The preface is beautiful—John just sent me a proof, the same day. You know how I love having you do it and how I thank you—it's so long! xxiii pages, which I take to be 23, which I think is a lot."[10]

Porter's introduction to *A Curtain of Green and Other Stories* was the first important critical essay to be published on Welty's fiction. By reading Welty through the distorted glass of her own experience and strong opinions about how fiction is written, Porter either foregrounded those aspects of Welty's stories that resembled her own or created a myth to explain how Welty could succeed and yet be different. Using almost verbatim the "little potted biography" that Welty had supplied, Porter played up Welty's provinciality and almost miraculous literary genesis: "Being the child of her place and time, profiting perhaps without being aware of it by the cluttered experiences, foreign travels, and disorders of the generation immediately preceding her, she will never have to go away and live among the Eskimos, or Mexican Indians; she need not follow a war and smell death [Hemingway] to feel herself alive; she knows about death already. She shall not need even to live in New York in order to feel that she is having the kind of experience, the sense of 'life proper to a serious author.' " Porter exaggerated Welty's isolation by saying that, in addition to self-exclusion from literary groups, she "had never discussed with any colleague or older artist any problem of her craft" until "after her first collection was ready to be published." Expanding her myth of Welty

9. Ibid., 61; Welty to Porter, February 22, March 16, 1941, Porter Papers.

10. Welty to Porter, May 1, 1941, and n.d. [1941], both in Porter Papers; Eudora Welty, "My Introduction to Katherine Anne Porter," in Magee, ed., *Friendship and Sympathy*, 128–29.

the *wunderkind*, Porter described her development as "a cellular growth in a most complex organism"—"a way of life and a mode of being which cannot be divided from the kind of human creature you were the day you were born." Welty was proof for Porter that the best writers (herself included) are not produced by schools of creative writing. They learn their craft by reading "early and omnivorously" in the classics—Greek and Roman poetry, history and fable, Shakespeare, Milton, Dante, the nineteenth-century French and Russian novelists—"and by discover[ing] contemporary literature," in authors like Yeats and Woolf, who are "in the air about her."[11]

Porter saw herself, a successful writer of short fiction, as uniquely suited to be Welty's champion against the literary establishment's unreasonable demands. Welty must, Porter advised, be leery of the "trap lying just ahead . . . and all short story writers know what it is—The Novel. Already publishers have told her, 'give us first a novel, and then we will publish your short stories.' "[12] Porter knew of the struggles which she, along with colleagues such as Tate, Lytle, and Gordon, had had with their publishers. In Welty, Porter saw a reenactment of her own history, characterized by no little success in thwarting those publishers and somehow remaining, primarily, a writer of short stories. Like Porter, Welty would continue to consider short fiction her forte but eventually move beyond it to the short novel and from there to the full-length novel. Here, of course, the "pupil" was destined to surpass the "teacher."

When the contents of *A Curtain of Green and Other Stories* were still unsettled, Welty enlisted Porter's help in persuading her publisher to include *The Robber Bridegroom*, which she described as "the thing I like best that I wrote, a long story, about 100 pages, really a tale, as wild as anything." Although Porter dutifully promoted its inclusion, both Russell and Woodburn, who anticipated a collection of stories involving the Natchez Trace, voted against the addition, and Welty agreed. On February 22, she wrote Porter, "Oh dear, about the Robber Bridegroom, my long story, I gave you the wrong impression, it was just an idle, grandiose wish wishing it were in, just to say how pleased I was about everything—a sort of sweeping feeling."[13] That decision ironically resulted in *The Robber Bridegroom*'s separate publication in 1942.

11. Katherine Anne Porter, introduction to *A Curtain of Green and Other Stories by Eudora Welty* (1941; rpt. New York: Harvest, 1979), xiv, xv.

12. Ibid., xviii.

13. Welty to Porter, February 15, 22, 1941, both in Porter Papers; Kreyling, *Author and Agent*, 62.

Without intending to, Welty had published her first (short) novel, which she appropriately dedicated to Katherine Anne Porter.

The publication of Welty's second collection of short stories, *The Wide Net and Other Stories* (1943), was the occasion of Robert Penn Warren's seminal essay "The Love and the Separateness in Miss Welty," first published in the spring 1944 issue of Ransom's *Kenyon Review*. Warren began by comparing *A Curtain of Green* with *The Wide Net*. The first collection demonstrated remarkable variety, whereas the second, in Warren's words, "represent[ed] a specializing, an intensifying, of one of the many strains which were present in *A Curtain of Green*." Instead of a range of moods and tones—ranging from fantasy to pathos—Warren found that "the stories are more nearly cut to one pattern." The reader enters "a special world," wherein all events occur within a "season of dreams," uniformly characterized by the "special tone and mood, the special perspective, the special sensibility with which they are rendered." And although Warren seemed disappointed in this new strain in Welty's fiction, he nonetheless emerged as Welty's defender against the likes of Diana Trilling of the *Nation*, who preferred the Eudora Welty of *A Curtain of Green*, who exhibited "a reliable and healthy wit" and "dialogue . . . as reportorial of its world as the dialogue of Ring Lardner."[14]

It is entirely proper that Warren should have defended *A Curtain of Green* because as editors of the *Southern Review*, he and Brooks were generally unreceptive to Welty's satiric and realistic offerings. They had, after all, nearly caused the loss of "Petrified Man" and had rejected "Keela, the Outcast Indian Maid." In this new collection, Welty, by intensifying her gift for lyrical impressionism, brought her separate stories into stylistic unity. Warren played the New Critic first by objecting to one kind of unity and then finding, despite himself, an acceptable "presiding idea" in both Welty collections—that "almost all of the stories deal with people who, in one way or another, are cut off, alienated, isolated from the world."[15] As soon as Warren had located a unifying theme in all of Welty's fiction, he could approve of her art.

Warren devoted a major section of the essay to "A Still Moment." Welty's "moment" involves the fusion of radically different perspectives—those of Lorenzo Dow, a backwoods preacher; James Murrell, a highway robber; and John James Audubon, artist and naturalist. In the same instant, the attention

14. Robert Penn Warren, "The Love and Separateness in Miss Welty," in Erskine, ed., *Robert Penn Warren Reader*, 196–97; Diana Trilling, "Fiction in Review," *Nation*, October 2, 1943, reprinted in *Critical Essays on Eudora Welty* ed. W. Craig Turner and Lee Ealing Harding (Boston: G. K. Hall, 1989), 39.

15. Warren, "Love and Separateness," 199.

of these very different individuals is riveted on a single arresting object: "In that quiet moment a solitary snowy heron flew down not far away and began to feed beside the marsh water."[16] From his reading of the story, Warren found reason to focus on only one member of the trilogy, Audubon, who shatters the stillness by shooting the heron. Contemplation of the tension inherent in Audubon's dilemma, as Welty portrays it, provoked in Warren his own moment of lyrical intensity: "Neither Lorenzo [the evangelist] nor Murrell [the outlaw] can 'love' the bird, and so escape from their own curse as did, again, the Ancient Mariner. But there is the case of Audubon himself, who does 'love' the bird, who can innocently accept nature. There is, however, an irony here. To paint the bird he must 'know' the bird as well as 'love' it, he must know it feather by feather, he must have it in his hand. And so he must kill it."[17] Years later, Warren composed one of his most important poetic sequences, *Audubon: A Vision*, around this same theme of love through knowledge. "A Still Moment" was not only seminal to *Audubon: A Vision* but must also have helped to shape "A Poem of Pure Imagination," Warren's essay on Samuel Taylor Coleridge's "Rime of the Ancient Mariner."

After close analyses of several other stories from *The Wide Net*, Warren closed his essay with a caveat—"It is possible that in trying to define the basic issue and theme of Miss Welty's stories, I have made them appear too systematic, too mechanical." Recognizing this downside of the New Critical agenda did not, however, prevent Warren from praising Welty's art in New Critical terms: "The method is similar to the method of much modern poetry, and to that of much modern fiction and drama . . . but at the same time it is a method as old as fable, myth, and parable." Warren predicted, however, that "the method, if pursued much farther, might lead to monotony and self-imitation and merely decorative elaboration." He suggested that Welty ought to [submit] "her vision more daringly to fact."[18] If Warren's essay reveals any trepidation about the direction Welty's development was taking, surely it was occasioned by his realization that her art was the logical result of New Critical methodology.

Warren's admiration of Welty's fiction led him and Brooks to include two of her stories in their first edition of *Understanding Fiction* (1943). Welty's conspicuous presence among the likes of Joyce, Poe, Maupassant, Faulkner,

16. Eudora Welty, *The Collected Stories of Eudora Welty* (New York: Harcourt Brace Jovanovich, 1980), 195.

17. Warren, "Love and Separateness," 200.

18. Ibid., 204–6.

Hawthorne, and Kipling no doubt had as much to do with the realities of publication as with critical appraisal. Having published "A Piece of News" and "Old Mr. Marblehall" in the *Southern Review*, Brooks and Warren had easy access to the stories without lengthy and expensive negotiations with other publishers. For Welty, however, their choice of her stories from among many others was a substantial validation of her literary importance.

Although the Fugitives' heirs generally acknowledged their mentors and were usually grateful for their assistance, they seldom if ever admitted any direct influence in their writing. Occasionally, the strands of intertextuality extended backward from mentee to mentor. Eudora Welty not only gave Robert Penn Warren and Katherine Anne Porter credit for their roles in her own career but also had an effect on their later writing. To Warren, she contributed the germ of a poetic sequence; to Porter, Welty contributed an important essay, "Katherine Anne Porter: The Eye of the Story," and, perhaps, the idea for a narrative essay, "A Defense of Circe."

Because Welty and Porter enjoyed a close professional relationship, as well as many artistic affinities, their two "Circe's" provide a unique opportunity for comparing and contrasting their narrative strategies. Welty's "Circe," initially published as "Put Me in the Sky" (in *Accent*, autumn 1949), in effect brings Homer's tale of the witch-goddess down to earth by giving it the texture of earthly existence. Porter's "A Defense of Circe," published in the June 1954 issue of *Mademoiselle*, gilds the subject and elevates her, and her hero, above the darkling plain of mere mortal existence.

When Cyrilly Abels requested " 'something' for *Mademoiselle*'s annual beauty number," Katherine Anne Porter "coincidentally" produced her "defense," which proved to be the only product of her Ann Arbor year. Did Porter read Welty's story before, during, or after composing her own? In a letter dated February 20, 1956, Porter praised Welty's *Place in Fiction*, calling it "next to the *Odyssey* . . . about my favorite reading matter now." But in the margin, in pen, she added, "I think our pieces about Circe so near together a strange coincidence—after thinking about it for some 15 years I finally got to it in March 1954 in Ann Arbor." By then, Porter could have read "Circe" in Welty's 1955 collection, *The Bride of the Innisfallen*. To Givner, however, Porter "described it [her "Circe"] as the only original idea she ever had."[19] She did not, however, consider it original enough for placement among her works of fiction but instead included it with her essays and occasional pieces. Unlike

---

19. Givner, *Katherine Anne Porter: A Life*, 411–13; Porter to Welty, February 20, 1956, Porter Papers.

Welty, whose fiction abounds in mythological allusions and topoi, Porter made no other direct use of Greek mythology in her short stories and short novels.

Welty's close friendship with Porter had suffered a temporary disjuncture in the late 1940s, which some attribute to Welty's publication of a full-length novel, *Delta Wedding*, twenty years before *Ship of Fools*. Not only had Welty preceded her mentor in the literary genre they had once jointly spurned, but she angered Porter by failing to mention her in "The Reading and Writing of Short Stories," which appeared in the *Atlantic Monthly* in 1949. When *The Golden Apples* came out the same year, Porter labeled it "technical virtuosity gone into a dizzy spin absolutely drunk on language, a personal showing off as shameless as a slackwire dancer with pinwheels." In time, however, the relationship was resumed, if never to be quite so strong, and by 1952, Porter was enthusiastically planning a visit to Jackson, where they might "catch up on our gossip, tie up floating ends into little bowknots, and just enjoy our visit."[20]

In 1965, the *Yale Review* published Welty's best-known essay, "Katherine Anne Porter: The Eye of the Story." Perhaps since the subtitle of the article became the title for Welty's volume of selected essays (1978), it is also her favorite. Not only did the essay allow Welty to show gratitude for Porter's introduction to *A Curtain of Green*, but it stands as testimonial to their long friendship. The essay centered, however, on an extended contrast between Porter's mode of fiction and Welty's own. The key word *eye* signifies the direction and focus of the writer's vision; and Katherine Anne Porter's "eye" turns inward. In effect, Welty had, by positioning Porter's art in opposition to her own, made it abundantly clear that she had never for a minute intended to imitate Porter. Perhaps because, as Givner records, 1965 was a triumphant year for Porter, with *Ship of Fools* out and *The Collected Stories* and other lucrative contracts in the works, she registered no objection to Welty's essay.[21]

Although less important to her career than Warren and Porter, Cleanth Brooks emerged from his *Southern Review* dealings with Eudora Welty as another valuable supporter and friend. In July 1993, Brooks looked back on their meeting: "Fairly early in her career she drove down from Jackson, Mississippi to Baton Rouge and called on my wife and me and we had a pleasant evening together. If I remember Warren was out of town, perhaps in Italy at

20. Givner, *Katherine Anne Porter: A Life*, 372, 371; Porter to Welty, February 13, 1952, Porter Papers.

21. Givner, *Katherine Anne Porter: A Life*, 474–75.

the time. At any rate a fast friendship quickly developed and we counted on Eudora Welty as one of our prime young authors." Brooks's comments on Welty's writing appeared in *Understanding Fiction*, as well as in several of his articles. In "Eudora Welty and the Southern Idiom," Brooks, in the role of dialectician, commended Eudora Welty for "works that make use of the resources of our language at its highest level." Using "Petrified Man," *Losing Battles*, and *The Optimist's Daughter* as his primary examples, Brooks commented on Welty's depiction of the lower socioeconomic strata of southern society but insisted that "like the good artist that she is, she never condescends to the folk culture or treats it with anything less than full artistic seriousness." His article "The Past Reexamined: *The Optimist's Daughter*" is a thoroughly sympathetic reading of that novel, and, as in the earlier essay, Brooks defended Welty's unpatronizing treatment of "poor white" characters. Clearly, Brooks approved of Welty's social realism, perhaps without realizing that, like most writers of the Fugitive legacy, she identified with the patrician characters—the Laurel Hands against the Wanda Fay Chisoms—in her fiction. And yet Welty does not write as a regionalist, or the *Southern Review* would have rejected her stories along with Mildred Haun's. Brooks's closing remark in the first essay made it clear that he admired Welty's fiction not only because it renders the "folk tradition" faithfully but also "incorporate[s] it into the written [tradition]."[22]

Although her writings include important and insightful essays and reviews, Eudora Welty has never considered herself a critic or a literary historian. She did not compose any overall assessment of the general state of letters in the South until the September 17, 1954, issue of the *Times Literary Supplement*, when she published an essay entitled "Place and Time: The Southern Writer's Inheritance."

Beginning with Faulkner, by her admission "the man right now," she soon moved to the more general topic of the southern writer and, in due course, to the Fugitives and their unique importance to her own generation: "Their little group flourished and reached out, for the reason that they were, first of all, a group of creative minds, charged to bursting point with the poetic impulse. This was too much to defeat. It is the Underground of all time." From Welty's perspective, the history of the Fugitive movement was defined and chronicled by the periodicals they brought into being. From the "original

22. Cleanth Brooks, letter to author, July 30, 1993; Cleanth Brooks, "Eudora Welty and the Southern Idiom," in *Eudora Welty: A Form of Thanks*, ed. Louis Dollarhide and Ann J. Abadie (Jackson: University Press of Mississippi, 1979), 3, 24.

organ . . . the little magazine called the *Fugitive*, green in the mind today for its poetry and criticism," she then turned to the *Southern Review*, as the "next established quarterly" of the Agrarians, and how these new literary magazines shaped her own generation of writers: "It is likely that the new crop, paying all respect and honor to what had been done before them, would have written their stories and poems just the same, without the agrarians: they simply would never have got published. The *Southern Review*, edited in Baton Rouge, La., by Robert Penn Warren and Cleanth Brooks and Albert Erskine . . . was of inestimable help to these new writers in giving them publication in austerely good company, under the blessing of discriminating editing, without ever seeking to alter or absorb them."[23] There could be no more eloquent or inclusive statement of the nature and scope of the Fugitive legacy.

23. Welty, "Place and Time: The Southern Writer's Inheritance," *Times Literary Supplement*, September 17, 1954, typescript, Welty Papers, 7–9.

13 / Peter Taylor and the Fugitives: Surrogate Fathers, Foster Son

> That miraculous group at Vanderbilt—there have not been many things like it. Their temperaments and their intellects and all these things, it's such a wonderful coincidence that they turned up at the same time. And it was very wonderful for me, coming along afterward . . . I knew that the South was what I was interested in, the only thing I knew anything about, and they gave me their ideas to latch onto about what it meant.
> —James Curry Robison, *Peter Taylor*

More than that of any other heirs to the Fugitive legacy, Peter Taylor's career was a paradigm of the legacy's role in the making of a writer. Yet paradoxically, Peter Taylor may have been more acutely affected than any of his peers by the anxiety of influence. His career was for many years marked by scrupulous avoidance of his mentors' primary artistic media, poetry and criticism, and by adherence to their areas of least involvement, fiction and drama. Taylor thereby avoided competition with his mentors and most intimate peers. On numerous occasions, Taylor attributed his disinclination toward the writing of criticism to his own relativism, his habit of seeing both sides of a question—a trait that seldom deters other critics and indeed may improve their vision. But reluctance to compete with the likes of Allen Tate, John Crowe Ransom, and Randall Jarrell might have played an even larger role.

Peter Taylor once said that at "just at the right psychological moment I came under the influence of Tate, Ransom, and Warren," in that order. Taylor gave Allen Tate credit for initiating and focusing his career. According to Taylor, Tate "helped me identify myself as to who I was, as a southerner." Tate "adopted" him when, as a student in his freshman English class at Southwestern, Taylor "wrote a paper, and in it I quoted my grandfather [former Tennessee governor Robert L. Taylor] saying, 'Speak not to me of the *New* South; there's only the Old South resurrected with the print of the nails in her hands.' " Allen Tate was, however, no Simeon, moved to cry out "*Nunc dimitis*" when he encountered the talented young writer. In fact, Tate dropped Taylor from his class because, as he said later, "the simple truth is that he did not need to know anything I could teach him. He had a perfection of style at the age of 18 that I *envied*." In a 1987 interview with James Curry Robison, Taylor called Tate's statement "rather an exaggeration," explaining that despite Tate's dismissal, he (Taylor)

> went on to his class and he began telling me I ought to read Chaucer, and I hadn't so every afternoon we would go and sit under the trees, and he would coach me in reading Chaucer. And he did that with other things and talked to me about literature generally. I went on with that class, that was in the spring, and in the summer I took a novel course under him—a creative writing course, really. He liked the things I would write for the papers in the class. Then I wrote some fiction, and he liked it immensely, and that really set me up and gave me to courage to go on and be a writer.

Taylor would later call Tate "the best teacher I ever had. He made literature seem important. And I don't know how he did it." It was, as Taylor *could* express later, "the drama of being a writer of literature—that was wonderful for a young man, to make you feel that what you're doing is important . . . [and] he liked my work from the beginning." Moreover, in class, "Tate talked about the *art* of fiction, taking it seriously as a form," although fiction was not Tate's forte.[1]

Tate continued to act as Taylor's friend and sponsor, both in front of and behind the scenes, after Taylor left Southwestern, first by sending two of his stories to Robert Penn Warren at the *Southern Review* without Taylor's knowledge. Second, as Taylor added in a 1985–86 interview, Tate was "responsible for my going to Vanderbilt to study under Ransom; he introduced

---

1. Robert Daniel, "The Inspired Voice of Mythical Tennessee," in *Conversations with Peter Taylor*, ed. Hubert H. McAlexander (Jackson: University Press of Mississippi, 1987), 47; Peter Taylor, interview by author, St. Augustine, Florida, March 17, 1994; Allen Tate, "Peter Taylor," *Shenandoah* 28 (1977): 10; James Curry Robison, *Peter Taylor: A Study of the Short Fiction* (Boston: Twayne, 1988), 136–37; Robert Brickhouse, "Peter Taylor: Writing, Teaching and Making Discoveries," in McAlexander, ed., *Conversations with Taylor*, 50; William J. Broadway, "A Conversation with Peter Taylor," ibid., 114; Barbara Thompson, "Interview with Peter Taylor," ibid., 146.

me to Eleanor [Eleanor Ross Taylor, his future wife]; he arranged a job for me with a New York publisher, after I was discharged from the army. . . . He was also a great manipulator; he was always telling various ones of us, 'Now this is what you must do'—some scheme to advance ourselves in the literary world."[2] Tate and Caroline Gordon also undoubtedly played a part in landing Taylor the teaching job at Greensboro that launched his academic career.

Allen Tate may also have had an indirect and subtle effect on the fiction Peter Taylor wrote. In an interview with Stephen Goodwin, Taylor remarked, "I vowed I would never write another line of criticism after doing a review of Allen Tate's novel, *The Fathers*, and my record is clean." "Assumptions of the Game," written for *Hika*, the Kenyon College literary magazine, might well have been more formative than Taylor later realized. Not only did Taylor call *The Fathers* a novel of manners, later to be his own specialty, but he also praised Tate for his masterful employment of point of view: "His adaption of the prose style along with the point of view of a Southern gentleman of the post-War era is the decisive technical device of the novel." Tate's strategy proved to be the one Taylor would gravitate toward in much of his own later fiction. At the same time, Peter Taylor astutely indicated that Allen Tate was essentially a poet and critic, not a writer of fiction, and that the novel, despite its virtues, was unlikely to become a durable and popular success.[3] It was therefore logical, from a Bloomian standpoint, that Taylor would imitate Tate's fiction, since Tate presented no rivalry where fiction was concerned, but avoid writing any criticism after that initially daring examination of his mentor's novel.

For years afterward, as subsequent correspondence between Taylor and Tate reveals, Peter trusted Allen's comments on his stories and frequently acted on them. On January 9, 1941, Tate wrote to say: "I have just read your new story, 'Sky Line,' and I want to congratulate you. It is not only the best thing you've ever done, it is the best story the S. R. has published in a coon's age." He was particularly complimentary of "the way you let the ostensible story (the boy's father) tell the main story of the boy's development into consciousness and responsibility. The overtones are beautifully managed." Tate

2. Thompson, "Interview with Taylor," 146; Hubert H. McAlexander, "A Composite Conversation with Peter Taylor," in McAlexander, ed., *Conversations with Taylor*, 124.

3. Stephen Goodwin, "An Interview with Peter Taylor," in McAlexander, ed., *Conversations with Taylor*, 19; Peter Taylor, "The Assumptions of the Game," *Hika* 5 (February 1939): 21–22. In *Peter Taylor: A Descriptive Bibliography* (Charlottesville: University Press of Virginia, 1988), Stuart Wright committed a possible Freudian slip in substituting "Grave" for "Game" in his listing of the title, possibly with Tate's "Ode to the Confederate Dead" in mind (86, Item C29).

advised him, however, "to delete the word *obscene* from the description of the girl." The word remains in the story, although on January 26, 1941, during Taylor's year at Baton Rouge, he wrote Tate to "thank you for troubling to write me about my story." And on January 24, 1946, when Taylor sent a revised and *renamed* version of "A Long Fourth" for inclusion in *A Southern Vanguard*, he commented that the new version contained "very little revision except of the sentences and phrases you encircled."[4]

John Crowe Ransom's impact on Peter Taylor began at Vanderbilt. Taylor had at first declined to attend his father's alma mater, but when the elder Taylor refused to supplement the scholarship that would have taken Peter to Columbia, father and son compromised. The elder Taylor knew and respected Tate, having met both him and Ransom at Vanderbilt.[5] It was Tate's intervention that landed Peter at Vanderbilt in 1936.

Not long afterward, Peter became involved in the effort to keep Ransom at Vanderbilt and, when the campaign failed, dropped out of school. David McDowell, a minor figure in the Fugitive legacy, told in "A Year Without Peter" how he, Robert Lowell, and Jarrell engaged in "a campaign to have Peter join us" at Kenyon College. Only when a scholarship materialized at Kenyon could Peter, against his father's opposition, once again be among the members of his newly adopted literary family. On May 13, 1938, Ransom informed Peter Taylor that he, Robie Macauley, and Jack Thompson were "the successful contestants for our literary prizes," adding, "One of whom is you, and I'm glad." The prize apparently carried with it a tuition grant, for in the spring of 1938, a jubilant Peter wrote to McDowell, "I read much at night and go *North* in winter."[6] Peter Taylor's writing career, under the aegis of the Fugitive legacy, was once again on track.

The nature of that career was, however, yet to be decided. At Kenyon, the emphasis was primarily on poetry, secondarily on criticism, least of all on fiction. Taylor therefore had to try his hand at poetry "to make myself felt." In a 1947 letter to Robert Penn Warren, Taylor conveyed as he did nowhere else the intensity of the pressure on him to become a poet: "The great hardship of my undergraduate days was my wide acquaintance among student poets. I don't remember ever meeting any 'talented young writer' who wrote fiction

4. Allen Tate to Taylor, January 9, 1941, Peter Hillsman Taylor Papers, Jean and Alexander Heard Library, Vanderbilt University, Nashville, Tenn.; Taylor to Tate, January 26, 1941, January 20, 1946, Tate Papers.

5. Taylor, interview by author.

6. David McDowell, "The Year Without Peter," *Shenandoah* 28 (1976–77): 36; Ransom to Taylor, May 13, 1938, Taylor Papers.

until I met Jean Stafford, the year I finished at Kenyon. While I was at Kenyon with Cal [Robert Lowell] and Randall and Nerber—and Harry Brown always on the horizon—I was driven by the desire for prestige, to writing poetry." Ransom subjected the poems that Taylor brought to his office to his familiar methodical approach: "When you gave him a poem to read, the first thing he did was to look at the poem and tap on the desk to make sure the meter was correct. Then he carefully checked the rhyme scheme. He would not discuss other elements of the poem until he had done that."[7]

Considering the predominance of poetry such as this in his apprentice writing at Kenyon, Peter Taylor might well have become a poet and a good one. This is not to suggest that he would have been a better poet than fictionist or that he would have equaled Jarrell, Lowell, and Berryman. It is likely, however, that Peter Taylor shaped his career as an exercise in *clinamen* by swerving away from the strategies of dominating precursors. Taylor realized later that in learning to write poetry, he picked up techniques that would be useful in writing fiction: "It seems now that what he taught me about writing was compression. And compression is what I have set great store by as a short story writer." Taylor frequently recounted how, when he once gave Ransom a story that contained a poem, Ransom gave him an "A" for the poem and only a "B" for the story.[8]

Taylor had begun to realize that although Ransom was reluctant to criticize his fiction, the principles that he stressed for poetry could be adapted to fiction. More important, Taylor learned that he would have to go it alone at Kenyon as a writer of fiction and to assert his autonomy within a circle of writers devoted to poetry and criticism.

If the combined influence of Tate and Ransom virtually *determined* the course of Peter Taylor's higher education and of his literary career, surely Randall Jarrell's impact was equally crucial and more enduring. Taylor's essay "Randall Jarrell" appeared in the memorial volume, *Randall Jarrell, 1914–1965*, which he edited with Robert Lowell and Robert Penn Warren. The vivid and moving memoir, which begins at Vanderbilt and Kenyon and continues through the remainder of Jarrell's lifetime, not only registers Taylor's near adoration of Jarrell but also suggests the extent and nature of his impact on Peter Taylor's writing.

7. Taylor, interview by author; Taylor to Robert Penn Warren, December 9, [1947], Warren Papers; Thompson, "Interview with Taylor," 147. Since Taylor usually dated his letters by month and day only, the years of their composition must be derived from contextual evidence. Lowell's nickname "Cal" is derived from Caliban and Caligula.

8. Thompson, "Interview with Taylor," 147; Taylor, interview by author.

At Vanderbilt in 1936, Taylor joined a faction of literary students who became "disciples" of Randall Jarrell. To young Peter the former Fugitive-Agrarians were the "gods of literary undergraduate students," and Nashville was still the "gathering place" for a circle of larger-than-life figures. Although other students drank beer with George Marion O'Donnell, Taylor and his fellows played touch football with Randall so that they could catch his words of wisdom and wit: "It was Randall's talk we wanted of course, and his talk on the sidelines and even while the game was in progress was electrifying. It was there that I first heard anyone analyze a Chekhov story. I have never since heard anything to equal it." It proved to be of no small consequence for Peter Taylor that Jarrell was enamored of Chekhov. Numerous critics have maintained that Peter Taylor's fiction—and only his among American writers—resembles Chekhov's. Then, however, Jarrell believed that Taylor had much to learn about the master, for example, that his literary virtues could survive any translation: "On the sidelines of one of those games I once suggested to him that probably we couldn't know just how good Chekhov's stories were unless we could read them in Russian. He laughed at me—somewhat cruelly, I'm afraid. . . . On that occasion, he said, 'Even in Constance Garnett's translation, Chekhov's stories are the best in the English language.' "⁹ Taylor no doubt experienced Chekhov thereafter through the filter of Jarrell's own reading. At Vanderbilt, Jarrell established an intellectual domination over Taylor that would persist throughout their relationship.

At Kenyon College, Taylor renewed his apostleship to Jarrell by becoming his student. He took Jarrell's course in American literature, for which the instructor was "frequently late." If Jarrell did not arrive until the required second bell, when students were entitled to leave the classroom, Peter and the more "devoted" students would remain for what became "more like a literary club than a class." Even on the tennis courts, Jarrell's student circle always had the feeling that he was their teacher as well as friend.¹⁰

Clearly, Randall Jarrell had an impact on the stories Taylor wrote at Kenyon. Taylor recalled that "Mr. Ransom just wouldn't pay much attention to my fiction; Jarrell was the only one there who did. He was much more interested, even then, in characters in poetry than any of the others were." Although Taylor was also writing poems that were similar to Jarrell's, there is no evidence that Jarrell ever commented on them, either in person or by let-

9. Peter Taylor, "Randall Jarrell," in Lowell, Taylor, and Warren, eds., *Randall Jarrell*, 242–43.
10. Ibid, 245–46.

ter. Mary Jarrell later conjectured that "it was, by all accounts, the contrasts between their creative interests that kept Peter and Randall together." She continued, "To be perfectly honest, I doubt if Randall would have felt quite so cozy if the *New Yorker* were continuously bringing out Peter's poetry."[11]

After Kenyon, Jarrell gave his time generously to encouraging and refining Taylor's career, but his patronage cut two ways. If he liked Taylor's stories, he would read them carefully and critique them in lengthy phone calls or epistles; if he disliked one of them totally, he would respond with hostility to the author. In his memoir, Taylor commented that "if you published something he didn't like, he behaved as though you had been disloyal to him in some way—or not that so much—more as if you had been disloyal to some other friend of his—your other self, that is, your artist self." Mary Jarrell recounts an incident when the Jarrells were on vacation with the Taylors and Randall, who had read "Venus, Cupid, Folly, and Time," and disliked it, refused to speak to Taylor.[12]

It appears that Jarrell's commentary on Taylor's stories, from the first, was colored by his notion of what role Peter Taylor would play in the literary world. To Barbara Thompson, Taylor recalled that "he wanted me to have a very light touch, Chekhovian, not to have much serious event in it. I think he really thought of me as the Southern regional writer of memoir stories. He used to say, 'Write all those stories you can, because that is a world that's gone, will never exist again, and this record of it should exist.' "[13] This was the same Jarrell who eschewed "southern subjects" in most of his writing.

Taylor seems to have accepted Jarrell's advice (and abuse) with too much complacency. Jarrell would sometimes sharpen the rapier of his wit by poking fun behind Taylor's back, as when he remarked to a mutual friend that Taylor the writer was "like a great white horse doing tatting." Taylor's response was to write that "I used to wish I could have been hiding under the sofa the night he brought forth that about the white horse." When the shoe was on the other foot, however, Jarrell saw things differently. In a 1977 conversation with Ruth Dean, Taylor remarked that literary friendships are valuable because of the "mutual exchange of criticism as well as praise."[14] Jarrell, however, wanted always to be on the giving end of the exchange.

11. Goodwin, "Interview with Taylor," 6; Mary Jarrell, "Peter and Randall," *Shenandoah* 28 (1976–77): 33.

12. Taylor, "Randall Jarrell," 246–47; M. Jarrell, "Peter and Randall," 32.

13. Thompson, "Interview with Taylor," 157.

14. Taylor, "Randall Jarrell," 250; Ruth Dean, "Peter Taylor: A Private World of Southern Writing," in McAlexander, ed., *Conversations with Taylor*, 32.

It is not surprising, therefore, that Peter Taylor's writing became more experimental, more serious, and more poetic after Jarrell's death in 1965. He came to recognize that despite the undeniable advantages of Jarrell's presence, "I don't think it was altogether good. In the end you have to throw over your mentor."[15] The poems of *In the Miro District*, written and published in the early seventies, may have come to fruition because Taylor was at last out from under Jarrell's domination.

An equally strong friendship between Peter Taylor and Robert Lowell also began at Kenyon when they roomed together in Douglass House, a Gothic-type structure that had been designated for transfer students. They got along, though temperamentally opposite, because of their passion for writing. In a 1982 interview with Robert Wilson, Taylor said of his college friendship with Lowell: "I found him to be very interesting. I've always been attracted to people who are not like me—it's the 'not me in thee' I like. He was so totally different. He was the intellectual and a poet and a classicist." In "Our Afterlife," Lowell's commemorative poem for Taylor, he writes, "Were we ever weaned / from our reactionary young masters, / by the *schadenfreude* of new homes?" Although they often ridiculed Jarrell behind his back, both realized the importance to their developing art of his confidently expert and copious comment on their writing, which began while all three were at Kenyon. Like Taylor, Lowell sometimes received negative feedback from their junior mentor: "Jarrell, if he liked your effort, would write you a long letter about it, and if he didn't he wouldn't speak to you. Cal had exactly that experience, too, and we would laugh about it."[16]

The relationship of Lowell and Taylor not unexpectedly bore fruit in their writing. At least one of Taylor's stories, "The Fancy Woman," was written in direct response to Lowell's reaction to another story, "The Spinster's Tale": "Lowell always teased me about that story. We were still at Kenyon when I wrote it, and he told me that *I* was prim and puritanical, that I didn't know anything about the world, that there wasn't enough of the roughness of life in my stories. So I vowed I'd show him, and I sat down and wrote the first sentence of 'The Fancy Woman': '*He wanted no more of her drunken palaver.*' "[17] Unlike other stories written at Kenyon, "The Spinster's Tale" and "The Fancy Woman" became permanent fixtures in his oeuvre, as well as precursors to all his other stories that focus on southern women.

15. Thompson, "Interview with Taylor," 157.
16. Robert Wilson, "Peter Taylor Remembers Robert Lowell," in McAlexander, ed., *Conversations with Taylor*, 36, 39; Robert Lowell, "Our Afterlife," *Shenandoah* 28 (1977): 5–6.
17. Goodwin, "Interview with Taylor," 10–11.

As early as 1948, Taylor had intended to write something about his Kenyon days, but it was not until 1952, when teaching brought him back to his alma mater, that he responded to a visitor's suggestion by producing the story entitled "1939." When William Broadway asked if "1939" was "about you and Lowell," Taylor replied, "It's almost literally true," so true that Jarrell said he ought to have "put in real names." According to Taylor, "Both Jean Stafford and Lowell were furious at first," although they had advised Taylor to pay "no attention" to relatives who objected to being used in stories. Despite his ambiguous reaction to the story, Lowell found inspiration in it for the kind of poetry that would soon transform his career. In a letter, he wrote, "I've been trying to do the same sort of thing with scenes from my childhood with my Grandfather, Old Aunt Sarah Cousin Belle etc. I want to invent a lot and forget a lot, but at the same time have the historian's wonderful advantage."[18]

Taylor's deliberate intention was, however, to construct two characters typical of the young men who, in the years just before World War II, chose to matriculate at colleges where they might sit at the feet of their literary idols: "We had all come to Kenyon because we were bent upon becoming writers of some kind or other and the new president of the college had just appointed a famous and distinguished poet to the staff of the English Department." The "famous and distinguished poet" was, of course, Ransom, and the atmosphere of incipient creativity and excitement was exactly that which Taylor, Lowell, Jarrell, MacDowell, Macauley, and others inhaled on that isolated campus. But in "1939," the narrator's focus is on himself and Jim Prewitt. The plot involves their Thanksgiving odyssey to New York, to visit their "fiancées" and to partake of " 'life's deeper and more real experience,' the kind that dormitory life seemed to deprive us of."[19] Taylor's story is, by his admission, the most autobiographical text in his literary corpus, wherein it stands as a unique rendering of the mixture of personal friendship and creative rivalry that characterized the Fugitive legacy.

Lowell wrote two poems to Peter Taylor, one early and one late. The first, "To Peter Taylor on the Feast of the Epiphany," appeared in the *Nation* for March 16, 1946, then in *Lord Weary's Castle*. Taylor is mentioned only in the first line—"Peter, the war has taught me to revere / The rules of this dark-

18. Broadway, "Conversation with Taylor," 113; McAlexander, "Composite Conversation," 120; Robert Lowell to Taylor, April 25, 1945, Taylor Papers.

19. Peter Taylor, "1939," in *The Collected Stories of Peter Taylor* (New York: Farrar, Straus & Giroux, 1969), 334, 336.

ness"—as a point of departure. The second, "Our Afterlife," was Lowell's contribution to the 1974 *Shenandoah* issue, *Peter Taylor at Sixty*. This time Lowell, now middle-aged and in his confessional mode, nostalgically deprecated the naïveté that characterized their youth:

> Peter, in our boyish years,
> 30 to 40,
> when Cupid was still the Christ of love's religion,
> time stood on its hands.

As he journeys by train to their place of reunion, Lowell is grateful that, after half a lifetime in the creative arena, he still can say to Peter Taylor, "Our loyalty to one another sticks like love."[20] The letters Taylor wrote to Lowell between 1943 and 1972 (now in Harvard University's Houghton Library) attest to that continuity.

For the remainder of Lowell's life, Taylor shared with his former schoolmate the variegated tapestry of his life as a writer, teacher, husband, and father, as well as private responses to the people and places both knew equally well. These letters offer few specifics about the actual writing of his stories and plays. They do indicate that Taylor frequently sent his stories to Lowell, as well as to Jarrell, before submitting them for publication. Lowell offered few suggestions but often responded with high praise. After "The Scoutmaster" appeared in *Partisan Review*, Lowell wrote, "I think it is one of the great stories of the age. The detail is incredibly acute and solid. . . . The way you have the boy narrate it is masterly. I had to rub my eyes to realize it was yours; not that I don't extremely admire some of your other stories, but with this one I think you can be said to have arrived."[21] Like Lowell, Taylor moved beyond his modernist beginnings, but he did so later and to a lesser extent. Taylor's experimentation in *Miro* with new genres—falling between strict generic lines of fiction, poetry, and drama—would finally result in a loosening of strict form in the interests of colloquial realism.

Robert Penn Warren's impact on Peter Taylor was no less crucial to Taylor's literary vocation than that of Tate, Ransom, Jarrell, and Lowell. By accepting his stories for publication in the *Southern Review*, Warren nurtured Taylor's early publishing career. Warren began his introduction to Taylor's first volume of fiction, *A Long Fourth and Other Stories*, with a simple account of how their relationship began: "In 1936 Allen Tate sent two stories by a

20. Lowell, *Poems*, 56; Robert Lowell, "Our Afterlife," 5, 6.
21. Lowell to Taylor, September 27, 1945, Taylor Papers.

boy in Memphis, Tennessee, to the office of the *Southern Review*. They were obviously the work of a very gifted young writer who had a flavor and a way of his own." On September 4, 1936, Warren wrote a letter to young "Mr. Taylor" that conveyed the importance of having a former Fugitive's recommendation to anyone wishing to publish in the *Southern Review*: "Both Brooks and I feel that Tate's enthusiasm for your work is entirely justified, and we are certain that we shall be able to use some of it in the near future." Warren expressed chagrin that by taking its time, the *Southern Review* forfeited the privilege of "introducing Peter Taylor's work to print." *River* beat them to it, but the *Southern Review* editors were able "to redeem themselves" by publishing three stories—"A Spinster's Tale," "Sky Line," and "The Fancy Woman"—in 1938, 1939, and 1940.[22]

Twenty-seven years later, in "Two Peters: Memory and Opinion," Warren looked back on a forty-year friendship that actually began when Taylor and Lowell arrived in Baton Rouge, newly graduated from Kenyon, to begin their graduate work at LSU. In several apologetic references, Warren suggested that, like Jarrell at Vanderbilt, Taylor put him somewhat on the defensive. Of his behavior during the seminar, Warren wrote: "Taylor read widely and dutifully and never opened his mouth without uttering a shrewd perception or wry criticism—all from the slightly askew angle of vision which is his and his alone." Warren would soon learn, however, that "the seminar [was] . . . to be deprived of the shrewd comments and wry criticism," when, as Warren humbly wrote, "Peter tactfully explained that graduate work was not for him. . . . He had to be a writer, he said, and he had to put all his eggs in one basket." And when he resigned from the seminar, Taylor, according to Warren, spoke to him after class "with grave kindness, more like a father explaining the facts of life to a young son."[23]

Taylor remained on campus for some months, leaving shortly before being drafted into the army in 1941. During those months of hanging on, said Warren, Taylor gave the Baton Rouge community the "benefit" of his charm and his stories, while he enjoyed continued association with Warren, the professor in question, and with Robert and Jean Lowell. On January 26, 1941, Taylor wrote to Tate: "During this fall I've had a room with the Warrens. They have left now, however, for Iowa, and the Lowells have moved into their

22. Robert Penn Warren, introduction to Peter Taylor, *A Long Fourth and Other Stories* (New York: Harcourt Brace Jovanovich, 1948), vii; Warren to Taylor, September 4, 1936, Taylor Papers.

23. Robert Penn Warren, "Two Peters: Memory and Opinion," *Shenandoah* 28 (1977): 8.

apartment. So I have a new landlord and landlady. The latter, I must say, I'm thankful for." After those two initial rejections, the *Southern Review* accepted his stories, like Katherine Anne Porter's, without criticism. Warren would call Taylor, here and on other occasions, "a gift of God to the *Southern Review.*"[24]

Around eight years after Taylor's year in Baton Rouge, Taylor wrote Warren that he "was thoroughly delighted when Cal said he had suggested to [Robert] Giroux that you be asked to write that introduction [to *A Long Fourth and Other Stories*]; I am sure there is nobody who understands better than you the sort of thing I was trying to do." In the introduction, Warren attributed the overall effect of Taylor's stories to "a natural style, one based on conversation and the family tale, with the echo of the spoken word, with the texture of the narrator's mind." Alluding to "A Spinster's Tale" and "The Fancy Woman," first published in the *Southern Review*, Warren wrote that "the most successful and rendered characters are women."[25] "The Fancy Woman," clearly Warren's favorite, appeared in two anthologies that Warren edited, the *Anthology of Short Stories from the Southern Review* (1953) and *A New Southern Harvest* (1957).

After completing his essay, Warren wrote to Taylor: "And here is the introduction. I am not proud and happy about it, and I throw it on your mercy. If anything seems too far off base, please say so and I'll try to adjust matters." When Taylor read the essay, however, he exclaimed: "It is perfect in every detail, and I have never seen a piece of writing more wonderfully organized. . . . I couldn't write you about it before now because I was afraid that in my rapture I would sound plain foolish."[26]

Three years later, Warren provided yet another boost to Taylor's career in his review for the *New York Times* of *A Woman of Means*. If his statement that "no description of mere mortals or events of *A Woman of Means* can indicate the particular kind of excitement it possesses" seems overblown, surely Warren, by observing that a reader of the novel experiences "the excitement of being constantly on the verge of deep perceptions and deep interpretations," captures the essence of Taylor's psychological strategy.[27] After this re-

24. Taylor to Tate, January 26, 1941, Tate Papers; Warren, "Two Peters," 8.

25. Taylor to Warren, December 9, 1947, Warren Papers; Warren, introduction to *A Long Fourth*, x.

26. Warren to Taylor, December 16, 1947, Taylor Papers; Taylor to Warren, December 21, 1947, Warren Papers.

27. Robert Penn Warren, Review of *A Woman of Means*, *New York Times Book Reviews*, June 11, 1950, 8.

view, however, Warren wrote no further evaluations of Taylor's writing until the *Shenandoah* sixty-year commemorative issue. As in the case of his refusal to review Andrew Lytle's *Velvet Horn*, Warren may well have feared that his close association with Taylor, as well as his membership in the "southern clique," would begin to make his judgment suspect.

As a bona fide member of the post-Fugitive group and an established writer of fiction, Peter Taylor would automatically be placed on any "short list" when the former Fugitives edited a textbook or anthology. He was not included, however, in the first editions of *An Approach to Literature* (1939) and *Understanding Fiction* (1943). "A Long Fourth" appeared in *A Southern Vanguard*, edited by Tate and John Peale Bishop, and "Skyline" appeared in Tate and Gordon's *House of Fiction* (1950). Warren used "The Fancy Woman" in his two collections of fiction from the *Southern Review*. It is likely, however, that Peter Taylor's early and frequent inclusion in the *Best American* and *O'Henry* collections of short stories made the former Fugitives' anthologies of less importance to his career than they might otherwise have been.

At Baton Rouge, Peter Taylor also formed a lifetime friendship with Cleanth Brooks and his wife, Tinkum. Letters exchanged over the years between Taylor and Brooks attest to strong mutual admiration. Brooks's most extensive treatment of a Taylor story appeared in the late sixties. On January 10, 1968, Brooks sent Taylor a copy of a lecture he had delivered on "Miss Leonora When Last Seen." Entitled "The Southern Temper," the essay was later published in *A Shaping Joy*. Brooks called it "a kind of belated thanks for your having written it" and modestly hoped that he had gotten "the point of the story sufficiently well and that I haven't flattened too many of its nuances putting it to the use that I have." On January 22, 1969, Taylor replied that he was "just delighted by all you had to say about my story. . . . It seems to me now that your interpretation states precisely what I was trying to say, though certainly when I wrote it I didn't see so clearly what it was about. (I no doubt couldn't have written it if I had.)."[28] It was the familiar story of the writer who knows not what he does and the critic whose response, though unique and even surprising in some respects to the writer, is influential enough to augment the text and forever shape responses to it.

Taylor was especially surprised by Brooks's comments on the function of Miss Leonora's disguises, put on when her "relation to a true community . . . lapses." According to Brooks, she either "adopts the disguise of creatures

28. Brooks to Taylor, January 10, 1968, and Taylor to Brooks, January 22, 1969, Brooks Papers.

whom she evidently regards as fakes and therefore as truly grotesque" or as an act of defiance. The author enthusiastically replied, "That hits the nail on the head. Her disguises are finally her ironic comment on the enemy to which she can no longer offer any other sort of resistance."[29]

Cleanth Brooks's final comment on Peter Taylor and his writing appeared in a special 1987 issue of the *Journal of the Short Story in English*. After reading "a collection of short plays by him" and *A Summons to Memphis*, Brooks called Taylor "one of our most distinguished writers of the short story."[30]

Brooks's slender commentary on Peter Taylor demonstrates how perfectly Taylor's writing adhered to the literary and philosophical values of Brooks and the New Criticism. The stories, based on a lifetime of personal memories and close observation, still lend themselves to the aesthetic categories of New Critical interpretation. Any incongruity can be handled as irony, and limitations in scope make close reading more possible. In other words, Taylor's short fiction can be creatively augmented by a Brooksean analysis. Far from charging Brooks with eccentric misreading, Taylor seemed only too happy for a trusted friend in the post-Fugitive circle to spell out the meanings of his own stories.

In conversation, Peter Taylor would not admit to having learned much about the writer's craft from either Lytle or Gordon and only as far as all three followed the example of Henry James. He added, however, "I was also influenced by Katherine Anne [Porter]." When asked, "In what way?" he replied, "Well, I just admired the stories—I don't know how to say it, but I think that she wrote the very best fiction of everybody in . . . that generation." The two became acquainted when Taylor invited Porter to participate in an Arts Forum that Taylor organized in 1951 at the Women's College at Greensboro. His letter of invitation of December 1, 1951, states extravagantly that "it would be impossible for me to write this letter without mentioning the great debt I feel to you for all that you have written. I hope you won't think it impertinent of me to give my opinion, which is that there is no better story than *Old Mortality* in any literature." Obviously flattered, Porter replied, "Of course I'll be happy to come to Greensboro—I was there in the spring of 1949 (I think) to collect my first, and maybe my last, honorary D.Litt. . . . I got an odd idea of the meaning of the honor, because another

29. Cleanth Brooks, "The Southern Temper," in Brooks, *A Shaping Joy*, 201; Taylor to Brooks, 22 Jan. 1969, Brooks Papers.

30. Cleanth Brooks, "A Tribute to Peter Taylor," *Journal of the Short Story in English* 9 (Autumn 1987): 37.

lady-author got one at the same time, and I thought secretly, if SHE is a D.Litt I am a rag dolly." Porter added, more humbly, "Thank you for your very good words about Old Mortality—more than good, overwhelming."[31]

After the visit, which apparently went well, Taylor became one of Porter's young "protégés," always on her list of the best writers of his generation. In 1954, Taylor sent her a copy of *The Widows of Thornton* and received, with her thanks, glowing compliments on the "freshness and clearness and deep-water feeling" of the stories, which so skillfully treated "all those born widows of the south."[32]

Like Taylor's other post-Fugitive mentors and peers, Porter obviously favored those Taylor stories in which the southern "lady" symbolizes the South in its troubled passage into the modern world. Since Porter had excelled in her portrayal of the women of "the old order," she was, in effect, designating Peter Taylor as her successor, a role that Taylor, in his admiration, must have valued. There were times, however, when he rebelled against the sometimes narrow advice and proscriptive preferences of his well-meaning friends, as in the following May 2, 1951, letter to Robert Lowell:

> I think all you say about my stories and my novel is true. . . . In fact I feel myself shifting into saying right now that Randall thinks that last story you saw is one of the two best things I've written. But I really tell you that in order to say also that Randall's high praise of that and of certain other stories of mine reveals just that he thinks of me as an "old fashioned writer" or that he thinks I am best when I am that. But he, like Red preferring "The Fancy Woman,["] and like nearly everybody about his contemporaries or more especially about his slightly-juniors, has preconceived ideas about what and how I should write.[33]

As Taylor's career matured, it became increasingly clear that the former Fugitives placed an unjustifiable emphasis on the stories centering on eccentric female characters. From Warren's introduction and textbook selections, to Brooks's "Tribute," to Porter's extravagant letters of praise, the post-Fugitive circle followed one another in foregrounding this aspect of Taylor's fiction at the expense of another story that demanded to be told, his own.

Because Peter Taylor told what was essentially his own story, his critics

---

31. Taylor, interview by author; Taylor to Porter, December 1, 1951, and Porter to Taylor, December 5, 1951, both in Porter Papers.
32. Porter to Taylor, May 17, 1954, Taylor Papers.
33. Taylor to Lowell, May 2, 1951, Lowell Papers.

and biographers, with his encouragement, have read his fiction as a realistic rendering of life among members of the upper middle class who led genteel, if sometimes not so prosperous lives in the cities of the upper South. He populated the fictional town of Thornton (based on Taylor's hometown of Trenton, Tennessee) with characters based on family members and their friends and drew most of his plots from recollections of their actual experiences. Steadily, however, Taylor proceeded to tell a parallel story, an episodic bildungsroman in which the narrator or protagonist loses his naïveté and is rudely thrust into a world that is undergoing a parallel alteration.

This particular strain, which Joseph A. Bryant has called "vintage Peter Taylor," may also be read as a trope of his role in the Fugitive legacy. When asked if his relationship with the former Fugitives might be a continuation of his father and son story and if the Fugitives might be considered his literary fathers, Taylor replied, "I don't think that's wrong," adding, "I became devoted to them."[34] With such brothers as Lowell and Jarrell and sisters like Porter and Eudora Welty to complete the family circle, Peter Taylor could proceed to tell, again and again, the story of his separation from one father and search for the approval of those surrogate fathers who enabled him to proceed with his life as a writer.

The stories in which this masked biography emerges occur throughout Taylor's career and are represented in every collection of his fiction. They include the seldom discussed "Skyline" and "The Scoutmaster" of the thirties; the novelette *A Woman of Means* at mid-century; "Porte-Cochere," "Miss Leonora When Last Seen," and "Dean of Men" from the fifties and sixties; and "In the Miro District" and "The Old Forest" from the seventies. Peter Taylor's protagonist comes of age in *A Summons to Memphis* (1986), in "Owl Mountain" and "The Oracle at Stoneleigh Court" from *The Oracle at Stoneleigh Court* (1993), and in his last novel, *In the Tennessee Country* (1994).

In "Skyline" and "The Scoutmaster," the central characters are children moving into adolescence while learning painful lessons about the moral fallibility and vulnerability of adults. Although points of view differ in the two stories, the distancing strategies result in essentially the same degree of modernist impersonality. In "The Scoutmaster," Taylor uses first person point of view, which forces the narrator to be retrospective rather than immediate. "Skyline" illustrates the more immediate Jamesian mode of narration by which events in the present are filtered through one consciousness at a time,

34. Joseph A. Bryant, Jr., "Peter Taylor and the Walled Gardens," *Journal of the Short Story in English* 9 (Autumn 1987): 65; Taylor, interview by author.

the favored point of view of the fiction writers of the Fugitive legacy (Lytle's "roving"). It is not surprising, therefore, that Allen Tate and Caroline Gordon chose "Skyline" for inclusion in *The House of Fiction* (1950).

"Skyline" is a poignant story that, as Albert J. Griffith has recognized, recalls James Joyce's *A Portrait of the Artist as a Young Man*, not to mention Eliot's *Waste Land*. In his introduction to *A Long Fourth*, Warren faulted the story, along with "Rain in the Heart," for lacking "the positive ironies of the other stories."[35] Given the literary environment in which Taylor wrote it, the story does stand out from the rest in the collection as consciously literary.

The surrogate Peter Taylors who appear in these stories are placed before a sickeningly deep chasm into which they must either leap or face a lifetime of cliff-hanging. They may love and admire the way their fathers' generation stubbornly avoided the unheroic present, but they cannot afford to embrace their fathers' position. For Taylor, the frequent retelling of the story became an act of separation and a declaration of independence. That Tate and Warren could regard these stories as the creation of an artist who could refine himself out of existence, to paraphrase Joyce, must have authenticated Taylor's act of rebellion. For Warren, it constituted "an irony blended out of comedy and sympathetic understanding."[36] Through these stories, written as he embraced the former Fugitives as surrogate fathers, Peter Taylor also became a fugitive from the repression and provincialism of his southern past.

"A Long Fourth," signature story for Taylor's first collection, contains an ironic allusion to Agrarianism, which by the middle forties was a phase of the Fugitive legacy that most of the participants would just as soon have forgotten. The grotesque sisters Kate and Helena embark on a campaign to make Son and Ann, the "Platonic" couple, as uncomfortable as possible. Knowing that the couple holds progressivist and egalitarian views, Helena protests, "You two are speaking as New Yorkers now . . . not as Southerners. Didn't it ever occur to you that the South has its own destiny? It has an entirely different tradition from the rest of the country. It has its own social institutions and must be allowed to work out its own salvation without interference." When Kate chimes in with a defense of secession and slavery, Son bursts out with, "Now the cat's out of the bag! I know what you girls have been reading and who you've probably been seeing—those fellows at the University in Nashville. You know what I mean, Ann! . . . the agrarian tradition." By the

---

35. Albert J. Griffith, *Peter Taylor*, rev. ed. (New York: Twayne, 1990), 16–17; Warren, introduction to Taylor, *A Long Fourth*, x.

36. Warren, introduction to Taylor, *A Long Fourth*, x.

late forties, Taylor was prepared to ridicule Agrarianism because it had been discredited both pragmatically and philosophically. Since Ransom, Tate, and Warren had moved on in their thinking—if Donald Davidson and Lytle had not—to trounce Agrarianism was not necessarily an act of impiety toward Taylor's friends and mentors. When asked if he was more interested in the Fugitives' ideas about writing than about Agrarian politics, Taylor replied, "It was both things, yes. . . . You see I studied with Ransom at Kenyon and was much interested in poetry *and* fiction, but . . . I was an ardent agrarian too."[37]

Taylor's early fiction culminated in *A Woman of Means*, completed during his first year teaching at the Woman's College in Greensboro, North Carolina, in 1946–47. Letters to Warren, as well as to Lowell, outline a complicated process of literary creation.

Taylor wrote to Warren that he was writing "a group of stories about a Tennesse [*sic*] family whose 1920–40 generations move north and east . . . to become 'hardware, insurance, and shoe people.' " He complained of being "stuck just now on the murder of the grandmother who thinks (senile dementia) or thought that she was pregnant by her grandson who has returned temporarily to the Tennessee farm." Taylor was also thinking of writing another story, which "takes place during the thirty hours that Charles Lindbergh was flying the Atlantic," about a "young hero's realization that neither his cultural or biological equilibrium is going to work in the world he is moving toward." Not until December 9, 1947, did Taylor inform Warren that both ideas had become part of his "novella," "about a Tennessee country boy whose father marries a rich widow in St. Louis and takes his son to live in her mansion there." Taylor was quick to insist that it "is not the story of my life" but rather is based on material of which he has "complete and thorough knowledge." On January 15, [1948?], Taylor wrote Lowell that "the novelette is done, and I'm now trying to get Doubleday to print it as a short novel since it would run to well over a hundred pages. . . . It's wonderful to have it off my chest and off my hands."[38]

In the same letter, Taylor commented that the basic idea of *A Woman of Means* had already become one of his staples: "If you read my new novelette and the other stories I've written recently you'll observe that my favorite stunt is to write about Southerners living out of the South. Somehow that situation fascinates me. I like to put a whole family (with its servants and a

37. Peter Taylor, "A Long Fourth," in *A Long Fourth*, 154–55; Taylor, interview by author.

38. Taylor to Warren, July 1, 1946, December 9, 1947, both in Warren Papers; Taylor to Lowell, January 15, [1948], Lowell Papers.

couple of old relatives) in Chicago or St. Louis or New York or Washington, and begin my story from there."[39] These "fugitive" stories became another aspect of Peter Taylor's family romance. On the personal level, Taylor drew from the fact that his father, an insurance lawyer, had moved his family from Trenton, Tennessee, to St. Louis, where they had to adjust to existence in a midwestern city while retaining physical and emotional ties with the rural South. Taylor was also aware that the former Fugitives, beginning with Ransom, had without noticeable reluctance experienced a similar displacement. On both levels, fleeing the South becomes a somewhat painful but deliberate assertion of independence to which the "fugitive" responds with unexpected resilience.

As in "Skyline" and "The Scoutmaster," Taylor records in *A Woman of Means* a tale of filial disappointment and eventual alienation. Griffith calls the novel an "amazing solo flight" for the maturing fiction writer Peter Taylor. He praises the novel's nonlinear structure as "a particularly apt adaptation of what has almost become the conventional handling of time in the post-Jamesian novel."[40] He might well have said "in the fiction of the Fugitive legacy," for in its skillful use of first person narrative, Taylor's first novel invites comparison with novels by Warren, Tate, Gordon, and Lytle, with which Taylor was undoubtedly familiar. Robert Penn Warren, the only former Fugitive to review the novel, crowned it with praise matched by few disinterested reviewers. But, New Critic that he was, Warren did not register how much of Taylor's own experience shaped the novel.

The Widows of Thornton came out in 1954 and presented, as the title indicates, a compendium of stories about southern women, both black and white: "A Wife of Nashville," "Their Losses," "What You Hear from 'Em?' "Two Ladies in Retirement," "Cookie," and "The Dark Walk." These were the kind of Peter Taylor stories that the members of the Fugitive circle liked best and praised most, Warren and Jarrell especially. Taylor dedicated the volume "To Allen and Caroline [Tate]."[41]

One story, "Porte-Cochère," represents, however, one of Taylor's darkest versions of the father-son saga. On September 25, 1948, Taylor wrote to Lowell from Bloomington: "Did I write you that my newest story is called 'Yellow Brick' and all takes place in an ugly yellow brick house (built about

---

39. Taylor to Lowell, January 15, [1948], Lowell Papers.

40. Griffith, *Peter Taylor*, 39.

41. Peter Taylor, *The Widows of Thornton* (1948, rpt. Baton Rouge: Louisiana State University Press, 1994).

1915) with a porte-cochere, an octagonal side porch, a sunparlor with wicker furniture, a study opening off the stairway, and a green tile roof? The man who built it and lives in it, of course, remembers other houses—old houses he lived in as a boy." The story, with a new title, appeared first in the *New Yorker* in July 1949. It is a cautionary tale about how failed communication between fathers and sons leads first to cruel mistreatment and finally to impotent isolation. The porte-cochère is directly under Old Ben's study, where he can monitor the comings and goings, as well as some of the conversation, of the grown children who dutifully but unwillingly visit on his birthday. As Robert Penn Warren brilliantly and chillingly delineated in *All the King's Men*, Old Ben is acting out the age-old "blood greed," whereby "when you get born your father and mother lost something out of themselves and they are going to bust a hame trying to get it back, and you are it."[42]

By the late 1950s, Taylor was in the double bind of having to assert his independence from both his biological and creative families. It is ironically appropriate, therefore, that his next collection of stories was entitled *Happy Families Are All Alike*. Published in 1959, the collection is dominated by stories of familial conflict such as "The Walled Garden" and "Venus, Cupid, Folly, and Time," which came out first in the *Kenyon Review* and was immediately disliked by Jarrell and Lowell. Included also is "*Je Suis Perdu*," in which (as in the much later story "Dean of Men") Taylor dramatized the mingled satisfactions and discomfitures that characterize the academic world, which, despite his early aloofness toward it, Taylor elected as his own. Like his former-Fugitive mentors, Taylor had discovered that the satisfactions of the literary life and community must be paid for by carrying what is aptly called an academic *load*.

"*Je Suis Perdu*" was first published in the *New Yorker* in June 1958 as "A Pair of Bright-Blue Eyes." In it a college professor on sabbatical in France confronts the conflicting demands of his academic and family roles, just as Taylor himself did during his 1955–56 Fulbright in Paris. Taylor achieves perfunctory distance from his protagonist by making him a historian who has obtained a grant to write a book "about certain Confederate statesmen and agents who, with their families were in Paris at the end of the Civil War, and who had to decide whether to go home and live under the new regime or remain permanently in Europe." Transferred to the 1920s, the expatriates making a similar decision might have been Allen Tate, Caroline Gordon, and

---

42. Taylor to Lowell, September 25, 1948, Lowell Papers; Robert Penn Warren, *All the King's Men* (New York: Random House, 1946; rpt. Bantam, 1956–81), 35.

Katherine Anne Porter—all of whom at one time or another during their so-journs abroad had ruefully observed, like Taylor's young professor, that "as far as research was concerned, he had soon found that there was nothing to be got hold of at the Bibliotheque Nationale or anywhere else in Paris that was not available at home."[43]

Perhaps Peter Taylor was finding the role of Fugitive legatee too binding, he who might have become a lawyer like his father or made a living in real estate. Perhaps his own European sojourn was but a facile, ultimately unsatis-factory imitation of the expatriate generation.

Peter Taylor's literary life in the 1960s continued, however, to revolve around his role as a Fugitive legatee. His newest short stories appeared either in the *New Yorker*, with which he had an ongoing relationship, or in the *Kenyon* or *Sewanee Reviews*. The decade of fiction coalesced in *Miss Leonora When Last Seen* in 1964 and *The Collected Stories of Peter Taylor* in 1969. In teaching assignments at Greensboro, Indiana University, Kenyon, and the University of Virginia, Taylor recapitulated the teaching careers of his mentors, still re-sisting the role of reviewer-critic. Letters to Lowell, Tate, and Warren con-vey Taylor's chagrin at being unable to contribute to the Ransom issue which the *Kenyon Review* published in 1964 to celebrate Ransom's seventy-fifth birthday and memorialize Philip Blair Rice, the *Kenyon* editor who died as a result of a traffic accident in 1952.[44] Ironically, the 1960s saw as well the tragic death of Randall Jarrell, to which Taylor responded with his best prose writing. These stories constitute neither a change in perspective nor a new interest for Taylor; rather they continue his filtration of his own experience at various stages.

The narrator of "Dean of Men" has, like his creator, held more than one academic position in more than one college town. Like Taylor, he sees over his shoulder a succession of paternal figures whom, in career crises, he emu-lates even as he despises their weaknesses. In a parable of the anxiety of in-fluence, however, he too has chosen the academic life rather than politics or the insurance business, in the vain hope that he may escape a reenactment of their professional humiliations and frustrations. These conflicts and their ef-fects emerge as the narrator accounts for his choice of careers: "I don't hon-estly know when I decided to go into college teaching, Jack. I considered doing other things—a career in the army or the navy. . . . One thing was cer-

43. Wright, *Peter Taylor*, 158; Robison, *Peter Taylor*, 170; Peter Taylor, "*Je Suis Perdu*," in *The Collected Stories of Peter Taylor* (New York: Farrar, Straus & Giroux, 1969), 489.

44. Janssen, *Kenyon Review*, 330.

tain, though. Business was just as much out of the question for me as politics had been for my father."[45] Other aspects of Taylor's own academic and personal life appear in the story, including the narrator's eventual return to the college where he was an undergraduate. With a young daughter and baby son, he (like the narrator of *"Je Suis Perdu"*) goes to Italy on a Fulbright fellowship, returning to find that a change in administration would shatter his former contentment as a member of the small college faculty.

As a creative writer rather than Ph.D. scholar, Taylor endured the same conflicts between need for security (tenure and full professorships being rare for those lacking doctorates) and freedom to create that plagued his mentors, the former Fugitives; and yet he followed their footsteps almost exactly. Taylor described these difficulties in several letters to Robert Lowell when the first of those transfers, from Greensboro to Bloomington, occurred in 1948. Like the young professor in "Dean of Men," the Taylors were short of funds. A letter of August 10, [1948], mentions selling their refrigerator to raise money for the move. Moreover, the specters of his Fugitive forebears Ransom and Tate haunted Taylor in his new job: "Here we are among all these young intellectual college professors, and I have never felt more out of place. When I wrote you last I had not really gotten the slant on them I have now. The most difficult to handle are the followers of Red and those of Ransom. They have taken over the opinions of those two men on every subject under the sun. And if ever I refer lightly to any aspect of Red's or Ransom's characters, I am given either a hurt or a baffled look." Taylor would return to the academic variation of his familiar plot once more in "The Old Forest." The narrator finally rebels by entering the academic world and taking his society-bred wife with him.[46] For Peter Taylor to leave the security of upper-middle-class urban society to become a writer and college professor was a parallel act of rebellion that would not have been possible had not the former Fugitives, as his teachers and surrogate fathers, offered him a viable alternative. For Taylor, as for his mentors, the groves of academe offered a graciously ordered, if sometimes insecure, Arcadia.

That *In the Miro District*, product of the late sixties and early seventies, has been called Taylor's best work was particularly pleasing to the author.[47] Taken as a whole, the volume is not only a collection of fine writing, but it also was the occasion of Peter Taylor's triumph over the anxiety of influence.

45. Peter Taylor, "Dean of Men," in *Collected Stories*, 24.
46. Taylor to Lowell, August 10, 29, [1948], Lowell Papers.
47. Taylor, interview by author.

Whereas his earliest stories came out a time when he felt most obligated to his literary "fathers" for his successes in the literary arena, these new stories and narrative poems show mastery over both mentors and peers and of the literary forms from which he had formerly felt excluded.

Two letters which Taylor wrote to Robert Penn Warren testify, nevertheless, how much Taylor still valued encouragement and feedback from the post-Fugitive circle. On August 8, 1974, Taylor, recovering from a heart attack that had left him in a state of depression, wrote that he was "sending these three stories to prove it. They are not quite stories and they are not quite poems, but they are what I am doing now. I'm doing a whole book of them. Their form is just something I can't help." Warren must have responded immediately to Taylor's creative outpouring, for, on August 30, Taylor wrote, "I can never thank you enough for reading my stories so carefully and for writing me about them. Your letter came at a particularly good time, just when I am about to do more work on 'The Hand of Emmagene.' Cal had much the same feeling that you do about the need of compression toward the beginning, and I am looking for ways of achieving that."[48] He was also apparently "determined to get away from" the anxiety of influence, from New Critical irony and its prohibition against writing his own personal story, as well as from their hegemony over the domain of poetry. Like many writers of his time, he felt the need for direct use of his own material and freedom to mix forms and genres.

The poems of *In the Miro District* combine attributes of fiction, poetry, and drama. When Barbara Thompson, in a 1987 interview, asked Peter Taylor about these "prose poems," he expressed preference for Lowell's term, "story poems," and then remarked that "every story in *The Miro District* was written in that form, originally. That is, I began them all that way, but if I got halfway through and found that they got too long, or I couldn't sustain it, or that the line ends were not significant, no longer functional, then I gave it up."[49] After revision, these lines fell into the sort of loose blank verse that both Jarrell and Lowell had used in many of their poems.

It is fortunate that *In the Miro District* did not, as Taylor first planned, consist entirely of poems, that "The Captain's Son" and "In the Miro District" worked out best as stories. A close reading of "In the Miro District" proves that Peter Taylor's debt to the former Fugitives, Robert Penn Warren especially, forms a subtextual ground bass throughout.

---

48. Taylor to Warren, August 8, 30, 1974, both in Warren Papers.
49. Thompson, "Interview with Taylor," 160–61.

In the August 30, 1974, letter to Warren, Taylor remarked on how his composition of "In the Miro District," the most important story in the volume, was also for him an assumption of mastery over both material and form: "There are subjects that are accessible to me now and that never seemed so before. One of them is about my grandfather's kidnapping by the Nightriders, at Reelfoot Lake. It may be more about me than about Grandfather, but it is fun making use of the stories he used to tell—even about his first meeting with General Forrest. He claimed he was the only man who ever called Forrest an S. O. B. and lived."[50] Personal material in Warren's poems from *Promises* on may also have helped to make Taylor's own family stories "accessible" to him. In fact, autobiographical storytelling, so important to Warren's later poetry, is the primary mechanism that advances the plot of "Miro."

There are allusions to the New Madrid (Reelfoot Lake) earthquake of 1811 that Warren used in *Brother to Dragons* and elsewhere and to John James Audubon, about whom Warren published his long poem. All of these particulars suggest not only Warren but also the other post-Fugitive writers. References to General Nathan Bedford Forrest, so important to the fiction of Andrew Lytle and Caroline Gordon, constitute by the time of Taylor's usage a coterie symbol for the fiction of the Fugitive legacy. Moreover, a duck-hunting incident recalls not only Lytle's "The Mahogany Frame," another story of male initiation that might have influenced Taylor, but also a minor recollected occurrence in *Flood*, Warren's novel of the early sixties. None of these allusions, conscious or unconscious, punctures the fabric of Taylor's story. Rather, they enrich it by enlarging its relevance. While Warren's close involvement in the writing of the story, as evidenced in their correspondence, may have inhibited somewhat Taylor's overt use of Warren in the story, it also made the implantations, and their subsequent enrichment of the story, stronger.

Late in the story, the narrator wondered, in a passage of more than common resonance, "if, merely as a result of being born when I was and where I was, at the very tail end of something, I was like nothing else at all, only incomparably without a character of my own."[51] Did Peter Taylor finally feel, like his narrator, that he "was at the tail end of something"? Did the character of the grandfather, in his new identity, become more like Tate or Lytle than Warren, always rehashing the war and assuming a privileged status as

50. Taylor to Warren, August 30, 1974, Warren Papers.
51. Peter Taylor, "In the Miro District," in *In the Miro District and Other Stories* (1977; rpt. New York: Ballantine, 1990), 182.

its historian? In his relationship with the former Fugitives, particularly with Warren, their only important writer of fiction, Peter Taylor may reflect in this passage his own belatedness.

Perhaps, however, Taylor and Warren actually felt little generational rivalry. Eleanor Clark once objected that when Taylor and his peers discussed LSU days, they made Robert Penn Warren seem to be of a "new generation." In a manner of speaking, Peter Taylor and Robert Penn Warren *were* by the seventies not only of the same literary generation but also about to change places within it. In the same (August 30, 1974) letter that proclaimed his new freedom and independence, Taylor also indicated that he still felt incapable of challenging his master in the genre that had won him such acclaim: "I am glad you're writing a new novel. I have given up ever being able to do one and this makes me able to enjoy other people's novels still more."[52] *A Summons to Memphis* nonetheless appeared in 1986, only three years before Warren's death and nine years after the publication of his last novel, *A Place to Come To*, for Warren had reserved his last years for the writing of poetry. Claiming the field of fiction for himself, Peter Taylor moved beyond the anxiety of influence.

From the beginning of his career, Peter Taylor was never able to "resist the opportunity to talk about his [old] teachers." In interview after interview, spanning more than half a century, the following comment became typical: "I was lucky in growing up in Tennessee when I did. There were writers of the first rank around, men like Tate and Lytle and Davidson and Ransom. They had almost the same background that I did, they were accessible to me—Lytle and my father were devoted friends—and I never felt the alienation from my background that some writers seem to feel."[53] Along with the other fiction writers of the Fugitive legacy, Taylor found that by incorporating the aesthetic values of the New Criticism with his own personal narrative, he could carve his own respectable niche in their patrician community.

Membership in that community became for Peter Taylor a sufficient compensation for what was, for many years, a modest literary reputation. Taylor consistently maintained that he "always had a lot of appreciative literary friends," that "it's all chance whether or not you become well known in your generation," and that his "concern is with how good what I write is and with the opinion of my peers." Even more forcefully, in a 1986 interview with J. H. E. Paine, Taylor maintained that "the most important group [of readers]

52. Taylor, interview by author; Taylor to Warren, August 30, 1974, Warren Papers.
53. Peter Taylor, postcard to author, 1992; Goodwin, "Interview with Taylor," 8.

to me . . . is my number of literary friends when I was growing up and through the years. It's what made it possible for me to go on without minding that I had no big reputation as a writer." He went on to mention Lowell, Jarrell, Stafford, Tate, and Warren, who, he extravagantly claimed, "really constituted all that I cared about as a public."[54] With the publication of *A Summons to Memphis*, which garnered the Pulitzer Prize, Taylor came to recognize that despite its indisputable value to a young writer, fame within the Fugitive circle was not enough to establish a writer's reputation. Only after the death of most of those peers was Peter Taylor able to claim the importance he had long deserved and the acclaim not only of his teachers, peers, and students but that of the critics and reading public as well.

54. Wendy Smith, *"P[ublisher's] W[eekly]* Interviews Peter Taylor," in McAlexander, ed., *Conversations with Taylor*, 64; J. H. E. Paine, "Interview with Peter Taylor, March 1, 1986," *Journal of the Short Story in English* 9 (Fall 1987): 14.

14 / Flannery O'Connor: The Last Direct Legatee

> Mrs. Tate is Caroline Gordon Tate, the wife of Allen Tate. She writes fiction as good as anybody, though I have not read much of it myself. They, with John Crowe Ransom and R. P. Warren, were prominent in the 20s in that group at Vanderbilt that called itself the Fugitives. The Fugitives are now here there and yonder. Anyway, Mrs. Tate has taught me a lot about writing.
>
> —Flannery O'Connor to "A"
> August 28, 1955

Uncomfortable with, if not especially anxious about, influence, Flannery O'Connor nevertheless was often willing to give credit to the former Fugitives and their heirs for aiding and abetting her career as a writer. Not only were they among her earliest teachers, but they furnished her, through their anthologies and textbooks, a theory of narration that was, if not always amenable to her purposes, at least worthy of consideration. Moreover, at the outset of her career, she relied on Allen Tate, John Crowe Ransom, Andrew Lytle, Robert Penn Warren, and their influential friends to recommend her for fellowships and to potential editors and publishers.[1]

O'Connor's ties with the post-Fugitive circle were strengthened by more than the fact that she grew up in the South and agreed with the premises of the Agrarian movement. Her ardent adherence to the beliefs and strictures of Roman Catholicism caused O'Connor to form especially strong bonds with those members of the group who were of the same religious affiliation. The Tates, Robert Lowell, and former Vanderbilt student and journalist Brainard

---

1. Portions of this discussion have appeared in Charlotte H. Beck, "Caroline Gordon and Flannery O'Connor: An Empowering Anxiety of Influence," *Flannery O'Connor Bulletin* 25 (1996–97): 194–213.

Cheney and his wife, Frances, were particularly supportive of O'Connor's career because she was Catholic and grounded her fiction in Roman Catholic theology. Lytle, Ransom, Warren, and the Tates were attracted to O'Connor because of her generally agrarian, antipositivist attitudes. All of the post-Fugitive writers recognized in O'Connor a writing talent so immense that they were intensely desirous of claiming her as one of their group. Through the continuing supportive presence of these fellow writers in her literary life, Flannery O'Connor therefore became part of the Fugitive legacy, perhaps, in a sense, the last major writer to benefit directly from the influence and sponsorship of that far-ranging group. It was Caroline Gordon, however, who became O'Connor's mentor and close friend for the remainder of her life and who played an invaluable role in the development of her genius.

O'Connor's life history made such allegiances particularly important. As Louise Westling remarks in *Sacred Groves and Ravaged Gardens*, O'Connor's illness (lupus) forced her, after "only five years of freedom at the University of Iowa, in New York and in rural Connecticut" to retreat "into the claustrophobic conventionality of mother's control in her Georgia hometown."[2] Fortunately, O'Connor had by then formed alliances that would be supportive throughout her short but luminous career. Beyond correspondence and the visits that letter writing encouraged, O'Connor occasionally participated in the affairs of the literary community. As her fame grew, she was frequently invited to lecture and to join conferences and symposia that were a way of life, not to mention a source of income, for the other members of her writing community. When her health permitted and when she could overcome her aversion to such events, O'Connor ventured afield to participate in them with respected colleagues. These too provide insight into the communal side, slight though it was, to O'Connor's writing career.

O'Connor became acquainted with the post-Fugitive group when, after majoring in the social sciences at Georgia College, Milledgeville, she left the South to study journalism at the State University of Iowa. Unable to comprehend her Georgia accent, Paul Engle handed her a pad of paper upon which she wrote, "My name is Flannery O'Connor. I am not a journalist. Can I come to the Writer's Workshop?" It so happened that Andrew Lytle, who became acting head of the school of writing during the spring and fall terms of 1947, taught O'Connor's class in fiction writing. Because the Fugitive circle never failed to involve one another in their peripatetic teaching stints (to share both the "wealth" and the weariness), Lytle invited both Allen Tate and

2. Westling, *Sacred Groves*, 121.

Robert Penn Warren to serve, as Tate described it, as "visiting writer[s] whose job was to 'criticize' the work of the young writers in the week I was there."[3] Both Tate and Warren consequently became acquainted with Flannery O'Connor and with her writing.

The experience must have been frustrating to O'Connor, for the former Fugitives were not immediately impressed. Tate wrote later that when he examined some early portions of *Wise Blood*, he "hadn't the vaguest idea of what she was up to; I offered to correct her grammar; I even told her that her style was dull, the sentences being flat and simple declarative." Warren suggested and O'Connor made certain changes in the story she submitted for his criticism.[4]

The bond that soon developed between Lytle and O'Connor was, however, instant. Their semirural, upper South background gave O'Connor and Lytle something in common. In "Literary Portraits" (1964), Lytle described their first encounter:

> Years ago at Iowa City in a rather informal class meeting I read aloud a story by one of the students. I was told later that it was understood that I would know how to pronounce in good country idiom the word *chitling*, which appeared in the story. At once it was obvious that the author of the story was herself not only southern but exceptionally gifted. The idiom for her characters rang with all the truth of the real thing, but the real thing heightened. It resembled in tone and choice of words all country speech I had ever heard, but I couldn't quite place it. And then I realized that what she had done was what any first-rate artist always does—she had made something more essential than life but resembling it. She had done this by the use of crucial words and the proper rhythm raised to a higher power. She was making her own language for the subject already seen to be uniquely her own.
>
> This, of course, was Flannery O'Connor.[5]

O'Connor's studies at Iowa also introduced her to the theories of fiction that the Fugitives espoused and to the literature they had helped to canonize.

---

3. Robert Giroux, introduction to *The Complete Stories of Flannery O'Connor* (New York: Farrar, Straus & Giroux, 1994), vii; Young and Sarcone, eds., *Tate-Lytle Letters*, xii–xxiii; Allen Tate, "Platitudes and Protestants," in *Critical Essays on Flannery O'Connor*, ed. Milton Friedman and Beverly Lyon Clark (Boston: G. K. Hall, 1985), 67.

4. Tate, "Platitudes," 67; Giroux, introduction to *Complete Stories of O'Connor*, vii.

5. Andrew Lytle, "Literary Portraits: Flannery O'Connor," in *Southerners and Europeans: Essays in a Time of Disorder* (Baton Rouge: Louisiana State University Press, 1988), 187.

In a 1955 letter to her anonymous correspondent "A," O'Connor wrote, "When I went to Iowa I had never heard of Faulkner, Kafka, Joyce, much less read them. Then I began to read everything at once, so much that I didn't have time I suppose to be influenced by any one writer. I read all the Catholic novelists, Mauriac, Bernanos, Bloy, Greene, Waugh; I read all the nuts like Djuna Barnes and Dorothy Richardson and Va. Woolf (unfair to the dear lady of course); I read the best Southern writers like Faulkner and the Tates, K. A. Porter, Eudora Welty and Peter Taylor." O'Connor was also introduced to a textbook that shaped her attitudes toward the writing of fiction. James Grimshaw believes that the narrative form that O'Connor regularly employed was "undoubtedly assimilated from Cleanth Brooks and Robert Penn Warren's *Understanding Fiction*." But although she was later to call *Understanding Fiction* the only book on "short-story form" that she continued to trust throughout her writing career, she recommended it not for its theory so much as for the fact that "it has a variety of stories . . . and you get some idea of the range of what can be done." To Ben Griffith she called it "a book that has been of invaluable help to me and I think would be to you." And to "A," who aspired to be a writer, O'Connor recommended "a textbook I used at Iowa. It is pure textbook and very uninviting and part of the value of it for me was that I had it in conjunction with Paul Engle who was able to breathe some life into it; but even without him, it might help you some—called Understanding Fiction, Brooks and Warren."[6]

After leaving Iowa, Flannery O'Connor naturally turned to the two most prestigious southern literary magazines, the *Kenyon Review* and the *Sewanee Review*, still in the hands of former Fugitive-Agrarians, as strong possibilities for placing her stories. Because of Andrew Lytle and Allen Tate, she had an entrée to the *Sewanee Review*, which published four of her stories (see Appendix). She was, however, to form a more fruitful relationship with the *Kenyon Review* and with its founder and editor, John Crowe Ransom. In time, like Porter, Welty, and Taylor, O'Connor began to place her stories in the national magazines that paid well, including *Esquire, Mademoiselle*, and the *Atlantic*; but she still felt allegiance to the southern journals edited by members of the post-Fugitive group and continued to publish in them even when doing so would cost her income and broad readership.

O'Connor became a protégé of Ransom and the *Kenyon Review* when, as

6. Sally Fitzgerald, ed., *Letters of Flannery O'Connor: The Habit of Being* (New York: Farrar, Straus & Giroux, 1979), 98, 283, 83, 192; James A. Grimshaw, Jr., *The Flannery O'Connor Companion* (Westport, Conn.: Greenwood Press, 1981), 19.

she reported in a letter to Sally Fitzgerald, she had a note from Ransom "saying there was such a thing as a *Kenyon Review* Fellowship in Fiction that they got from Rockerfeller [*sic*] money and would I like to apply, that Robt Fitzgrld [*sic*] & Peter Taylor had mentioned me to him." She applied for the fellowship, submitting "The Life You Save" and "The River"; by December 20, 1952, O'Connor had received word that she would receive the fellowship and that Ransom would publish one of the two stories. On the same day, she wrote to the Fitzgeralds: "Merry Christmas from Grimrack. I got the Kenyon Fellowship, thanks no doubt to your saying to him this summer that I was an existing writer." On December 30 she wrote again to thank Sally and Robert for giving her a subscription to the *Review* and for allowing her the pleasure of seeing her story with "Mr. Shiftlet [of "The Life You Save"] and somebody like Yvor Winters, blank wall to blank, between two unintelligible poems." On January 25, 1953, she reported to the Fitzgeralds: "*The Kenyon Review* sent me a thoousand [*sic*] bucks the other day, no note, no nothing; just the dough. My kinfolks think I am a commercial writer now and really they are proud of me."[7] The story appeared in the spring 1953 issue.

"A Circle in the Fire," the next story that Ransom accepted, appeared a year later, in the spring 1954 issue, not long after the *Review* renewed her fellowship for the following year. Beginning to feel "rich" with literary success and the monetary gains therefrom, she wrote to the Fitzgeralds: "I sold a story to *Kenyon* and another to *Harper's Bazaar*. I don't know if I ought to buy AT&T or go in for colored rental property."[8]

Though grateful for the *Kenyon Review*'s sponsorship, O'Connor was able to stand her ground against any unreasonable objections from its editor. On November 14, 1954, she wrote to Caroline Gordon: "Mr. Ransom took the Artificial Nigger for the Kenyon but I think without enthusiasm. He complained it was very flat and had no beautiful sentences in it. I rewrote it but there still ain't any beautiful sentences. It may be too long." When the story first crossed Ransom's desk, however, he was reluctant to print it because of its title, as he wrote to Robert Penn Warren the following April: "We have the best serio-comic story Flannery O'Connor has yet written. . . . But it's entitled 'The Artificial Nigger.' I was for using it but Phil [Rice] pointed out how sensitive the people of color are, so I wrote and proposed to her another title. Her reply was in effect that the responsibility would be ours, we could change the title if we liked, but she believed that if the people who read her

7. Fitzgerald, ed., *Letters of Flannery O'Connor*, 46, 48–50, 54.
8. Ibid., 66.

title would also read the story they would see that the only reflection on any-body is on the whites. We kept her title." It was one of the stories that owes both its final form and publication to the joint efforts of the group. As she reports in letters to Robert Giroux (who edited her first collection, *A Good Man Is Hard to Find*, in the same year), both Ransom and Caroline Gordon read "The Artificial Nigger" and made suggestions before its first publication in the *Kenyon Review*. The version that appeared in the collection was written after O'Connor had "conferred with Caroline about the story . . . and . . . consequently [rewritten] it." In 1958, however, she wrote to Cecil Dawkins that "I have always listened with profit to what he [Ransom] has had to say about my stories—except when he wanted me to change the title of The Arti-ficial Nigger."[9]

O'Connor continued to send Ransom her stories, though more of them actually appeared in magazines where they could earn more money. On Janu-ary 1, 1957, she wrote to the Fitzgeralds, "I have got the O. Henry prize this year—$300—for the thing that was in the *Kenyon* this summer" ("Green-leaf"). As she explained to Elizabeth McKee on March 15, "I finished the story ["Greenleaf"] I was working on, and after some deliberation, sent it to Mr. Ransom. It is a good story and I am sure *Harper's Bazaar* would have taken it and paid twice as much as *Kenyon* but Mr. Ransom has been very good to me and I would like as long as he's there . . . to send him a story every year."[10]

In hindsight it appears not only that the five stories that O'Connor pub-lished in the *Kenyon Review* were among her best but also that receiving the Kenyon Fellowship was key to her growing confidence that she could succeed as a writer. As editors of literary reviews, the former Fugitives and their pro-tégés came to accept O'Connor's approach to writing and praise her for it—despite their resistance to stories containing regional dialect. By 1954, when Lytle was in the throes of writing *The Velvet Horn*, Tate would hold up O'Connor's handling of dialect as a model for Lytle to emulate: "Just read her 'The Circle of Fire,' in the *Kenyon*. She has instinctively hit upon what seems to me the essentials of the matter. The local idiom is recreated cheifly [*sic*] through word order and rhythm, with an occasional local idiom, and all done with the *minimum* of distorted, or phonetic, spelling." Andrew Lytle remained an O'Connor partisan and booster throughout her career. After

9. O'Connor to Caroline Gordon, November 14, 1954, Flannery O'Connor Papers, Flan-nery O'Connor Collection, Ina Dillard Russell Library, Georgia College, Milledgeville, Ga.; Young and Core, eds., *Selected Letters of Ransom*, 376; Fitzgerald, ed., *Letters of Flannery O'Connor*, 73, 297.

10. Fitzgerald, ed., *Letters of Flannery O'Connor*, 192, 146.

publishing *The Violent Bear It Away* (1960), she wrote to Lytle, "I feel better about the book, knowing you think it works. I expect it to get trounced but that won't make any difference if it really does work. There are not many people whose opinion on this I set store by."[11]

Membership in the Fugitive network also brought O'Connor her first major critical attention. In 1961, Andrew Lytle, now editor of the *Sewanee Review*, wrote to "brother" Allen Tate: "Both Peter Taylor and Flannery [O'Connor] have reached that stage where they need a concentrated appraisal. Say two or three pieces on them. But not only that. Let them give me something, a story or piece of fiction, to go with the criticism. I think this will lighten somewhat, without lessening, the heavy effect which criticism makes in a quarterly. Peter has agreed, and I've written Flannery." One may assume that Tate's response was favorable, and when Lytle sounded Ransom out on the notion, he also offered moral support—"That's a fine idea of yours about a critics' get together on a story by Peter Taylor and Flannery O'Connor. I'm for it."[12] With Tate's and Ransom's encouragement, Lytle proceeded with plans for an O'Connor issue of the *Sewanee Review*.

The "piece of fiction" required for the issue proved to be a difficult assignment for Flannery O'Connor. In November 1961, she wrote to John Hawkes (who was working on his famous article "Flannery O'Connor's Devil" for the issue): "I had brief notes from Andrew a couple of times lately. In fact he has a story of mine but I haven't heard from him whether he's going to use it or not." Lytle did accept the story, but not before she labored on it for many months and, even as late as January 1962, was not yet satisfied with it. In May, when the issue was in press, she wrote to her agent Elizabeth McKee that "I have decided that I don't like it and am going to try to persuade Andrew not to use it. However, I'm afraid it is too late."[13] The summer 1962 issue of the *Kenyon Review* did indeed feature O'Connor and her a new story, "The Lame Shall Enter First." The autumn 1962 issue was on Taylor, with "At the Drugstore" as his original inclusion. Neither Ransom nor Tate contributed to either issue.

Andrew Lytle and the *Sewanee Review* continued to be one of O'Connor's mainstays near the end of her life when the grind of writing and publishing were proving more and more strenuous for her. One of her last stories, "Rev-

---

11. Young and Sarcone, eds., *Tate-Lytle Letters*, 239; Fitzgerald, ed., *Letters of Flannery O'Connor*, 373.

12. Young and Sarcone, eds., *Tate-Lytle Letters*, 314; Ransom to Lytle, n.d., Lytle Papers.

13. Fitzgerald, ed., *Letters of Flannery O'Connor*, 456, 460, 475.

elation," was submitted to Lytle early in 1964, just before she began planning her last collection of stories, *Everything That Rises Must Converge*.[14]

It would be difficult to exaggerate Lytle's role in O'Connor's literary career. Had she not become his protégé before sending her fiction to Ransom, she might have been another writer whose stories Ransom did not "like quite enough." But because she did have both talent and Lytle's sponsorship, Ransom and Lytle, through their literary magazines, were able to provide O'Connor with a respectable showcase for her fiction. Cognizant of her debt to these editors, O'Connor continued to send them her best efforts. Of the nine stories in *Everything That Rises Must Converge*, four were published first in the *Sewanee* and *Kenyon Reviews*.

After being introduced to Robert Penn Warren, first through *Understanding Fiction* and then, in person, at Iowa, O'Connor had little personal contact with him except through his friends in the post-Fugitive group. Their next encounter may have been in connection with O'Connor's unsuccessful application in 1948 for a Guggenheim Fellowship. When Harcourt published *Wise Blood* in 1948, O'Connor included Warren's name, along with those of Lytle, Robie Macauley, and John Palmer, as persons whom "a good word might be squeezed out of" in the form of a review. Likewise, when her second novel, *The Violent Bear It Away*, was in press, Warren, along with Lytle and "the Lowells," was on her list to Robert Giroux of "several people that I would like to see the book when it gets all the corrections in it." After Warren reviewed the novel favorably, she sent her anonymous correspondent "A" some first-response letters "just for your entertainment, as considered preferable to television," including one "from Red Warren [that] pleased me no end as I really didn't expect him to like the book."[15]

Although O'Connor's great respect for Warren was a combination of personal and artistic admiration, she was a careful reader of all his fiction who did not hesitate, on grounds of friendship, to point out his strengths and weaknesses. As she wrote to Maryat Lee, "Warren is a lovely man. That *Band of Angels* is probably not his best by far. I suggest you read *All the King's Men*. I have his long dramatic poem *Brother to Dragons* if you would like me to send it to you."[16]

O'Connor was again in the company of one of her first mentors on April 23, 1959, when she and Robert Penn Warren were interviewed by a group of

14. Ibid., 565.
15. Ibid., 34, 353, 390.
16. Ibid., 396.

Vanderbilt University students and faculty members. A typically garrulous, informal Warren and an unusually loquacious O'Connor revealed some striking similarities in the way each approached the task of writing fiction. Against the formalist implications of New Critical theory, both, for example, rejected the notion of writing from a formal outline:

> Miss O'Connor: I just don't outline.
> Mr. Warren: I had an outline once, and it took me two years to pull out of it. You think you've got your work done.

As to the selection of a theme and foreknowledge of a conclusion, their answers were again similar:

> Miss O'Connor: I think it's better to begin with the story, and then you know you've got something. Because the theme is more or less something that's in you, but if you intellectualize it too much you probably destroy your novel. . . .
> Mr. Warren: I think people can freeze themselves by their hasty intellectualizing of what they are up to.

When the conversation turned to how a writer knows enough to write, both agreed that experience—coming from living all one's life in a certain region, from grounding in a certain theological perspective, and from reading other writers—allows an author first to internalize and afterward to create. Both also agreed that to be identified as a regional writer was a "trap" that had to be avoided.[17]

This meeting of the youngest Fugitive with the youngest Fugitive legatee established that against the implications of formalism in New Critical theory, Robert Penn Warren was, like O'Connor, essentially romantic in his approach to writing fiction. Had their relationship been stronger, O'Connor might well have rebelled more confidently against the rigidly structured, monovocal Jamesian mode of fiction so strictly insisted upon by Lytle and Gordon.

Robert Lowell and Flannery O'Connor became fast friends after her residence at Yaddo in 1948–49, but apparently she had either met him or heard a lot about him earlier from the Tates. By November 1948, at any rate, it appears that Lowell had taken up Flannery as a sort of protégé, recommending

17. "An Interview with Flannery O'Connor and Robert Penn Warren," in *Conversations with Flannery O'Connor*, ed. Rosemary M. Magee (Jackson: University Press of Mississippi, 1987), 19, 20, 36.

her for the Guggenheim she did not receive but, more important, introducing her to Robert Giroux at Harcourt, who became her lifelong friend and editor. Ian Hamilton recounts how O'Connor sided with Lowell in the chaotic Yaddo witch-hunt in which he was the most vocal denouncer of Elizabeth Ames and the Yaddo management. The incident drove Lowell, in one of his manic phases, toward Catholicism (and into the bosom of his Catholic friends) more strongly than ever. As Hamilton puts it, "Friends like [Sally] Fitzgerald, Tate and O'Connor were ready to view the whole incident as a symptom of [Lowell's] 'reconversion'—although O'Connor had been worried by Lowell's insistence that she was a saint."[18] Robert Lowell and his second wife, Elizabeth Hardwick, remained O'Connor's correspondents thereafter when illness had forced her to return home to Georgia.

Lowell served often as O'Connor's loyal reader and reviewer. When he responded favorably to "Enoch and the Gorilla," published in *New World Writing* in 1952, she replied: "I was powerful glad to hear from you and I am pleased that you like the gorilla. I hope you'll like the whole thing." In 1953, when he praised "A Good Man Is Hard to Find," O'Connor wittily replied, "I'm glad you liked the story. That is my contribution to Mother's Day throughout the land." Since fiction was certainly not Lowell's medium, his contribution to O'Connor's career was exclusively that of a (Catholic) friend and respected fellow writer of the post-Fugitive group. In the years that followed, O'Connor frequently asked for news of the Lowells as they lived and worked in Europe and the United States. In 1956 she summed up her friendship with Robert Lowell: "You ask about Cal Lowell. I feel almost too much about him to be able to get to the heart of it. He is a kind of grief to me. I first knew him at Yaddo. We were both there one fall and winter. At that time he had left his first wife, Jean Stafford, and the Church. To make a long story short, I watched him that winter come back into the Church. I had nothing to do with it but of course it was a great joy to me." For O'Connor, Lowell's aberrant behavior, though heartbreaking, did not invalidate his literary judgment. His encouraging letter about *The Violent Bear It Away* evoked a warm response: "I'll keep your letter about the book nearby when the trouncing begins."[19]

If Flannery O'Connor's debt to the male cohort of the Fugitive legacy was strong, her ties to the female side were perhaps stronger. In fact, although Louise Westling believes that O'Connor "could have achieved her own voice

18. Fitzgerald, ed., *Letters of Flannery O'Connor*, 7, 8; Hamilton, *Robert Lowell*, 149.
19. Fitzgerald, ed., *Letters of Flannery O'Connor*, 35, 57, 152, 372.

and developed her particular literary strengths without female allies," she readily admits that for O'Connor, those "close women friends," rather than literary associates, were in a tangential way important to O'Connor's career.[20]

There is a strong possibility that Caroline Gordon is the strong precursor that O'Connor had first to please but ultimately to resist in asserting her own genius and that her struggles with point of view were the battleground on which O'Connor fought for her creative autonomy. That autonomy having been achieved, she began (as her letters to various correspondents establish) to distance herself from Gordon, only to proceed, in her final collection of stories, in remarkably Gordonian methods. Gordon met O'Connor indirectly when Robert Fitzgerald sent Caroline the manuscript for *Wise Blood*, identifying the writer as southern and Catholic. Gordon responded with enthusiasm: "The girl is a real novelist (I wish that I had had as firm a grasp on my subject matter when I was her age!) At any rate, she is already a rare phenomenon: A Catholic novelist with a real dramatic sense, one who relies more on her technique than her piety." She was particularly interested in how much better O'Connor wrote about "freaks" than did Frederick Buechner and Truman Capote. Gordon compared O'Connor's writing of dialogue favorably with some of Ernest Hemingway's. Hazel Motes's rejoinder "Blind myself" (on page 142 of the manuscript) led her to remark, "If this girl is capable of writing a line like that she is certainly capable of making the revisions this manuscript needs." Those revisions involved what Gordon referred to as "certain technical imperfections [that] deprive it of its proper frame of reference and actually limit its scope."[21]

These first suggestions from Gordon did not survive, although O'Connor obviously welcomed them and used them in her first revision. By late September, she wrote to ask the Fitzgeralds if they thought "Mrs. Tate would read the revised version." Gordon answered affirmatively in October, and in November she sent her new protégé "nine pages of comments," which, in O'Connor's words, "increased my education thereby." That "education" shaped the final revision of *Wise Blood*.[22]

That constructive experience led Flannery O'Connor to accept Gordon as a mentor with whom she was congenial from the standpoints of region, gender, and, most of all, spiritual commitment. Westling calls Gordon "more a

---

20. Westling, *Sacred Groves*, 63.

21. Sally Fitzgerald, "A Master Class: From the Correspondence of Caroline Gordon and Flannery O'Connor," *Georgia Review* 33 (1979): 828.

22. Ibid., 830–31.

coach than a model, a critic who helped O'Connor refine the mechanics of her craft" and one whose "professional encouragement was essential in O'Connor's isolated life."[23] Clearly Gordon's specific suggestions for textual emendation and revision shaped O'Connor into a writer whose style, though possessed of its own singular qualities, was well within the New Critical parameters and therefore acceptable to the publishing establishment.

At first O'Connor accepted Gordon's comments on *Wise Blood* humbly and gratefully. In September 1951, she wrote to Mavis McIntosh, "Bob Giroux and Mrs. Tate made some suggestions for improving my book and I have been working on these and have by now come up with another draft of it." During the same month, O'Connor wrote to Sally Fitzgerald asking, "Do you think Mrs. Tate would [read her revised manuscript]? All the changes are efforts after what she suggested in that letter and I am much obliged to her." Specifically, as she informed Robert Giroux, Caroline "thought that some places went too fast for anybody to get them; also that I needed some preparation for the title." In this, her first major publication, Flannery O'Connor was clearly willing to revise extensively, even at the last minute, to act on Gordon's suggestions. Like most writers, however, O'Connor was afraid to make too many substantive changes so close to publication, wanting to know "about how much can I mess around on the proofs without costing myself a lot of money." On January 23, 1952, O'Connor wrote to Robert Giroux, "The corrected galleys and the manuscript are enclosed. I hope the corrections and insertions are plain and not too numerous. They were all suggested by Caroline."[24]

With *Wise Blood* in print, Flannery O'Connor mapped out her next major publication project. On January 1, 1953, she wrote to Elizabeth and Robert Lowell: "I'm getting up a collection of stories that I'm going to call *A Good Man Is Hard to Find*. I send them all to Caroline and she writes me wherein they do not meet the mark."[25] All of the stories had indeed been revised in response to Gordon's letters of advice and previously published in various journals.

After receiving Gordon's comments on "The Artificial Nigger," O'Connor wrote to Giroux that she was "consequently rewriting it." An unpublished letter to Gordon reports: "I have a new story called 'The Artificial Nigger,' that I want to send you if you are not too busy & if you are really in

23. Westling, *Sacred Groves*, 64.
24. Fitzgerald, ed., *Letters of Flannery O'Connor*, 25, 27, 29, 30, 65.
25. Ibid., 65.

Minnesota. Apparently Harcourt is going to put out my collection of stories in August. I have ten & have gone over them and removed all such words as 'Squinch,' 'skrunch,' 'scrwnch,' etc."[26]

The worksheets to the story show, among other things, a struggle with beginnings as well as endings. Some of those revisions came, no doubt, in response to Gordon's letter, which begins with the sort of caveat that frequently accompanies a communication between a mentor and a particularly talented mentee: "As usual, I think you have improved your story by revision. (one reason that makes me reluctant to advise you is the danger that in reworking a story you will lose some of the good stuff. People nearly always do. But I don't think you do.)" Gordon proceeds to suggest that the first paragraph be more "elevated," that she should observe what a "high and mighty tone" James Joyce uses in the beginning of "Araby," a story with less important subject matter.[27]

Clearly "The Artificial Nigger," which Ransom also liked, is her most sympathetic and least characteristic story. Robert J. Brinkmeyer finds that "because of the narrator's less severe perspective, 'The Artificial Nigger' is not as searing as much of O'Connor's other work; its characters and situations . . . less extreme and charged."[28] It may well have been Gordon's advice that caused O'Connor to make this story at once more literary and more objective, less marked by her passionate and violent vision, and more organically, "New Critically," unified.

In her revision of "Good Country People," O'Connor was obviously at the apex of her relationship with Caroline Gordon. *A Good Man Is Hard to Find* was near publication when O'Connor wrote to Robert Giroux: "I have just written a story . . . that Allen and Caroline both say is the best thing I have written and should be in this collection." And in a letter dated February 19, 1955, Gordon outlined her reaction to the story in which she reacted to the story:

> GOOD COUNTRY PEOPLE is a master-piece. Allen and I are in complete accord on that . . . what a tone! It's a terrific story—terrific in more than one sense. . . .
>
> I have, of course being me, a few strictures, minor ones to which you may well pay no attention, having got the job done in such a masterly fashion.

26. Ibid., 73; O'Connor to Gordon, October 27, 1954, O'Connor Papers.

27. Gordon to O'Connor, n.d. [1954], ibid.

28. Robert H. Brinkmeyer, Jr., *The Art and Vision of Flannery O'Connor* (Baton Rouge: Louisiana State University Press, 1989), 74.

The child: Allen and I both wonder a little about calling her the child. And that brings up that old debil [*sic*], View-point . . . from whose viewpoint do you call her the child? . . . If it is from her mother's viewpoint, then it might be well to make that fact clear.[29]

Because worksheets to "Good Country People" are not among O'Connor's papers at Georgia College, only the final published version of the story remains to demonstrate how O'Connor responded to Gordon's letter. At some point, O'Connor added the following sentence to page 1: "Mrs. Hopewell thought of her as a child though she was thirty-two years old and highly educated."[30] No doubt she also added the concrete detail that Gordon advised.

With the publication of *A Good Man Is Hard to Find*, Flannery O'Connor had come of age as a writer, and yet she still gave Caroline Gordon credit for the success of her stories and for helping her to perfect her style. O'Connor was by then ready, moreover, to demonstrate peerage with her mentor by becoming her critic. A year earlier, she had published a review of Gordon's *The Malefactors* in the small Catholic journal called *Bulletin* (in which she published all of her criticism). With the mission of the periodical as well as her own priorities in mind, O'Connor emphasized the religiosity of the novel, how the "novel's protagonist, a poet who is not producing," is finally led to "return to his wife, who, in the meantime and after an attempt at suicide, has found her way to the Church." Alluding indirectly to Gordon's obviously biographical subtext, O'Connor praised the "sure knowledge of her craft" that Gordon brings to what most readers, she fears, will "look upon . . . merely as a *roman a clef*." She closed the short review by calling Gordon's novel "undoubtedly the most serious and successful fictional treatment of a conversion by an American writer to date."[31]

In 1957 she also reviewed Gordon's textbook *How to Read a Novel*, recommending it to her Catholic readers with the following wry comment: "By now all are familiar with the famous ad found in a diocesan paper: 'Let a Catholic do your termite work.' In connection with literature, which is almost as dangerous as termites, this fraternal attitude abounds. Miss Gordon's

29. Fitzgerald, ed., *Letters of Flannery O'Connor*, 75; Gordon to O'Connor, February 19, 1955, O'Connor Papers.

30. O'Connor, "Good Country People," in *Three by Flannery O'Connor* (New York: Signet, 1962), 243.

31. Leo J. Zubar, comp., and Carter W. Martin ed., *The Presence of Grace and Other Book Reviews by Flannery O'Connor* (Athens: University of Georgia Press, 1983), 16.

book can therefore be recommended on the grounds that it is a Catholic who is writing." Gordon's book, O'Connor states, should challenge Catholics to "read more slowly" and thereafter to form literary judgments more carefully and on aesthetic criteria, which, she maintains, are related as well to "moral insight."[32] Taken together, these reviews go far to explain the Gordon-O'Connor relationship. Clearly Caroline Gordon, as *Catholic* critic and fiction writer, demonstrated for O'Connor an acceptable and imitable fusion of faith and work. Because Gordon had expounded and practiced a literary aesthetic marked by firm critical principles apart from doctrine, O'Connor felt empowered to work on similar assertions and, moreover, to consider it "moral" to do so.

In 1958, the journal *Critique*, which had already featured Gordon in one of its issues, devoted its fall issue to O'Connor and to J. F. Powers. Gordon contributed a brief but perceptive article, "Flannery O'Connor's *Wise Blood*," to the O'Connor issue. Calling O'Connor "one of the most original among younger American writers," Gordon complained that "her originality has been to some extent obscured by the resemblance of her work to the work of other American writers who belong, roughly, to the same literary generation," especially Truman Capote, Carson McCullers, and Tennessee Williams. Gordon concluded by astutely describing "all of her characters [as] displaced persons . . . [who are] 'off center,' out of place, because they are victims of a rejection of the Scheme of Redemption. They are lost in that abyss which opens for man when he sets up as God."[33] In so condensing O'Connor's overriding theme, Gordon set the tone and direction for O'Connor criticism for a generation to come.

Pleased with the article, O'Connor wrote "A" that "I enclose you Caroline's piece which the more I read the better I like." To Gordon she wrote, in appreciation, "I guess they sent you a copy of *Critique*. It helped to have you say something good about the novel." O'Connor had, however, to correct Gordon on two errors: the way she stated the name of "Haze's church"—Gordon had written "the Church of Christ Without Christ" rather than "The Church Without Christ"—and on a detail concerning where Hazel Motes reads the ad for "Leora Watt's friendly bed."[34]

By 1959, when O'Connor had almost finished *The Violent Bear It Away*, she

32. O'Connor, review of "How to Read a Novel," by Caroline Gordon, in Magee, ed., *Friendship and Sympathy*, 68–69.

33. Fitzgerald, ed., *Letters of Flannery O'Connor*, 287; Caroline Gordon, "Flannery O'Connor's Wise Blood," in Magee, ed., *Friendship and Sympathy*, 70–77.

34. Fitzgerald, ed., *Letters of Flannery O'Connor*, 299, 305.

had begun to feel somewhat less needful of and confident in Gordon's editorial suggestions. In January, according to letters to Dawkins and "A," O'Connor had finished the novel and sent it to Gordon for her "say." The typescript returned to its author with "everything commented upon, doodles, exclamation points, cheers, growls. You can know that she [Gordon] . . . reads every word and reacts to every one she reads." O'Connor added, however, that her novel would not be out for some time because she was "again very dissatisfied with it, in spite of Caroline and her enthusiasm." O'Connor was, moreover, beginning to trust other readers, like the Fitzgeralds and Catherine Carver (her editor at Farrar, Straus and Giroux). To the latter she wrote: "You have done me an immense favor that nobody else could have or would have done. Caroline read it but her strictures always run to matters of style. She swallows a good many camels while she is swatting the flies—though what she has taught me has been invaluable and I can never thank her enough."[35]

After the publication and critical success of her second novel, O'Connor was no longer in need of Gordon's tutelage. She now looked to Caroline Gordon's three novels from the fifties—*Women on the Porch, The Strange Children*, and especially *The Malefactors*—for viable models, both formally and thematically. Like Gordon in these novels, O'Connor had dedicated her writing to the "almost insurmountable problem" of writing convincingly of the action of supernatural grace in a conversion experience. Ironically, these same three novels, which may be attributed in part to Gordon's own anxiety of influence, would a decade later exert similar pressures on some of O'Connor's late stories. These products of O'Connor's creative maturity are not just about epiphanies and conversions, but also, like Gordon's, about conversions of agnostic intellectuals.

As evidence of her own anxiety of influence, O'Connor's correspondence began to express increasing irritation with Gordon's magisterial vetting of the stories. Fatigue, always mixed with gratitude, surfaced in several 1961 letters to various correspondents. In July she wrote to Cecil Dawkins: "We have just had a weekend of Caroline. She read a story that I have been working on and pointed out to me how it was completely undramatic and a million other things that I could have seen myself if I had had the energy." To "A," shortly afterward, she wrote: "Ashley [Brown] and Caroline were strenuous as usual. I had a story that I had written a first draft sort of on and Caroline thought as usual that it wasn't dramatic enough (and she was right) and told me all the things that I tell you when I read one of yours. She did think the structure

35. Ibid., 316, 317, 321, 328.

was good and the situation. All I got to do is write the story. This one is called 'The Lame Shall Enter First.' "[36]

But even while she began to question her mentor, O'Connor was composing stories (all with the exception of "The Partridge Festival" to be collected in *Everything That Rises Must Converge*), which began to resemble Gordon's not only in plot and characterization but in other respects, especially in the simplification of point of view. O'Connor had been impressed initially by the Jamesian use of third limited, center of revelation perspective, which Gordon harped on continually in her teaching and writing. In mid-career, with Gordon as authority, O'Connor had clearly and forcefully explained the method to her own disciple, "A": "She [Gordon] is a disciple of James, and James started this business of telling a story through what he called a central intelligence—like he did with Strether in *The Ambassadors* and like she does with Claiborn [in *Malefactors*]. Start writing a novel and you will soon discover this to be a problem. She follows a kind of modified use of the central intelligence and the omniscient narrator, but she never gets in anybody else's mind but Claiborn's and that's quite something to do." O'Connor's approach to point of view had varied from use of a Jamesian central intelligence in *Wise Blood* to a mixture of old-fashioned authorial omniscience with shifting centers of revelation in her middle stories and in *The Violent Bear It Away*, only to return to Jamesian centers of revelation in the late stories. Robert Brinkmeyer's Baktinian and Ted R. Spivey's deconstructive approaches have proven fruitful in explaining why, in this middle period, the fifties, O'Connor's narrative strategy defies New Critical analysis.[37] In *Everything That Rises Must Converge*, a tightly controlled center of revelation became her normal mode of narration. No longer the dialogic performances characteristic of *A Good Man Is Hard to Find*, these are Jamesian stories in which the reader is mainly limited to the thoughts of the major character, relieved only by the dramatic scenes which Gordon continually urged O'Connor to employ. Notably immune to the pressure of influence were O'Connor's characteristically black humor and devastating apocalyptic irony.

The title story, "Everything That Rises Must Converge," is securely con-

36. Ibid., 444–46.
37. Ibid., 157; Ted R. Spivey, "Flannery O'Connor, the New Criticism and Deconstruction," *Southern Review* n.s., 23 (1987): 271–80. Citing O'Connor's letter to Ben Griffith (Fitzgerald, ed., *Letters of Flannery O'Connor*, 69), in which she passes on Gordon's advice that "the om. nar. never speaks like anyone but Dr. Johnson," Brinkmeyer argues that in Baktinian terms, O'Connor creates two voices, that of the "narrative consciousness" and, "standing apart from it . . . is O'Connor, author and Catholic" (Brinkmeyer, *Art and Vision*, 58).

trolled by the cynical reflections of Julian, the would-be liberal who, until his epiphanic moment at the end of the story, feels so very superior to his childlike mother.[38] The center of revelation in "Greenleaf" is the simpleminded mother, Mrs. May, who parodically reenacts the myth of Europa and the bull (a favorite of Gordon's). "A View of the Woods" allows no corrective except the reader's intelligence for the hubristic thoughts of grandfather Mark Fortune. "The Enduring Chill" and "The Comforts of Home," with their emasculated intellectual narrators in control, strongly resemble "Everything That Rises." In these stories, O'Connor follows the Jamesian-Gordonian demand for objectivity by filtering the narrative through the eyes of protagonists apparently divorced by gender and experience from the author; and yet, just as there is clearly a Henry James prototype in all his stories, O'Connor's male narrators share many traits, and their uncomfortable family situations, with their author.

Gordon continued, however, to have the first word on most of O'Connor's stories, notably "The Partridge Festival" and "The Lame Shall Enter First." In the summer of 1960, she wrote to "A": "I enclose you Caroline's words on the 'Partridge' story. At first reading I thought she was just being technical but on consideration I saw she was right, so I enclose you what I did about it and as you can plainly see it is much better." And when she did finally finish "The Lame Shall Enter First," in November 1961, she wrote Gordon that "I think you would approve of it now, but I am not going to afflict you with it because I know you have a million things to do."[39] This was the new O'Connor story that Lytle published in the *Sewanee Review* commemorative issue.

Lecturing to a session of the 1995 Southern Women Writers' Conference at Berry College in Rome, Georgia, Sally Fitzgerald read and commented on three unpublished letters in which Caroline Gordon responded to "The Enduring Chill." After reading O'Connor's first draft of the story, Gordon attacked the problem of point of view. She advised O'Connor to move slowly from the narrative observer's stance into Asbury's thoughts, where the perspective would remain except for sections of dialogue. Despite her usual preference for the Jamesian central intelligence, Gordon advised O'Connor not to relinquish authorial control entirely but to remain the superior intellect guiding the central intelligence.[40]

38. Sarah Gordon has discovered in O'Connor's letters to Maryat Lee that O'Connor's characterization of Julian owes much to Lee's account of similar experience she had on a train (lecture, January 25, 1995, Georgia College, Milledgeville). As in "Good Country People" and "Revelation," O'Connor also reflects on her own intellectual mismatch with her mother.

39. Fitzgerald, ed., *Letters of Flannery O'Connor*, 401, 454.

40. Sally Fitzgerald, "Roman Arches and Pillars of Wisdom," lecture to the Southern Women Writer's Conference, April 12, 1996, Berry College, Rome, Ga.

Gordon's primary focus, however, was on structure. Believing that every story ought to be constructed like a Roman arch, Gordon advised that key supporting images (i.e., columns) be embedded in the story in the beginning, middle, and end. These images would surreptitiously suggest the hovering presence of the "HG" (Holy Ghost) lying in wait for the unsuspecting Asbury. The first of these "columns" would be the "red sun," which Gordon believed should be prepared for by a progression from the physical to the spiritual—not thrust in "flat footed" in a single sentence. O'Connor accordingly revised the sentence to read "a startling white-gold sun, like some strange potentate from the east, was rising beyond the black woods that surrounded Timberboro."[41] On Gordon's advice, O'Connor had positioned her all-important first "pillar of wisdom."

After perusing O'Connor's second draft, Gordon went to work on the middle of the story, which, she advised, should contain a "peripity," perhaps some remembered event that had occurred in New York involving "fooling around on the edge of religion." Accordingly, O'Connor has Asbury remember attending a lecture on the Vedanta, where he has a brief encounter with Ignatius Vogle, S.J. Thinking this black-clad priest a "man of the world, someone who would have understood the unique tragedy of his death" prepares for Asbury's disappointing dialogue with Father Finn, from Purgatory, Vogle's grotesque opposite number. The placement of this medial "pillar" apparently satisfied Gordon.[42]

After reading O'Connor's third revision, Gordon again attacked the opening of the story, recommending more preparation for Asbury's transition to his new environment. O'Connor added the image of the "exotic temple for a god he didn't know" and changed the word "peak" to "turret"—again so as not to be "flat-footed." When O'Connor also improved the ending, in which Asbury finally submits to his disappointing illness and to the HG's icy presence, the all-important final column was in place, and Gordon was pleased. The third letter did not close, however, without a sermon on O'Connor's "grammar" and prose style, extolling the superiority of periodic over loose sentences. Gordon's unrelenting attention to form and syntax, even late in O'Connor's career, was still filing away the rough edges of O'Connor's prose.[43]

Though O'Connor finally felt strong enough in her own talent to "ignore"

41. O'Connor, "The Enduring Chill," *Complete Stories*, 357; S. Fitzgerald, "Roman Arches."
42. Fitzgerald, "Roman Arches."
43. Ibid.

Gordon's advice, she nonetheless submitted to her judgment until the last. After O'Connor's death, Gordon wrote to Katherine Anne Porter: "Flannery sent me all of the stories she wrote until a few years ago when, as she put it, she 'let me off the hook.' It's no light chore reading and commenting on the work of a genius, and I was thankful when she did let me off that hook. But last year she sent me two stories and I knew then that she thought her days were numbered." The years 1962 and 1963, during which Gordon was, apparently, "off the hook," O'Connor kept up with Gordon's activities second hand.[44] O'Connor's last two stories, "The Lame Shall Enter First" and "Parker's Back," were, however, once again subjected to Gordon's critical eye.

During her terminal period of illness, O'Connor saw and heard from Gordon less often. In June 1964, she wrote to Ashley Brown that Caroline had "breezed in one weekend. She visited Fr. Charles at the monastery and they came out to see me. She has dyed her hair the color of funnytoor polish. Startling effect." At about the same time, she was in the throes of composing her last story, "Parker's Back," about which she wrote, revealingly, to "A": "You sound like Caroline to the teeth. I sent it to her same time as I sent it to you and got a telegram back saying some mechanical details would follow but she thought it unique, that I had succeeded in dramatizing a heresy. Well not in those terms did I set out but only thinking that the spirit moveth where it listeth." To "A" 's reply, O'Connor continued: "No Caroline didn't mean the tattoos were the heresy. Sarah Ruth was the heretic—the notion that you can worship in pure spirit. Caroline gave me a lot of advice about the story but most of it I'm ignoring. She thinks every story must be built according to the pattern of the Roman arch and she would enlarge the beginning and the end, but I'm letting it lay. I did well to write it at all."[45]

The worksheets for "Parker's Back" reveal that O'Connor did not let it lay; in fact, she wrote and revised several versions, especially of the story's beginning. Her initial inclination was to start with a prosaic, third person omniscient commentary, replete with the homely similes that characterize such early stories as "The Artificial Nigger."[46] In final form, the entire story, with the exception of several dramatic scenes in dialogue, is filtered through a central narrative consciousness, Parker's, exactly as Gordon might have directed.

Besides Gordon, other female members of the post-Fugitive group joined

44. Gordon to Porter, November 10, 1965, Porter Papers; Fitzgerald, ed., *Letters of Flannery O'Connor*, 486.
45. Fitzgerald, ed., *Letters of Flannery O'Connor*, 584, 593–94.
46. O'Connor, worksheets for "Parker's Back," O'Connor Papers.

O'Connor's outer circle of friends and supporters. Long before O'Connor had been introduced to Katherine Anne Porter in person, she had gotten to know Porter through her writing; and near the end of her career, O'Connor regarded Porter as one of the few southern writers who was "successfully cosmopolitan in fiction," a quality she herself envied.[47]

Porter and O'Connor first met in April 1958, when, as she reported to Ashley Brown, "Miss Katherine Anne read in Macon a few weeks ago and had lunch with us the next day. . . . She told somebody in Macon that my stories reminded her of Scheverell Sitwell and George Garrett. Who please tell me is George Garrett? I hope nobody awful." That their meeting had more than casual significance is apparent from a letter to "A," only a few days later, in which the subject of the protracted and tenuous task of novel-writing came up for discussion: "I'm glad you are on the short novel. Let it be what it will. Miss Katherine Anne and her 27 years [writing *Ship of Fools*] is giving me nightmares. It's not so much perfectionism—it's that a novel is like a machine, it either runs or it don't. If it don't run, she's right to keep it with her until it does. If it never runs, she's right not to inflict it on the public; but how awful to spend 27 years on what won't run. This is what I hope I will be spared."[48]

O'Connor met Porter a second time on October 28, 1960, when she joined O'Connor, Caroline Cordon, and Madison Jones at Wesleyan College in Macon, Georgia, at a panel discussion entitled "Recent Southern Fiction."

Although Porter and O'Connor were not to see each other again after the Wesleyan conference, Porter continued to feel a certain bond with her fellow southern writer. After O'Connor's death, Porter wrote a short, sentimental eulogy entitled "Gracious Greatness," which recaptures the impression that Flannery made on her during and after their two—or was it three?—meetings. Declining to "speak of her work because we all know what it was," Porter focused on how O'Connor appeared to her on the three occasions when they were together. To see O'Connor in her "old-fashioned southern village very celebrated in southern history," among her peacocks and nonliterary neighbors, verified Porter's belief that "the atmosphere in which her genius developed and her life was lived and her work was done" was in fact "the best possible way for a genius to live."[49]

Because O'Connor superficially resembled Eudora Welty in remaining

47. Flannery O'Connor, *Mystery and Manners*, ed. Robert Fitzgerald and Sally Fitzgerald (New York: Farrar, Straus & Giroux, 1969), 199.

48. Fitzgerald, ed., *Letters of Flannery O'Connor*, 277, 279–80.

49. Katherine Anne Porter, "Gracious Greatness," in Magee, ed., *Friendship and Sympathy*, 78.

closely associated with a single southern community, it was inevitable that critics and reviewers would compare the two writers again and again—although neither would support their contentions. When asked if her view of and relationship to what is generally called "the southern community" were like that of Welty or Faulkner, O'Connor replied, "I don't know how Eudora Welty or Faulkner looks at it. I only know how I look at it and I don't feel that I am writing about the community at all." In fact, O'Connor's literary community did *not* include Welty, whose acquaintance she made when both attended a literary conference in the spring of 1962 at Converse College in South Carolina. Just afterward O'Connor wrote to Cecil Dawkins that she "really liked Eudora Welty—no presence whatsoever, just a real nice woman. She read a paper on 'Place in Fiction.' It was very beautifully written but a little hard to listen to as anything like that . . . is written to be read." When in 1972 Linda Kuehl asked Welty if she did "ever feel part of a literary community, along with people like Flannery O'Connor, Carson McCullers, Katherine Anne Porter or Caroline Gordon," Welty replied, "I'm not sure there's any dotted line connecting us up, though all of us knew about each other and all of us, I think, respected and read each other's work and understood it. And some of us are friends of long standing." To Jan Nordby Gretlund, in 1978, Welty commented pointedly that she could not "imagine . . . three more different writers than Katherine Anne Porter, Flannery O'Connor and myself."[50]

What relationship there was between Welty and O'Connor seemed to be marked, therefore, by personal admiration and professional rivalry. That O'Connor did not always approve of Welty's writing is made clear in her September 1963 letter to "A," in which she calls a Welty story just published in the *New Yorker* (no doubt "Where Is the Voice Coming From?" in the July 6 issue) "the kind of story that the more you think about it the less satisfactory it gets. What I hate most is its being in the *New Yorker* and all the stupid Yankee liberals smacking their lips over typical life in the dear old dirty Southland." For her part, Welty was once reported to have asked in a response to an O'Connor passage that seemed overloaded with obscure theological significance, "Is there a Catholic in the class?"[51] The central obstacle to a close

50. "Recent Southern Fiction: A Panel Discussion," in Magee, ed., *Conversations with Flannery O'Connor*, 70; Fitzgerald, ed., *Letters of Flannery O'Connor*, 471; Linda Kuehl, "Interview with Eudora Welty," in *Conversations with Eudora Welty*, ed. Peggy Whitman Prenshaw (Jackson: University Press of Mississippi, 1984), 80; Jan Nordby Gretlund, "An Interview with Eudora Welty," ibid., 218.

51. Fitzgerald, ed., *Letters of Flannery O'Connor*, 537; Alice Walker, "Beyond the Peacock: The Reconstruction of Flannery O'Connor," in Friedman and Clark, eds., *Critical Essays on Flannery O'Connor*, 79.

relationship between the two writers was, probably, their very different religious convictions. Welty could not join O'Connor, Gordon, and Porter within the Roman Catholic segment of the post-Fugitive circle.

In the beginning of Flannery O'Connor's literary life, allegiance with the Fugitive legacy was clearly a matter of associating with writers with whom she could identify and whom she could respect in a time when to be called a "southern writer" was by no means always a compliment. In "The Fiction Writer and His Country," O'Connor made it very clear where her admiration lay: "Most readers these days must be sufficiently sick of hearing about Southern writers and Southern writing and what so many reviewers insist upon calling the 'Southern school.' No one has ever made plain just what the Southern school is or which writers belong to it. Sometimes, when it is most respectable, it seems to mean the little group of Agrarians that flourished at Vanderbilt in the twenties." In one of her last letters to "A," O'Connor reported that "I am reading for the first time *I'll Take My Stand* which is out in a paperback. It's a very interesting document. It's futile of course like 'woodman, spare that tree,' but still, the only time real minds have got together to talk about the South."[52]

Although O'Connor both approved of and codified the political philosophies of the Agrarians in her fiction, it was to the Nashville group as writers that she consistently proclaimed her allegiance. In one of her last interviews, for *Atlanta Magazine*, O'Connor put it all into words: "The best American writing has always been regional. . . . But to be regional in the best sense you have to see beyond the region. For example, the Fugitives at Vanderbilt in the '20s felt that the South they knew was passing away and they wanted to get it down before it went, but they had a larger vision than just the South. They were against what they saw coming, against the social planner, fellow traveller spirit that came along in the next ten years. They looked to past and future to make a judgement in their own times."[53] Flannery O'Connor's stories and novels augmented the former Fugitives' efforts to "get it down before it went." As the last important figure in the Fugitive legacy, O'Connor and her fiction stand both as judgment and prophecy.

52. O'Connor, *Mystery and Manners*, 28; Fitzgerald, ed., *Letters of Flannery O'Connor*, 566.
53. "Southern Writers Are Stuck with the South," in Magee, ed., *Conversations with O'Connor*, 109.

Afterword

By the 1960s, both the Fugitives (by then generally referred to as Fugitive-Agrarians) and their heirs had moved into the autumns and summers, respectively, of their creative lives. By then, the notion of literary movements and networking had become irrelevant to many emerging writers. The literary arena had opened up considerably, and scores of magazines were available to publish their writing. Frederick J. Hoffman, Charles Allen, and Carolyn F. Ulrich's *Little Magazine* estimated that six hundred little magazines were published in English between 1912 and 1946, most of which lasted for only a few issues.[1] In contrast, the most recent issue of *Poet's Market* (1994) lists seventeen hundred magazines that publish poetry, while the 1989 edition of *Novel and Short Story Writer's Market* names nineteen hundred periodical publishers of fiction. Such proliferation of places to publish does indeed provide more opportunities, but it also spreads the cohort of readers very thinly and tends to isolate individual writers from one another and into ever smaller, more specialized

1. Frederick J. Hoffman, Charles Allen, and Carolyn F. Ulrich, *The Little Magazine in America: A History and a Bibliography* (Princeton: Princeton University Press, 1946); Elliott Anderson and Mary Kinzie, eds., *The Little Magazine in America: A Modern Documentary History* (Yonkers, N.Y.: Pushcart Press, 1978), 8–9.

literary communities. The writers of the Fugitive and Agrarian legacy and those whom they in turn befriended perhaps found it easier to claim prominence in a less crowded arena.

Moreover, an increasing number of colleges and universities now have departments of creative writing and writers in residence. Like the former Fugitives and their heirs, many new writers are finding it possible to make a living in academia. From among their legions of students, some excellent writers have no doubt emerged, but surely their teachers are less and less likely to play a role in the development of their careers.

As an offshoot of the counterculture movements of the late sixties and seventies, moreover, ethnic minorities, feminists, gay rights groups, and other enclaves are beginning to demand recognition. These initiatives have resulted in affirmative action in regard to hiring of college teachers and in movements to dismantle the official canon of literary texts to be offered to college and university students. All of these alterations have helped to weaken networks like the Fugitive legacy, which held shared notions of literary excellence and in which personal relationships undergirded professional activities. Coincidentally, the aesthetic and interpretive paradigms the New Criticism helped to canonize have come under attack from the European-based advocates of newer critical theories, from structuralists to poststructuralists to deconstructionists. To a surprising degree, all that the Fugitive legacy has come to represent has been opposed by these new forces, who have proved by their open opposition just how influential that legacy has become. And yet, though attenuated, the Fugitive legacy is still very much with us, not only through its attackers but also by virtue of those writers who in large and small ways were and still are literary descendants of the Fugitives' legatees.

Among the most successful of those poets of the middle and late twentieth century who were indebted to the former Fugitives was James Dickey. After beginning his college education at Clemson and serving in the U.S. Air Force in World War II, Dickey transferred to Vanderbilt, where, in the words of Richard J. Calhoun, "his interest in literature grew" because of Fugitives' "strong literary reputation." After obtaining his baccalaureate degree, Dickey remained at Vanderbilt as a graduate fellow in creative writing and began to publish his poetry, first in student magazines and then in the *Sewanee Review*. With Allen Tate and Andrew Lytle as judges, Dickey won a *Sewanee Review* fellowship in creative writing. Lytle then hired Dickey to teach creative writing at the University of Florida, but the sensational content of his poetry caused so much controversy that he was forced to resign. After publishing two collections of poetry, *Into the Stone* (1960) and *Drowning with Others* (1962), however, Dickey's status as a major poet was assured.[2]

In the violent naturalism that often surfaces both in his poetry and fiction, Dickey demonstrates his kinship to Robert Penn Warren, the former Fugitive whom he most admired. Warren and Dickey wrote perceptive reviews of each other's poetry that underscored their similarities. Reviewing Warren's *Promises: Poems, 1954–56* for the *Sewanee Review*, Dickey recognized Warren's ability to "give you the sense of poetry as a thing of final importance to life" but criticized Warren's "over-inflated" language and "outrageous" uses of the pathetic fallacy, charges that could surely be leveled against Dickey himself. He ultimately justified all such excesses in the service of Warren's (and his own) ultimate theme: "man's ageless, age-old drive toward self-discovery." In 1976, Warren reviewed Dickey's "The Zodiac," a sequential poem that, in its fusing of violence and lyrical beauty, might have been written by Warren himself. Though he faults the poem for its structural shortcomings, Warren finally praises its "audacity of imagery, assemblage of rhythms, [and] power of language."[3] In 1983, Warren dedicated his last sequential poem, "Chief Joseph of the Nez Perce," to James Dickey.

Other well-known poets with Fugitive-Agrarian connections are Edwin Godsey, a student of Davidson's at Vanderbilt; Anthony Hecht and James Wright, World War II veterans who studied with Ransom at Kenyon; Mona Van Duyns and Josephine Miles, whom Ransom sponsored and published through the *Kenyon Review*; W. D. Snodgrass, who studied with Robert Lowell at Iowa and was a protégé of Randall Jarrell; and Philip Levine, who studied with Lowell and John Berryman at Iowa. They are joined by a host of southern poets such as Donald Justice, Jonathan Williams, Miller Williams, Dabney Stuart, James Applewhite, Betty Adcock, and Fred Chappell, who have inherited the sensibilities and communal spirit that characterized the Southern Renaissance in general and the Fugitive legacy in particular.

The post-Fugitive influence on fiction writers has been surprisingly strong given the movement's genesis in poetry and criticism. Jesse Hill Ford, Elizabeth Spencer, Madison Jones, and Robert Drake are among the former Vanderbilt students who benefited from contact with the former Fugitives

2. Richard Calhoun, "James Dickey," in *Fifty Southern Writers After 1900: A Bibliographical Sourcebook*, ed. Joseph M. Flora and Robert Bain (New York: Greenwood Press, 1987), 137.

3. James Dickey, "In the Presence of Anthologies," *Sewanee Review* 66 (1958): 307, 309; Robert Penn Warren, "*The Zodiac*: A Poem About the Ambitions of Poetry," *New York Times Book Review*, November 14, 1976, 8.

and their heirs and have gone on to distinguish themselves in the writing of novels and stories.[4] Madison Jones (1925–) was born in Nashville and received his baccalaureate degree from Vanderbilt in 1949, where he studied literature and writing with Donald Davidson. Jones's relationship with the post-Fugitive group continued at the University of Florida, where he received his M.A. under Andrew Lytle in 1951. In 1955–56, when Jones was recipient of a *Sewanee Review* fellowship, he also taught freshman composition at the University of Tennessee in Knoxville.[5] Though Jones's fiction has received high praise from Allen Tate, Flannery O'Connor, and James Dickey, it has sometimes put off critics and common readers because, in the words of David K. Jeffrey, it "reflect[s] its author's traditional social values and stern Puritanism." The moral landscape of Madison Jones's novels is darkened by conflicts, often ending tragically, involving morally bankrupt, alienated individuals. Not surprisingly, Allen Tate once called him a "southern Thomas Hardy." Robert Penn Warren reviewed Jones's first novel, *The Innocent*, in the spring 1957 issue of the *Sewanee Review*, praising its author for his "basic seriousness of intention, and on his deep, natural sense of fiction." At this writing, Jones has published eight novels, as well as short stories and literary criticism. Since 1956 he has taught at Auburn University in Auburn, Alabama, where he is writer-in-residence.[6]

Robert Drake (1930–) received a B.A. from Vanderbilt University, where he was a student of Donald Davidson, and a Ph.D. from Yale University, where he was a friend, if never a student, of Cleanth Brooks. Drake has pub-

4. Jesse Hill Ford (1928–), a product of Vanderbilt, later studied fiction writing with Andrew Lytle at the University of Florida. Donald Davidson wrote the foreword to Ford's third novel, *The Conversion of Buster Drumwright*, published in 1964 by Vanderbilt University Press (Martha E. Cook, "Old Ways and New," in *The History of Southern Literature*, ed. Louis D. Rubin, Jr., et al. [Baton Rouge: Louisiana State University Press, 1985], 531).

Elizabeth Spencer (1921–), a distant relative of the Agrarian Stark Young, came to Vanderbilt on an M.A. fellowship in creative writing. Though she never studied with Donald Davidson, she has credited him with introducing her and her novel *Fire in the Morning* to David Clay of the New York publishing firm of Dodd, Mead, who published it in 1984. Spencer's Fugitive-Agrarian connections may have helped her to receive a Kenyon Review fellowship in 1957, as well as the post of associate editor of the *Sewanee Review* under Andrew Lytle in 1961. She never identified with the Fugitive-Agrarians, however, because she strongly disagreed with their politics.

5. M. E. Bradford, "Madison Jones," in Rubin et al., eds., *History of Southern Literature*, 523.

6. David K. Jeffrey, "Madison Jones," in *Contemporary Fiction Writers of the South: A Bio-Bibliographical Sourcebook*, ed. Joseph M. Flora and Robert Bain (Westport, Conn.: Greenwood Press, 1993), 261; Bradford, "Madison Jones," 526, 523; Warren, "A First Novel," review *The Innocent* by Madison Jones, *Sewanee Review* 65 (1957): 352.

lished six collections of short stories, or tales, which he has described as "short, succinct, and usually narrated in the first person," in which "the theme and form are one." Jeffrey Folks has called Drake's fiction "a significant historical record of a time and place"—the west Tennessee town of Ripley, which is thinly disguised in his fiction as Woodville. Cleanth Brooks, in his review of *The Burning Bush*, Drake's second collection of stories, found in them an expression of "a pattern of values, and an attitude toward reality that derive from a living community."[7]

Other fiction writers in the Fugitive-Agrarian community had their own literary progeny. Katherine Anne Porter's students and protégés included William Humphrey, George Garrett, and Walter Clemons. Caroline Gordon not only advised Flannery O'Connor but also Walker Percy, who sent his first novel to Gordon for her comments and received a "thirty-page single-spaced letter" in reply.[8] A host of others, including William Styron (a close friend of Robert Penn Warren), Reynolds Price, and Madison Smartt Bell, are products of universities other than Vanderbilt, LSU, or Kenyon but have read Warren, Tate, Gordon, Lytle, Welty, Peter Taylor, and O'Connor closely enough to imbibe their style and ethos along with the formidable influence of William Faulkner.[9]

So large is the Fugitive-Agrarian legacy's continuing impact on criticism and critical theory that it is nearly impossible to select the most prominent of the Fugitives' and Agrarians' heirs among contemporary critics. Surely deserving of mention, however, are Walter Sullivan and Thomas Daniel Young.

Sullivan was introduced to the former Fugitives in 1943, when, at the age of nineteen, he took Donald Davidson's advanced writing course at Vanderbilt. "Davidson was the first writer I ever encountered," Sullivan later wrote, "and I was impressed with him not only because of the poems and books he had published, but because of the other writers he knew and spoke of in class with intimate affection." Sullivan's thirty-five-year friendship with Allen Tate

7. Robert Drake, "My Own House of Fiction," *Mississippi Quarterly* 45 (1992): 127–31; Jeffrey J. Folks, "A Southern Realist: The Short Stories of Robert Drake," *Mississippi Quarterly* 45 (1992): 159–65.

8. Waldron, *Close Connections*, 284.

9. Bell, educated at Princeton, formed connections with Allen Tate and Andrew Lytle through his parents, who were Vanderbilt students, and by seeing Tate and Lytle during summer vacations when he was a small child. Attracted to the Agrarian "ideology," Bell turned to their writings—and those of Robert Penn Warren and Flannery O'Connor—as models for his own (Mary Louise Weaks, "An Interview with Madison Smartt Bell," *Southern Review* n.s., 30 [January 1994]: 1–12).

began in April of the same year, when he was invited to spend a weekend at the home of Tate and Caroline Gordon at Monteagle, Tennessee. Robert Lowell, Jean Stafford, Peter Taylor, and Eleanor Ross, Taylor's future wife, were also there—providing young Sullivan an immediate introduction to the post-Fugitive circle. *Allen Tate: A Recollection* (1988) is an intimate and revealing account of that friendship and of Sullivan's subsequent dealings with the group.[10]

During the 1950s, after graduate studies, Sullivan joined the faculty of Vanderbilt University, where he helped to keep the Fugitives' name alive. As a literary critic, Sullivan has specialized in contemporary southern fiction. His first collection of essays, *Death by Melancholy* (1972), makes mostly unflattering comparisons between contemporary southern fiction writers and the giants that immediately preceded them. In *A Requiem for the Renaissance: The State of Fiction in the Modern South* (1976), Sullivan sounded a warning against forces that threaten to negate the accomplishments of the Fugitives and their generation. A third collection of essays, *In Praise of Blood Sports*, was published in 1990. Sullivan has also emerged as a writer of fiction with three novels to his credit, *Sojourn of a Stranger* (1957), *The Long, Long Love* (1959), and *A Time to Dance* (1995), along with several short stories.

In "From Pachuta to the World: The Lowdown on Thomas Daniel Young," foreword to *The Vanderbilt Tradition: Essays in Honor of Thomas Daniel Young*, Louis D. Rubin, Jr., has vividly, though facetiously, summarized Young's journey from a small town in southern Mississippi to Vanderbilt and a lifelong immersion in the study of the Fugitives and Agrarians.[11] As a Vanderbilt graduate student, Young made the Fugitives his major interest. Thereafter, beginning with a study of Donald Davidson, which he coauthored with M. Thomas Inge, Young produced an impressive catalog of scholarly books on the Fugitives, most notably Ransom, including *John Crowe Ransom: Critical Essays and a Bibliography* (1968) and the definitive biography of Ransom, *Gentleman in a Dustcoat*, in 1975. Young's editions of the Fugitives' and Agrarians' letters include *The Literary Correspondence of Donald Davidson and Allen Tate*, with John T. Fain (1974); *The Republic of Letters in America: The Correspondence of John Peale Bishop and Allen Tate* (1981); *Selected Letters of John Crowe Ransom*, with George Core (1985); and *The Tate-Lytle Letters*, with Elizabeth Sarcone (1987). Along with his many critical books

10. Sullivan, *Allen Tate*, 2–3.
11. Louis D. Rubin, Jr., "From Pachuta to the World: The Lowdown on Thomas Daniel Young," in Winchell, ed., *Vanderbilt Tradition*, xiii–xx.

and articles, these texts have become essential to any study of southern literature, especially of the Fugitives and Agrarians.

To these must be added the names of Louise Cowan, a student of Davidson, who wrote the first history of the Fugitive movement and sponsored
Caroline Gordon during her teaching stint at the University of Dallas in
1972; Ashley Brown, loyal friend and able critic of Caroline Gordon and
Flannery O'Connor; and George Core, close friend of Andrew Lytle, who
has edited the *Sewanee Review* since 1973. Like Randall Jarrell, after Brooks
the best-known critic of the Fugitive legacy, these scholar-critics have employed more than one critical method and philosophy in their explorations of
literary texts.

It was Cleanth Brooks, in person and in print, who nonetheless became
the stalking-horse for contemporary literary theorists. Until his death in the
spring of 1994, Brooks was ever prepared to correct, amend, or, if need be,
boldly attack his younger adversaries in print and in public. Brooks's final
statements may now be read in the posthumous collection, *Community, Religion, and Literature*, a diverse group of essays, three of which—"The Primacy
of the Linguistic Medium," "The Primacy of the Author," and "The Primacy of the Reader"—respond to deconstruction, new historicism, and
reader response, respectively. Jewel Spears Brooker, who characterizes the
collection as "quintessential Brooks," that is, "civilized, courteous, and generous," finds it remarkable that Brooks remained to the last "a critic under
attack who finds something to praise, some genuinely fine point to remark,
in almost every opponent."[12] But perhaps Brooks always mediated between
apparently disparate critical approaches, for he began as a synthesizer of Eliot
with Richards and Tate with Ransom.

If the New Criticism came into disrepute after 1970, it has remained very
much alive as a point of departure for all its detractors. Typical is Frank Lentricchia's remark in *After the New Criticism*: "If my title suggests that the New
Criticism is dead . . . I must stipulate that in my view it is dead in the way that
an imposing and repressive father-figure is dead. I find many traces (perhaps
'scars' is the word) of the New Criticism and of nineteenth-century thought
in the fixed and identifiable positions we have come to know as contemporary
theory." The essays published in *The New Criticism and Contemporary Literary
Theory*, edited by William J. Spurlin and Michael Fischer, serve to verify and
augment Lentricchia's statement by locating continuities and similarities be-

12. Jewell Spears Brooker, "In Conclusion: Literature and Culture in the Last Essays of
Cleanth Brooks," *South Atlantic Review* 60 (November 1995): 130.

tween the New Criticism and such varied approaches as reader-response theory, new black aesthetic criticism, deconstruction, new historicism, and lesbian criticism.[13]

The Fugitives' continuing legacy to criticism nonetheless lies not only in critics friendly to and influenced by the former Fugitives and their heirs but in the New Criticism as a method still taught and practiced by readers from high school students to college professors. One needs only to attend regional sessions of the Modern Language Association and the numerous conferences held each year on individual writers to realize that among the presentations by feminists, queer theorists, historicists, and deconstructionists, a surprising number of New Critical explications and close readings are still in evidence. These presentations are still popular and well received because they allow the listeners to delve again into individual stories, poems, and essays and to retain criticism's focus on imaginative rather than merely theoretical writing.

It seems to be the practicality of the New Criticism that so energizes opponents. As contemporary literary theories move into the classroom, they too begin to lose some of their arcane mystery and become more directly related to the literature they profess to discuss. Such simplification and domestication may prove, as for the New Criticism, the real test of their viability. Untold numbers of teachers of literature and their students still benefit from the Brooks and Warren way of reading because it opens up to them—along with the important historical, sociological, and philosophical baggage of the story, poem, or play—the elements of the text itself. As Robert Heilman has put it, southern critics gave "impetus" to the creation of "a new order of teacher critics . . . [as well as] a more competent general reader.[14]

By the mid-eighties, the former members of the post-Fugitive and post-Agrarian communities were among those who wanted to enlarge their circle to include the best members of a new and growing generation of southern writers. To "recognize and promote the considerable amount of good writing being done in the post-Renascence South," in Mark Winchell's words, Cleanth Brooks and twenty-five like-minded literary colleagues met in 1987 to organize the Fellowship of Southern Writers. Although critics Brooks, Louis Rubin, and George Core—with novelist George Garrett—played the major roles in founding the organization, its primary function was to honor

13. Frank Lentricchia, *After the New Criticism* (Chicago: University of Chicago Press, 1980), xiii; "Contents," in Spurlin and Fischer, eds., *New Criticism and Contemporary Literary Theory*, vii–ix.

14. Heilman, *Southern Connection*, 256.

poets, fiction writers, and playwrights. To that purpose, the fellowship obtained corporate funding for six yearly awards: the Hanes Prize for Poetry, the Hillsdale Prize for Fiction, the Bryan Family Foundation Award for Playwriting, the Chubb Life American Award honoring Robert Penn Warren, the Cleanth Brooks Medal for Distinguished Achievement in Southern Letters, and the fellowship's own award for nonfiction.[15]

The post-Fugitive circle was represented in the newly formed association by Brooks, Robert Penn Warren, Eudora Welty, Peter Taylor, and Andrew Lytle, who was elected its first chancellor. By 1993, the membership consisted of twenty-seven living members, Warren and Walker Percy having died in the interim: A. R. Ammons, Wendell Berry, Fred Chappell, James Dickey, Ellen Douglas, Ralph Ellison, Horton Foote, Shelby Foote, John Hope Franklin, Ernest Gaines, Blyden Jackson, Madison Jones, C. Eric Lincoln, Romulus Linney, Andrew Lytle, Reynolds Price, Mary Lee Settle, Lewis P. Simpson, Lee Smith, Monroe K. Spears, Elizabeth Spencer, William Styron, Walter Sullivan, Peter Taylor, Eudora Welty, C. Vann Woodward, and Charles Wright.[16] Although some worthy writers were no doubt excluded, this group seems sufficiently varied to prove that the fellowship was not founded merely to be an extension of the founders' circle of personal friends.

From time to time, the post-Fugitive circle has nonetheless been accused, with some justice, of having excluded certain southern writers who functioned outside of its conservative definition of the function and content of good literature. Reasons for such apparent snobbery were many, but for the most part they were aesthetic or personal rather than political. As formalists and conservatives, the former Fugitives tended to ally themselves with the genteel, or traditional, direction in literature and thus to distance themselves from free-form advocates like the Imagists, from various brands of regionalists, and from such political persuasions as Marxism. Writers like Thomas Wolfe confounded the New Critics by producing novels too prolix and (apparently) formless to conform to the rigors of close reading and to be manageable under the umbrella of a single governing theme. Other talented writers like James Agee were too radically polemic for the members of the Fugitive circle, to whom literature and literary criticism were matters beyond the realms of economic and political struggle. In "What Does Poetry Communicate?" from *The Well Wrought Urn*, Cleanth Brooks expressed what be-

15. Winchell, *Cleanth Brooks and the Rise of Modern Criticism*, 436.
16. Ibid., 437.

came the Fugitives' basic attitude, that "the poet [and hence all imaginative writers] is most truthfully described as a *poietes*, or maker, not as an expositor or communicator."[17] Writers of other persuasions might pursue their objectives at their pleasure, but the former Fugitives and their heirs have remained adamant in believing that literature was primarily a fine art, secondarily a means of communication.

When charged with creating a narrowly defined literary canon, Brooks and his fellow New Critics consistently expressed surprise that a small contingency of hardworking writers and editors were perceived as having so much power. Apparently the Fugitive legacy has remained unaware of its own strength, perhaps because it has always functioned informally, through personal and professional association. As the circle widened, the Fugitives' heirs in turn formed supportive alliances with younger writers with similar backgrounds and objectives. Many and fruitful were their associations with literary folk from other regions and modes of thought, but their first obligations clearly were to members of the network. Young writers who became associated with members of that charmed circle—as teachers, mentors, or editors—may well have tailored their attitudes and subsequent writing to what they perceived to be the post-Fugitive mind-set. Surely, when the New Criticism and its tenets held sway (roughly between 1940 and 1960), many writers must have thought it desirable to cultivate such qualities as imagistic density, authorial objectivity, and thematic unity in their compositions. That other priorities existed and eventually had to be acknowledged led quite naturally to the reactions against the New Critics and their proponents that now prevail. But if writers were good enough, they found their own alliances—in New York and elsewhere—and did not blame their lack of success on exclusion from the post-Fugitive circle.

It was not so much a certain style or content that these very different writers inherited from the Fugitive-Agrarian legacy as it was a concatenation of shared attitudes toward life and literature and, more important, a need to join forces with writers of like minds. In *The Southern Writer in the Postmodern World*, Fred Hobson identified as southern attitudes—also shared by other people in traditional societies—"a religious sense, a closeness to nature, a great attention to and affection for place, a close attention to family, a preference for the concrete and a rage against abstraction." These qualities attracted and still attract writers outside the South, but most of these, like John Berryman and Robert Lowell before them, continue to have allegiances with

17. Cleanth Brooks, "What Does Poetry Communicate?," in *Well Wrought Urn*, 75.

southern writers and an attraction to their attitudes and beliefs. In a 1985 interview, David Madden insisted that the writers of the post-Fugitive circle did not consciously boost one another, but because their "paths crossed," they were able to "push one another ahead." Peter Taylor once called it "the way things used to be done," and Walker Percy said of his contact with Caroline Gordon that "the valuable thing was the relationship with her."[18]

In a letter to the author, the noted critic Ashley Brown remarked that "the Fugitives did have the legacy that you are discussing, and it has gone outside the South long before now."[19] No longer a southern phenomenon, not limited to the writers of the Southern Renaissance, the Fugitive legacy has left its mark on contemporary American literature in myriad ways. As new networks form and new legacies are passed down, they will no doubt continue to extend the valuable asset of friendship and mentoring to new generations just as the Fugitives did. The influence will still be accompanied by anxiety, and much of what occurs will be the result of reaction more than action; but there will remain the impact of those writers with the talent, energy, and generosity to make of their lives and work a generative and nurturing force.

18. Fred Hobson, *The Southern Writer in the Postmodern World* (Athens: University of Georgia Press, 1991), 3; Madden interview; Waldron, *Close Connections*, 159, 284.
19. Ashley Brown, letter to author, March 11, 1995.

Appendix / Dates and Places of Publication of Selected Works of Fugitive Legatees

EARLY POEMS OF RANDALL JARRELL, JOHN BERRYMAN, AND
ROBERT LOWELL

Date	First Publisher	Title

RANDALL JARRELL (POEMS PUBLISHED 1933–1940)

1933	*American Review*	"Fear"
1933	*American Review*	"O Weary Mariners"
1933	*American Review*	"The Man with the ax . . ."
1933	*American Review*	"Above the waters . . . "
1933	*American Review*	"The cow wandering . . . "
1934	*New Republic*	"Zeno"
1935	*Westminster*	"Poem" (later "Jack")
1935	**Southern Review**	"And did she dwell"
1935	**Southern Review**	"Looking back in my mind"
1936	**Southern Review**	"A Man sick with whirling"
1936	**Southern Review**	"A Description of Some Confederate Soldiers"
1936	**Southern Review**	"The Indian"
1936	**Southern Review**	"A Poem (Fat, Aging)"

Names of periodicals edited by the former Fugitives are in bold type.

Date	First Publisher	Title
1936	*Southern Review*	"Old Poems"
1936	*Southern Review*	"Kirilov on a Skyscraper"
1936	*Southern Review*	"An Old Song"
1937	*Transition*	"Because of me, because . . . "
1937	*Transition*	"Enormous love . . . asking"
1937	*Southern Review*	"The Automaton"
1937	*Southern Review*	"A Poem ('When Achilles fought and fell')"
1937	*Southern Review*	"A Poem (Love . . . Separate Being)"
1937	*Southern Review*	"A Poem (The hanged man . . .)"
1937	*Southern Review*	"A Poem (O the dummies . . . window)"
1937	*Southern Review*	"A Poem (Falling in love . . . simple)"
1937	*Southern Review*	"A Dialogue . . . Soul"
1937	*Southern Review*	"The Machine Gun"
1938	*Pursuit*	"Housman" and "Auden's . . . Style"
1938	*Kenyon Review*	"The Winter's Tale"
1939	*Southern Review*	"On the Railway Platform"
1939	*Southern Review*	"A Poem (Over . . . capitals)"
1939	*Southern Review*	"A Poem (A Picture . . . Paper)"
1939	*Southern Review*	"A Poem (Up in the sky)"
1939	*Southern Review*	"A Poem (When you and I . . .)"
1939	*Southern Review*	"1938: The Spring Dances"
1939	*Hika*[1]	"The Poet . . . ," " . . . Butcher," and "Rachel" (parodies Frost)
1939	*Partisan Review*	"A Story"
1939	*Poetry*	"The Ways and the Peoples"
1940	*Partisan Review*	"A Nursery Rhyme"
1940	*Partisan Review*	"The Refugees"
1940	*Kenyon Review*	"For an Emigrant" (later "For the New World . . .")
1940	*New Directions*	*Five Young American Poets*: "The Rage for the Lost Penny": "The See-er of Cities" "A Poem for Someone Killed in Spain" "Eine Kleine Nachtmusik" "The Bad Music" "A Little Poem" "For the Madrid" "Che Faro Senza Euridice"

1. *Hika* was Kenyon College's literary magazine, edited by Robert T. S. Lowell in 1939.

Date	First Publisher	Title

JOHN BERRYMAN (POEMS PUBLISHED 1934–1940)

Date	First Publisher	Title
1934	*Columbia Review*	"Delinquency . . . Portion"
1935	*Columbia Review*	"Essential"
1935	*Columbia Poetry 1935*	"Ars Poetica"
1935	*Columbia Poetry 1935*	"Blake"
1935	*Columbia Poetry 1935*	"Lead Out the Weary Dancers"
1935	*Columbia Poetry 1935*	"Apostrophe"
1935	*Columbia Poetry 1935*	"Ivory"
1935	*The Nation*	"Note on E. A. Robinson"
1935	*Columbia Review*	"Elegy: Hart Crane"
1935	*Columbia Review*	"Thanksgiving"
1935	*Columbia Review*	"Words to a Young Man"
1936	*Columbia Review*	"Notation"
1936	*Columbia Review*	"The Witness"
1936	*Columbia Review*	"The Ancestor"
1936	*Columbia Review*	"Trophy"
1938	**Southern Review**	"Night and the City and Other Poems"
1938	**Southern Review**	"Night and the City"
1938	**Southern Review**	"Note for a Historian"
1938	**Southern Review**	"The Apparition"
1938	**Southern Review**	"Toward Statement"
1938	*20th Century Verse*	"The Trial"
1939	**Kenyon Review**	"Letter to His Brother"
1939	**Kenyon Review**	"Nineteen Thirty-Eight"
1939	*New Republic*	"World Telegram"
1939	*Partisan Review*	"The Statue"
1939	*Partisan Review*	"On the London Train"
1939	*Nation*	"The Disciple"
1940	**Southern Review**	"Desires of Men and Women"
1940	**Southern Review**	"Conversation"
1940	**Southern Review**	"Homage to Film"
1940	**Southern Review**	"Song from Cleopatra"
1940	**Southern Review**	"Meditation"
1940	New Directions Press	*Five Young American Poets*: "The Statue" "Nineteen Thirty-eight" "The Curse" "Desires of Men and Women" "World Telegram" "On the London Train"

Date	First Publisher	Title
		"Conversation"
		"The Return"
		"Ceremony and Vision"
		"Song from 'Cleopatra' "
		"Winter Landscape"
		"Letter to His Brother"
		"Caravan"
		"The Apparition"
		"Meditation"
		"Parting as Descent"
		"Sanctuary"
		"The Disciple"
		"The Trial"
		"Night and the City"

ROBERT LOWELL (POEMS WRITTEN OR PUBLISHED 1937–1944)

1937	Unpublished[2]	"A Month of Meals with Madox Ford"
1937	Unpublished[2]	"An Afternoon in an Umbrella Tent at Benfolly"
1939	*Kenyon Review*	"The Cities' Summer Death"
1939	*Kenyon Review*	"The Dandelion Girls"
1943	*Chimera*	"The Park Street Cemetary"
1943	*Partisan Review*	"The Capitalist's Meditation by the Civil War Monument"
1943	*Partisan Review*	"Salem"
1943	*Partisan Review*	"Concord"
1943	*Partisan Review*	"Song of the Boston Nativity"
1943	*Sewanee Review*	"Leviathan"
1943	*Sewanee Review*	"Dea Roma"
1943	*Sewanee Review*	"Death from Cancer on Easter" [later part 1 of "In Memory . . . Winslow"]
1943	*Sewanee Review*	"On the Eve . . . Conception"
1943	*Sewanee Review*	"Prayer for the Jews"
1943	*Kenyon Review*	"Satan's Confession"
1944	Cummington Press	*Land of Unlikeness*: "In Memory of Arthur Winslow" "A Suicidal Nightmare" "The Bomber" [Doreski 64–65]

2. Unpublished poems found in Lowell's 1935 notebooks are quoted by permission of the Houghton Library, Harvard University.

Date   First Publisher   Title
                                    "Concord Cemetery after the Tornado"
                                    "Napoleon Crosses the Berezina"
                                    "Scenes from the Historic Comedy"
                                    "The Slough of Despond"
                                    "Christ for Sale"
                                    "The Crucifix"
                                    "The Wood of Life"
                                    "Cisterians in Germany"
                                    "The Drunken Fisherman"
                                    "Children of Light"
1944   *Sewanee Review*   "France"
1944   *Sewanee Review*   "Colloquy in Black Rock Connecticut"
1944   *Partisan Review*   "The Quaker Graveyard in Nantucket"

SHORT FICTION OF LYTLE, GORDON, PORTER, WELTY, TAYLOR,
AND O'CONNOR PUBLISHED IN VARIOUS PERIODICALS

Date   First Publisher   Title

ANDREW LYTLE (STORIES PUBLISHED 1932–1945)
1932   *Virginia Quarterly Review*   "Old Scratch in the Valley"
1935   *Virginia Quarterly Review*   "Mr. MacGregor"
1936   **Southern Review**   "Jericho, Jericho, Jericho"
1939   *Hika*   "How Nuno Tovar Came to Cross the Ocean
                                        Sea"
1942   **Kenyon Review**   "Alchemy"
1945   **Sewanee Review**   "The Guide" (later "The Mahogany Frame")

CAROLINE GORDON (STORIES PUBLISHED 1929–1950)
1929   *Gyroscope*   "Summer Dust"
1930   *Gyroscope*   "The Long Day"
1931   *Hound and Horn*   "The Ice House"
1931   *Scribner's Magazine*   "Mr. Powers"
1932   *Hound and Horn*   "The Captive"
1933   *Criterion*   "Old Red"
1933   *Yale Review*   "Tom Rivers"
1934   *Scribner's Magazine*   "To Thy Chamber Window, Sweet"
1935   *Scribner's Magazine*   "The Last Day in the Field"
1935   **Southern Review**   "A Morning's Favor"
1935   *Scribner's Magazine*   "One More Time"
1937   **Southern Review**   "The Women on the Battlefield"
1937   *Mademoiselle*   "The Brilliant Leaves"

Date	First Publisher	Title
1938	**Southern Review**	"The Enemy"
1939	**Southern Review**	"Frankie and Thomas and Bud Asbury"
1944	Maryland Quarterly	"The Forest of the South"
1944	Mademoiselle	"All Lovers Love the Spring"
1945	Harper's	"Hear the Nightingale Sing"
1945	**Sewanee Review**	"The Olive Garden"
1947	Mademoiselle	"The Petrified Woman"
1948	Harper's Bazaar	"The Presence"
1950	**Sewanee Review**	"The Waterfall"

KATHERINE ANNE PORTER (STORIES PUBLISHED 1922–1960)

1922	Century Magazine	"Maria Concepcíon"
1923	Century Magazine	"The Martyr"
1924	Century Magazine	"Virgin Violeta"
1927	New Masses	"He"
1928	transition	"Magic"
1928	Second American Caravan	"Rope"
1929	Gyroscope	"Theft"
1929	transition	"The Jilting of Granny Weatherall"
1930	**Hound and Horn**	"Flowering Judas"
1932	Scribner's Magazine	"The Cracked Looking Glass"
1932	Virginia Quarterly Review	"Hacienda"
1934	Virginia Quarterly Review	"That Tree"
1935	Virginia Quarterly Review	"The Grave"
1935	**Southern Review**	"The Circus"
1936	Signatures	"Noon Wine"
1936	**Southern Review**	"The Old Order"
1936	**Southern Review**	"The Journey"
1938	**Southern Review**	"Old Mortality"
1938	**Southern Review**	Pale Horse, Pale Rider
1939	Harper's Bazaar	"The Downward Path to Wisdom"
1941	Accent	"The Source"
1941	**Southern Review**	"The Leaning Tower"
1944	The Leaning Tower and Other Stories	"The Witness"
1944	The Leaning Tower and Other Stories	"The Last Leaf"
1960	Atlantic Monthly	"Holiday"

EUDORA WELTY (STORIES PUBLISHED 1936–1966)

1936	Manuscript	"Death of a Traveling Salesman"

Date	First Publisher	Title
1936	*Tanager* (Grinnell College)	"The Doll"
1936	*Manuscript*	"Magic"
1937	*Prairie Schooner*	"Lily Daw and the Three Ladies"
1937	*River*	"Retreat"
1937	**Southern Review**	"A Piece of News"
1937	*Prairie Schooner*	"Flowers for Marjorie"
1937	**Southern Review**	"A Memory"
1938	**Southern Review**	"Old Mr. Grenada"
1938	**Southern Review**	"A Curtain of Green"
1938	*Prairie Schooner*	"The Whistle"
1939	**Southern Review**	"Petrified Man"
1939	**Southern Review**	"The Hitch-hikers"
1940	*New Directions in Prose and Poetry*	"Keela, The Outcast Indian Maiden"
1941	*Atlantic Monthly*	"A Worn Path"
1941	*Atlantic Monthly*	"Why I Live at the P.O."
1941	**Southern Review**	"Clytie"
1941	*Decision*	"A Visit of Charity"
1941	*Atlantic Monthly*	"Powerhouse"
1941	*Harper's Bazaar*	"The Key"
1941	*Harper's Bazaar*	"The Purple Hat"
1942	*Harper's Bazaar*	"First Love"
1942	*American Prefaces*	"A Still Moment"
1942	*Harper's Magazine*	"The Wide Net"
1942	*Harper's Bazaar*	"The Winds"
1942	*Yale Review*	"Asphodel"
1942	*Atlantic*	"Livvie Is Back"
1943	*Philadelphia Inquirer*	"The Robber Bridegroom"
1947	*Atlantic*	"Hello and Goodbye"
1951	*Harper's Bazaar*	"The Burning"
1951	*New Yorker*	"The Bride of the Innisfallen"
1952	*New Yorker*	"Kin"
1954	*Harper's Bazaar*	"Going to Naples"
1963	*New Yorker*	"Where Is the Voice Coming From?"
1966	*New Yorker*	"The Demonstrators"

PETER TAYLOR (STORIES PUBLISHED 1937–1960)

1937	*River* (Oxford, Miss.)	"The Party"
1937	*River*	"The Lady Is Civilized"
1938	*Hika*	"A Departure"

Date	First Publisher	Title
1939	Hika	"Memorable Evening"
1939	Hika	"Mimsy Were the Borogoves"
1939	Hika	"The Life Before"
1939	Hika	"Middle Age" (later "Cookie") from *The Wanderer*
1940	Hika	"Winged Chariot" (later "Sky Line")
1940	**Southern Review**	"A Spinster's Tale"
1941	**Southern Review**	"Sky Line"
1941	**Southern Review**	"The Fancy Woman"
1941	New Republic	"Like the Sad Heart of Ruth" (later "A Walled Garden")
1942	American Prefaces	"The School Girl"
1945	**Sewanee Review**	"Rain in the Heart"
1945	Partisan Review	"The Scout Master"
1946	**Sewanee Review**	"A Long Fourth"
1947	**Kenyon Review**	"Allegience"
1948	Harper's Bazaar	"Casa Anna" (from *A Woman of Means*)
1949	**Sewanee Review**	"The Death of a Kinsman" (play)
1949	New Yorker	"Dudley for the Dartmouth Cup" (from *A Woman of Means*)
1949	New Yorker	"Porte-Cochère"
1949	New Yorker	"A Wife of Nashville"
1950	New Yorker	"Their Losses"
1951	New Yorker	"What You Hear from 'Em?"
1951	New Yorker	"Two Ladies in Retirement"
1951	New Yorker	"Bad Dreams"
1954	Harper's Bazaar	"The Dark Walk"
1955	New Yorker	"A Sentimental Journey" (later "1939")
1956	**Kenyon Review**	"Tennessee Day in St. Louis" (play)
1957	New Yorker	"The Other Times"
1958	New Yorker	"The Unforgivable" (later "Promise of Rain")
1958	**Kenyon Review**	"Venus, Cupid, Folly, and Time"
1958	New Yorker	"A Pair of Bright-Blue Eyes" (later "*Je Suis Perdu*")
1959	New Yorker	"Cousins, Family Love, Family Life, All That" (later "The Little Cousins")
1959	**Kenyon Review**	"Who Was Jesse's Friend and Protector" (later "A Friend and Protector")
1959	New Yorker	"Heads of Houses"

Date	First Publisher	Title
1959	New Yorker	"Guests"
1960	New Yorker	"Miss Leonora When Last Seen"

FLANNERY O'CONNOR (STORIES PUBLISHED 1946–1971)

1946	Accent	"The Geranium"
1948	Sewanee Review	"The Train" (later chapter 1 of Wise Blood)
1948	Mademoiselle	"The Capture"
1949	Partisan Review	"The Heart of the Park" (later chapter 5 of Wise Blood)
1949	Tomorrow	"The Woman on the Stairs" (later "Stroke of Good Fortune")
1949	Partisan Review	"The Peeler" (later chapter 3 of Wise Blood)
1952	New World Writing	"Enoch and the Gorilla" (later chapter 11 of Wise Blood)
1953	Kenyon Review	"The Life You Save May Be Your Own"
1953	Sewanee Review	"The River"
1953	Harper's Bazaar	"A Late Encounter with the Enemy"
1954	Kenyon Review	"A Circle in the Fire"
1954	Harper's Bazaar	"A Temple of the Holy Ghost"
1954	Sewanee Review	"The Displaced Person"
1955	Kenyon Review	"The Artificial Nigger"
1955	Harper's Bazaar	"Good Country People"
1955	New World Writing	"You Can't Be Poorer than Dead" (later chapter 8 of The Violent Bear it Away)
1956	Kenyon Review	"Greenleaf"
1957	Partisan Review	"A View of the Woods"
1958	Harper's Bazaar	"The Enduring Chill"
1960	Kenyon Review	"The Comforts of Home"
1961	The Critic (Chicago)	"The Partridge Festival"
1961	New World Writing	"Everything That Rises Must Converge"
1962	Sewanee Review	"The Lame Shall Enter First"
1963	Esquire	"Why Do the Heathen Rage?"
1964	Sewanee Review	"Revelation"
1956	Esquire	"Parker's Back"
1970	North American Review	"Wildcat"
1970	Atlantic	"The Barber"
1971	Mademoiselle	"The Crop"

Bibliography

Manuscripts

John Berryman Papers, Manuscript Division, University of Minnesota Libraries, St. Paul, Minn.

Cleanth Brooks Papers. Yale Collection of American Literature, Beinecke Rare Book and Manuscript Library, Yale University, New Haven, Conn.

Donald Davidson Papers. Jesse E. Wills Collection, Jean and Alexander Heard Library, Vanderbilt University, Nashville, Tenn.

Caroline Gordon Papers. Firestone Library, Princeton University, Princeton, N.J.

Kenyon Review Papers. Kenyon College Special Collections in the Olin Library, Kenyon College, Gambier, Ohio.

Robert Lowell Papers. Houghton Library, Harvard University, Cambridge, Mass.

Andrew Nelson Lytle Papers. Special Collections, Jean and Alexander Heard Library, Vanderbilt University, Nashville, Tenn.

Flannery O'Connor Papers. Flannery O'Connor Collection, Ina Dillard Russell Library, Georgia College, Milledgeville, Ga.

Frank Lawrence Owsley Papers, Special Collections, Jean and Alexander Heard Library, Vanderbilt University, Nashville, Tenn.

Papers of Katherine Anne Porter. Special Collections, University of Maryland Libraries, College Park, Md.

Southern Review Papers. Beinecke Rare Book and Manuscript Library, Yale University, New Haven, Conn.

Allen Tate Papers. Firestone Library, Princeton University, Princeton, N.J.

Peter Hillsman Taylor Papers. Special Collections, Jean and Alexander Heard Library, Vanderbilt University, Nashville, Tenn.

Robert Penn Warren Papers. Yale Collection of American Literature, Beinecke Rare Book and Manuscript Library, Yale University, New Haven, Conn.

Eudora Welty Papers. Mississippi Department of Archives and History, Archives and Library Division, Jackson, Miss.

Personal Interviews and Communications

Brooks, Cleanth. Interview by author. New Haven, January 10, 1988.
———. Interview by author. New Haven, August 7, 1991.
———. Interview by author. Atlanta, Ga., November 15, 1991.
———. Letter to author. July 30, 1993.
Brown, Ashley. Letter to author. March 11, 1995.
Jarrell, Mary von Schrader. Interview by author. Greensboro, N.C., August 1984.
———. Letter to author. January 23, 1980.
Madden, David. Interview by author. Baton Rouge, La., July 16, 1985.
Still, James. Interview by author. Lexington, Ky., August 16, 1986.
Taylor, Peter. Interview by author. St. Augustine, Fla., March 17, 1994.
———. Postcard to author. 1992.
Warren, Robert Penn. Annotations to author's manuscript. 1984.
Young, Thomas Daniel. Interview by author. Atlanta, Ga., October 30, 1985.

Published Sources

Allums, Larry. "From Classical to Christian: Versions of the Hero in the Novels of Caroline Gordon." *Southern Review* n.s., 28 (1990): 63–70.

Altieri, Charles. *Enlarging the Temple: New Directions in American Poetry in the Sixties.* Lewisburg, Pa.: Bucknell University Press, 1979.

Anderson, Elliott, and Mary Kinzie, eds. *The Little Magazine in America: A Modern Documentary History.* Yonkers, N.Y.: Pushcart Press, 1978.

Axelrod, Steven Gould. *Life and Art.* Princeton: Princeton University Press, 1978.

Baum, Catherine, and Floyd Watkins. "Caroline Gordon and The Captive.'" *Southern Review* n.s., 7 (1971): 447–62.

Bawer, Bruce. *The Middle Generation: The Lives and Poetry of Delmore Schwartz, Randall Jarrell, John Berryman, and Robert Lowell.* Hamden, Conn.: Archon Books, 1986.

Bayley, Isabel, ed. *Letters of Katherine Anne Porter.* New York: Atlantic Monthly Press, 1990.

Beck, Charlotte H. "Caroline Gordon and Flannery O'Connor: An Empowering Anxiety of Influence." In *Flannery O'Connor Bulletin* 25 (1996–97): 194–213.

———. "Randall Jarrell and Robert Penn Warren: Fugitive Fugitives." *Southern Literary Journal* 17 (1984): 82–91.

——. " 'Solely *The Southern Review*': A Significant Moment in the Poetic Apprenticeship of John Berryman." In *Recovering Berryman: Essays on a Poet*, edited by Richard J. Kelly and Alan K. Lathrop. Ann Arbor: University of Michigan Press, 1993.

Berryman, John. *Collected Poems, 1937–1971*. Edited by Charles Thornbury. 1989. Reprint. New York: Noonday, 1991.

Bloom, Harold. *The Anxiety of Influence: A Theory of Poetry*. New York: Oxford University Press, 1973.

Blotner, Joseph. *Robert Penn Warren: A Biography*. New York: Random House, 1997.

Brinkmeyer, Robert H., Jr. *The Art and Vision of Flannery O'Connor*. Baton Rouge: Louisiana State University Press, 1989.

——. *Katherine Anne Porter's Artistic Development: Primitivism, Traditionalism, and Totalitarianism*. Baton Rouge: Louisiana State University Press, 1993.

Brooker, Jewell Spears. "In Conclusion: Literature and Culture in the Last Essays of Cleanth Brooks." *South Atlantic Review* 60 (November 1995): 129–36.

Brooks, Cleanth. *Community, Religion, and Literature: Essays by Cleanth Brooks*. Columbia: University of Missouri Press, 1995.

——. "Eudora Welty and the Southern Idiom." In *Eudora Welty: A Form of Thanks*, edited by Louis Dollarhide and Ann J. Abadie. Jackson: University Press of Mississippi, 1979.

——. *Modern Poetry and the Tradition*. Chapel Hill: University of North Carolina Press, 1939.

——. "The New Criticism: A Brief for the Defense." *American Scholar* 43–44 (1943): 285–95.

——. "The Past Re-examined: *The Optimist's Daughter*." *Mississippi Quarterly* 26 (1972–73): 577–87.

——. *A Shaping Joy: Studies in the Writer's Craft*. New York: Harcourt Brace Jovanovich, 1971.

——. "A Tribute to Peter Taylor." *Journal of the Short Story in English* 9 (Autumn 1987): 37–38.

——. "The Vision of W. B. Yeats." *Southern Review* 4 (Summer 1938): 116–42.

——. *The Well Wrought Urn: Studies in the Structure of Poetry*. New York: Harcourt Brace Jovanovich, 1947.

——. "The Woman and Artist I Knew." In *Katherine Anne Porter and Texas: An Uneasy Relationship*, edited by Clinton Machann and William Bedford Clark. College Station: Texas A&M University Press, 1990.

Brooks, Cleanth, John T. Purser, and Robert Penn Warren, eds. *Sophomore Poetry Manual*. Baton Rouge: Louisiana State University Press, 1936. Beinecke Rare Book and Manuscript Library, Yale University, New Haven, Conn.

Brooks, Cleanth, and Robert Penn Warren, eds. *Modern Rhetoric*. New York: Harcourt Brace Jovanovich, 1970.

——. *Understanding Fiction*. 1st ed. New York: Appleton-Century-Crofts, 1943.

Brooks, Cleanth, Robert Penn Warren, and John Thibaut Purser, eds. *An Approach to Literature: A Collection of Prose and Verse with Analyses and Discussions*. Baton Rouge: Louisiana State University Press, 1936.

Browne, Elizabeth, comp. *"Kenyon Review" Index: 25 Years Cumulative Compilation, 1939–1963*. New York: AMS Reprint Co., Arno, 1984.

Bryant, Joseph A., Jr. "Peter Taylor and the Walled Gardens." *Journal of the Short Story in English* 9 (Autumn 1987): 65–72.

Burton, Linda, ed. *Stories from Tennessee*. Knoxville: University of Tennessee Press, 1983.

Calhoun, Richard. "James Dickey." In *Fifty Southern Writers After 1900: A Bibliographical Sourcebook*, edited by Joseph M. Flora and Robert Bain. New York: Greenwood Press, 1987.

Cook, Martha E. "The Artistry of *I'll Take My Stand*." *Mississippi Quarterly* 33 (1980): 425–32.

Cowan, Louise. *The Fugitive Group: A Literary History*. Baton Rouge: Louisiana State University Press, 1959.

Cutrer, Thomas W. *Parnassus on the Mississippi: "The Southern Review" and the Baton Rouge Literary Community, 1935–1942*. Baton Rouge: Louisiana State University Press, 1984.

Davidson, Donald. "The Southern Writer and the Modern University." In *Southern Writers in the Modern World*. Athens: University of Georgia Press, 1958.

———, ed. *American Composition and Rhetoric*. 4th ed. New York: Scribner's, 1959.

Dickey, James. "In the Presence of Anthologies." *Sewanee Review* 66 (1958): 294–314.

Doreski, William. *The Years of Our Friendship: Robert Lowell and Allen Tate*. Jackson: University Press of Mississippi, 1990.

Drake, Robert Y. "Donald Davidson and the Ancient Mariner." *Vanderbilt Alumnus* 49 (1964): 18–22.

———. "My Own House of Fiction." *Mississippi Quarterly* 45 (1992): 127–31.

Erskine, Albert, ed. *A Robert Penn Warren Reader*. New York: Random House, 1989.

Fain, John T., and Thomas Daniel Young, eds. *The Literary Correspondence of Allen Tate and Donald Davidson*. Athens: University of Georgia Press, 1974.

Ferguson, Suzanne. *The Poetry of Randall Jarrell*. Baton Rouge: Louisiana State University Press, 1971.

Fitzgerald, Sally. "A Master Class: From the Correspondence of Caroline Gordon and Flannery O'Connor." *Georgia Review* 33 (1979): 827–46.

———. "Roman Arches and Pillars of Wisdom." Lecture to the Southern Women Writer's Conference, Berry College, Rome, Ga., April 12, 1996.

———, ed. *Letters of Flannery O'Connor: The Habit of Being*. New York: Farrar, Straus & Giroux, 1979.

Fitz-Piggott, Jill. "The Dominant Chord and the Different Voice: The Sexes in Gordon's Stories." In *The Female Tradition in Southern Literature*, edited by Carol S. Manning. Urbana: University of Illinois Press, 1993.

Flynn, Richard. *Randall Jarrell and the Lost World of Childhood*. Athens: University of Georgia Press, 1990.

Folks, Jeffrey J. "A Southern Realist: The Short Stories of Robert Drake." *Mississippi Quarterly* 45 (1992): 159–65.

Ford, Ford Madox. "A Stage in American Literature." *Bookman* 74 (1931): 371–76.

Freistat, Rose Ann C. *Caroline Gordon as Novelist and Woman of Letters*. Baton Rouge: Louisiana State University Press, 1984.

Friedman, Milton, and Beverly Lyon Clark, eds. *Critical Essays on Flannery O'Connor*. Boston: G. K. Hall, 1985.

Gelpi, Albert. "The Reign of the Kingfisher: Robert Lowell's Prophetic Poetry." In *Robert Lowell: Essays on the Poetry*, edited by Stephen Gould Axelrod and Helen Dees. New York: Cambridge University Press, 1986.

Gilbert, Sandra, and Susan Gubar. *The War of the Words*. Vol. 1 of *No Man's Land: The Place of the Woman Writer in the Twentieth Century*. New Haven: Yale University Press, 1987.

Givner, Joan. "The Genesis of Ship of Fools." *Southern Literary Journal* 9 (1970): 14–30.

———. *Katherine Anne Porter: A Life*. Athens: University of Georgia Press, 1991.

———, ed. *Katherine Anne Porter: Conversations*. Jackson: University Press of Mississippi, 1987.

Goodman, Charlotte Margolis. *Jean Stafford: The Savage Heart*. Austin: University of Texas Press, 1990.

Gordon, Caroline. *Aleck Maury, Sportsman*. New York: Scribner's, 1934.

———. *The Collected Short Stories of Caroline Gordon*. New York: Farrar, Straus & Giroux, 1981.

———. "Flannery O'Connor's *Wise Blood*." *Critique* 2 (1958): 3–10.

———. *The Garden of Adonis*. New York: Scribner's, 1937.

———. *How to Read a Novel*. New York: Viking, 1958.

———. "Katherine Anne Porter and the ICM." *Harper's*, November 1964, 146–48.

———. *The Malefactors*. New York: Harcourt, Brace, 1956.

———. *None Shall Look Back*. 1937. Reprint. Nashville: Sanders, 1992.

———. *Penhally*. 1931. Reprint. Nashville: J. S. Sanders, 1991.

———. *The Strange Children*. New York: Scribner's, 1951.

Gordon, Caroline, and Allen Tate, eds. *The House of Fiction: An Anthology of the Short Story with Commentary*. New York: Scribner's, 1950.

Gordon, Sarah. Lecture. Georgia College, Milledgeville, Ga., January 25, 1995.

Gretlund, Jan Nordby. "Three on Katherine Anne Porter." *Mississippi Quarterly* 36 (1983): 117–30.

Griffith, Albert J. *Peter Taylor*. Rev. ed. New York: Twayne, 1990.

Grimshaw, James A., Jr., *The Flannery O'Connor Companion*. Westport, Conn.: Greenwood, 1981.

———, ed. *Cleanth Brooks and Robert Penn Warren: A Literary Correspondence*. Columbia: University of Missouri Press, 1998.

Gross, Harvey. *Sound and Form in Modern Poetry: A Study of Prosody from Thomas Hardy to Robert Lowell*. Ann Arbor: University of Michigan Press, 1964.

Hamilton, Ian. *Robert Lowell: A Biography*. New York: Random House–Viking, 1982.

Heilman, Robert B. *The Southern Connection*. Baton Rouge: Louisiana State University Press, 1991.

Hobson, Fred. *The Southern Writer in the Postmodern World*. Athens: University of Georgia Press, 1991.

Hoy, Pat C. "The Wages of Sin: Terminal Considerations in Lytle's 'Jericho, Jericho, Jericho.' " *South Atlantic Review* 49 (1984): 107–11.

Janssen, Marian. *The Kenyon Review, 1939–1970: A Critical History*. Baton Rouge: Louisiana State University Press, 1990.

Janssens, G. A. M. *The American Literary Review: A Critical History, 1920–1950*. The Hague: Mouton, 1968.

Jarrell, Mary. "Peter and Randall." *Shenandoah* 28 (1976–77): 28–34.

———, ed. *Randall Jarrell's Letters: An Autobiographical and Literary Selection*. Boston: Houghton Mifflin, 1985.

Jarrell, Randall. *The Complete Poems*. New York: Farrar, Straus & Giroux, 1969.

———. *Poetry and the Age*. New York: Random House, 1953.

———. "Poetry in War and Peace." In *Kipling, Auden & Co*. New York: Farrar, Straus & Giroux, 1980.

———. *The Third Book of Criticism*. New York: Farrar, Straus & Giroux, 1969.

Jeffrey, David K. "Madison Jones." In *Contemporary Fiction Writers of the South: A Bio-Bibliographical Sourcebook*, edited by Joseph M. Flora and Robert Bain. Westport, Conn.: Greenwood, 1993.

Jonza, Nancylee Novell. *The Underground Stream: The Life and Art of Caroline Gordon*. Athens: University of Georgia Press, 1995.

Justus, James H. "The Mariner and Robert Penn Warren." In *Robert Penn Warren: Critical Perspectives*, edited by Neil Nakadate. Lexington: University Press of Kentucky, 1981.

Kalstone, David. *Becoming a Poet: Elizabeth Bishop with Marianne Moore and Robert Lowell*. Edited by Robert Hemenway. New York: Noonday-Farrar, 1989.

Kenner, Hugh. "The Pedagogue as Critic." In *The New Criticism and After*, edited by Thomas Daniel Young. Charlottesville: University Press of Virginia, 1976.

Kreyling, Michael. *Author and Agent: Eudora Welty and Diarmuid Russell*. New York: Farrar, Straus, & Giroux, 1991.

Laughlin, James, ed. *Five Young American Poets*. New York: New Directions, 1940.

Lentricchia, Frank. *After the New Criticism*. Chicago: University of Chicago Press, 1980.

Liberman, M. M. "Some Observations on the Genesis of *Ship of Fools*: A Letter from Katherine Anne Porter." *PMLA* 84 (1936): 135–37.

Lowell, Robert. *Day by Day*. Baton Rouge: Louisiana State University Press, 1977.

———. *Land of Unlikeness*. New York: Cummington Press, 1944.

———. "Our Afterlife." *Shenandoah* 28 (1977): 5–7.

———. *Poems, 1938–1949.* London: Faber, 1950.

———. *Robert Lowell, Collected Prose,* edited by Robert Giroux. New York: Farrar, Straus & Giroux, 1987.

———. "Two Poems." *Kenyon Review* 1 (1939): 32–33.

Lowell, Robert, Peter Taylor, and Robert Penn Warren, eds., *Randall Jarrell, 1914–1965.* New York: Farrar, Straus & Giroux, 1967.

Lucas, Mark. *The Southern Vision of Andrew Lytle.* Baton Rouge: Louisiana State University Press, 1986.

Lytle, Andrew. *At the Moon's Inn.* Indianapolis: Bobbs-Merrill, 1941.

———. *Bedford Forrest and His Critter Company.* 1931. Reprint. Nashville: Sanders, 1992.

———. *The Hero with the Private Parts.* Baton Rouge: Louisiana State University Press, 1966.

———. "Literary Portraits: Flannery O'Connor." In *Southerners and Europeans: Essays in a Time of Disorder.* Baton Rouge: Louisiana State University Press, 1988.

———. *The Long Night.* Indianapolis: Bobbs-Merrill, 1936.

Macauley, Robie. "*The Kenyon Review,* 1939–1970." *Tri-Quarterly* 43 (1978): 71–77.

Magee, Rosemary M., ed. *Conversations with Flannery O'Connor.* Jackson: University Press of Mississippi, 1987.

———. *Friendship and Sympathy: Communities of Southern Women Writers.* Jackson: University Press of Mississippi, 1992.

Makowsky, Veronica A. *Caroline Gordon: A Biography.* New York: Oxford, 1989.

Mariani, Paul. *Dream Song: The Life of John Berryman.* New York: Morrow, 1990.

Matterson, Stephen. *Berryman and Lowell: The Art of Losing.* Totowa, N.J.: Barnes & Noble, 1988.

McAlexander, Hubert H., ed. *Conversations with Peter Taylor.* Jackson: University Press of Mississippi, 1987.

McClure, Heather, ed. *Women Writers of the Short Story: A Collection of Critical Essays.* Englewood Cliffs, N.J.: Prentice-Hall, 1980.

McDowell, David. "The Year Without Peter." *Shenandoah* 28 (1976–77): 34–86.

McLuhan, Marshall. "An Ancient Quarrel in Modern America (Sophists vs. Grammarians)." In *The Interior Landscape: The Literary Criticism of Marshall McLuhan,* edited by Eugene McNamara. New York: McGraw-Hill, 1969.

Meiners, R. K. *Everything to Be Endured: An Essay on Robert Lowell and Modern Poetry.* Columbia: University of Missouri Press, 1970.

Miles, Josephine. *The Continuity of Poetic Language: Studies in English Poetry from the 1540's to the 1940's.* Berkeley: University of California Press, 1951.

Myers, Jeffrey. *Manic Power: Robert Lowell and His Circle.* New York: Arbor House, 1987.

O'Connor, Flannery. *The Complete Stories of Flannery O'Connor.* New York: Farrar, Straus & Giroux, 1994.

―――. "Good Country People." In *Three by Flannery O'Connor*. New York: Signet, 1962.

―――. *Mystery and Manners*. Edited by Robert Fitzgerald and Sally Fitzgerald. New York: Farrar, Straus & Giroux, 1969.

Ozick, Cynthia. "A Critic at Large: T. S. Eliot at 101." *New Yorker*, November 20, 1989, 119–54.

Paine, J. H. E. "Interview with Peter Taylor, March 1, 1986. *Journal of the Short Story in English* 9 (Fall 1987): 14–35.

Polk, Neal. "Andrew Nelson Lytle: A Bibliography of His Writings." *Mississippi Quarterly* 23 (1970): 435–91.

Porter, Katherine Anne. "Dulce et Decorum Est." *New Republic*, March 31, 1937, 244–45.

―――. Introduction to *A Curtain of Green and Other Stories by Eudora Welty*. 1941. Reprint. New York: Harvest, 1979.

Prenshaw, Peggy Whitman, ed. *Conversations with Eudora Welty*. Jackson: University Press of Mississippi, 1984.

Pritchard, William H. *Randall Jarrell: A Literary Life*. New York: Farrar, Straus & Giroux, 1990.

Ransom, John Crowe. "Apologia for Modernism, a Review of *Modern Poetry and the Tradition* by Cleanth Brooks." *Kenyon Review* 2 (1940): 247–51.

―――. "Constellation of Five Poets." *Kenyon Review* 3 (1941): 377–380.

―――. "Fiction Harvest." *Southern Review* 2 (Autumn 1936): 399–418.

―――. "Why Critics Don't Go Mad." *Kenyon Review* 14 (1952): 331–39.

―――. *The World's Body*. Baton Rouge: Louisiana State University Press, 1938.

Robison, James Curry. *Peter Taylor: A Study of the Short Fiction*. Boston: Twayne, 1988.

Rollins, J. Barton. "Robert Lowell's Apprenticeship and Early Poems." *American Literature* 52 (1980): 67–83.

Rubin, Louis D., Jr. *The Wary Fugitives: Four Poets and the South*. Baton Rouge: Louisiana State University Press, 1978.

―――. *Writers of the Modern South*. Seattle: University of Washington Press, 1963.

Rubin, Louis D., Jr., et al., eds. *The History of Southern Literature*. Baton Rouge: Louisiana State University Press, 1985.

Schmidt, Peter. *The Heart of the Story: Eudora Welty's Short Fiction*. Jackson: University Press of Mississippi, 1991.

Simpson, Eileen. *Poets in Their Youth: A Memoir*. New York: Random House, 1982.

Simpson, Lewis P. Panel on the New Criticism at Tennessee Homecoming Celebration, Nashville, Tenn., 1987.

―――, ed. *The Possibilities of Order: Cleanth Brooks and His Work*. Baton Rouge: Louisiana State University Press, 1976.

Simpson, Lewis P., James Olney, and Jo Gulledge, eds. *The Southern Review and Modern Literature, 1935–1985*. Baton Rouge: Louisiana State Press, 1988.

Smithson, William T. *The Methodist Pulpit, South*. [an anthology of sermons] (1859). Special Collections, Hoskins Library, University of Tennessee, Knoxville.

Spears, Monroe. "The Function of Literary Quarterlies." In *American Ambitions: Selected Essays on Literary and Cultural Themes*. Baltimore: Johns Hopkins University Press, 1987.

———. "The *Sewanee Review* and the Southern Renascence." *South Carolina Review* 25 (Fall 1992): 7–11.

Spivey, Ted. R. "Flannery O'Connor, the New Criticism, and Deconstruction. *Southern Review* n.s., 23 (1987): 271–80.

Spurlin, William J., and Michael Fischer, eds. *The New Criticism and Contemporary Literary Theory, Connections and Continuities*. New York: Garland Press, 1995.

Squires, Radcliffe. "The Underground Stream: A Note on Caroline Gordon's Fiction." *Southern Review* n.s., 7 (1971): 467–79.

Staples, Hugh B. *Robert Lowell: The First Twenty Years*. London: Faber, 1962.

Sullivan, Walter. *Allen Tate: A Recollection*. Baton Rouge: Louisiana State University Press, 1988.

Tate, Allen. "A New Star." *Nation* 131 (1930): 352–53.

———. "Peter Taylor." *Shenandoah* 28 (1977): 10.

———. "A Southern Mode of the Imagination." In *Essays of Four Decades*. Chicago: Swallow Press, 1968.

Taylor, Peter. "The Assumptions of the Game." *Hika* 5 (February 1939): 21–22.

———. *The Collected Stories of Peter Taylor*. New York: Farrar, Straus & Giroux, 1969.

———. "In the Miro District." In *In the Miro District and Other Stories*. 1977. Reprint. New York: Ballantine, 1990.

———. *A Long Fourth and Other Stories*. New York: Harcourt Brace Jovanovich, 1948.

———. "The Old Forest." In *The Old Forest and Other Stories*. New York: Ballantine, 1986.

———. *The Widows of Thornton*. 1948. Reprint. Baton Rouge: Louisiana State University Press, 1994.

Tinterelli, Rhonda Cabot. "*The Southern Review*, 1935–1942: The Intellectual History of a Cultural Quarterly." Ph.D. dissertation, Louisiana State University, 1980.

Titus, Mary. "Katherine Anne Porter's Miranda: The Agrarian Myth and Southern Womanhood." In *Redefining Autobiography in Twentieth-Century Women's Fiction*, edited by Janice Morgan and Colette T. Hall. New York: Garland Press, 1991.

Trilling, Diana. "Fiction in Review." *Nation*, October 2, 1943. Reprinted in *Critical Essays on Eudora Welty*, edited by W. Craig Turner and Lee Ealing Harding. Boston: G. K. Hall, 1989.

Waldron, Ann. *Close Connections: Caroline Gordon and the Southern Renaissance*. Knoxville: University of Tennessee Press, 1987.

Warren, Robert Penn. *All the King's Men*. 1946. Reprint. New York: Bantam, 1956–81.

———. "Andrew Lytle's *The Long Night*: A Rediscovery." *Southern Review* n.s., 7 (1971): 130–40.

———. "Brooks and Warren." *Humanities* 6 (April 1985): 1–4.

————. "The Fiction of Caroline Gordon." *Southwest Review* 20 (1935): 5–10.

————. "A First Novel." *Sewanee Review* 65 (1957): 352.

————. Review of *A Woman of Means*. *New York Times Book Review*, June 11, 1950, 8.

————. "Then and Now . . . A Review in Review." *LSU Outlook*, January 1981, n.p.

————. "Two Peters: Memory and Opinion." *Shenandoah* 28 (1977): 8–10.

————. "University Tribute: Introductory Remarks on the Occasion of the University Press–Historical Book Club Tribute." *Alumni News* (University of North Carolina, Greensboro) 54 (Spring 1966): 23ff.

————. "*The Zodiac*: A Poem About the Ambitions of Poetry." *New York Times Book Review*, November 14, 1976, 8.

————, ed. *Katherine Anne Porter: A Collection of Critical Essays*. Englewood Cliffs, N.J.: Prentice-Hall, 1979.

Weaks, Mary Louise. "An Interview with Madison Smartt Bell." *Southern Review* n.s., 30 (January 1994): 1–12.

Wellek, René. *A History of Modern Criticism, 1757–1950*. Vol. 6, *American Criticism, 1900–1950*. New Haven: Yale University Press, 1986.

Wells, Henry W. *Poet and Psychiatrist: Merrill Moore, M.D.* New York: Twayne, 1955.

Welty, Eudora. *The Collected Stories of Eudora Welty*. New York: Harcourt Brace Jovanovich, 1980.

————. "Place and Time: The Southern Writer's Inheritance." *Times Literary Supplement*, September 17, 1954. Typescript, Welty Papers. Jackson, Miss.

Westling, Louise H. *Sacred Groves and Ravaged Gardens: The Fiction of Eudora Welty, Carson McCullers, and Flannery O'Connor*. Athens: University of Georgia Press, 1985.

Winchell, Mark Royden. *Cleanth Brooks and the Rise of Modern Criticism*. Charlottesville: University Press of Virginia, 1996.

————, ed. *The Vanderbilt Tradition: Essays in Honor of Thomas Daniel Young*. Baton Rouge: Louisiana State University Press, 1991.

Wood, Sally, ed. *The Southern Mandarins: Letters of Caroline Gordon to Sally Wood, 1924–1937*. Baton Rouge: Louisiana State University Press, 1984.

Wright, Stuart. *Peter Taylor: A Descriptive Bibliography*. Charlottesville: University Press of Virginia, 1988.

————. *Randall Jarrell: A Descriptive Bibliography, 1929–1983*. Charlottesville: University Press of Virginia, 1986.

Yaeger, Patricia S. " 'Because a Fire Was in My Head': Eudora Welty and the Dialogic Imagination." In *Welty: A Life in Literature*, edited by Albert J. Devlin. Jackson: University Press of Mississippi, 1987.

Young, Thomas Daniel. "Cleanth Brooks at Vanderbilt." Unpublished essay, Cleanth Brooks Papers, Yale University, New Haven, Conn.

————. *Gentleman in a Dustcoat: A Biography of John Crowe Ransom*. Baton Rouge: Louisiana State University Press, 1976.

Young, Thomas Daniel, and George Core, eds. *Selected Letters of John Crowe Ransom*. Baton Rouge: Louisiana State University Press, 1985.

Young, Thomas Daniel, and John Hindle, eds. *Selected Essays of John Crowe Ransom*. Baton Rouge: Louisiana State University Press, 1984.

Young, Thomas Daniel, and Elizabeth Sarcone, eds. *The Tate-Lytle Letters: The Correspondence of Andrew Lytle and Allen Tate*. Jackson: University Press of Mississippi, 1987.

Zesner, David. "Experiment at Kenyon." *Dallas Morning News*, September 5, 1948.

Zubar, Leo J., comp., and Carter W. Martin, ed. *The Presence of Grace and Other Book Reviews by Flannery O'Connor*. Athens: University of Georgia Press, 1983.

Index